THE PEACEFUL SETTLEMENT OF INTER-STATE CYBER DISPUTES

With cyberspace becoming a domain of inter-state conflict and confrontation, this book is one of the first studies of the ways in which international law can facilitate the peaceful settlement of inter-state cyber disputes.

By employing theoretical and practical inquiries and analysis, the book examines the legal parameters of cyber dispute settlement; explores critical questions about the role of dispute settlement institutions and methods; and identifies and addresses related challenges.

The book begins by considering the legal definition of a cyber dispute and the scope of the good faith obligation of states in settling their cyber disputes peacefully. It then examines the role of certain institutions (International Court of Justice, national courts, the EU, the Security Council) and methods (judicial, diplomatic, countermeasures, arbitration, conciliation, fact-finding) in the settlement of cyber disputes. It also discusses how data disputes can be settled and whether new and specialised mechanisms are needed.

The book provides scholars, practitioners, and law students with immediate knowledge and understanding of the role of international law in the peaceful settlement of cyber disputes, as well as how international dispute settlement as a discipline and practice can apply to this new field.

The Peaceful Settlement of Inter-State Cyber Disputes

Edited by
Nicholas Tsagourias
Russell Buchan
and
Daniel Franchini

•HART•
OXFORD • LONDON • NEW YORK • NEW DELHI • SYDNEY

HART PUBLISHING

Bloomsbury Publishing Plc

Kemp House, Chawley Park, Cumnor Hill, Oxford, OX2 9PH, UK

1385 Broadway, New York, NY 10018, USA

29 Earlsfort Terrace, Dublin 2, Ireland

HART PUBLISHING, the Hart/Stag logo, BLOOMSBURY and the Diana logo are trademarks of Bloomsbury Publishing Plc

First published in Great Britain 2024

A catalogue record for this book is available from the British Library.

A catalogue record for this book is available from the Library of Congress.

Library of Congress Control Number: 2024944190

ISBN: HB: 978-1-50996-091-0
ePDF: 978-1-50996-093-4
ePub: 978-1-50996-092-7

Typeset by Compuscript Ltd, Shannon

FOREWORD

> Peace is not merely a distant goal that we seek, but a means by which we arrive at that goal.
>
> – Martin Luther King, Jr.

This volume sits at the intersection of two important – but amorphous – issues: (a) the obligation of states to peacefully settle their disputes; and (b) that obligation's ability to regulate state behaviour vis-à-vis cyberspace. The first occupies an unusual place in public international law. On the one hand, the peaceful settlement obligation undoubtedly constitutes a pillar of the modern international legal order. UN Charter Article 2(3) directs all Member States to 'settle their international disputes by peaceful means in such a manner that international peace and security, and justice, are not endangered'. Article 33 catalogues various modalities for doing so with respect to disputes 'likely to endanger international peace and security'. Treaties like the charters of the Organization of American States (OAS) and the Arab League contain similar commitments to say nothing of those dispute settlement mechanisms embedded directly into various bilateral and multilateral treaty commitments.[1] Moreover, the general modalities of peaceful settlement (eg, negotiation, arbitration, mediation, conciliation, and judicial settlement) are almost daily indicia of the ongoing life of international law.

On the other hand, the 'obligation' of peaceful settlement itself remains remarkably underdeveloped. Scholarship on its contours is limited (at least relative to its more prominent Article 2 cousin – the prohibition on the use of force). The peaceful settlement obligation's contents are, moreover, unclear; competing candidates characterise it as an obligation for states: (a) to settle all disputes; (b) to settle only those disputes endangering international peace and security; (c) to settle international legal disputes; or (d) to forgo using force when engaged in dispute settlement. State practice remains quite limited; states rarely invoke the obligation in specific cases, let alone protest perceived violations. For its part, the International Court of Justice (ICJ) has proffered requirements for finding the existence of a justiciable 'dispute' – eg, a disagreement on a point of law or fact, a conflict of legal views

[1] See, eg, Charter of the Organization of American States, Feb. 27, 1967, 2 UST 2394, Art 3 (g)-(i); Pact of the League of Arab States, Mar. 22, 1945, 70 UNTS 237, Art 5. For examples of treaty-specific dispute settlement regimes, see, eg, Marrakesh Agreement Establishing the World Trade Organization, Apr. 15, 1994, 1869 UNTS 299, Annex 2; United Nations Convention on the Law of the Sea, Dec. 10, 1982, 1833 UNTS 397, pt XV.

or interests between two parties[2] which are positively opposed[3] and that can be objectively determined,[4] while (perhaps) requiring the respondent's awareness of such positive opposition.[5] Aside from the navigational hurdles this poses for the ICJ's own role in peaceful dispute settlement, its doctrine risks becoming the last word on the scope of the obligation overall (in lieu of simply speaking to the boundaries of judicial settlement specifically).

Meanwhile, cyberspace – a socio-technical system comprised of information and communication technologies (ICTs), including but not limited to, the Internet – has become ubiquitous, impacting almost every human endeavour. In so doing, it has garnered rising attention from states concerned with the ever-expanding humanitarian, economic, and national security costs and benefits of the digital age. Upholding data privacy, building resilience against disinformation and election interference, and stopping ransomware and other forms of cybercrime have all become banners around which states seek to regulate via domestic – and in the case of the EU, regional – measures. At the same time, states have questioned whether and what 'rules of the road' govern their own (increasing) operations online, including acts of cyber espionage, influence operations, offensive cyber-attacks, alongside defensive measures by potential victims. A consensus that existing international law governs such behaviour has not precluded existential questions of *which* international law rules do so, and interpretative issues with the precise behaviors existing international law prohibits, permits or requires of states. The sufficiency of the extant law is also contested; claims that existing principles can be applied to achieve a peaceful, safe, and secure online environment are juxtaposed against arguments that cyberspace deserves its own self-contained legal regime, whether by treaty or otherwise. The Internet's well-known attribution problem (where anonymity is a default feature of the technical architecture) further complicates international relations; technical, political, and legal challenges persist in knowing precisely who is doing what online. In short, the digital

[2] See, eg, *The Mavrommatis Palestine Concessions* (Judgment of 30 August 1924) PCIJ Rep Series A No 2, 11 para 19; see also *Applicability of the Obligation to Arbitrate Under Section 21 of the United Nations* (Advisory Opinion of 26 April 1988) [1988] ICJ Rep 12, 27; *Northern Cameroons (Cameroon v United Kingdom)* (Cameroon Preliminary Objections, Judgment of 2 December 1963) [1963] ICJ Rep 15, 27; *Case Concerning East Timor (Portugal v Australia)* (Judgment of 30 June 1995) [1995] ICJ Rep 90, 99.

[3] See, eg, *South West Africa Cases (Ethiopia v South Africa; Liberia v South Africa) (Preliminary Objections*, Judgment of 21 December 1962) [1962] ICJ Rep 319, 328; *Armed Activities on the Territory of the Congo (New Application: 2002) (Democratic Republic of the Congo v Rwanda)* (Jurisdiction and Admissibility, Judgment of 3 February 2006) [2006] ICJ Rep 6, 40.

[4] See, eg, *Application of the Convention on the Elimination of All Forms of Racial Discrimination (Georgia v Russian Federation)* (Preliminary Objections, Judgment of 1 April 2011) [2011] ICJ Rep 70, 84; *Interpretation of Peace Treaties with Bulgaria, Hungary and Romania* (Advisory Opinion of 30 March 1950) [1950] ICJ Rep 65, 74.

[5] See *Obligations Concerning Negotiations Relating to Cessation of the Nuclear Arms Race and to Nuclear Disarmament (Marshall Islands v United Kingdom)* (Preliminary Objections, Judgment of 5 October 2016) [2016] ICJ Rep 833, 849; *Application of the Convention on the Prevention and Punishment of the Crime of Genocide (Gambia v Myanmar)* (Preliminary Objections, Judgment of 22 July 2022) [2022] ICJ Rep 477, 496.

environment has provided a massive new platform for international relations and international law, broadening and deepening the range of issues on which states may agree *and* disagree.

The present volume will undoubtedly advance the conversation on both international law's role in governing cyberspace while foregrounding the particular role(s) peaceful settlement can play in doing so. For my part, I read it to make – at least – four clarifying contributions. For starters, one of the volume's chief contributions is its acknowledgement that for all the inter-state issues over (and in) cyberspace, the number of actual disputes (at least those that the ICJ would consider justiciable) remains limited. To be sure, some disputes may be inferred from the divergent positions evident in the recent proliferation of national statements on the application of international law to cyberspace. But competing regulatory policies in other areas (eg, on data privacy) have not matured into disputes per se, nor have states invoked international law in their attributions of foreign state/state-sponsored cyber-operations, precluding the law's application to the claims and denials that follow. Some might be inclined to take this finding as grounds for demurring any international law analyses until more cyber disputes ripen into reality.

This volume, however, proves such topics are well worthy of current attention by states and scholars alike. Most of the chapters are framed to explore the *potential* of peaceful settlement and its modalities to ensure the stability and security of cyberspace. Hence, readers will receive a primer on the law of peaceful settlement as it exists in judicial and non-judicial contexts, unpacking principles like good faith that drive its performance, or follow-on commitments to preserve confidentiality, protect legitimate expectations, and prohibit aggravation. These inquiries are, moreover, situated in ways that call attention to cyber-specific issues, like the potential for an ongoing data exfiltration cyber-operation (or one deploying ransomware) to disrupt and conflict with the processes by which dispute settlement mechanisms proceed. Different chapters anticipate how the various vehicles for pursuing settlements – negotiation, arbitration, conciliation, fact-finding – may intersect with different types of 'cyber' disputes, whether over who authored a particular cyber operation, the applicable rules of international law for cyber-attacks, or the extraterritorial reach of state regulations on data privacy. The growing number of states' 'cyber diplomats' and inter-state 'cyber dialogues' signal the emergence of such disputes is likely only a matter of time. The status quo thus highlights a need for more experts specialised in the intersection of digital technologies with international law to better advise states or otherwise participate in various dispute settlement processes. The result is a set of ready-made templates that future international lawyers may employ to navigate the future of international relations in cyberspace towards more peaceful outcomes.

Second, the chapters push the boundaries of the subject-matters usually examined in discussing peaceful settlement, expanding the timelines under consideration and the roster of relevant participants. For example, the role of domestic courts is highlighted, particularly their capacity to help *avoid* cyber disputes from arising in the first place (ie, a domestic court ruling may preclude that court's government agencies from acting in ways that would lead to disputes with foreign states). The EU's role (whether to resolve intra-EU disputes among Member States or the potential of a 'Brussels' effect' globalising those dispute settlement modalities the EU prefers) models the potential for regional international organisations to productively engage with inter-state cyber disputes. And where the geopolitical environment produces cyber operations threatening international peace and security, Chapter VII of the UN Charter creates room for a significant UN Security Council role. Moreover, these approaches – surveying ways to avoid inter-state disputes entirely or focusing on the utility of third party, non-state actors – need not apply to cyberspace alone. Hence, the current volume reads as a case-study for identifying new prospects for peaceful settlement across all international relations.

Third, whatever its general utility for public international law, this volume also anticipates various ways cyber operations will challenge whether – and, more importantly, *how well* – the peaceful settlement obligation can operate. Here, the attribution problem looms large, particularly in redressing state and state-sponsored cyber operations that are conducted in secret and without acknowledgement (ie, covertly). The uncertainty of the contours and contents of the applicable international law will undoubtedly further unsettle efforts to resolve disputes over the international wrongfulness of certain behaviors, to say nothing of available remedies. The volume recognises, moreover, that peaceful settlement as an international law obligation does not exist in isolation, anticipating that ongoing debates over other international law tools like countermeasures (particularly those of the collective or third-party variety) can impact the availability and operation of peaceful settlement methods themselves. Meanwhile, as states invoke 'sovereignty' to nationalise and regulate 'their' networks and 'their' contents, a more fragmented Internet suggests a future with more potential for normative fragmentation and diverging, if not contradictory, dispute settlement outcomes.

The potential for fragmentation highlights a fourth and final import for a volume such as this – reinforcing the multiple purposes peaceful dispute settlement serves. Obviously, as its very title suggests, peaceful *settlement* functions to resolve particular disputes between particular states. Yet, the *peaceful* modifier evinces more public purposes, namely the preservation of international peace and security, and (as Article 2 of the Charter highlights) justice. Given current geopolitical tensions and the risks and realities of regional and global conflict, the utility of peaceful settlement to such public purposes alone justifies the effort in compiling a volume such as this.

At the same time, the practice of pursuing peaceful settlement – that is, the outputs of various processes like binding agreements, judicial decisions, fact-finding reports, etc – will have a constitutive role for international law's application to cyberspace. Even if only a 'subsidiary' source of international law, by agreeing to third-party dispute settlement (eg, an ICJ decision), states may help resolve more than their cyber dispute; a single decision can speak to – and resolve – broader uncertainties about the availability and application of international law.

As such, a volume that at first glance focuses only on a relatively obscure standard of international law's intersection with digital technologies is better seen as laying a necessary foundation for states to address the application of international law to cyberspace overall. Moreover, such applications of international law to cyberspace will not stay in cyberspace; what dispute settlement processes and outcomes say about duties like non-intervention and due diligence online are likely to reverberate and evolve their contours and contents outside the digital environment as well.

The Peaceful Settlement of Inter-State Cyber Disputes thus marks an important contribution to a topic that will undoubtedly require more expansive discussion in the years ahead. Hopefully, the expertise and experience reflected in the current effort can catalyse further conversations on topics like the potential of the Security Council to work on cyber (and other) disputes under Chapter VI of the UN Charter or the role(s) private ICT companies can play in facilitating inter-state dispute settlement. For now, it stands alone as a first stop; a carefully curated resource for examining the implications of the intersection of new digital technologies with the public international law we all rely on to achieve peaceful co-existence in both the 'real' world and the ICT environment we call cyberspace.

Duncan B Hollis
Philadelphia, April 2024

CONTENTS

PART III
METHODS

CONTRIBUTORS

Constantine Antonopoulos LLB (Thrace); LLM (Cantab); PhD (Nottingham) is Professor of Public International Law Faculty of Law at the Democritus University of Thrace. He is a member of several academic societies, including the British Institute of International and Comparative Law; American Society of International Law; European Society of International Law; International Law Association (member of the board of the Hellenic Branch); Hellenic Society of International Law and International Relations; and the International Law Association, *Committee on the Use of Force* (2009-present).

Annegret Bendiek Dr habil is a political scientist and Senior Researcher in the research division 'EU/Europe' at the German Institute for International and Security Affairs (SWP), where she leads the 'European Repository of Cyber Incidents' since March 2022. In 2022, she held a visiting professorship at Carleton University in Ottawa, Canada. In 2022 and 2023, she served as a Substitute Professor in 'European Integration' and 'European Governance' at Osnabrück University. In 2014, Dr Bendiek was seconded to the Policy Planning Staff of the German Federal Foreign Office for the project 'Review 2014: Rethinking Foreign Policy'. Prior to that, in 2013, she was a Robert Bosch Fellow at the Transatlantic Academy 'The Future of the Liberal Order' and a Visiting Fellow at the German Marshall Fund in Washington, DC.

Russell Buchan is Professor of International Law at the University of Reading. Professor Buchan is a former British Academy Innovation Fellow at the Foreign, Commonwealth and Development Office.

Daniel Franchini is Lecturer in International Law and Deputy Director of the Sheffield Centre for International and European Law at the University of Sheffield.

Dr Iakovos V Iakovidis, Ambassador, Ministry of Foreign Affairs of Greece. Prior to that he served in Geneva, Brussels and New York. Dr Iakovidis holds a PhD from the University of Athens and a DEA in Droit international public et organisations from University of Paris I: Panthéon-Sorbonne. Dr Iakovidis was also Max Weber Fellow at the European University Institute and the Robert Schuman Centre for Advanced Studies.

Andraz Kastelic PhD is the lead cyber stability researcher at the Security and Technology Programme of the United Nations Institute for Disarmament Research (UNIDIR). Prior to joining UNIDIR, Andraz held various research positions in different international organisations and research institutions around the world. Andraz holds a PhD in International Law and an MA in Diplomacy.

Matthias C Kettemann is Professor of Innovation, Theory and Philosophy of Law and head of the Department for Theory and Future of Law at the University of Innsbruck. He leads the University's Quantum Ethics Lab and heads research programmes at the Humboldt Institute for Internet and Society in Berlin and the Leibniz Institute for Media Research in Hamburg. After studying law in Graz, Geneva and at Harvard Law School he taught in Frankfurt, Heidelberg, and Jena.

Robert Kolb is Professor of Public International Law at the University of Geneva. He is a former staff member of the ICRC. He is a member of the section on the law of armed conflicts of the Swiss Army.

Joanna Kulesza PhD is the Executive Director of the Lodz Cyber Hub research centre at the University of Lodz and an Assistant Professor of international law at the Faculty of Law and Administration. Her expertise spans public international law, internet governance, human rights, and cybersecurity. Joanna represents European Internet users at the At-Large Advisory Committee within the Internet Corporation for Assigned Names and Numbers and leads cybersecurity due diligence efforts within the European and Chinese working group on the application of international law in cyberspace led by the EUISS, GCSP and CICIR. Formerly, she chaired the Advisory Board of the Global Forum on Cyber Expertise (2019–2022) and was a member of the Scientific Committee of the European Union Agency for Fundamental Rights.

Tomohiro Mikanagi is Legal Advisor, Director-General for International Legal Affairs Bureau, Ministry of Foreign Affairs, Japan. He is a Former Visiting Fellow and current Partner Fellow of the Lauterpacht Centre for International Law, University of Cambridge. He has served in London, New York, and Beijing as a diplomat.

Martin Müller is a PhD researcher at the University of Innsbruck's Department for Theory and Future of Law and Legal Officer in the 'European Repository of Cyber Incidents' project. After his law studies in Frankfurt, he is currently pursuing his PhD in the field of online platform regulation and the role of public authorities. Prior to his academic career, he has worked for an international law firm in the practice group of 'Digital Law' specialising in copyright and data protection law.

Nicholas Tsagourias is Professor of International Law at the University of Sheffield.

Pål Wrange (PhD, LLM) is Professor of public international law at Stockholm University and the director of the Stockholm Centre for International Law and Justice. He is currently a member of the Swedish government's Advisory Committee on International Law, a member of the Permanent Court of Arbitration, and of the OSCE Court of Conciliation as well as a member of the board of the Swedish National Human Rights Institution. Professor Wrange has been a visiting scholar and fellow at Harvard Law School, the European University Institute, the University of Melbourne, and the University of Oxford and is a member of a number of international scientific advisory and editorial boards, in addition to various senior administrative positions at Stockholm University. Professor Wrange is a former principal legal advisor at the Swedish Ministry for Foreign Affairs, where he first encountered issues relating to international law and cyberspace as a member of an inter-agency committee on information operations in 2001. As a legal advisor he represented Sweden i.a. in the ICC Assembly of States Parties and in the EU working party on international law. Professor Wrange has also worked as consultant and advisor to the European Union, governments, and NGOs and has clerked in a district court in Stockholm.

ABBREVIATIONS

AI	artificial intelligence
APT	advanced persistent threat
ARF	ASEAN Regional Forum
ARSIWA / ASR	Articles on the Responsibility of States for Internationally Wrongful Acts / Articles on State Responsibility
ASEAN	Association of Southeast Asian Nations
CAR	Central African Republic
CBMs	confidence-building measures
CCDCOE	NATO Cooperative Cyber Defence Centre of Excellence
CERD	International Convention on the Elimination of All Forms of Racial Discrimination
CERT-EU	Computer Emergency Response Team of the EU institutions
CFSP	Common Foreign and Security Policy (EU)
CICTE	Inter-American Committee against Terrorism
CIDCC	Cyber and Information Domain Coordination Centre
CIL	customary international law
CISA	Cybersecurity and Infrastructure Security Agency (USA)
CJEU	Court of Justice of the European Union
CLOUD Act	Clarifying Lawful Overseas Use of Data Act, 2018
CNIL	Commission nationale de l'informatique et des libertés
CoE	Council of Europe
CRRT	Cyber Rapid Response Teams
CTC	SC Counter-Terrorism Committee
CTED	SC Counter-Terrorism Executive Directorate
CyCLONe	Cyber Crisis Liaison Organisation Network

DDoS	distributed-denial-of-service
DOJ	Department of Justice
DPRK	Democratic People's Republic of Korea
ECHR / ECtHR	European Court of Human Rights
EEC / EC	European Economic Community / Economic Community
ECOWAS	Economic Community of West African States
EEAS	European External Action Service
ENISA	European Network and Information Security Agency
EU	European Union
EUCDCC	European Union Cyber Defence Coordination Centre
EU-INTCEN	European Union Intelligence and Situation Centre
FATF	Financial Action Task Force
FBI	US Federal Bureau of Investigation
FISA	US Foreign Intelligence Surveillance Act of 1978
FSIA	US Foreign Sovereign Immunities Act of 1976
FTA	free trade agreement
GATT	General Agreement on Tariffs and Trade
GDPR	General Data Protection Regulation
GGE	Group of Governmental Experts on Developments in the Field of Information and Telecommunications in the Context of International Security
ICC	International Criminal Court
ICCPR	International Covenant on Civil and Political Rights
ICJ	International Court of Justice
IcSP	Instrument contributing to Stability and Peace
ICT	information and communications technology/ies
ICTY	International Criminal Tribunal for the former Yugoslavia
IETF	Internet Engineering Task Force
IIL	Institute of International Law

ILC	International Law Commission
IT	information technology/ies
ITLOS	International Tribunal for the Law of the Sea
ITU	International Telecommunication Union
LE	legitimate expectations
MFN	Most Favoured Nation
MLAT	mutual legal assistance treaty
NAFTA	North American Free Trade Agreement
NATO	North Atlantic Treaty Organization
NGO	non-governmental organisation
NIS	network and information security
NSA	US National Security Agency
OAS	Organization of American States
OECD	Organisation for Economic Co-operation and Development
OEWG	Open-Ended Working Group on Security of and in the Use of Information and Communications Technologies 2021–2025
OHCHR	United Nations Office of the High Commissioner for Human Rights
OPCW	Organisation for the Prohibition of Chemical Weapons
OSCE	Organization for Security and Co-operation in Europe
P5	five permanent members of the UNSC
PCA	Permanent Court of Arbitration
PCIJ	Permanent Court of International Justice
PESCO	Permanent Structured Cooperation
PLA	People's Liberation Army (China)
PoC	Points of Contact
PRST	presidential statement
RGB	Reconnaissance General Bureau (North Korea)
SCA	Stored Communications Act of 1986 (USA)

SPE	Sony Pictures Entertainment
TEU	Treaty on European Union
TFEU	Treaty on the Functioning of the European Union
UK	United Kingdom
UN	United Nations
UNCITRAL	United Nations Commission on International Trade Law
UNGA / GA	United Nations General Assembly
UNIDIR	United Nations Institute for Disarmament Research
UNODA	United Nations Office for Disarmament Affairs
UNODC	United Nations Office on Drugs and Crime
UNSC / SC	United Nations Security Council
US	United States (adjective)
USA	United States of America (noun)
VASP	virtual asset service provider
VCLT	Vienna Convention on the Law of Treaties
WTO	World Trade Organization

TABLE OF CASES

Australia

Canada

Court of Justice of the European Union

European arbitration

European Court of Human Rights

France

International arbitration

International Court of Justice (including Permanent Court of International Justice)

International Criminal Tribunal for the Former Yugoslavia

International Tribunal for the Law of the Sea

Iran/US Claims Tribunal

Italy

NAFTA Arbitration Tribunal

Permanent Court of Arbitration

United Kingdom

UN Human Rights Committee

UNCITRAL Ad Hoc Tribunal

United States of America

World Trade Organization

Other

TABLE OF STATUTES

Belarus

China

Uganda

United States of America

TABLE OF INTERNATIONAL INSTRUMENTS

Treaties

EU documents

GATT documents

UN documents

US documents

Introduction

RUSSELL BUCHAN, DANIEL FRANCHINI
AND NICHOLAS TSAGOURIAS

Disputes are a persistent feature of international relations. Cyberspace is no exception, with existing offline disputes migrating to cyberspace and new cyber-specific disputes emerging. Cyber disputes can appear in many forms: factual, economic, political, strategic, military, legal or a combination thereof.

Disputes can potentially disrupt the international order and endanger international peace and security.[1] For this reason, there have been many initiatives throughout history to forge a culture of peaceful settlement of disputes and to develop mechanisms to facilitate such settlement.[2]

In the contemporary international order established by the United Nations (UN), the peaceful settlement of international disputes is one of its guiding principles and goals. It is enshrined in Article 2(3) of the UN Charter, which reads: 'all Member States shall settle their international disputes by peaceful means in such a manner that international peace and security, and justice, are not endangered'.

Article 2(3) of the UN Charter is complemented by Article 33(1),[3] which also lays down a non-exhaustive list of modalities for settling disputes likely to endanger international peace and security.[4]

[1] D Franchini and R Buchan, 'The Obligation of Peaceful Settlement of International Disputes: Status, Nature, Content, and Scope' in R Buchan, D Franchini and N Tsagourias (eds), *The Changing Character of Dispute Settlement: Challenges and Prospects* (Cambridge, Cambridge University, 2023) 15; H Kelsen, *Peace through Law* (Chapel Hill, University of North Carolina Press, 1944) 32: 'Nothing is more dangerous to peace than the existence of a conflict which is not settled.'

[2] See, eg, Treaty of Amity, Commerce and Navigation, between His Britannic Majesty and the United States of America, by their President, with the Advice and Consent of their Senate (London, 19 November 1794); Convention for the Pacific Settlement of International Disputes (The Hague, 29 July 1899); Convention for the Pacific Settlement of International Disputes (The Hague, 18 October 1907); Covenant of the League of Nations (Paris, 28 June 1919) Arts 12 and 13; League of Nations Protocol for the Pacific Settlement of International Disputes (Geneva, 2 October 1924); General Act for the Pacific Settlement of International Disputes (Geneva, 26 September 1928).

[3] DD Caron and C Tomuschat, 'Article 2, para 3 UN Charter' in A Zimmermann et al (eds), *The Statute of the International Court of Justice: A Commentary*, 3rd edn (Oxford, Oxford University Press, 2019) 125.

[4] Art 33 of the Charter of the United Nations (San Francisco, 26 June 1945) reads: 'The parties to any dispute, the continuance of which is likely to endanger the maintenance of international peace and security, shall, first of all, seek a solution by negotiation, enquiry, mediation, conciliation, arbitration, judicial settlement, resort to regional agencies or arrangements, or other peaceful means of their own choice.'

The obligation to settle disputes peacefully has been reaffirmed in many UN resolutions, the most important of which is the Declaration on Friendly Relations.[5] Nowadays, it has acquired customary law status.[6] This means that all international legal persons have an obligation to settle their disputes peacefully.[7]

The peaceful settlement of disputes – being a guiding principle of the contemporary international order as well as a rule of international law – applies to cyberspace to the extent that states have confirmed the application of international law and the UN Charter to this domain and recognised the threat that malicious cyber activities pose to international peace and security.[8]

The 2021 Group of Governmental Experts (GGE) report, for example, provides:

> An affected State's response to malicious ICT activity attributable to another State should be in accordance with its obligations under the Charter of the United Nations and other international law, including those relating to the settlement of disputes by peaceful means and internationally wrongful acts. States could also avail of the full range of diplomatic, legal and other consultative options available to them, as well as voluntary mechanisms and other political commitments that allow for the settlement of disagreements and disputes through consultation and other peaceful means.[9]

The 2021 GGE report thus reaffirms states' commitment to settle their cyber disputes peacefully by using diverse means and methods, including informal and

[5] UNGA, 'Declaration on Principles of International Law Concerning Friendly Relations and Co-operation among States in Accordance with the Charter of the United Nations' (24 October 1970) UN Doc A/RES/2625(XXV) (the Friendly Relations Declaration) Annex. See also UNGA, 'Manila Declaration on the Peaceful Settlement of International Disputes' (15 November 1982) UN Doc A/RES/37/10 (the Manila Declaration); UNGA, 'Declaration on the Prevention and Removal of Disputes and Situations which May Threaten International Peace and Security and on the Role of the United Nations in this Field' (5 December 1988) UN Doc A/RES/43/51.

[6] *Case Concerning Military and Paramilitary Activities in and against Nicaragua (Nicaragua v United States of America)* (Merits, Judgment of 27 June 1986) [1986] ICJ Rep 14 para 290. See also *Request for Interpretation of the Judgment of 15 June 1962 in the Case Concerning the Temple of Preah Vihear (Cambodia v Thailand)* (Judgment of 11 November 2013) [2013] ICJ Rep 281 paras 105–06; *Accordance with International Law of the Unilateral Declaration of Independence in Respect of Kosovo* (Advisory Opinion of 22 July 2010) [2010] ICJ Rep 403 para 80.

[7] See, eg, Arts 14, 35, 36, 52 and 98 of the UN Charter; *Reparation for Injuries Suffered in the Service of the United Nations* (Advisory Opinion of 11 April 1949) [1949] ICJ Rep 174, 177.

[8] 'States … are increasingly concerned about the implications of the malicious use of ICTs for the maintenance of international peace and security, and subsequently for human rights and development. In particular, concern was expressed regarding the development of ICT capabilities for purposes that undermine international peace and security. Harmful ICT incidents are increasing in frequency and sophistication, and are constantly evolving and diversifying. Increasing connectivity and reliance on ICTs without accompanying measures to ensure ICT security can bring unintended risks, making societies more vulnerable to malicious ICT activities. Despite the invaluable benefits of ICTs for humanity, their malicious use can have significant and far-reaching negative impacts.' UNGA, 'Final Substantive Report of the Open-Ended Working Group on Developments in the Field of Information and Telecommunications in the Context of International Security' (10 March 2021) UN Doc A/AC.290/2021/CRP.2 para 15.

[9] UNGA, 'Report of the Group of Governmental Experts on Advancing Responsible State Behaviour in Cyberspace in the Context of International Security' (14 July 2021) UN Doc A/76/135 para 25.

voluntary ones. By explicitly mentioning such methods, the report appeals to states' ingenuity and incentivises states to settle their cyber disputes peacefully.

The 2021 Open-Ended Working Group (OEWG) final report reaffirmed this obligation. It reads:

> States also reaffirmed that States shall seek the settlement of disputes by peaceful means such as negotiation, enquiry, mediation, conciliation, arbitration, judicial settlement, and resort to regional agencies or arrangements, or other peaceful means of their own choice.[10]

The new OEWG vowed to explore the application of international law to cyber operations, including the peaceful settlement of disputes, with a view to identifying areas of convergence and consensus. As the 2023 progress report noted, states reaffirmed the application of Articles 2(3) and 33 of the UN Charter to cyberspace.[11]

Individual states have also affirmed the application of this principle to cyberspace. According to Canada:

> A central, and at times overlooked, rule of international law is the obligation of every State, under the UN Charter, to seek the settlement of disputes by peaceful means. This is closely related to the prohibition of the threat or use of force. Like that prohibition, it applies in cyberspace just as it does elsewhere. Thus, Canada considers that in line with the UN Charter, in case of disputes States may seek solutions through negotiation, enquiry, mediation, conciliation, arbitration, judicial settlement, and resort to regional agencies or arrangements, or other peaceful means of their own choice.[12]

And for Costa Rica:

> In accordance with Article 2(3) of the UN Charter, States 'shall settle their international disputes by peaceful means in such a manner that international peace and security, and justice, are not endangered'. Likewise, under Article 33(1) of the Charter, in the case of a dispute 'the continuance of which is likely to endanger the maintenance of international peace and security', States 'shall, first of all, seek a solution by negotiation, enquiry, mediation, conciliation, arbitration, judicial settlement, resort to regional agencies or arrangements, or other peaceful means of their own choice.' They must do so in good faith. Both provisions encapsulate the customary principle of peaceful settlement of disputes, which applies to factual or legal disputes involving cyber operations.[13]

[10] UNGA, 'Final Substantive Report of the OEWG' UN Doc A/AC.290/2021/CRP.2 para 35.

[11] UNGA, 'Developments in the Field of Information and Telecommunications in the Context of International Security' (1 August 2023) UN Doc A/78/265 para 30.

[12] Government of Canada, 'International Law Applicable in Cyberspace' (April 2022) www.international.gc.ca/world-monde/issues_development-enjeux_developpement/peace_security-paix_securite/cyberspace_law-cyberespace_droit.aspx?lang=eng para 41.

[13] Ministry of Foreign Affairs of Costa Rica, 'Costa Rica's Position on the Application of International Law in Cyberspace' (21 July 2023) docs-library.unoda.org/Open-Ended_Working_Group_on_Information_and_Communication_Technologies_-_(2021)/Costa_Rica_-_Position_Paper_-_International_Law_in_Cyberspace.pdf para 17.

Other states that explicitly mentioned this principle include Estonia,[14] Japan,[15] Kenya,[16] Singapore,[17] and Switzerland.[18] The Common African Position on the application of international law in cyberspace not only recognises the importance of the obligation to settle cyber disputes peacefully but also recognises the potential of using ICTs for the peaceful settlement of disputes.[19]

The Tallinn Manual 2.0 provides that states 'must attempt to settle their international disputes involving cyber activities that endanger international peace and security by peaceful means' and continues by saying, 'if States attempt to settle their international disputes involving cyber activities that do not endanger international peace and security, they must do so by peaceful means'.[20]

The Tallinn Manual distinguishes disputes that may endanger international peace and security whose peaceful settlement is mandatory from other disputes whose settlement is not mandatory but, at minimum, their settlement should not be forcible. This seems to diverge from Article 2(3), which does not make such a distinction, although it should be admitted that the scope of disputes which can endanger international peace and security can be quite broad.[21]

Having provided an overview of the import of this obligation to cyberspace, the immediate question is, what does the obligation of peaceful settlement entail when applied to cyber disputes? First, the obligation of peaceful settlement covers all cyber disputes regardless of their nature. This is reflected in the attendant dispute settlement mechanisms, which cater to different types of disputes. While a distinction is often made between political and legal disputes, no criteria for their classification are provided. Indeed, international disputes are often multifaceted.[22]

[14] UNGA, 'Official Compendium of Voluntary National Contributions on the Subject of How International Law Applies to the Use of Information and Communications Technologies by States Submitted by Participating Governmental Experts in the Group of Governmental Experts on Advancing Responsible State Behaviour in Cyberspace in the Context of International Security Established Pursuant to General Assembly Resolution 73/266' (13 July 2021) UN Doc A/76/136, 29.

[15] Ministry of Foreign Affairs of Japan, 'Basic Position of the Government of Japan on International Law Applicable to Cyber Operations' (28 May 2021) www.mofa.go.jp/files/100200935.pdf 6.

[16] UNGA, 'Official Compendium' UN Doc A/76/136, 54.

[17] ibid 83.

[18] Swiss Federal Department of Foreign Affairs, 'Switzerland's Position Paper on the Application of International Law in Cyberspace' (May 2021) www.eda.admin.ch/dam/eda/en/documents/aussenpolitik/voelkerrecht/20210527-Schweiz-Annex-UN-GGE-Cybersecurity-2019-2021_EN.pdf 2.

[19] African Union, 'Common African Position on the Application of International Law to the Use of Information and Communication Technologies in Cyberspace' (29 January 2024) docs-library.unoda.org/Open-Ended_Working_Group_on_Information_and_Communication_Technologies_-_(2021)/CAP_Communiques_FULL_0e34eb5799.pdf.

[20] MN Schmitt (ed), *Tallinn Manual 2.0 on the International Law Applicable to Cyber Operations*, 2nd edn (Cambridge, Cambridge University Press, 2017) Rule 65.

[21] See UNSC, 'Resolution 2532 (2020) Adopted by the Security Council on 1 July 2020)' (1 July 2020) UN Doc S/RES/2532 (2020) in relation to COVID-19. The Common African Position explicitly says that the obligation of peaceful settlement is not limited to disputes that may endanger peace and security. See above n 19, para 35.

[22] As the International Court of Justice jurisprudence indicates, the Court does not dismiss cases because of their political aspects but entertains their legal aspects. *United States Diplomatic and Consular Staff in Tehran (United States of America v Iran)* (Judgment of 24 May 1980) [1980] ICJ Rep 3

That said, the distinction may play a role in the choice of means and the basis upon which a dispute will be settled. In this regard, how the parties package their dispute, for example, in factual, political, economic, legal or other terms, the nature of their claims, the type of dispute settlement modality they chose, and the nature of the prescription they seek are critical in categorising the dispute.

Second, the obligation of peaceful settlement is one of conduct and not result. If a cyber dispute arises, states should seek a peaceful settlement, which means that states should act in good faith to settle their dispute.[23] Good faith also entails that states should seek alternative means of settlement in case of failure and not aggravate the dispute with their actions.[24] This raises the question of whether lawful reactions such as countermeasures or acts of retorsion can aggravate a dispute.[25] States also have a free choice of means when settling their disputes,[26] whereas all dispute settlement mechanisms are subject to state consent. While state consent and the freedom in the choice of means may affect the swift settlement of cyber disputes, states are nonetheless bound to seek peaceful settlement and not aggravate the situation.

Third, the obligation of peaceful settlement requires that no force should be used to settle a dispute.[27] This means that Article 2(3) is closely linked to the prohibition of the use of force enshrined in Article 2(4) of the UN Charter and customary law. However, these obligations are not conditional on each other, as in the League of Nations Covenant.[28] Thus, failure to settle a dispute does not make the resort to force lawful because the prohibition on the use of force and

para 36 ('no provision of the Statute or Rules contemplates that the Court should decline to take cognizance of one aspect of a dispute merely because that dispute has other aspects, however important'; *Border and Transborder Armed Actions (Nicaragua v Honduras)* (Jurisdiction and Admissibility, Judgment of 20 December 1988) [1988] ICJ Rep 69 para 54.

[23] The Manila Declaration paras 1, 5 and 11. *Aerial Incident of 10 August 1999 (Pakistan v India)* (Jurisdiction of the Court, Judgment of 21 June 2000) [2000] ICJ Rep 12 para 53 ('The choice of those means admittedly rests with the parties under Article 33 of the United Nations Charter. They are nonetheless under an obligation to seek such a settlement, and to do so in good faith in accordance with Article 2, paragraph 2, of the Charter').

[24] Friendly Relations Declaration, Second Principle, para 4: 'States … shall refrain from any action which may aggravate the situation so as to endanger the maintenance of international peace and security'; the Manila Declaration para 8; Manila Declaration on the Peaceful Settlement of International Disputes, above n 5, para 8. SR Ratner, 'The Aggravating Duty of Non-Aggravation' (2021) 31 *European Journal of International Law* 1307.

[25] See Franchini and Buchan (n 1) 39. See also Buchan (ch 9 in this volume).

[26] Friendly Relations Declaration, Second Principle, para 5. *Obligation to Negotiate Access to the Pacific Ocean (Bolivia v Chile)* (Judgment of 1 October 2018) [2018] ICJ Rep 507 para 165; *South China Sea Arbitration*, Philippines v China, Award, PCA Case No 2013-19, ICGJ 495 (PCA 2016), 12th July 2016, paras 1171–79; *Fisheries Jurisdiction (Spain v Canada)* (Jurisdiction, Judgment of 4 December 1998) [1998] ICJ Rep 432 para 56 ('disputes are required to be resolved by peaceful means, the choice of which, pursuant to Article 33 of the Charter, is left to the parties'); *Case Concerning the Factory at Chorzów* (Merits, Judgment of 13 September 1928) PCIJ Rep Series A No 17, 32; *Rights of Minorities in Upper Silesia (Minority Schools) (Germany v Poland)* (Judgment of 26 April 1928) PCIJ Rep Series A No 15, 22; *Status of Eastern Carelia* (Advisory Opinion of 23 July 1923) [1923] PCIJ Rep Series B No 5, 27.

[27] *Military and Paramilitary Activities in and against Nicaragua* [1986] ICJ Rep 14 para 290; *Maritime Boundary (Guyana v Suriname)* (2007) 30 RIAA 1 paras 483–84.

[28] Arts 12 and 13 of the League of Nations Covenant.

the obligation to settle disputes peacefully are independent injunctions. Yet, the obligation to settle disputes peacefully underpins the efficacy of the obligation not to use force.

Be that as it may, the question that can be asked is whether the advent of cyber disputes presents specific legal challenges regarding their peaceful settlement. In our opinion, certain challenges are common in the offline and online world, alongside distinct cyber-specific challenges.

A common challenge is the uneven implementation of this obligation across different fields of international law due to the fact that it is dependent on state consent. Power differentials and the involvement of essential state interests contribute further to this situation.

Turning to cyber-specific challenges, most cyber operations are conducted covertly and remain unattributed. Even if they become known, acting states do not acknowledge them, whereas victim states prefer to respond in kind, that is, covertly. Moreover, attribution or the particulars of the operation are usually shrouded by ambiguity.

Another challenge arises from the lack of clarity regarding the scope and content of international law when applied to cyberspace. This prevents international law from becoming a tool of dispute settlement. In an uncertain legal environment, states do not want to pre-empt their legal views, knowing that their approach, as well as the dispute settlement process itself, can have law-generative effects. Of course, states can use other more political processes to settle their cyber disputes. However, such processes create their own legacy and expectations and contribute to some form of regulation. For this reason, states prefer informal and non-binding mechanisms which may play a role in dispute settlement but frustrate or delay its formalisation in cyberspace.

This relates to another challenge, namely, the fact that current debates about the regulation of cyberspace evolve around certain fundamental questions, such as whether new rules are required and which changes in the existing law are needed, or which institutions and stakeholders should be involved in the regulation of cyberspace. For all these, there are divergent regulatory preferences which fall within the political realm.

Another challenge is that in the offline world, there is a process of centralisation, institutionalisation, multiplication, and judicialisation of dispute settlement in many fields, often accompanied by regionalisation and specialisation. Although most of these processes depend directly or indirectly on state consent and may be blamed for fragmenting the dispute settlement process, this network of institutions and processes indeed provides more opportunities for the settlement of disputes.[29] Also, in the physical world, there is more emphasis on preventing disputes, for example, through monitoring, good offices, good practices, or reporting. Cyberspace currently lacks many of these features. Although existing mechanisms

[29] A Peters, 'International Dispute Settlement: A Network of Cooperational Duties' (2003) 14 *European Journal of International Law* 1.

and processes could, in principle, address cyber disputes, they require reforms to overcome jurisdictional, factual, or other obstacles that make them unavailable for cyber disputes.

This leads to the next question: whether and to what extent existing mechanisms and processes are suitable to deal with cyber disputes, what changes are needed or whether new mechanisms should be designed, and what their form and processes will be. Another issue to consider is who can have locus standi before cyber dispute settlement mechanisms and, more specifically, whether non-governmental organisations (NGOs), individuals, private companies, or generally non-state actors can use them in addition to states and international organisations. This is important because cyberspace and cyber disputes may have many stakeholders. Related to this is the question of what form their appearance should take and what function they will serve. Issues of procedure also warrant attention, for example, what evidence should be used and how evidence will be presented and probed.

Broader questions should also be considered. If dispute settlement serves international peace and security, what is the meaning and content of peace and security in cyberspace? Is it only the absence of war or also the absence of the structural causes that can lead to conflict and war?[30] What does 'peaceful' mean in the peaceful settlement of disputes? Does it only mean the absence of force or also a modicum of justice? Finally, what does settlement mean? Does it mean the resolution of the dispute or its management?

These questions provide the trigger to this book together with the realisation that whereas the scholarship and practice on the peaceful settlement of international disputes are dense and articulate,[31] little attention has been devoted to the peaceful settlement of cyber disputes, even though cyberspace has become a highly conflictual environment. This led to a two-day international conference held in March 2021 at the University of Sheffield under the auspices of the Sheffield Centre for International and European Law on the peaceful settlement of cyber disputes.[32] The issues covered at the conference were new and challenging, but all distinguished participants – academics and practitioners – offered great insights distilled from their knowledge and experience.

This present volume draws from that conference but also includes new chapters and contributors. This volume is the first academic study of how the peaceful settlement of inter-state cyber disputes should be understood and practised by

[30] J Galtung, 'Peace: Negative and Positive' in NJ Young (ed), *Oxford International Encyclopaedia of Peace, Volume 3* (Oxford, Oxford University Press, 2010) 352–56.

[31] Indicatively see D French, M Saul and ND White (eds), *International Law and Dispute Settlement: New Problems and Techniques* (London, Bloomsbury Publishing, 2010); Y Tanaka, *The Peaceful Settlement of International Disputes* (Cambridge, Cambridge University Press, 2018); JG Merrills and E de Brabandere, *Merrill's Dispute Settlement*, 7th edn (Cambridge, Cambridge University Press, 2022); DB Hollis and E Tikk, 'Peaceful Settlement in International Law' (2022) 57 *Texas International Law Journal* 1; Buchan, Franchini and Tsagourias (n 1).

[32] For the conference report, see University of Sheffield School of Law, 'The Peaceful Settlement of Cyber Disputes' (4–5 March 2021) www.sheffield.ac.uk/law/research/centres-and-institutes/sciel/events/peaceful-settlement-cyber-disputes.

assessing the adequacy of current actors and methods and considering alternatives. In this regard, the book offers academics and practitioners a roadmap not only for analysis and assessment but also for projection regarding the peaceful settlement of cyber disputes.

The book has three main goals: its first goal is to reassess the meaning and parameters of dispute settlement as they apply to cyber disputes; the second is to explore several critical questions regarding the actors and methods of dispute settlement; and the third is to identify and address where possible any challenges and difficulties that arise in order to make the dispute settlement regime suitable for cyber disputes.

The structure and content of the book are based on these considerations.

The book opens with a chapter by Nicholas Tsagourias, which explains the transformation of a cyber dispute into an international legal dispute. The chapter then explains what an international legal dispute consists of and applies this to four cyber scenarios in order to consider whether they give rise to a legal dispute. The first scenario concerns disagreements over cyber facts by looking into attribution; the second concerns disagreements over points of international law and legal interests; the third concerns disagreements in multilateral fora; and the fourth concerns covert cyber operations and the legal issues they may give rise to.

The second chapter by Robert Kolb and Andraz Kastelic evaluates the doctrine of good faith in the context of peaceful settlement of cyber disputes. After outlining the specific obligations stemming from this doctrine and reviewing it in the cyber domain, the chapter concludes that the general, well-established rules on the settlement of disputes remain applicable to cyberspace, albeit with some adjustments and adaptations. The chapter then considers specific rules as they apply to dispute settlement in the information and communications technology (ICT) domain: first, the obligation to preserve confidentiality, which is imperative in the era of prevalent, mass remote intelligence collection via digital technologies; second, the prohibition of aggravation, which prohibits not only aggravating conduct but also dereliction of due diligence in respect of potentially aggravating cyber operations from a particular territory; third, the obligation to protect legitimate expectations, which can be created through unilateral declarations or state practice in the absence of a codified legal regime dedicated to the governance of state conduct in cyberspace; and fourth, the obligation of disclosure, which is at worst non-existent and at best emerging in disputed state ICT conduct.

The third chapter by Daniel Franchini considers the role of domestic courts in the settlement of cyber disputes. It claims that domestic courts play a crucial role in settling international cyber disputes. It then examines two avenues through which domestic courts engage in this domain. First, they can serve as 'gatekeepers' by reviewing executive and legislative actions and ensuring that malicious cyber operations originating from their state adhere to international obligations ('internal engagement'). This approach helps pre-empt the emergence of international disputes. Second, domestic courts can target state-sponsored malicious cyber operations from abroad through legal proceedings against individuals, state officials and private cyber contractors ('external engagement'). This enables domestic courts to advance claims against other states, develop international norms applicable to cyberspace, and, in certain instances, contribute to the settlement of international disputes.

The fourth chapter by Constantine Antonopoulos discusses the role of the International Court of Justice as a probable forum for settling cyber disputes. It argues that the particularities of cyberspace may raise questions of jurisdiction, for example, questions about the existence of a dispute, as well as the question about the admissibility of applications instituting proceedings, for example, questions on *locus standi* or the application of the *Monetary Gold* principle. Moreover, cyber claims may be raised by or against a plurality of states, leading to the joinder of cases by the Court. The chapter concludes by saying that the particularities of cyberspace militate for a more liberal or flexible approach to objections to jurisdiction or admissibility and the evaluation of evidence at the merits stage.

The fifth chapter by Annegret Bendiek, Martin Müller, and Matthias Kettemann focuses on the European Union's (EU's) internal and external cyber policy, principally expressed in its Cybersecurity Strategy. It analyses three elements of that strategy and positions them within its framework and the EU's overarching goal of achieving digital sovereignty. It first analyses the EU's approach to digital sovereignty as the generic concept behind its digital policy. It then turns to cyber resilience, cyber diplomacy, and cyber defence to show that the Union's cyber policies have internal normative foundations and produce several external effects. Finally, it discusses the Union's contribution to the peaceful settlement of cyber conflicts.

The sixth chapter by Tomohiro Mikanagi explores how the UN Security Council can contribute to the settlement of disputes involving malicious cyber operations that threaten international peace and security. Faced with such operations and the possible involvement of states, the Security Council should try to find out who the perpetrator is and examine the claims relating to the possible involvement of states. If the Council is not able to take decisive action, such as the condemnation of certain actors or the adoption of targeted sanctions, it can still condemn certain cyber activities as being unacceptable for the maintenance of international peace and security. In this regard, the UN GGE and OEWG have contributed to the clarification of which cyber operations are unacceptable by indicating that malicious cyber operations with serious impacts on critical infrastructure could threaten international peace and security. The chapter finally argues that the Security Council and other UN organs should continuously pay attention to the potential threat to international peace and security posed by malicious cyber operations and consider various options for addressing the associated risks.

The seventh chapter by Iakovos Iakovidis focuses on the role of cyber diplomacy in settling disputes. It claims that the peaceful settlement of disputes and the avoidance of force are also compelling in cyberspace. The chapter then assesses the role of cyber diplomacy in the form of bilateral, regional and global negotiations.

In this regard, it considers the UN GGE and OEWG processes as well as the UN Cybercrime Treaty. Its overriding claim is that cyber diplomacy uses old but also devises new tools to enhance cooperation, build trust, and settle disputes peacefully in cyberspace.

The eighth chapter by Joanna Kulesza considers international law measures for the settlement of inter-state data disputes. The chapter compares and contrasts the European approach to data with its clear dichotomy between personal and non-personal information with other regional approaches, particularly those of the US and China. The chapter looks at the EU's attempts to enforce extraterritorial jurisdiction with the General Data Protection Regulation and its 'Brussels effect' in light of the *Schrems* judgments. It also reviews existing measures targeting disinformation and online hate speech when confronted with national cybersecurity challenges. These examples allow for the identification of key challenges to the free flow of data as well as specific challenges to individual privacy and national security. They are then analysed with reference to existing international law instruments for solving inter-state disputes and with due regard to judicial and non-judicial means of dispute resolution.

The ninth chapter by Russell Buchan examines the role of collective and third-party countermeasures in implementing state responsibility for internationally wrongful cyber activity. The chapter draws a critical distinction between these doctrines: collective countermeasures involve indirectly injured states taking countermeasures against wrongdoing states to help protect *erga omnes (partes)* obligations, whereas third-party countermeasures involve non-injured states taking countermeasures on behalf of injured states to help protect the latter's legal rights against wrongdoing states. The chapter finds insufficient evidence of state practice and *opinio juris* to conclude that these doctrines are established in customary international law. However, in response to the sharp rise in malicious cyber activity, it recognises that state practice and *opinio juris* are growing in favour of collective countermeasures.

The tenth chapter by Pål Wrange claims that states are reluctant to settle their cyber disputes in the public eye and even more unwilling to involve third parties. There are several reasons for that, such as lack of agreement on the content of the law, difficulties in proving the facts of a dispute – especially relating to attribution – and the need for particular expertise. Nevertheless, the well-established and tried mechanisms of arbitration, conciliation and fact-finding (inquiry) are flexible and can be adjusted to accommodate at least some difficulties. Other methods could also be useful in the settlement of cyber disputes, for example, bilateral commissions. It concludes by saying that because states are obligated to settle cyber disputes peacefully, particularly those endangering international peace and security, they should be more creative in finding ways to overcome any challenges in this respect.

All in all, the book offers valuable insights into how the legal and institutional pillars of the system of dispute settlement apply to cyber disputes and, for this reason, it will provide knowledge and guidance to scholars, policymakers and practitioners, not only those specialising in cyber law but also those interested in international dispute settlement in general.

PART I

Concepts

1

Cyber Disputes as International Legal Disputes

NICHOLAS TSAGOURIAS*

I. Introduction

Cyberspace, with the resources and opportunities it offers, has become an important domain of state interaction in political, economic, social, military, cultural, and legal terms. As a result, inter-state disputes may arise, exacerbated by cyberspace's factual and technological complexity and the normative and regulatory uncertainty that currently characterises it.

If disputes arise, states are under an obligation to settle them peacefully.[1] This obligation is central to maintaining international peace and security and the rule of law in the global society.[2] It is also an obligation that applies to cyberspace, as the United Nations (UN) Group of Governmental Experts on Developments in the Field of Information and Telecommunications in the Context of International Security (GGE) and Open-Ended Working Group on Security of and in the Use of Information and Communications Technologies (OEWG) reports recognise.[3]

Cyber disputes appear in many different forms: political, economic, military, social, and factual, but this chapter explores the question of when cyber disputes become legal disputes and, indeed, international legal disputes. Distinguishing

* I would like to thank Dr Massimo Lando, Dr Daniel Franchini and Professor Russell Buchan for their invaluable comments on earlier drafts of this chapter. The usual disclaimer applies.

[1] Arts 2(3) and 33 of the Charter of the United Nations (San Francisco, 26 June 1945).

[2] D Franchini and R Buchan, 'The Obligation of Peaceful Settlement of International Disputes' in R Buchan, D Franchini and N Tsagourias (eds), *The Changing Character of International Dispute Settlement: Challenges and Prospects* (Cambridge, CUP, 2023) 15–44.

[3] UNGA, 'Report of the Group of Governmental Experts on Developments in the Field of Information and Telecommunications in the Context of International Security' (22 July 2015) UN Doc A/70/174 para 26; UNGA, 'Report of the Group of Governmental Experts on Advancing Responsible State Behaviour in Cyberspace in the Context of International Security' (14 July 2021) UN Doc A/76/135 para 25; UNGA, 'Final Substantive Report of the Open-Ended Working Group on Developments in the Field of Information and Telecommunications in the Context of International Security' (10 March 2021) UN Doc A/AC.290/2021/CRP.2 para 35.

legal disputes from other disputes is important because they acquire their own ontology even if they unfold within a broader context[4] and thus require a distinct conceptual framework of analysis. International law will define the substance of the dispute, explain which behavioural patterns are relevant to the dispute, demarcate the boundaries within which disputants and dispute resolution institutions perform their roles, and define the nature of the settlement. In short, international law becomes the applicable framework for disposing of the dispute.

To answer the question of when cyber disputes become international legal disputes, the chapter will first explain how inter-state disagreements, controversies or grievances over cyber matters become disputes and, indeed, international legal disputes. The chapter will then explain what an international legal dispute consists of and apply this definition to four cyber scenarios in order to consider whether they give rise to a legal dispute. The first scenario concerns disagreements over cyber facts by focusing on cyber attribution; the second concerns disagreements over points of international law or conflict of legal interests; the third concerns disagreements over international law in multilateral settings; and the fourth concerns covert cyber operations and the legal issues they give rise to. The last section contains concluding thoughts about the current status of cyber disputes.

Before proceeding, certain clarifications are in order. First, the chapter focuses on inter-state cyber disputes. Consequently, it will not deal with cyber disputes between and among states, individuals and companies. Second, the chapter focuses on international legal disputes, and thus, the use of the term 'legal dispute' should always be interpreted as referring to international legal disputes. Third, the definition of 'international legal dispute' adopted in this chapter is a generic one and not a technical definition for adjudication purposes.[5] This is because courts may have their own jurisdiction and admissibility criteria but also because legal disputes may be settled through non-judicial mechanisms.

[4] *United States Diplomatic and Consular Staff in Tehran (United States of America v Iran)* (Judgment of 24 May 1980) [1980] ICJ Rep 3 paras 36–37; *Aegean Sea Continental Shelf Case (Greece v Turkey)* (Judgment of 19 December 1978) [1978] ICJ Rep 3 para 31; *Case Concerning Military and Paramilitary Activities in and against Nicaragua (Nicaragua v USA)* (Jurisdiction and Admissibility, Judgment of 26 November 1984) [1984] ICJ Rep 392 paras 101, 105–06; *Application of the Interim Accord of 13 September 1995 (The Former Yugoslav Republic of Macedonia v Greece)* (Judgment of 5 December 2011) [2011] ICJ Rep 644 para 37.

[5] *Nuclear Tests (Australia v France)* (Judgment of 20 December 1974) [1974] ICJ Rep 253 para 55; *Obligations Concerning Negotiations Relating to Cessation of the Nuclear Arms Race and to Nuclear Disarmament (Marshall Islands v United Kingdom)* (Preliminary Objections, Judgment of 5 October 2016) [2016] ICJ Rep 833, Declaration of President Abraham, 858, para 3. RY Jennings, 'Reflections on the Term "Dispute"' in RSJ Macdonald (ed), *Essays in Honour of Wang Tieya* (Dordrecht, Martinus Nijhoff, 1993) 401, 403: 'A "legal dispute" in a technical and realistic sense is accordingly, one which has been … processed, or reduced, into a form suitable for decision by a court of law; *i.e.* a series of specific issues for decision.' See also Antonopoulos (ch 4 in this volume).

II. Legal Disputes and the Transformation Process

Disputes between states arise from conflicts. A conflict can be defined as a general situation of hostility, contestation, or competition between states.[6] Conflicts are woven into the fabric of every society, with international society being no exception. In cyberspace, inter-state conflicts can be strategic, political, military, technological, or economic, with states resorting to certain activities to strengthen their position and affect, change, or modify their competitors' position. In a conflictual environment, a dispute may arise through a process of transformation. It is, therefore, important to explain how conflicts are transformed into disputes and, indeed, international legal disputes because disputes are constructs arising in a particular context under certain conditions, requiring agency and a certain level of interaction between the parties.

The transformation of a conflict into a dispute involves a process of 'naming, blaming, and claiming'.[7] Naming refers to the recognition of the existence of divergent views or that something wrong has happened. Blaming refers to the identification of the wrongdoer or the opposing party, in other words, the attribution of the opposite view or wrongdoing to another actor. Claiming is the process of communicating a claim to the other party which is contested in whole or in part by that party in the sense of rejecting the claim or presenting a counterclaim.[8] Such contestation is the essence of the dispute, and as the International Court of Justice (ICJ) explained, for a dispute to exist, 'the claim of one party is positively opposed by the other'.[9]

It follows that a dispute is transformed into an international legal dispute when the aforementioned steps are framed in international law terms. To explain, an international legal dispute comes into existence when divergent views on

[6] JG Collier and AV Lowe, *The Settlement of Disputes in International Law* (Oxford, Oxford University Press, 2000) 1.

[7] WL Felstiner, RL Abel and A Sarat, 'The Emergence and Transformation of Disputes: Naming, Blaming, Claiming' (1980) 15 *Law & Society Review* 631–54.

[8] *South West Africa Cases (Ethiopia v South Africa; Liberia v South Africa)* (Preliminary Objections, Judgment of 21 December 1962) [1962] ICJ Rep 319, 328; *Obligations Concerning Negotiations* (n 5) para 37.

[9] *South West Africa Cases* (n 8) 328; *Certain Property (Liechtenstein v Germany)* (Preliminary Objections, Judgment of 10 February 2005) [2005] ICJ Rep 6 para 24; *Obligations Concerning Negotiations* (n 5) para 37. In the words of Judge Morelli, 'a manifestation of the will, at least of one of the parties, consisting in the making of a claim or of a protest is a necessary element for a dispute to be regarded as existing. By this manifestation of the will the party in question asserts the requirement of the realization of an interest of its own'. *South West Africa Cases* (n 8), dissenting opinion of Judge Morelli, 567. Also p 568: 'whether there was present an opposing attitude on the part of Ethiopia and Liberia or on the part of one or other of these two States, such an attitude could consist only in a manifestation of will: either in a prior claim designed to secure a course of conduct by South Africa different from that in fact pursued; or in a subsequent protest against that course of conduct'. See also *Obligations Concerning Negotiations* (n 5), separate opinion of Judge Owada, 879, paras 6–7.

international law are identified or when wrongfulness is characterised as such based on international law (naming), which are attributed to a particular state (blaming), and an international law-based claim and counterclaim are put forward (claiming).

Being a construct, a dispute requires transforming agents. The primary transforming agents for an international legal dispute are states. They can transform their dispute into an international legal dispute by using international law vocabulary when naming, blaming, and claiming, and by appealing to international law and international law methods to settle the dispute. This suggests that the transformation of a dispute into an international legal dispute is an agent-driven process. The ICJ has repeatedly asserted that whether a dispute exists is a matter of objective determination,[10] which appears to contradict the previous statement. In fact, there is no contradiction because the Court is referring to the evidence needed to prove the existence of a dispute which derives from states' conduct. If the conduct of states or their statements evidence opposing views on a particular matter, a legal dispute exists, notwithstanding any assertions to the opposite.[11]

Being a construct, a dispute also requires some interaction and communication between the disputants in the form of blaming and claiming. The ICJ labelled this aspect of the transformation process as 'awareness' in that the other party should be 'aware or could not have been unaware' of the claims[12] but awareness is a communicative act not requiring knowledge of the specificities of the claim.

Although the process of transformation is engineered and managed by the parties to the dispute, certain factors may accelerate this process and contribute to the emergence of a legal dispute. One such factor is the existence of a particular 'trigger' event and its seriousness,[13] for example, the occurrence of a severe

[10] *Interpretation of Peace Treaties with Bulgaria, Hungary and Romania* (Advisory Opinion of 30 March 1950) [1950] ICJ Rep 65, 74; *Alleged Violations of Sovereign Rights and Maritime Spaces in the Caribbean Sea (Nicaragua v Colombia)* (Preliminary Objections, Judgment of 17 March 2016) [2016] ICJ Rep 3 para 50; *Obligations Concerning Negotiations* (n 5) para 39.

[11] See, eg, *Applicability of the Obligation to Arbitrate Under Section 21 of the United Nations Headquarters Agreement of 26 June 1947* (Advisory Opinion of 26 April 1988) [1988] ICJ Rep 12, 28 paras 34–44.

[12] *Obligations Concerning Negotiations* (n 5) paras 49–51. Also see *Obligations Concerning Negotiations Relating to Cessation of the Nuclear Arms Race and to Nuclear Disarmament (Marshall Islands v India)* (Jurisdiction and Admissibility, Judgment of 5 October 2016) [2016] ICJ Rep 255; *Obligations Concerning Negotiations Relating to Cessation of the Nuclear Arms Race and to Nuclear Disarmament (Marshall Islands v Pakistan)* (Jurisdiction and Admissibility, Judgment of 5 October 2016) [2016] ICJ Rep 552. This caused strong dissent. See *Obligations Concerning Negotiations* (n 5), dissenting opinion of Judge Cançado-Trindade, para 13; dissenting opinion of Judge Robinson, para 5; dissenting opinion of Judge Crawford, paras 3–5. See Antonopoulos (ch 4 in this volume).

[13] 'An event may or may not have occurred before. But if it is particularly salient, vivid, serious, disruptive, rapid, or continuous it may trigger a naming process.' J Fitzgerald and R Dickins, 'Disputing in Legal and Nonlegal Contexts: Some Questions for Sociologists of Law' (1980) 15 *Law & Society Review* 681, 685; D Coates and S Pernord, 'Social Psychology and the Emergence of Disputes' (1980) 15 *Law & Society Review* 655, 655.

cyberattack on critical state infrastructure. The background context of the dispute or the existence of third parties who may support or oppose the claims can also influence this process.[14]

To give an example of the transformation process notwithstanding certain ambiguity surrounding statements and facts, in 2020, the United Kingdom (UK) attributed to Russia attacks on organisations involved in the COVID-19 vaccine development.[15] The British Foreign Secretary condemned them as 'unacceptable' and noted that international law and the norms of responsible state behaviour must be respected and that perpetrators should be held accountable.[16] The Russian ambassador denied the accusations, saying they make 'no sense' and 'to attribute any kind of computer hackers to any country, it is impossible'.[17] The Kremlin spokesperson, Dmitry Peskov, said, 'We can say one thing – Russia has nothing to do with these attempts and we do not accept such accusations.'[18] What we can see here is that the UK is naming a particular act (cyberattacks on vaccine developers) as wrongful, blames (attributes them to) Russia and claims that international law has not been respected, which Russia denies.[19]

The dispute took place in a context of political antagonism between the UK and Russia, a health emergency, and competition over vaccines. The seriousness of the trigger event in this context catalysed the process of naming, blaming, and claiming. Although intellectual property theft is quite common, obtaining secret information about the design of vaccines early on during a worldwide battle for vaccines was a particularly serious event that raised the stakes. The process of transformation was also facilitated by the involvement of other states, such as the United States of America (US) and Canada, which supported the UK claims.[20]

Having explained the process of transformation of a dispute, the next question is what an international legal dispute consists of. The Permanent Court of International Justice (PCIJ) provided the traditional definition in the *Mavrommatis*

[14] Fitzgerald and Dickins (n 13) 684–86.

[15] National Cyber Security Centre, 'Advisory: APT29 Targets COVID-19 Vaccine Development' (16 July 2020) www.ncsc.gov.uk/news/advisory-apt29-targets-covid-19-vaccine-development.

[16] UK Foreign and Commonwealth Office, 'UK Condemns Russian Intelligence Services Over Vaccine Cyber Attacks' (16 July 2020) www.gov.uk/government/news/uk-condemns-russian-intelligence-services-over-vaccine-cyber-attacks; UK Foreign and Commonwealth Office, 'UK Condemns Cyber Actors Seeking to Benefit from Global Coronavirus Pandemic' (5 May 2020) www.gov.uk/government/news/uk-condemns-cyber-actors-seeking-to-benefit-from-global-coronavirus-pandemic.

[17] AFP, 'Russia's Ambassador to UK Denies Coronavirus Vaccine-Hacking Claims' (19 July 2020) www.theguardian.com/world/2020/jul/19/russias-ambassador-to-uk-denies-coronavirus-vaccine-hacking-claims.

[18] Z Cohen, L McGee and A Marquardt, 'UK, US and Canada Allege Russian Cyberattacks on Covid-19 Research Centers' (17 July 2020) edition.cnn.com/2020/07/16/politics/russia-cyberattack-covid-vaccine-research/index.html.

[19] It is important to note that the statements are quite ambiguous. Demanding Russia to respect international law may imply that it breached international law when it attacked the COVID-19 laboratories. Invoking 'responsible behaviour' can also be framed in legal terms if it involves general international law principles such as good faith or due diligence.

[20] Cohen, McGee and Marquardt (n 18).

case, according to which a dispute is 'a disagreement on a point of law or fact, a conflict of legal views or of interests' between parties.[21] Although not characterised by its exactness, the *Mavrommatis* definition is broadly accepted. It has acquired customary law status,[22] and it is for this reason that I will use it in this chapter. More specifically, it includes three categories of legal disputes: (i) disagreement over facts; (ii) disagreement over points of law; and (iii) conflicts of legal views or interests in the sense of rights and privileges. Since the second and third categories seem to overlap, an international legal dispute, according to this definition, is one over facts or points of law.

III. Cyber Disputes: Four Scenarios

In this section, I will apply the *Mavrommatis* definition to four cyber scenarios in order to determine whether they give rise to an international legal dispute. The first scenario concerns disagreements over cyber facts in the context of cyber attribution; the second concerns disagreements over points of international law and conflicts of legal interests; the third concerns disagreements over international law in multilateral settings; and the fourth concerns legal questions arising from covert operations. The scenarios build on the *Mavrommatis* categories but also reflect areas and issues where cyber disagreements currently arise.

A. Disagreement Over Cyber Facts and Cyber Attribution

Cyberspace is an environment where the discovery and ascertainment of facts[23] are quite complex, leading to disputes over their existence. This is because cyber operations can be multi-staged, use proxy servers and false flags, perpetrators can falsify or hide their identities, and facts can be non-physical.

Factual disputes in cyberspace often evolve around the issue of attribution. Attribution refers to the process of establishing the facts associated with a malicious cyber operation through reverse engineering in order to identify its

[21] *The Mavrommatis Palestine Concessions* (Judgment of 30 August 1924) PCIJ Rep Series A No 2, 11.

[22] *Case Concerning Certain German Interests in Polish Upper Silesia* (Preliminary Objections, Judgment of 25 August 1925) PCIJ Rep Series A No 6, 14; *Interpretation of Peace Treaties with Bulgaria, Hungary and Romania* (Advisory Opinion of 30 March 1950) [1950] ICJ Rep 65, 74; *Applicability of the Obligation to Arbitrate* [1988] ICJ Rep 12 para 35; *Case Concerning East Timor (Portugal v Australia)* (Judgment of 30 June 1995) [1995] ICJ Rep 90 para 22; *Armed Activities on the Territory of the Congo (New Application: 2002) (Democratic Republic of the Congo v Rwanda)* (Jurisdiction and Admissibility, Judgment of 3 February 2006) [2006] ICJ Rep 6, 40, para 90; *Territorial and Maritime Dispute Between Nicaragua and Honduras in the Caribbean Sea (Nicaragua v Honduras)* (Judgment of 8 October 2007) [2007] ICJ Rep 659 para 130.

[23] A fact is 'an event or state of affairs known to have happened or existed'. J Law (ed), *A Dictionary of Law*, 10th edn (Oxford, Oxford University Press, 2022); RM Mosk, 'The Role of Facts in International Dispute Settlement' (2003) 304 *Collected Courses of the Hague Academy of International Law* 9–179.

perpetrator,[24] which can be a state or an advanced persistent threat (APT)[25] sponsored by a state or acting independently.

To give just a few examples where attribution was contested by disputing or denying the facts, Russia dismissed the attribution of the 2016 Democratic National Committee (DNC) hack for demanding 'some proof'.[26] Regarding the hacking of the Bundestag in 2015, which Germany attributed to Russia based on 'hard evidence', Russia rejected Germany's allegations as proofless.[27] When, in 2020, Norway accused Russia of committing a cyberattack against its Parliament, Russia rejected the accusation as groundless and claimed that no evidence was provided.[28] Regarding the SolarWinds cyberattack attributed to Russia,[29] Russia denied responsibility and said the accusations lacked evidence.[30]

When Albania suffered a wave of cyberattacks targeting governmental services between July and September 2022,[31] it attributed the attacks to Iran,[32] as did other

[24] Facts can be proven through evidence which can be physical, technical, or virtual. Evidence can include, for example, hardware, software, network traffic, malware, IP addresses, documents, statements, infrastructure, tools, and techniques/tactics and procedures (TTP) used for the cyberattack. See also F Skopik and T Pahi, 'Under False Flag: Using Technical Artifacts for Cyber Attack Attribution' (2020) 3 *Cybersecurity* 1–20.

[25] According to the US National Institute for Standards and Technology's definition, an advanced persistent threat (APT) is 'An adversary with sophisticated levels of expertise and significant resources, allowing it through the use of multiple different attack vectors (e.g., cyber, physical, and deception), to generate opportunities to achieve its objectives which are typically to establish and extend its presence within the information technology infrastructure of organizations for purposes of continually exfiltrating information and/or to undermine or impede critical aspects of a mission, program, or organization, or place itself in a position to do so in the future; moreover, the advanced persistent threat pursues its objectives repeatedly over an extended period of time, adapting to a defender's efforts to resist it, and with determination to maintain the level of interaction needed to execute its objectives.' NIST, 'advanced persistent threat' csrc.nist.gov/glossary/term/advanced_persistent_threat.

[26] L Smith-Spark, 'Russia Challenges US to Prove Campaign Hacking Claims or Shut Up' (16 December 2016) edition.cnn.com/2016/12/16/europe/russia-us-hacking-claims-peskov/index.html.

[27] C Cimpanu, 'Russia says Germany has not Provided any Evidence of Bundestag Hack' (1 June 2020) www.zdnet.com/article/russia-says-germany-has-not-provided-any-evidence-of-bundestag-hack/; Russian News Agency, 'Russia Rejects Claims It was Behind Cyberattack on Bundestag in 2015' (4 June 2020) tass.com/politics/1164165.

[28] BBC News, 'Norway Blames Russia for Cyber-Attack on Parliament' (13 October 2020) www.bbc.co.uk/news/world-europe-54518106.

[29] CISA, 'Joint Statement by the Federal Bureau of Investigation (FBI), the Cybersecurity and Infrastructure Security Agency (CISA), the Office of the Director of National Intelligence (ODNI), and the National Security Agency (NSA)' (5 January 2021) www.cisa.gov/news-events/news/joint-statement-federal-bureau-investigation-fbi-cybersecurity-and-infrastructure; The White House, 'Fact Sheet: Imposing Costs for Harmful Foreign Activities by the Russian Government' (15 April 2021) www.whitehouse.gov/briefing-room/statements-releases/2021/04/15/fact-sheet-imposing-costs-for-harmful-foreign-activities-by-the-russian-government/.

[30] AFP, 'Russia Denies Role in U.S. Cyber Attacks' (21 December 2020) www.themoscowtimes.com/2020/12/21/russia-denies-role-in-us-cyber-attacks-a72426; BBC News, 'SolarWinds Hack: Russian Denial "Unconvincing"' (18 May 2021) www.bbc.co.uk/news/technology-57156197.

[31] CISA, 'Iranian State Actors Conduct Cyber Operations Against the Government of Albania' (23 September 2022) www.cisa.gov/news-events/cybersecurity-advisories/aa22-264a. Microsoft Threat Intelligence, 'Microsoft Investigates Iranian Attacks against the Albanian Government' (8 September 2022) https://www.microsoft.com/en-us/security/blog/2022/09/08/microsoft-investigates-iranian-attacks-against-the-albanian-government/.

[32] Albanian Government, 'Videomessage of Prime Minister Edi Rama' (7 September 2022) www.kryeministria.al/en/newsroom/videomesazh-i-kryeministrit-edi-rama/.

states.[33] In its letter to the UN, Albania stated: 'A thorough in-depth investigation conducted in cooperation with specialized partner agencies on cyberterrorism has now confirmed, beyond any doubt, that the cyberattack was a State-sponsored aggression carried out by four groups, orchestrated and sponsored by the Islamic Republic of Iran'.[34] It continued by saying that it 'holds the Islamic Republic of Iran directly responsible for this irresponsible and unprovoked cyberattack' and then went on to severe diplomatic relations with Iran. Iran rejected 'any kind of unwarranted attribution', characterising the accusations as 'unsubstantiated' and 'unfounded'. It added, 'given the nature and technical characteristics of cyberspace and the challenges of attribution in the Information and Communication Technology (ICT) environment, Iran warns of the negative consequences of falsified and forged attribution to the States'.[35]

At its basis, cyber attribution is technical; it involves technical investigations to establish the technical source of a malicious cyber operation. This involves gathering, analysing and assessing information about the tools used for the attack or the attack process.[36] Even if the means, methods, and skills for conducting technical attribution have been improved, technical attribution faces many difficulties and limitations, and its determinations can be disputed. Consequently, factual disputes over cyber attribution should be settled peacefully using any available mechanisms such as fact-finding.[37]

Attribution also has a legal dimension. It is a mechanism for attributing wrongful acts to states and engaging their legal responsibility.[38] As a legal institution,

[33] The White House, 'Statement by NSC Spokesperson Adrienne Watson on Iran's Cyberattack Against Albania' (7 September 2022) www.whitehouse.gov/briefing-room/statements-releases/2022/09/07/statement-by-nsc-spokesperson-adrienne-watson-on-irans-cyberattack-against-albania/; UK Foreign, Commonwealth and Development Office, 'UK Condemns Iran for Reckless Cyber Attack Against Albania' (7 September 2022) www.gov.uk/government/news/uk-condemns-iran-for-reckless-cyber-attack-against-albania.

[34] UNGA and UNSC, 'Letter Dated 7 September 2022 from the Permanent Representative of Albania to the United Nations Addressed to the Secretary-General and the President of the Security Council' (9 September 2022) UN Doc A/76/943-S/2022/677.

[35] UNSC, 'Letter Dated 10 September 2022 from the Permanent Representative of the Islamic Republic of Iran to the United Nations Addressed to the Secretary-General and the President of the Security Council' (12 September 2022) UN Doc S/2022/685. It added: 'The Islamic Republic of Iran reiterates once again its persistent position that cyberspace and the ICT environment must be used exclusively for peaceful purposes and that States must act cooperatively and in full compliance with applicable international law' (para 3); 'While warning against any provocative and unwarranted measure taken under the guise of alleged claims, the Islamic Republic of Iran reserves its inherent right to respond, in accordance with international law and the United Nations Charter, to any threat, attack, or wrongful act that targets its interests, critical and civilian infrastructure, decisively and proportionately and whenever it deems necessary' (para 6).

[36] N Tsagourias and M Farrell, 'Cyber Attribution: Technical and Legal Approaches and Challenges' (2020) 31 *European Journal of International Law* 941, 947–51.

[37] N Tsagourias and F Middleton, 'Fact-Finding and Cyber Attribution' in R Buchan, D Franchini and N Tsagourias (eds), *The Changing Character of International Dispute Settlement* (Cambridge, CUP, 2023) 439–466.

[38] ILC, 'Draft Articles on Responsibility of States for Internationally Wrongful Acts, with Commentaries' in *Yearbook of the International Law Commission. 2001, Volume II, Part Two: Report of the Commission to the General Assembly on the Work of its Fifty-Third Session, as Corrected* (New York, UN, 2008) (ARSIWA), Art 2; Tsagourias and Farrell (n 36) 941–67.

attribution is fact-dependent, but which facts are relevant, how they will be assessed,[39] and which facts will be attributed to a state are determined by international law.[40]

If attribution is both a technical and a legal institution, the immediate question is under what circumstances factual attribution disputes can become legal disputes. For this to happen, factual disputes over attribution should be used to support the formulation of opposing legal claims. For example, factual disputes should be used as the basis of divergent claims about the scope, application or interpretation of the legal criteria of attribution and can further be used as the basis of opposing claims about the subject of a legal obligation, the existence of a violation, the existence of state responsibility. Put differently, if the existence or interpretation of facts underpinning attribution are disputed to counter consequential legal claims supported by these facts, a legal dispute comes into existence.[41] It is a legal dispute with a factual underbelly in contrast to a purely factual dispute over attribution because the parties seek legal vindication of their claims instead of factual vindication.

For example, suppose that France accuses Finland of violating its sovereignty through an intrusive cyber operation attributed to Finland based on factual evidence. France's position is that sovereignty is a rule that applies to cyberspace and that any unauthorised cyber intrusion constitutes a violation of its sovereignty.[42] Finland rejects the allegation, claiming that the presented facts do not satisfy any of the international law attribution criteria; that even if it were the author of the operation, there was no intrusion; and that, even if there was intrusion, it was not into governmental infrastructure and no damage was caused. This reflects Finland's view that sovereignty is a rule that applies to cyberspace, but only cyber operations that intrude into governmental infrastructure or cause damage violate this rule.[43] In this case, the factual dispute – whether the operation is attributed to Finland; whether there was an intrusion; whether governmental infrastructure was intruded; and whether any damage was caused – underpins opposing legal claims (whether there is a violation of the principle of sovereignty) and thus the dispute is a legal one.

[39] For the interplay between law and facts in adjudication, see *Pulp Mills on the River Uruguay (Argentina v Uruguay)* (Judgment of 20 April 2010) [2010] ICJ Rep 14 para 168: 'the Court will make its own determination of the facts, on the basis of the evidence presented to it, and then it will apply the relevant rules of international law to those facts which it has found to have existed'. Similarly, *Certain Activities Carried Out by Nicaragua in the Border Area (Costa Rica v Nicaragua) and Construction of a Road in Costa Rica Along the San Juan River (Nicaragua v Costa Rica)* (Judgment of 16 December 2015) [2015] ICJ Rep 665 para 176.

[40] For the attribution criteria in the law of state responsibility, see ARSIWA Arts 4–11.

[41] For example, in *Application of the Convention on the Prevention and Punishment of the Crime of Genocide (Gambia v Myanmar)* (Preliminary Objections, Judgment of 22 July 2022) [2022] ICJ Rep 477 para 72, the ICJ established the existence of a legal dispute as well as awareness from Myanmar's rejection of the Fact Finding Mission's reports which established the facts underlying crimes.

[42] République Française, Ministère des Armées, *Droit International Appliqué aux Opérations dans le Cyberespace* (Paris, Ministère des Armées, 2019).

[43] Finland, 'International Law and Cyberspace: Finland's National Position' (2020) um.fi/documents/35732/0/Cyber+and+international+law%3B+Finland%27s+views.pdf/41404cbb-d300-a3b9-92e4-a7d675d5d585?t=1602758856859, 1–3.

Reverting now to the examples mentioned above, it appears that none of them gave rise to a legal dispute. Regarding Russia's 2016 DNC hack, President Obama described the attack as a violation of 'established international norms of behavior' but not as a violation of international *law*.[44] The USA went on to impose sanctions on individuals and entities involved in the hack,[45] but these are acts of retorsion not predicated on a violation of international law. Indictments were also issued against individuals, but this is a domestic law issue. Regarding the hacking of the German Parliament, Germany's claim was not formulated in international law language either. The German Chancellor said it was an 'unpleasant' and 'outrageous' event and damaged trust, but she did not utter an international law-based accusation. A Russian operative, Dmitry Sergeyevich Badin, was indicted for the attack under German law, and after the indictment, the German Federal Prosecutor issued an international arrest warrant against him.[46] If questions of extradition were to arise with Germany and Russia holding different views on whether Badin should be extradited, this would be an international legal dispute that may also involve factual questions of attribution. The EU also imposed restrictive measures on Badin and other individuals and entities involved in the attack without raising international law questions, but to 'prevent, discourage, deter and respond to continuing and increasing malicious behaviour in cyberspace'.[47] Likewise, Norway made an attribution claim based on its investigation and assessment of the facts, but it did not make any normative claim by holding, for example, Russia responsible for violating international law.

Regarding the SolarWinds hack, the USA imposed sanctions and other measures on Russian entities and nationals[48] to 'make clear that this behavior was unacceptable'.[49]

Regarding the 2022 attacks on Albania, Albania branded them as irresponsible.[50] The only legal dispute that may have arisen is regarding Iran's allegation that

[44] (Emphasis added.) The White House, Office of the Press Secretary, 'Statement by the President on Actions in Response to Russian Malicious Cyber Activity and Harassment' (29 December 2016) obamawhitehouse.archives.gov/the-press-office/2016/12/29/statement-president-actions-response-russian-malicious-cyber-activity.

[45] Federal Register, 'Executive Order 13757 of December 28, 2016, 82 Fed. Reg. 1' www.federalregister.gov/documents/2017/01/03/2016-31922/taking-additional-steps-to-address-the-national-emergency-with-respect-to-significant-malicious.

[46] J Schuetze, 'Could the German International Arrest Warrant Against a GRU Hacker Prompt European Sanctions?' (26 May 2020) www.cfr.org/blog/could-german-international-arrest-warrant-against-gru-hacker-prompt-european-sanctions.

[47] Council Implementing Regulation (EU) 2020/1536 of 22 October 2020 of Implementing Regulation (EU) 2019/796 concerning restrictive measures against cyber-attacks threatening the Union or its Member States [2022] OJ L35I/1.

[48] The White House, 'Executive Order on Blocking Property with Respect to Specified Harmful Foreign Activities of the Government of the Russian Federation' (15 April 2021) www.whitehouse.gov/briefing-room/presidential-actions/2021/04/15/executive-order-on-blocking-property-with-respect-to-specified-harmful-foreign-activities-of-the-government-of-the-russian-federation/.

[49] The White House, 'Background Press Call by Senior Administration Officials on Russia' (15 April 2021) www.whitehouse.gov/briefing-room/press-briefings/2021/04/15/background-press-call-by-senior-administration-officials-on-russia/.

[50] The same line was followed by other states as well. For example, the US said: 'Iran's conduct disregards norms of responsible peacetime State behavior in cyberspace, which includes a norm on

Albania violated the 1961 Vienna Convention on Diplomatic Relations and the 1963 Vienna Convention on Consular Relations.[51]

Another issue raised by attribution is that it is often performed by private cybersecurity companies whose findings may be rejected by the accused state. Does this give rise to an international legal dispute? For example, China reacted to the Mandiant APT1 Report[52] by saying it lacked 'technical proof' that 'many hacking attacks were carried out using hijacked IP addresses' and since hacking was 'a cross-border, deceptive business, it was hard to pin down where attacks originated'.[53] In another instance, when Recorded Future, a cybersecurity company, attributed the intelligence gathering operation against the Vatican by RedDelta in 2020, which took place during discussions concerning the renewal of the 2018 China-Vatican provisional agreement concerning the appointment of Catholic bishops in China,[54] the Chinese foreign ministry denied any involvement, calling the report 'groundless speculation'.[55] In the present writer's opinion, attribution disputes between states and private companies do not amount to international legal disputes, as understood here. That is because one party to the dispute is a

refraining from damaging critical infrastructure that provides services to the public. Albania views impacted government networks as critical infrastructure. Malicious cyber activity by a State that intentionally damages critical infrastructure or otherwise impairs its use and operation to provide services to the public can have cascading domestic, regional, and global effects; pose an elevated risk of harm to the population; and may lead to escalation and conflict.' The White House (n 33).

[51] UNSC, 'Letter Dated 10 September 2022' UN Doc S/2022/685 para 8: 'Furthermore, following the unilateral termination of bilateral diplomatic relations by the Albanian Government on September 7, 2022, the police forces of the Republic of Albania breached the obligations under international law and used force for entering Iran's diplomatic missions in Tirana, without Iran's consent. While strongly condemning such unlawful acts, the Islamic Republic of Iran re-emphasizes that such intrusion is a flagrant violation of international law, specifically the principle of inviolability of diplomatic and consular premises, as well as States' obligations under the 1961 Vienna Convention on Diplomatic Relations and the 1963 Vienna Convention on Consular Relations, which required all States to take all appropriate steps to protect diplomatic and consular premises from any intrusion or damage and to prevent any disturbance of the peace of these missions or impairment of their dignity and any attack on diplomatic premises, agents and consular officers.'

[52] For example, the 2013 APT1 report by Mandiant attributed cyber espionage operations to China because, as the report said, 'It is time to acknowledge the threat is originating in China, and we wanted to do our part to arm and prepare security professionals to combat that threat effectively. The issue of attribution has always been a missing link in publicly understanding the landscape of APT cyber espionage. Without establishing a solid connection to China, there will always be room for observers to dismiss APT actions as uncoordinated, solely criminal in nature, or peripheral to larger national security and global economic concerns. We hope that this report will lead to increased understanding and coordinated action in countering APT network breaches.' Mandiant, 'APT1: Exposing One of China's Cyber Espionage Units' https://www.mandiant.com/sites/default/files/2021-09/mandiant-apt1-report.pdf.

[53] BBC News, 'China Condemns Hacking Report by US Firm Mandiant' (20 February 2013) www.bbc.co.uk/news/world-us-canada-21515259.

[54] Insikt Group, 'Chinese State-Sponsored Group "RedDelta" Targets the Vatican and Catholic Organizations' (28 July 2020) www.recordedfuture.com/reddelta-targets-catholic-organizations/. Also, Council on Foreign Relations, 'Cyber Operations Tracker: Operations by Country' www.cfr.org/cyber-operations/.

[55] Associated Press, 'Vatican Allegedly Hacked by China Ahead of Key Talks' (29 July 2020) https://apnews.com/article/religion-technology-hong-kong-china-hacking-86d667d57bca41ddbc6f289d48f2dfe0.

private entity, and the dispute is not framed in legal language but is mainly about the existence, interpretation, and adequacy of facts. If a private company's attribution findings are adopted by a state which then goes on to make a legal claim against another state based on such attribution, an international legal dispute will arise. No international legal dispute also arises when private cybersecurity companies dispute attribution findings among themselves. For example, private cybersecurity companies disagreed on the entity or the state responsible for the 2018 Winter Olympics cyberattack,[56] but that did not give rise to a legal dispute.

To conclude, cyber attribution disputes have not thus far given rise to legal disputes because they are not framed in international law terms, and facts are not used to support or deny legal claims.[57] Instead, states denounce behaviours attributed to other states as 'irresponsible', 'unfriendly', 'harmful' or 'reckless', but stop short of invoking international law or framing the exchanges in legal language.

This is because attribution has become an instrument of statecraft used to achieve political objectives such as micro or macro deterrence and defence.[58] There are instances, however, where attribution could have been linked to legal claims, although they were not pursued further. President Biden, for example, referring to Russia's attempted interference in the 2022 US midterm elections,[59] said, 'It's a pure violation of our sovereignty.'[60] Russia rejected the claim by saying, 'We hold that meddling in the internal affairs of sovereign states is unacceptable, this is an integral part of our nation's policy.'[61] These statements allude to the international law principles of sovereignty and non-intervention.

On another occasion, the USA and its allies condemned China's irresponsible and destabilising behaviour regarding IP theft by saying:

> Much of the MSS activity alleged in the Department of Justice's charges stands in stark contrast to the PRC's bilateral and multilateral commitments to refrain from engaging in cyber-enabled theft of intellectual property for commercial advantage.[62]

[56] A Greenberg, 'The Untold Story of the 2018 Olympics Cyberattack, the Most Deceptive Hack in History' (17 October 2018) www.wired.com/story/untold-story-2018-olympics-destroyer-cyberattack/.

[57] US Office of the Director of National Intelligence, 'A Guide to Cyber Attribution' (14 September 2018) dl.icdst.org/pdfs/files3/db004a6f55f96c056a23fc4efc6a23ac.pdf.

[58] J Bateman, 'The Purposes of U.S. Government Public Cyber Attribution' (28 March 2022) https://carnegieendowment.org/2022/03/28/purposes-of-u.s.-government-public-cyber-attribution-pub-86696; FJ Egloff, 'Public Attribution of Cyber Intrusions' (2020) 6 *Journal of Cybersecurity* 1–12.

[59] A Wahlstrom et al, 'Information Operations Targeting 2022 U.S. Midterm Elections Include Trolling, Narratives Surrounding Specific Races, Politicians' (18 December 2022) www.mandiant.com/resources/blog/information-operations-2022-midterm-elections.

[60] The White House, 'Remarks by President Biden at the Office of the Director of National Intelligence' (27 July 2021) www.whitehouse.gov/briefing-room/speeches-remarks/2021/07/27/remarks-by-president-biden-at-the-office-of-the-director-of-national-intelligence/.

[61] Tass, Russian News Agency, 'Democrats Blame Russia to Justify Their Coming Defeat in US Midterms, Says Speaker' (7 November 2022) tass.com/politics/1533009.

[62] The White House, 'The United States, Joined by Allies and Partners, Attributes Malicious Cyber Activity and Irresponsible State Behavior to the People's Republic of China' (19 July 2021)

The commitments referred to are the Obama–Xi agreement, according to which the two states should avoid conducting or supporting cyber-enabled intellectual property theft.[63] Again, the claim was not pursued in legal terms, nor was China's reaction framed in legal terms but in terms of 'right' and 'wrong'.[64]

In relation to the 2020 cyberattack against Georgia, which was attributed to Russia, Georgia issued a statement condemning the cyberattack 'which goes against international norms and principles, once again infringing Georgia's sovereignty'.[65] Russia rejected the allegation, asserting that the Georgian government had not provided any proof.[66] In this case, a legal dispute could have arisen regarding the question of whether attribution facts can support a claim of violation of the international law rule of sovereignty. Again, this line of contestation was not pursued.

www.whitehouse.gov/briefing-room/statements-releases/2021/07/19/the-united-states-joined-by-allies-and-partners-attributes-malicious-cyber-activity-and-irresponsible-state-behavior-to-the-peoples-republic-of-china/.

[63] The White House, 'Remarks by President Obama and President Xi of the People's Republic of China in Joint Press Conference' (25 September 2015) obamawhitehouse.archives.gov/the-press-office/2015/09/25/remarks-president-obama-and-president-xi-peoples-republic-china-joint.

[64] A foreign ministry spokesman said: 'The United States ganged up with its allies to make unwarranted accusations against Chinese cybersecurity,' and 'This was made up out of thin air and confused right and wrong. It is purely a smear and suppression with political motives.' China also accused the US of cyber attacks without raising international law. J McDonald, 'China Rejects Hacking Charges, Accuses US of Cyberspying' (20 July 2021) apnews.com/article/technology-business-china-hacking-6cd7d59f1b6aa4a0539d987e5340b705.

[65] UNGA and UNSC, 'Protracted Conflicts in the GUAM Area and Their Implications for International Peace, Security and Development: Identical Letters dated 21 February 2020 from the Permanent Representative of Georgia to the United Nations Addressed to the Secretary-General and the President of the Security Council' (24 February 2020) UN Doc A/74/714-S/2020/135. Other states have condemned the cyber attacks, branding them as irresponsible or reckless but without invoking international law. See UK Foreign and Commonwealth Office and National Cyber Security Centre, 'UK Condemns Russia's GRU Over Georgia Cyber-Attacks' (20 February 2020) www.gov.uk/government/news/uk-condemns-russias-gru-over-georgia-cyber-attacks; US Department of State, 'The United States Condemns Russian Cyber Attack Against the Country of Georgia' (20 February 2020) 2017–2021.state.gov/the-united-states-condemns-russian-cyber-attack-against-the-country-of-georgia/. Australia stated: 'The international community – Russia included – has agreed that international law and norms of responsible state behaviour apply in cyberspace. This malicious cyber activity contradicts Russia's attempts to claim it is a responsible actor in cyberspace and demonstrates a continuing pattern of reckless Russian GRU cyber operations against a number of countries.' Australia, Minister for Foreign Affairs, 'Attribution of Malicious Cyber Activity in Georgia by Russian Military Intelligence' (21 February 2020) www.foreignminister.gov.au/minister/marise-payne/media-release/attribution-malicious-cyber-activity-georgia-russian-military-intelligence. However Canada stated: 'Canada strongly condemns these malicious activities. These actions are aimed at sowing discord in Georgia ahead of their parliamentary elections later this year and show blatant disregard for international law, norms and agreements.' Government of Canada, 'Canada Condemns Russia's Malicious Cyber-Activity Targeting Georgia' (20 February 2020) www.canada.ca/en/global-affairs/news/2020/02/canada-condemns-russias-malicious-cyber-activity-targeting-georgia.html.

[66] L King and S Ayres, 'Russia Directed 2019 Cyberattack on Former Republic of Georgia, U.S. and Allies Say' (20 February 2020) www.latimes.com/world-nation/story/2020-02-20/russia-behind-sweeping-2019-cyber-attack-in-georgia.

B. Disagreement Over Points of International Law and Conflicts of Legal Interests

Under this scenario, the dispute will evolve around questions of whether an international law right, duty, or interest exists under treaty or customary law; the scope and content of said right, duty, or legal interest; the existence of a breach; the incurrence of responsibility; and the existence and application of international law defences.

To give an example, in the Georgia/Russia incident mentioned above, and assuming the question of attribution was settled, the legal dispute would evolve around the following questions: whether sovereignty is a rule of international law; whether it applies to cyberspace; what is its content and scope in cyberspace;[67] whether the impugned operation amounted to violation of Georgia's sovereignty; whether Russia can be held responsible; whether there are any defences to Russia's conduct; and whether reparations are owed and how.

To remain within the theme of sovereignty, suppose that France claims that the UK violated its sovereignty because a cyber operation attributed to the UK intruded into its sovereign space without its consent. The UK rejects the allegation, claiming there is no violation because there is no rule of sovereignty in international law.[68] In this case, a legal dispute exists between France and the UK as to whether sovereignty is a rule that applies to cyberspace. Also, in the scenario mentioned earlier involving France and Finland, even if France and Finland agree that sovereignty is a rule that applies to cyberspace, there will still be a legal dispute over the scope and content of the rule and, more specifically, whether any non-consensual intrusion can breach this rule or only operations that cause damage or target governmental infrastructure.

Will a legal dispute arise if legal claims are framed in general terms? States may condemn a particular cyber operation as violating international law but stop short of specifying which rule or rules have been violated.

In the *Georgia v Russia* (2011) case, the Court distilled the existence of a dispute from general statements which identified the subject matter of a legal claim but did not specify any treaties (in that case, the International Convention on the Elimination of All Forms of Racial Discrimination (CERD) as the basis of Georgia's application to the ICJ) or specific rules.

[67] According to the PCIJ, even abstract interpretative disputes are disputes. As it said, 'there seems to be no reason why States should not be able to ask the Court to give an abstract interpretation of a treaty; rather would it appear that is one of the most important functions which it can fulfil'. *Case Concerning Certain German Interests in Polish Upper Silesia, (Germany v Poland)* (Merits, Judgment of 25 May 1926) [1926] PCIJ Rep Series A No 7, 18.

[68] UK Attorney General's Office, 'Cyber and International Law in the 21st Century' (23 May 2018) www.gov.uk/government/speeches/cyber-and-international-law-in-the-21st-century; UK Attorney General's Office, 'International Law in Future Frontiers' (19 May 2022) www.gov.uk/government/speeches/international-law-in-future-frontiers.

For the Court, such legal claims were 'on a subject-matter capable of falling under CERD'.[69]

In the *Nuclear Tests* case, the legal dispute was equally framed in general terms. Australia claimed that conducting nuclear tests violates rules of international law without specifying them. France claimed that nuclear tests did not violate any rule of international law and asked Australia to state which specific rules they violated. Australia responded that it disagrees with the French view and is 'convinced that the conducting of the tests violates rules of international law' and said, 'It is clear that in this regard there exists between our two Governments a substantial legal dispute.'[70] The ICJ, in turn, said that it is the Court's duty to isolate the real issue in the case and identify the object of the claim.[71] Yet, the dispute became without object due to the French declaration that it would not carry out nuclear tests.

The Channel Tunnel Arbitration Tribunal also confirmed this broader approach by saying, 'International tribunals have been willing to discern a dispute from general exchanges of correspondence manifesting a difference of view without requiring the claim to have been made out with any particularity.'[72]

From the above it can be said that general statements demonstrating opposing legal views – for example, statements that a violation of international law has been committed or not – can give rise to a legal dispute. Whether a court can entertain the dispute is a different question, raising jurisdictional and admissibility questions.[73]

If a dispute, as was said, involves claims and counterclaims, what happens if the accused state remains silent? Suppose that state A claims that a cyber operation attributed to state B breached its international law rights, but state B does not respond by either denying the allegation or offering a legal justification. Would such silence be dispositive of the existence of a legal dispute? According to the ICJ's jurisprudence, the existence of a dispute can be inferred 'from the failure

[69] *Application of the Convention on the Elimination of All Forms of Racial Discrimination (Georgia v Russian Federation)* (Preliminary Objections, Judgment of 1 April 2011) [2011] ICJ Rep 70 para 181. The ICJ also said: 'While it is not necessary that a State must expressly refer to a specific treaty in its exchanges with the other State to enable it later to invoke that instrument before the Court the exchanges must refer to the subject-matter of the treaty with sufficient clarity to enable the State against which a claim is made to identify that there is, or may be, a dispute with regard to that subject-matter.' ibid para 30. *Case Concerning Military and Paramilitary Activities in and against Nicaragua* (n 4) para 83.

[70] *Nuclear Tests* (n 5) dissenting opinion of Judge Barwick, 427. For the exchanges between Australia and France, see ibid 423–27.

[71] *Nuclear Tests* (n 5) 262–63, para 29.

[72] *Channel Tunnel Group Limited and France-Manche SA v United Kingdom and France* (Partial Award, 30 January 2007) [2007] PCA Case No 2003-06 para 142.

[73] In the *Marshall Islands* case, the ICJ rejected the application because the statements relied on by the Marshall Islands to prove the existence of a legal dispute were general, not articulating an alleged breach by the respondent state. *Obligations Concerning Negotiations* (n 5) paras 49–51. See also *Dispute Over the Status and Use of the Waters of the Silala (Chile v Bolivia)* (Judgment of 1 December 2022) [2022] ICJ Rep 614 para 46.

of a State to respond to a claim in circumstances where a response is called for'.[74] The Court has not explained what these circumstances are. It can be said that an allegation of a breach of international law is such a circumstance because, if it remains unchallenged, it may affect the legal position or interests of the silent state.[75] This view can also be supported by the general presumption based on good faith that states comply with international law, and consequently, contrary claims are to be rebutted. Following this line of reasoning, if a state remains silent when accused of breaching international law, no dispute arises because it is inferred that it accepts the allegation. This statement, however, requires further prodding. States may remain silent due to political, military, or economic considerations or because they want to de-escalate the situation. There may also be legal considerations for not protesting, for example, because states do not have diplomatic relations, do not recognise each other, or do not want to express their *opinio juris* on a particular matter given the uncertainty surrounding the content of legal rules in cyberspace. Furthermore, a state may remain silent because it does not have a functioning government[76] or the technological capacity to support its opposition. More critically, though, silence may imply opposition and rejection of the claim, particularly if the silent state does nothing to redress the situation or does not formally accept the opposite claim.[77] For this reason, it can be said that silence can be dispositive of the non-existence of a legal dispute only if that is the only reasonable inference.

This leads to the next finding that the existence of a legal dispute can be inferred from a state's conduct. For example, state A claims that state B violated international law by engaging in a certain type of conduct. Although state B remains silent, it continues to engage in the same type of conduct against state A. In this

[74] *Application of the Convention on the Elimination of All Forms of Racial Discrimination* (n 69) para 30; *Land and Maritime Boundary Between Cameroon and Nigeria (Cameroon v Nigeria)* (Preliminary Objections, Judgment of 11 June 1998) [1998] ICJ Rep 275 para 89; *South China Sea Arbitration (Philippines v China)* (Award on Jurisdiction and Admissibility of 29 October 2015) 33 RIAA 1 para 163; *Case Concerning the Temple of Preah Vihear (Cambodia v Thailand)* (Merits, Judgment of 15 June 1962) [1962] ICJ Rep 6, 23; ILC, Draft Conclusions on the Identification of Customary International Law in UNGA, 'Report of the International Law Commission (30 April–1 June and 2 July–10 August 2018) UN Doc A/73/10 Conclusion 10(3) legal.un.org/ilc/texts/instruments/english/draft_articles/1_13_2018.pdf. Draft conclusions on subsequent agreements and subsequent practice in relation to the interpretation of treaties, in UNGA, 'Report of the International Law Commission (30 April–1 June and 2 July–10 August 2018) UN Doc A/73/10 Conclusion 10 (2) legal.un.org/ilc/texts/instruments/english/draft_articles/1_11_2018.pdf; IC McGibbon, 'The Scope of Acquiescence in International Law' (1954) 31 *British Yearbook of International Law* 143–86.

[75] McGibbon (n 74) 144. To give another example, it was held '[i]f it had been considered that Honduras was being deprived of territory to which she was entitled … , it can hardly be doubted that these assertions by Guatemala … would have been followed by protest and opposition on the part of Honduras'. *Honduras Borders (Guatemala v Honduras)* (1933) 2 RIAA 1307, 1328. *Application of the Convention on the Prevention and Punishment of the Crime of Genocide (The Gambia v Myanmar)* (Provisional Measures, Order of 23 January 2020) [2020] ICJ Rep 3 para 28.

[76] *Territorial Sovereignty and Scope of the Dispute (Eritrea v Yemen)* (1998) 22 RIAA 209 paras 415, 502; *Maritime Delimitation in the Indian Ocean (Somalia v Kenya)* (Judgment of 12 October 2021) [2021] ICJ Rep 206 para 79.

[77] *Applicability of the Obligation to Arbitrate* (n 11) paras 28–38; *Application of the Convention on the Prevention and Punishment of the Crime of Genocide (Gambia v Myanmar)* (Preliminary Objections, Judgment of 22 July 2022) para 71.

case, a legal dispute arises because engaging in a course of conduct inconsistent with the claim advanced by state A indicates rejection of the claim.[78] If state B ceases said conduct towards state A but engages in the same type of conduct vis-a-vis other states, does the legal dispute cease to exist? The answer is negative not only because of the previous conduct towards state A but also because by engaging in similar conduct against another state, state B continues to contest the international law rule regulating the impugned conduct. Whether, in this case, the dispute can be brought before a court is a different issue raising jurisdictional and admissibility questions.

To conclude, legal disputes can arise in cyberspace due to disagreements about the identification, application, or interpretation of international law. However, international practice indicates that states have stopped short of invoking international law when complaining about malicious operations.[79] For example, Albania did not invoke international law in relation to the 2022 cyberattacks. In its letter to the United Nations, it said: 'The actions and conduct of the Islamic Republic of Iran are a blatant breach of the norms of responsible peacetime State behaviour in cyberspace, which include refraining from damaging critical infrastructure that provides services to the public.'[80] Albania severed its diplomatic relations with Iran, expelled Iranian diplomats and its police entered Iranian diplomatic premises, but it did not explicitly justify its actions under the 1961 Vienna Convention on Diplomatic Relations and the 1963 Vienna Convention on Consular Relations. Iran claimed that Albanian's actions violated these Conventions. A legal dispute would have thus come into existence because following the *Georgia v Russia* (2011) ruling discussed earlier, Albania's actions fell under the Conventions. A factual dispute

[78] *Applicability of the Obligation to Arbitrate* (n 11), 28–30; *Land and Maritime Boundary Between Cameroon and Nigeria* [1998] ICJ Rep 275 paras 90–93. To follow the ICJ's reasoning, if the conduct and its legal assertions are juxtaposed with statements opposing said conduct, there is a legal dispute, although in that case, the ICJ focused on the issue of lack of awareness. *Obligations Concerning Negotiations (Marshall Islands v United Kingdom)* (n 5) para 57. In the words of Judge Donoghue '… . even in the absence of an explicit statement of the Respondent's opposition to the claim, there would have been a basis for the Court to infer opposition from an unaltered course of conduct.' Declaration of Judge Donoghue, ibid para 8.

[79] Efrony and Shany highlight how 'remarkable' it is having 'so little in the practice of victim states to indicate that [their international legal rights] actually guide their conduct when confronted by cyber-operations'. D Efrony and Y Shany, 'A Rule Book on the Shelf? Tallinn Manual 2.0 on Cyber-operations and Subsequent State Practice' (2018) 112 *American Journal of International Law* 583, 654.

[80] UNGA and UNSC, 'Letter Dated 7 September 2022' UN Doc A/76/943-S/2022/677. It contemplated invoking Art 5 of the North Atlantic Treaty (Washington DC, 4 April 1949) (the collective self-defence provision), but eventually, it did not. See M Miller, 'Albania Weighed Invoking NATO's Article 5 Over Iranian Cyberattack' (5 October 2022) www.politico.com/news/2022/10/05/why-albania-chose-not-to-pull-the-nato-trigger-after-cyberattack-00060347. See also NATO's statement in relation to the attacks which does not invoke international law: '3. We promote a free, open, peaceful and secure cyberspace. We pursue efforts to enhance stability and reduce the risks of conflict by promoting respect for international law, and the voluntary norms of responsible state behaviour in cyberspace, as recognised by all members of the United Nations. We call on all States to respect their international commitments to upholding a norms-based approach to cyberspace.' NATO, 'Statement by the North Atlantic Council Concerning the Malicious Cyber Activities Against Albania' (8 September 2022) www.nato.int/cps/en/natohq/official_texts_207156.htm.

of whether the police entered Iranian diplomatic premises before or after the expulsion of diplomats would have also come into existence.[81] That said, neither state engaged in a legal or factual dispute and, furthermore, these disputes do not concern cyber matters.

Also, when President Obama was asked whether the Sony attack[82] attributed to North Korea[83] was a violation of international law, he branded it as an act of cyber vandalism.[84] The Stuxnet attack in 2010 against the Iranian centrifuges is another glaring example where international law was not invoked by Iran, which was the victim of the attack.[85] Thus, at this juncture, states avoid elevating their disagreements into legal disputes.

C. Disagreements Over International Law in Multilateral Settings

The scenario discussed in this section is whether disagreements over international law voiced in multilateral settings can generate a legal dispute. For example, the GGE was able to produce consensus-based reports on the application of international law to cyberspace in 2013[86] and 2015[87] but failed to produce a report in 2017. Reportedly, its failure was due to disagreements among certain states regarding the inclusion of references to self-defence, countermeasures, and humanitarian law.[88] Can this demonstrate the existence of a legal dispute between these states? The answer is negative, and I will explain the reasons.[89]

[81] L Semini, 'Albanian Police Force Their Way into Iranian Embassy as Diplomats Expelled' (8 September 2022) www.timesofisrael.com/albanian-police-force-open-iranian-embassy-as-diplomats-expelled/.

[82] G Leupp, 'A Chronology of the Sony Hacking Incident' (29 December 2014) www.counterpunch.org/2014/12/29/a-chronology-of-the-Sony-hacking-incident/.

[83] The White House, 'Statement by the Press Secretary on the Executive Order Entitled "Imposing Additional Sanctions with Respect to North Korea"' (2 January 2015) obamawhitehouse.archives.gov/the-press-office/2015/01/02/statement-press-secretary-executive-order-entitled-imposing-additional-s.

[84] The White House, 'Remarks by the President in Year-End Press Conference' (9 December 2014) obamawhitehouse.archives.gov/the-press-office/2014/12/19/remarks-president-year-end-pressconference.

[85] N Falliere, LO Murchu and E Chien, 'W32.Stuxnet Dossier Version 1.3' (November 2010) www.wired.com/images_blogs/threatlevel/2010/11/w32_stuxnet_dossier.pdf; R Buchan and N Tsagourias, *Regulating the Use of Force in International Law: Stability and Change* (Cheltenham, Edward Elgar, 2021) ch 5.

[86] UNGA, 'Report of the Group of Governmental Experts on Developments in the Field of Information and Telecommunications in the Context of International Security' (24 June 2013) UN Doc A/68/98.

[87] UNGA (n 3).

[88] M Schmitt, 'The Sixth United Nations GGE and International Law in Cyberspace' (10 June 2021) www.justsecurity.org/76864/the-sixth-united-nations-gge-and-international-law-in-cyberspace/; AM Sukumar, 'The UN GGE Failed. Is International Law in Cyberspace Doomed as Well?' (4 July 2017) www.lawfaremedia.org/article/un-gge-failed-international-law-cyberspace-doomed-well; A Henriksen, 'The End of the Road for the UN GGE Process: The Future Regulation of Cyberspace' (2019) 5 *Journal of Cybersecurity* 1–9.

[89] In addition to the explanations provided in this section, one should also consider the fact that GGE/OEWG reports are consensual, and therefore, it is difficult to identify the subject matter of any

In the first place, disagreements, different opinions, and opposite views are common in every social setting. Still, as explained earlier, they do not constitute disputes unless transformed into disputes.[90] Also, opposition as the threshold for the existence of a dispute is not the same as having opposite views. The GGE and OEWG processes aim to initiate discussions and reach, if possible, consensus on the norms, principles, and rules that apply or should apply to cyberspace. States may have different views, but they are not required to agree, react, or reject the views expressed by other states or assert their rights or interests.

Second, the nature of disagreements in the GGE or OEWG is political rather than legal. For example, Cuba – one of the countries blamed for the failure of the 2017 GGE – stated that 'to convert cyberspace into a theatre of military operations and to legitimize, in that context, unilateral punitive force actions, including the application of sanctions and even military action by States claiming to be victims of illicit uses of ICTs' would turn cyberspace into a 'Law of the Jungle', in 'which the interests of the most powerful States would always prevail to the detriment of the most vulnerable'. Regarding humanitarian law, the Cuban representative said references to it 'would legitimize a scenario of war and military actions in the context of ICT'.[91] For Russia, as it appears from its statements, new technologies can not fit neatly under existing international humanitarian law.[92] For China, mentioning the law of armed conflict would speed up 'the arms race

legal dispute or the parties to the dispute. Even if reports were adopted by voting, any opposition identified by studying voting patterns is too abstract because states do not make their reasoning or, indeed, legal reasoning clear when they vote for or against a proposal. See *Obligations Concerning Negotiations* (n 5) para 56.

[90] The PCIJ opined that 'a difference of opinion does exist as soon as one of the Governments concerned points out that the attitude adopted by the other conflicts with its own views': *Case Concerning Certain German Interests in Polish Upper Silesia* (n 22), 14. The PCIJ interpreted, in that case, Art 23 of the German–Polish Convention on Upper Silesia (Geneva, 15 May 1922), which gave the PCIJ jurisdiction with respect to 'differences of opinion respecting the construction and application' of Arts 6–22 of the Convention. As a threshold for the establishment of a dispute, it is very low. C Tomuschat, 'Article 36' in A Zimmermann et al (eds), *The Statute of the International Court of Justice: A Commentary*, 3rd edn (Oxford, Oxford University Press, 2019) 11.

[91] M Rodriguez, 'Declaration by Miguel Rodríguez, Representative of Cuba, at the Final Session of Group of Governmental Experts on Developments in the Field of Information and Telecommunication in the Context of International Security' (23 June 2017) www.justsecurity.org/wp-content/uploads/2017/06/Cuban-Expert-Declaration.pdf. Also see MG Markoff, 'Explanation of Position at the Conclusion of the 2016–2017 UN Group of Governmental Experts (GGE) on Developments in the Field of Information and Telecommunications in the Context of International Security, Remarks' (23 June 2017) 2017–2021.state.gov/explanation-of-position-at-the-conclusion-of-the-2016-2017-un-group-of-governmental-experts-gge-on-developments-in-the-field-of-information-and-telecommunications-in-the-context-of-international-sec/. For the views of China and Russia, see E Korzak, 'UN GGE on Cybersecurity: The End of an Era?' (31 July 2017) thediplomat.com/2017/07/un-gge-on-cybersecurity-have-china-and-russia-just-made-cyberspace-less-safe/. Also see A Väljataga, 'Back to Square One? The Fifth UN GGE Fails to Submit a Conclusive Report at the UN General Assembly' ccdcoe.org/incyder-articles/back-to-square-one-the-fifth-un-gge-fails-to-submit-a-conclusive-report-at-the-un-general-assembly/#footnote_0_3011.

[92] UN Office for Disarmament Affairs, 'Open-Ended Working Group' disarmament.unoda.org/open-ended-working-group/: 'Statements / Contributions by Member States on the Zero and First (1st) Draft' and 'Comments by Member States on the Initial Pre-Draft of the OEWG Report'.

and militarization in cyberspace'; therefore, the 'application of existing laws of armed conflict to cyberspace requires further scrutiny'.[93]

States, in other words, were referencing international law in the GGE to support their strategic interests and preferences about the nature of cyber regulation. Even if one were to say there was a conflict of interests, it was not a conflict of legal interests for a legal dispute to arise.[94] It should also be noted that disagreements about how to regulate a new area, whether new law is required or what legal changes are needed, are political rather than legal. This is because lawmaking in international law is a political process.[95]

Third, the GGE/OEWG are diplomatic fora whose aim is to forge consensus among states on the normative framework that should apply to cyberspace to maintain a peaceful and stable cyber environment. To view them as places where legal disputes are elicited will affect their nature and function and will lead to an exponential increase in cyber disputes.

That being said, suppose now that states participate in negotiations to reach agreement on the scope and content of the rules regulating the use of force in cyberspace. A group of states contends that self-defence in cyberspace includes pre-emptive self-defence, a view rejected by another group of states which claims that such an interpretation is outside the law and that self-defence in cyberspace should be triggered only if there is an actual armed attack. Because such differences of opinion on the scope and content of the right to self-defence subsist during the negotiations, no agreement is reached. Does this give rise to a legal dispute?

In my opinion, what was said earlier about negotiations applies to this case, namely that no legal dispute arises, but the dispute is political about the content of the legal regulation of cyberspace or about changes in the law. This scenario should be distinguished from the *South West Africa* cases where the dispute was deemed to have been formed based on exchanges within the UN. In that case, the UN was the legally competent forum to discuss the obligations of the Mandatory toward the inhabitants of the Mandated Territory having succeeded the League of Nations and its Members.[96] Thus, negotiations took place within the UN to settle the dispute regarding the rights and obligations of the Mandatory. As the Court went on to say, even if the dispute within the UN may appear different from the one before the Court, the questions at issue are identical. The same can be said when there is an obligation under a treaty regime to reach a negotiated agreement,

[93] M Xinmin, 'Key Issues and Future Development of International Cyberspace Law' (2016) 2 *China Quarterly of International Strategic Studies* 119–33.

[94] *South West Africa Cases (Ethiopia v South Africa; Liberia v South Africa)* (Second Phase, Judgment of 18 July 1966) [1966] ICJ Rep 6 para 50: 'But the existence of an "interest" does not of itself entail that this interest is specifically juridical in character.'

[95] L Oppenheim and H Lauterpacht (eds), *International Law: A Treatise*, 7th edn (London, Longmans, 1952) vol II, 4. See MN Shaw (ed) and S Rosenne, *Rosenne's Law and Practice of the International Court: 1920–2015*, 5th edn (Leiden, Brill Nijhoff, 2016) I.1: 'the consequence of a *political* event is the creation of a new *legal* norm' (emphasis added).

[96] *South West Africa Cases* (n 8) 343–46.

as in the *Marshall Islands* case, where a dispute can emerge from exchanges within the regime's institutions or during negotiations.[97] That said, whether such disputes are justiciable is a different question because other conditions may need to be fulfilled, for example, *locus standi*,[98] or following the *Marshall Islands* judgment, specificity and awareness.

Another scenario concerns a controversy between two states regarding a malicious cyberattack. These states have in the past expressed divergent views about the content of related international rules in multilateral settings. Can such views be considered to prove the existence of a legal dispute in this case? As was said, the existence of a dispute is a matter of objective determination. For this reason, such divergent views are a factor to be taken into account to prove the existence of a legal dispute. This depends on the context, content, or author of such exchanges and will be assessed with evidence related to the dispute at hand.

In another instance, the ICJ opined that declarations, admissions or proposals during prior negotiations will not be considered if the negotiations have not led to an agreement.[99] The Court dismissed the role of such statements to facilitate negotiations as a means of dispute settlement by removing the risk that such statements would bind states if negotiations fail and states resort instead to judicial settlement. This, however, describes a different situation from the case at hand, which is about the added evidentiary value of views expressed in multilateral fora in the construction of a legal dispute.

To conclude, the juxtaposition of states' positions in multilateral fora such as the GGE/OEWG, even on matters of international law, does not give rise to a legal dispute unless there is a legal obligation to negotiate, in which case their opposing legal views can lead to the emergence of a legal dispute. They can be used however as evidence to support the existence of a legal dispute on a related matter.

D. Covert Cyber Operations

This scenario considers the question of whether covert cyber operations and the legal issues surrounding them may give rise to a legal dispute. This is important because cyber operations are often covert, and when they become known, often well after they are completed, they remain unacknowledged or partially

[97] In the *Marshall Islands* case, although the Court said that in this case, statements in international fora did not prove the existence of a dispute, it did not deny that there may be situations where they will. *Obligations Concerning Negotiations* (n 5) paras 49–58.

[98] The *South West Africa* case is different because it involved *erga omnes* obligations and obligations arising from the League of Nation's mandate system for South West Africa.

[99] *Case Concerning the Factory at Chorzów* (Jurisdiction, Judgment of 26 July 1927) [1927] PCIJ Rep Series A No 9, 19; *Factory at Chorzów* (Merits, Judgment of 13 September 1928) PCIJ Rep Series A No 17, 62–66; *Case Concerning Maritime Delimitation and Territorial Questions Between Qatar and Bahrain (Qatar v Bahrain)* (Jurisdiction and Admissibility, Judgment of 1 July 1994) [1994] ICJ Rep 112 para 40.

acknowledged. The Stuxnet attack targeting Iran's nuclear reactors is a case in point.[100] The attack reportedly took place in 2009 and 2010 but came to light in 2011 through journalistic reports based on interviews of current and past US officials.[101] Although, according to these reports, the attack was devised and executed by Israel and the USA, neither state acknowledged the attack.[102] Iran downplayed the attack and attributed it to 'enemies of Iran' instead of blaming particular states.[103]

If a malicious cyber operation is secret and remains unknown to the affected state, there is no naming, blaming, and claiming. Such operations are non-existent (non-events) for purposes of dispute formation. However, can a legal dispute arise when a state speculates that another state has engaged in an unlawful cyber operation against it? This scenario differs from the one discussed earlier regarding disputes over facts because there are no facts, just speculation. In my opinion, there is no dispute in this case. This situation is similar to hypothetical disputes which according to the ICJ are not real disputes.[104] Moreover, if hypothetical or speculative disputes were to be treated as real disputes, there would be endless possibilities of disputes arising between states, something which would destabilise the international legal order.

If a malicious cyber operation becomes known but remains unacknowledged and the victim state goes on to condemn it without blaming a particular state, no dispute arises because no transformation takes place. There is certainly naming in the sense of naming a particular operation as wrongful, but there is no blaming of a particular state. Even if the victim state claims that its legal rights or interests have been violated, this is not in response to a prior legal claim – verbal or factual – put forward by a state since the conduct remains unacknowledged. Furthermore, to the extent that the operation remains unacknowledged, it is not clear to which facts and legal views the affected state responds or whether they are correct representations of facts and legal views because in most cases of unacknowledged operations, facts and legal views are presented by third parties, for example, the media.[105]

[100] N Falliere, LO Murchu and E Chien, 'W32.Stuxnet Dossier Version 1.4' (February 2011) www.wired.com/images_blogs/threatlevel/2011/02/Symantec-Stuxnet-Update-Feb-2011.pdf.

[101] W Broad, J Markoff and D Sanger, 'Israeli Test on Worm Called Crucial in Iran Nuclear Delay' (15 January 2011) www.nytimes.com/2011/01/16/world/middleeast/16stuxnet.html; D Sanger, 'Obama Order Sped Up Wave of Cyberattacks Against Iran' (1 June 2012) www.nytimes.com/2012/06/01/world/middleeast/obama-ordered-wave-of-cyberattacks-against-iran.html.

[102] Sanger (n 101); E Nakashima and J Warrick, 'Stuxnet was Work of U.S. and Israeli Experts, Officials Say' (2 June 2012) www.washingtonpost.com/world/national-security/stuxnet-was-work-of-us-and-israeli-experts-officials-say/2012/06/01/gJQAlnEy6U_story.html.

[103] Reuters, 'Iran Says Cyber Foes Caused Centrifuge Problems' (29 November 2010) www.reuters.com/article/iran-ahmadinejad-computers-idAFLDE6AS1L120101129/.

[104] *Dispute Over the Waters of the Silala* [2022] ICJ Rep 614 para 48; *Northern Cameroons (Cameroon v United Kingdom)* (Preliminary Objections, Judgment of 2 December 1963) [1963] ICJ Rep 15 paras 33–34; *Question of the Delimitation of the Continental Shelf Between Nicaragua and Colombia Beyond 200 Nautical Miles from the Nicaraguan Coast (Nicaragua v Colombia)* (Preliminary Objections, Judgment of 17 March 2016) [2016] ICJ Rep 100 para 123.

[105] As Daniel Bethlehem wrote, 'in very many cases one cannot make assumptions about what the law is, or reach considered conclusions on whether conduct is lawful or unlawful, until one has considered

If a malicious operation is acknowledged by the acting state and condemned by the victim state as a violation of international law, a legal dispute arises because conduct can reveal the legal attitude of the acting state on a particular matter in view also of the fact that covert state conduct is usually subject to internal legal scrutiny. This conclusion becomes stronger if the acting state offers legal justifications upon acknowledging it, even in general terms. As explained earlier, the juxtaposition of general legal justifications and facts surrounding a particular conduct can help in establishing the legal position of the acting state on a specific matter and project a legal claim communicated to the affected state which, if rejected, gives rise to a legal dispute.

Can it, however, be said that there is no dispute when the acting state acknowledges a covert operation without offering a justification because covert operations are ipso facto unlawful? This is a broadly held view,[106] which, if accepted, would mean that no legal dispute will arise because the parties' views about the unlawfulness of the operation coincide. However, the view that covert operations are ipso facto unlawful is not an accurate representation of reality and is based on presumptions. States engage in lawful covert operations for security or other reasons, and covert operations as was said are not immune from internal legal scrutiny. It should also be added that there is no rule of international law requiring states to always act publicly. It is, therefore, important to carefully assess the facts before any inference is made about the existence of legal disputes in such cases. As was said earlier, a dispute can arise on the basis of facts or the 'attitude' of states.[107]

One issue that needs mentioning is whether the timing of the acknowledgement plays any role for a dispute to arise. In my opinion, it plays no role, provided that the states involved transform it into a present-day legal dispute. A dispute will thus arise as soon as an operation (ongoing or completed) is acknowledged by a state and is opposed by another state. That said, because a legal dispute is a construct, states may decide not to trigger a dispute after the passage of time.

In conclusion, it can be said that covert cyber operations may give rise to a dispute depending on the circumstances. That having been said, covert operations can also be viewed as mechanisms of dispute avoidance or containment. By not acknowledging an act and not making claims, disputes are avoided. The states involved can downplay the incident, deny that it happened or ignore it.

the invisible conduct as well as the visible'. D Bethlehem, 'The Secret Life of International Law' (2012) 1 *Cambridge International Law Journal* 23, 36. For how the ICJ assessed media and other reports and its interpretation of non-denials, see *Case Concerning Military and Paramilitary Activities in and against Nicaragua (Nicaragua v United States of America)* (Merits, Judgment of 27 June 1986) [1984] ICJ Rep 14 paras 83–91.

[106] R Falk, 'CIA Covert action and International Law' (1975) 12 *Proceedings of American Society of International Law* 1079; WM Reisman and JE Baker, *Regulating Cover Action: Practices, Contexts, and Policies of Covert Coercion Abroad in International and American Law* (New Haven, Yale University Press, 1992) 13; A D'Amato, 'Custom and Treaty: A Response to Professor Weisburd' (1988) 21 *Vanderbilt Journal of Transnational Law* 459, 469.

[107] *Applicability of the Obligation to Arbitrate* (n 11) para 38; *United States Diplomatic and Consular Staff in Tehran* (n 4) para 46.

Iran's reaction to the Stuxnet attack is a case in point. Moreover, and in a rather perverse manner, covert operations can maintain at least the veneer of international legality by not explicitly challenging international law.

IV. Conclusion

Cyberspace has all the ingredients for legal disputes to arise. There are factual problems and problems with the identification, application, interpretation, and enforcement of international law, which can form the subject matter of international legal disputes. In the preceding sections, I explained how a cyber dispute can be transformed into an international legal dispute. I also considered scenarios from existing practice where this may be the case.

Notwithstanding the potential for legal disputes to arise, as the scenarios have shown, states have not presented their disagreements in legal language and have not claimed that a legal dispute exists. There are many reasons for this state of affairs, and I will mention some of them.

First, the international legal edifice in cyberspace is still under construction. In an uncertain legal environment, the law cannot act as a stable regulatory tool, and states cannot trust the law to settle disputes. This may change in the future, but for now, states prefer to use other processes and soft mechanisms to manage their behaviour in cyberspace. For example, acts of cyber espionage are not condemned as violations of international law but as unfriendly acts, because the question of whether cyber espionage per se or its methods and effects are unlawful is not settled and, moreover, states engage in comparable activities.[108] This situation can explain why international law was not invoked regarding the SolarWinds attack.[109]

Second, states do not want to tie themselves to certain interpretations of international law before the normative content of cyberspace is stabilised because that may disadvantage them towards their competitors. States prefer normative ambiguity, allowing them to test the boundaries of international law and the boundaries of their conduct.

Third, there is the difficulty in attributing cyber operations to states either factually or legally or both. Attribution, as I explained, is the gatekeeper to international law, but even if the factual difficulties are overcome and attribution mechanisms have improved, the legal difficulties of attribution remain.

[108] MN Schmitt (ed), *Tallinn Manual 2.0 on the International Law Applicable to Cyber Operations*, 2nd edn (Cambridge, Cambridge University Press, 2017) 168–74 (Rule 32); R Buchan, *Cyber Espionage and International Law* (Oxford, Hart Publishing, 2018).

[109] A Lubin, 'SolarWinds as a Constitutive Moment: A New Agenda for the International Law of Intelligence' (23 December 2020) www.justsecurity.org/73989/solarwinds-as-a-constitutive-moment-a-new-agenda-for-the-international-law-of-intelligence/; J Goldsmith, 'Quick Thoughts on the Russia Hack' (16 December 2020) www.lawfaremedia.org/article/quick-thoughts-russia-hack. *Contra* R Buchan, 'Eye on the Spy: International Law, Digital Supply Chains and the SolarWinds and Microsoft Hacks' (31 March 2021) voelkerrechtsblog.org/eye-on-the-spy/.

Fourth, and related to the above, most cyber operations are covert. Consequently, they fall below the radar of states, and even if states become aware of such operations, they prefer to respond in kind. The covert nature of the majority of cyber operations also slows down the law-making process in cyberspace by denying it the benefits of practice and *opinio juris* either in support or against a particular behaviour or legal interpretation.

Fifth, framing claims in legal terms and instigating a legal dispute ushers states into a new relationship phase by invoking responsibility and reparations.[110] This is a novel state of affairs with legal, political, financial, and other consequences, but states may want to avoid getting entangled in such relations.

Sixth, legal disputes are often linked to third-party – judicial or arbitral – dispute settlement mechanisms where states lose their autonomy and discretionary power in managing the dispute. For this reason, they prefer to maintain the non-legal character of cyber disputes and thus influence their outcome.

In conclusion, there is inter-state conflict in cyberspace and a layer of inter-state conduct which is informed by political and strategic considerations but falls below the threshold of a legal dispute. All this may change, however, if the legal regulation of cyberspace matures and densifies through treaties or the evolution of customary rules and when the legal capacity of states in cyberspace increases.

[110] ARSIWA Arts 42 and 48.

2

Good Faith in the Context of the Resolution of Cyber Disputes

ROBERT KOLB AND ANDRAZ KASTELIC*

I. Introduction

It is a complete understatement that the importance of cyberspace grew exponentially in recent years. Examples abound, but it will suffice to mention all the cyber-activities surrounding the war in Ukraine.[1] The question posed in this chapter is to what extent disputes relating to cyberspace – in times of peace or armed conflict – are subject to the general rules of dispute settlement law and to what extent, on the contrary, they are different and call for separate solutions. This chapter does not, however, focus on dispute resolution law in general but on the role that the principle of good faith plays in it.[2] To this end, in the first part the chapter will first present the functions of good faith in dispute settlement (the *lex generalis*) and will then determine the inflections, departures and derogations of the principle of good faith in the particular domain of cyber disputes (the *lex specialis*) in the second part. The chapter will not present the law of dispute resolution, which is assumed to be known,[3] neither will there be a general presentation of the role and functions of good faith in international law; for which we refer to monographs on this principle.[4] Let us therefore delve immediately *in medias res*.

* The views expressed in the publication are the sole responsibility of the individual authors. They do not necessary reflect the views or opinions of the United Nations, United Nations Institute for Disarmament Research, its staff members, or sponsors.

[1] See, eg, the Reports by the Center for Strategic Cyberspace and International Studies: D Swan, 'Cyber Intelligence Report – Cyberwarfare: Russia vs Ukraine' (*CSIS*, 18 March 2022) cscis.org/2022/03/20/cyberwarfare-russia-vs-ukraine.

[2] See the Introduction to this volume.

[3] See, eg, JG Merrills and E de Brabandere, *International Dispute Settlement*, 7th edn (Cambridge, Cambridge University Press, 2022). See also the Introduction to this volume.

[4] R Kolb, *Good Faith in International Law* (Oxford, Hart Publishing, 2017).

II. The General Law: Good Faith in International Dispute Settlement

The law of the peaceful settlement of international disputes rests on two interrelated pillars: the principle of cooperation and the principle of consent. The first principle is triggered by the fact that the process of settlement is based on a common effort. There can be success only if there is a minimum level of loyalty and coordinated effort. The second principle is based on the fact that all means of settlement – from negotiation to judicial or arbitral proceedings – suppose the acceptance of the states involved. Good faith (bona fides) plays a major role in both pillars of the law of peaceful dispute settlement: it is a polar star in all cooperative efforts (loyalty, non-abuse, spirit of benevolence and effort, etc) and in all consensual bonds (*pacta sunt servanda*, bona fides).[5] In the context of cooperation, its aim it to protect the common finalities of the dispute settlement process. In the context of consent, it operates as a limitation on the true (but hidden) will of the parties in favour of considering the objective meaning of certain conduct and what others could and should have expected from such conduct. In view of the foregoing, the principle of good faith legally dominates the pacific settlement of international disputes.[6]

The particular obligations we will consider in this chapter flow from the principle of good faith but are free-standing obligations under customary and conventional international law having been regularly mentioned and applied by courts and commentators. However, they still remain linked to their nourishing principle of bona fides, which continues to provide interpretive guidance in their specific context.

There are different obligations deriving from good faith which apply to dispute settlement, with a particular focus on the negotiations phase. Before we discuss this cluster of obligations, it should be noted that how they apply depends on the context (eg, negotiations on mere interests, on conclusion of a legal bond, on the existence or not of an obligation to negotiate, on closeness of the negotiating states or tensions among them, etc) and on whether the negotiations are geared to the solution of the substantive dispute, or whether the negotiations concern the establishment of another mode of settlement for the dispute, for example arbitration.

A. Preservation of the Object and Purpose of the Process

An important part of the good faith obligation concerns the *preservation* (not necessarily the furthering) *of the object and purpose of the process*, in particular the subject matter to which the negotiations relate. To negotiate means to enter into a phase of common effort for the achievement of a certain aim. To allow one or other of the parties to conduct itself in such a way as to render the whole process futile or nugatory is incompatible with good faith, that is with the very object of negotiations. In

[5] See, eg, Art 26 of the Vienna Convention on the Law of Treaties (Vienna, 23 May 1969) (VCLT).

[6] L Delbez, *Les principes généraux du droit international public*, 3rd edn (Paris, Pichon et Durand-Auzias, 1964) 41.

a sense, not negotiating 'in good faith' is not truly negotiating at all; it is rather abusing the notion of negotiations for other aims.[7] In the latter case, from a legal point, negotiations ought simply to be suspended or terminated. Upon closer inspection, negotiation has a general and a special object: the first concerns all that is necessary to ensure that negotiations *as such* remain meaningful;[8] the second concerns the *specific object* of one particular negotiation, such as the sharing of a financial effort.

Regarding the general object and purpose of negotiations, good faith elicits a series of material obligations which have been described in case law in the following terms:

(i) Negotiations must be conducted in a meaningful way, ie, with a true intention to progress and potentially to conclude. This is not the case if a party refuses to take into account the adverse party's positions or immediately rejects all reasonable proposals.[9]
(ii) During negotiations, measures causing disproportionate harm to the other party(ies) and offering little advantage to one's own party should be avoided.[10]
(iii) The contempt for agreed procedures is contrary to good faith and possibly also to some legal engagement.[11] Duties of good faith may imply keeping discussions confidential, especially when it was so agreed.
(iv) The manifestly unjustified interruption of negotiations, for example in order not to be confronted with a reasonable proposal of the other party, is contrary to good faith. It will be sanctionable only in extreme cases.[12]
(v) In some cases of a closer relationship between parties, for example the existence of a strong agreement between them to negotiate or to agree, good faith may imply an obligation to accept a reasonable compromise.[13]
(vi) There is a general duty not to aggravate the dispute by deliberate acts during the negotiation (again, only manifest abuses can lead to a breach).[14]

[7] See the *Tacna-Arica Question (Chile v Peru)* (1925) 2 RIAA 921, 929–30.

[8] It has rightly been said that to negotiate otherwise than in good faith is surely not to negotiate at all: H Thirlway, 'The Law and Procedure of the ICJ (1960–1989): General Principles and Sources of Law' (1989) 60 *British Yearbook of International Law* 1, 25.

[9] *North Continental Shelf Sea Cases (Germany v Denmark; Germany v Netherlands)* (Judgment of 20 February 1969) [1969] ICJ Rep 3, 47; *Delimitation of the Maritime Boundary in the Gulf of Maine Area (Canada v USA)* (Judgment of 12 October 1984) [1984] ICJ Rep 246, 299; *Tacna-Arica Question* (n 7), 929–30; *Lake Lanoux Case (Spain v France)* (1957) 12 RIAA 281, 307–08, 311, 315; *Claims Arising out of Decisions of the Mixed Graeco-German Arbitral Tribunal Set Up under Article 304 in Part X of the Treaty of Versailles (Greece v Germany)* (1972) 19 RIAA 27, 57 (*German External Debts*); *Delimitation of the Maritime Boundary (Guyana v Suriname)* (2007) 30 RIAA 1, 130. See also UNGA, 'Manila Declaration on the Peaceful Settlement of International Disputes' (15 November 1982) UN Doc A/RES/37/10 para I(10).

[10] *Apportionment of Property of Local Authorities* (1953) 13 RIAA 501, 521.

[11] *Lake Lanoux Case* (n 9) 307.

[12] ibid.

[13] *German External Debts* (n 9) 56; *Lake Lanoux Case* (n 9) 308, 311, 315; *Government of Kuwait v American Independent Oil Company (AMINOIL)* (1984) 66 ILR 518, 578.

[14] *Case Concerning the Agreement of 27 March 1946 (United States v France)* (1979) 54 ILR 303, 338–39: 'It is tempting to assert that when parties enter into negotiations, they are under a general

Regarding the special object of negotiations, it is protected by rules analogous to the ones under Article 18 of the Vienna Convention on the Law of Treaties (VCLT) of 1969. It touches on obligations in the phase before the treaty comes into force. These duties are mainly of abstention.[15] The basic point is to preserve the object of negotiations from unilateral alterations and impairments rendering the common process nugatory. Here are some scattered examples. In the *Samoa* case (1902), the sole arbitrator determined that during the negotiation on the new constitutional regime in a place where more than one government had rights, the United States of America (US) could not militarily intervene without consulting one other party. The military intervention unilaterally modified the situation on which the negotiations bore.[16] It was incompatible with good faith. In the *Fisheries Jurisdiction* case (*UK v Iceland*, 1974), the International Court of Justice (ICJ) stated that negotiations in good faith on fish stocks presupposed that conservation issues relating to those stocks had to be taken into account during the negotiations.[17] This implied a limitation of the fishing practised by Iceland and the United Kingdom (UK). In the *Delimitation of the Maritime Boundary (Guyana v Suriname)* case of 2007, the arbitral tribunal held, based on some provisions of the Montego Bay Convention on the Law of the Sea (1982), that no permanent physical changes should be unilaterally affected in the area in dispute pending the final agreement on delimitation. Such changes would breach the obligation to negotiate in good faith and to preserve the specific object of the negotiation.[18]

As transpires from the above, the protection of the general object of negotiations gives rise to a series of flexible general rules, whereas the protection of the special objects of a negotiation tailors more idiosyncratic rules according to the particular circumstances. The general law is thus supplemented by a more particular law, the latter adding to the former (and not derogating from it).

duty not to aggravate the dispute, this general duty being a kind of emanation of the principle of good faith.' The tribunal however – rightly – refused to consider that this implies an obligation to abstain from all counter-measures in that phase: 'The Arbitral Tribunal does not believe that it is possible, in the present state of international relations, to lay down a rule prohibiting the use of counter-measures during negotiations, especially where such counter-measures are accompanied by an offer for a procedure affording the possibility of accelerating the solution of the dispute.' In this volume, see the Introduction and Wrange (ch 10).

[15] JF O'Connor, 'L'accord anglo-irlandais de 1985' (1985) 31 *Annuaire Français de Droit International* 191, 197; E Jiménez de Aréchaga, 'International Law in the Past of a Century – General Course on Public International Law' (1978) 159 *Recueil des Cours de l'Academie de Droit International de la Haye* 2, 200.

[16] USA, *Papers Relating to the Foreign Relations of the United States, Volume 43 (1902)* (Washington DC, United States Government Printing Office, 1903) 446: 'Pending instruction from the three treaty powers … those powers were bound upon principles of international good faith to maintain the situation thereby created until by common accord they had otherwise decided.'

[17] *Fisheries Jurisdiction (United Kingdom v Iceland)* (Merits, Judgment of 25 July 1974) [1974] ICJ Rep 3, 31 para 71 and 78.

[18] *Maritime Boundary* (n 9) 133.

B. Protection of Legitimate Expectations

A second potentially important limb of good faith during negotiations concerns the *protection of legitimate expectations*. What are such legitimate expectations (hereafter LE), which the law recognise as giving rise to specific rules? Generally, the engagement of parties in a common negotiation process creates some minimal needs of mutual confidence. On the one hand, negotiations must remain flexible.[19] A strict legal straitjacket would be self-defeating, unreal and illusory. On the other hand, a complete absence of rules protecting legitimate mutual expectations would jeopardise the usefulness of negotiations and undermine the credibility of the whole process.

As the ICJ ruled in the *Obligation to Negotiate an Access* case between Bolivia and Chile in 2018, such LE are not a free-standing principle in public international law.[20] However, the Court failed to take into account the fact that such LE can be part and parcel of the principle of good faith. The very core of the principle of good faith evolved around the protection of LE as most expressions of the principle demonstrate such as ratification of treaties by conduct, preconventional obligations under Article 18 of the VCLT, acquiescence, estoppel, and prescription.[21] The concept of LE coalesced around specific rules and principles of international law in various contexts, all of them linked to the general principle of good faith. Moreover, case law exists where the principle of good faith even served as a basis for directly posing LE duties and consequently finding breaches of the law. These examples are discussed extensively elsewhere[22] but an older case will illustrate that LE considerations have a considerable pedigree in international law and are not an invention of modernity. In the *Portendick* arbitration case of 1843, the French minister for the navy and the colonies informed the British ambassador in Paris that there was no intention on the part of the French government to close the port of Portendick, located in Senegal. Following disturbances in the African territory, ten months after this declaration, the port was subjected to a closure. The arbitral tribunal set up to hear the case also confirmed the legality and validity of the closure by France. The UK did not challenge the legality of the closure. It simply criticised the absence of any notification of the closure through diplomatic channels and in a timely manner. Such notification seemed to be even more necessary in view of the assurances given previously, creating LE. Not knowing of the closure, several ships flying the British flag sailed for the port of Portendick.

[19] The necessary flexibility in negotiations is emphasised in the UNGA, 'Manila Declaration on the Peaceful Settlement of International Disputes' UN Doc A/RES/37/10 para I(10).

[20] *Obligation to Negotiate Access to the Pacific Ocean (Bolivia v Chile)* (Judgment of 1 October 2018) [2018] ICJ Rep 507 paras 160–62.

[21] R Kolb, *La bonne foi en droit international public* (Paris, Presses universitaires de France, 2000) 177ff.

[22] ibid 150ff.

Faced with the new situation and unable to anchor at the port, they suffered damage. The arbitrators sanctioned the trust and confidence that a state may reasonably place in the word of another by awarding damages only for the ships whose captains effectively ignored the closure. It held that:

> France will have to compensate the claimants for the damages and prejudices to which they would not have been exposed if the said government … had simultaneously notified this measure to the English government; that France, on the contrary, despite the omission of this official notification of the blockade, owes no compensation for the losses suffered as a result of commercial operations in which the claimants engaged after, by other means, they had positively informed of the formation of the blockade of the Portendick.[23]

In this sense, it is apparent that the principle of good faith can become the source of specific rights or obligations[24] although in the context of dispute settlement, the good faith–LE link has not yet hardened into a well-defined set of rules. The necessary flexibility of negotiations and other political means of settling disputes acts, to some extent, as an obstacle to engendering detailed LE obligations. In contrast, in the arbitral and judicial process, good faith–LE obligations are ordinarily woven into procedural rules, for example through time-limits or admissibility of documents at particular stages of the proceedings.

That said, the good faith–LE link can take one of three shapes in the context of dispute settlement: (1) an argument brought forward cannot be heard in view of previous assurances or conduct (*petitio non est audienda*); (2) certain points must be considered accepted or abandoned under the principles of acquiescence, estoppel or prescription; (3) conduct rendering the settlement process nugatory or aggravating the dispute considerably is deemed contrary to the object and purpose of the process.[25] A court could sanction these duties by not admitting an argument or considering a point to be settled. Further, sometimes the LE created by acquiescence or estoppel-like conduct does not give rise to new rights or obligations but is used as an element in the interpretive process. The following examples are indicative.

[23] A de Lapradelle and N Politis, *Recueil des arbitrages internationaux, t I (1798–1855)* (Paris, A Pedone, 1905) 526 (translation by the authors).

[24] For example, the Swiss International Law Directorate admitted that under international law Switzerland could be bound by the declarations and related expectations it deliberately created towards another state: see L Caflisch, 'La pratique suisse en matière de droit international public 2018' (2019) 29 *Swiss Review of International and European Law* 607–57, 633ff.

[25] Also consider the definition of LE in the context of international investment law. Thus, in *International Thunderbird Gaming Corporation v The United Mexican States* (Award of 26 January 2006) UNCITRAL para 147, the tribunal considered that 'the concept of "legitimate expectations" relates … to a situation where a Contracting Party's conduct creates reasonable and justifiable expectations on the part of an investor (or investment) to act in reliance on said conduct, such that the failure by the NAFTA Party to honor those expectations could cause the investor (or investment) to suffer damages'. The proximity of this definition with estoppel is manifest. See on the question the succinct exposé of A Reinisch, *Advanced Introduction to International Investment Law* (Cheltenham, Edward Elgar, 2020) 58ff.

The arbitral tribunal in the *Sarropoulos v Bulgaria* case of 1927 considered the conduct of the Greek government during negotiations as the starting point of the renunciation of some claims[26] (based on its face value, ie, the LE raised by it).[27] In the *European Office of Patents* case of 1997, the arbitral tribunal found that, because of its attitudes during the negotiation (and thereafter), Belgium acquiesced in the new regime of taxation.[28] A LE was thus created and had to be honoured. In the *Pedra Branca / Pulau Batu Puteh, Middle Rocks and South Ledge* case (2008), the ICJ emphasised that Malaysia did not raise an argument during the phase of bilateral negotiations.[29] The Court used this fact to corroborate a presumption of regularity linked to a letter of 1953 and the competence of a minister to take a certain action. Contrariwise, explicit opposition during negotiations excludes the formation of acquiescence and thus of LE. The International Tribunal for the Law of the Sea (ITLOS) ruled accordingly in the *Ghana v Ivory Coast* case of 2017.[30] The ICJ took a similar position in the *Maritime Delimitation* case between Kenya and Somalia (2021).[31] It held that the fact that negotiations were called for shows that no prior boundary had been agreed or acquiesced to.

The extent of these good faith obligations depends among others on the precise relations between the parties, the particular law applicable (or possibly the power to settle the dispute on the basis of equity), the previous conduct in which they indulged, and the general geopolitical situation (relaxed or tense). Relevant duties vary in intensity according to context. There are several factors which tend to increase the scope and intensity of relevant obligations (which case law has taken into account), for example:

(i) the existence of agreements creating a situation of cooperation, eg, mandates or trusteeships; special agreements for arbitral or judicial settlement; etc;[32]
(ii) negotiations among members of an international organisation, where there are special duties of good faith owed to each other, eg, under Article 2(2) of the UN Charter;[33]

[26] *Sarropoulos v Bulgarian State* (Case No 291, 14 February 1927) (1932) 4 ADIL 424, 425–26.

[27] See K Hobér, *Extinctive Prescription and Applicable Law in Interstate Arbitration* (Uppsala, Iustus Förlag, 2001) 289.

[28] *Rémunération des services de recherche fournis par l'Office européen des brevets à l'Etat Belge* Case *(Belgique c Organisation européenne des brevets)* (Arbitral Award of 15 December 1997) (1997) 30 *Revue Belge de Droit International* 380–407, 381ff.

[29] *Sovereignty over Pedra Branca / Pulau Batu Puteh, Middle Rocks and South Ledge (Malaysia v Singapore)* (Judgment of 23 May 2008) [2008] ICJ Rep 12 para 219.

[30] *Delimitation of the Maritime Boundary in the Atlantic Ocean (Ghana v Côte d'Ivoire)* (Judgment of 23 September 2017) ITLOS Reports 2017, 4, para 191.

[31] *Maritime Delimitation in the Indian Ocean (Somalia v Kenya)* (Judgment of 12 October 2021) [2021] ICJ Rep 206 para 69.

[32] See, eg, the Dissenting Opinion of C de Visscher in *International Status of South West Africa* (Advisory Opinion of 11 July 1950) [1950] ICJ Rep 128, 188.

[33] See, eg, the *Interpretation of the Agreement of 25 March 1951 between the WHO and Egypt* (Advisory Opinion of 20 December 1980) [1980] ICJ Rep 73, 92ff.

(iii) the presence of an agreement to negotiate, to consult, or to conclude an agreement, according to its precise terms and scope;[34]
(iv) the fact that the negotiations are about a shared resource, trans-boundary cooperation, environmental issues, etc;[35]
(v) the general and special relations between parties, eg, closely allied or friendly nations (like Switzerland and Liechtenstein) or adversaries (like the USA and North Korea or Russia).

Further, it must be noted that good faith does not oblige states to negotiate in the first place.[36] How and if states want to resolve their dispute is a matter for other norms of international law.[37] But once the decision to negotiate (or to engage in any other settlement process) is taken and carried through, the obligations mentioned accompanies the process.

C. Prohibition of the Abuse of Rights

A third aspect of good faith during negotiations relates to the prohibition of *abuse of rights*. First, it is forbidden to resort to prohibited means of negotiation, such as fraud (ie, the deliberate inclusion of the other party into error by spreading false information, etc).[38] Treaty law provides specific sanctions for fraudulent behaviour – for example, Article 49 of the VCLT. In the law related to peaceful dispute settlement, the issue is not the voiding of some process, but rather the prohibition of fraudulent behaviour as such. Fraud is manifestly incompatible with negotiations in good faith.[39] Second, it may occur that the purpose of the negotiations is misappropriated. Negotiations can sometimes be used, not with a view to reach an agreement, but with a view to misuse power for unmentionable ends, eg, attempt to gain time for a military invasion.[40] In such cases there is no will to reach a solution to the dispute; rather, the point is to take advantage from the negotiation

[34] See, eg, *German External Debts* (1972) 19 RIAA 27, 56.

[35] See, eg, *Lake Lanoux Case* (n 9), 307ff. See also M Bernad and A de Eulate, 'La coopération transfrontalière régionale et locale' (1993) 243 *Recueil des Cours de l'Academie de Droit International de la Haye* 293–418, 305ff, 396ff.

[36] See *Obligation to Negotiate Access to the Pacific Ocean* [2018] ICJ Rep 507, para 91. See also the UNGA, 'Manila Declaration on the Peaceful Settlement of International Disputes' UN Doc A/RES/37/10 para I(10), emphasising the free choice of means principle, which implies a right to refuse entering into a particular means dispute settlement, including negotiation.

[37] On the issue, see, eg, DN Hutchinson, 'The Material Scope of the Obligation under the United Nations Charter to Take Action to Settle International Disputes' (1992) 14 *Australian Yearbook of International Law* 1, 1ff, 47ff; CF Murphy, 'The Obligation of States to Settle Disputes by Peaceful Means' (1973) 14 *Virginia Journal of International Law* 57–74.

[38] See Art 49 of the VCLT. Fraud leads to the voidability of the concluded agreement.

[39] The close link between fraud and good faith is regularly noted: see, eg, T Rensmann, 'Article 49' in O Dörr and K Schmalenbach (eds), *Vienna Convention on the Law of Treaties: A Commentary* (Heidelberg, Springer, 2012) 835–48, 835.

[40] See, eg, G Geamanu, 'Théorie et pratique des négociations and droit international' (1980) 166 *Recueil des Cours de l'Academie de Droit International de la Haye* 365–448, 413.

to pursue ends which will injure the interests of the other party. In other words, the negotiation is used as a weapon against the other party(ies). Such behaviour does not deserve legal protection. But proving and sanctioning such abuses is difficult and the lines between permitted self-interest and prohibited ruthlessness are fine. Under international law there is no general duty to behave in an unselfish way. A state may give priority to its interests and legal positions. As the old adage says, 'you do not harm anyone when you exercise your rights'. However, there is always a limit to such freedom. Thus, action can be considered abusive and contrary to legal principle when it is based on *détournement de pouvoir* (action which abuses a legal entitlement to pursue other ends than the ones allowed), arbitrariness (action which shocks the sense of elementary justice because it is entirely devoid of a proper basis), or possibly also action which prioritises a state's own interest in a shocking way (notably if an insignificant interest is given priority over a manifestly essential one). That said, there is no international case law on such situations in the context of dispute settlement.

A specific area in which practice exists is the notion of 'abuse of procedure' in the process of a dispute settlement organ, notably a tribunal. Abuse of procedure consists in the use of procedural instruments and entitlements with a fraudulent, malevolent, dilatory, vexatious or frivolous intent. The aim is to harm another or to secure an undue advantage for oneself, with the intent to deprive the proceedings (or some other related proceedings) of their proper object and purpose or outcome, or to use the proceedings for aims alien to the ones for which the procedural rights at stake have been granted (eg, pure propaganda).[41] Abuse of procedure is not presumed. It must be clearly established by evidence presented or by judicial scrutiny of available evidence *proprio motu*. Written rules on abuse of procedure developed in certain branches of international law. In human rights law (writ large), petitions and communications are declared inadmissible when there is an abuse of procedure. This has been the case, for example, under the mandate system at the League of Nations and under the UN trusteeship system;[42] and later under former Article 27(2) of the European Convention on Human Rights (now Article 35(3)),[43] Rule 99(c) of the Rules of Procedure of the Human Rights

[41] On abuse of procedure in international law, see M Gestri, 'Considerazioni sulla teoria dell'abuso del diritto alla luce della prassi internazionale' (1994) 77 *Rivista di Diritto Internazionale* 5, 27ff, 43ff. As was said by the Australian High Court in *CSR Ltd v Cigna Insurance Australia Ltd* (1997) 118 ILR 380, 409–10: 'The counterpart of a court's power to prevent its process being abused is its power to protect the integrity of those processes once set in motion.'

[42] E Schwelb, 'The Abuse of the Right of Petition' (1970) 3 *Revue des droits de l'homme* 313–332, 313ff, 324–26.

[43] 'The Court shall declare inadmissible any individual application … which it considers … an abuse of the right of application.' See, eg, D Appanah, 'A la recherche posthume de l'intention du requérant: l'identification délicate de la requête abusive au sens de la Convention' (2015) 26 *Revue trimestrielle des droits de l'homme* 1053–070, 1053ff; K Jungwiert, 'Sur la requête abusive devant la Cour européenne des droits de l'homme' in P Titiun and P Dumaine (eds), *Essays in Honor of JP Costa* (Paris, Dalloz, 2011) 329–335, 329ff.

Committee under the CCPR,[44] Article 56(3) of the African Charter on Human and Peoples' Rights (requests written in disparaging or insulting language),[45] or Article 22(2) of the Convention against Torture (1984).[46] International administrative law and international investment case law are replete with references to misuse of authority and procedure.[47] Further, Article 294 of the Montego Bay Convention gives the tribunal chosen by parties the power to scrutinise whether the claimant's request related to the coastal state's exercise of its sovereign rights under Article 297 constitutes an abuse of procedure, and to declare it inadmissible *in limine litis*.[48]

At the ICJ, the principle of abuse of procedure was invoked in several cases: for example *Ambatielos* (abuse of process by excessive delay prior to the presentation of the claim to the Court);[49] *Right of Passage over Indian Territory* (abuse of process by starting proceedings too rapidly after lodging an optional declaration – a 'surprise attack');[50] *Barcelona Traction* (abuse of process by introducing a new case based on the same arguments as those used in discontinued proceedings);[51] *Military and Paramilitary Activities in and against Nicaragua* (abuse of process because of the futility of the proceedings and the intention to make political propaganda out of a request for the indication of interim measures);[52] *Border and Transborder Armed Actions* (abuse of process by recourse to the ICJ in parallel with the so-called 'Contadora' negotiating process; abuse of process because of the political motivation of the application and its artificial character);[53] *Arbitral Award of 31 July 1989* (abuse of process by invoking a declaration by the president of the tribunal to cast doubt on the validity of the award);[54] *Certain Phosphate Lands in Nauru* (abuse of process in that Nauru was asking of the respondent an attitude that

[44] International Covenant on Civil and Political Rights, Rules of procedure of the Human Rights Committee, UN Doc CCPR/C/3/Rev.12, 4 January 2021. See also Gestri (n 41) 31; A Cassese, 'The Admissibility of Communications to the United Nations on Human Rights Violations' (1972) 5 *Revue des droits de l'homme* 375–393, 375ff.; *KL v Denmark* (Communication No 72/1979, Decision of 31 July 1980) in Human Rights Committee, 'Selected Decisions under Optional Protocol' (1985) UN Doc CCPR/C/OP/I, 26.

[45] Gestri (n 41) 32–33; GM Palmieri, 'Aperçu du règlement intérieur de la Commission africaine des droits de l'homme et des peuples' in GM Palmieri (ed), *La Charte africaine des droits de l'homme et des peuples* (Padova, CEDAM, 1990) 128.

[46] Gestri (n 41) 33.

[47] Kolb (n 4) 170ff, 249ff.

[48] MH Nordquist (ed), *United Nations Convention on the Law of the Sea, 1982: A Commentary* (Dordrecht, Martinus Nijhoff, 1989) vol 5, 75ff.

[49] *Ambatielos Case (Greece v United Kingdom)* (Merits: Obligation to Arbitrate, Judgment of 19 May 1953) [1953] ICJ Rep 10 para 23.

[50] *Right of Passage over Indian Territory (Portugal v India)* (Preliminary Objections, Judgment of 26 November 1957) [1957] ICJ Rep 125 paras 146–47.

[51] *Barcelona Traction, Light and Power Company, Limited (Belgium v Spain)* (Preliminary Objections, Judgment of 24 July 1964) [1964] ICJ Rep 6 paras 24–25.

[52] *Military and Paramilitary Activities in and against Nicaragua (Nicaragua v United States of America)* (Provisional Measures, Order of 10 May 1984) [1984] ICJ Rep 169 paras 21–25.

[53] *Border and Transborder Armed Actions (Nicaragua v Honduras)* (Jurisdiction and Admissibility, Judgment of 20 December 1988) [1988] ICJ Rep 69 paras 51ff and 94.

[54] *Arbitral Award of 31 July 1989 (Guinea-Bissau v Senegal)* (Judgment of 12 November 1991) [1991] ICJ Rep 53 paras 26–27.

Nauru itself had not respected);[55] *Genocide* (abuse of process in making a request for interim measures motivated by political considerations and abusive repetition of the request for such measures);[56] *Aerial Incident of 10 August 1999* (abuse of process by invoking a reservation to a declaration under the optional clause the content of which was allegedly directed solely against Pakistan and was thus said to be discriminatory);[57] *Avena and Others* (abuse of process by delaying the presentation of claims);[58] *Criminal Proceedings* (*Equatorial Guinea v France*, Preliminary Objections, 2018) (abuse of procedure by trying to impose the unilateral determination of a building as an embassy);[59] *Application of the Genocide Convention* (*Gambia v Myanmar*, Preliminary Objections, 2022) (abuse of procedure when a state brings a case on behalf of an international organisation in order to circumvent the restriction *ratione personae* of Article 34(1) of the Statute)[60] but also in other proceedings.[61] The ICJ rejected all these pleas of abuse on the basis of the facts and the evidence at hand. It continued to do so in its most recent judgment on the allegations genocide brought by Ukraine against Russia.[62]

That said, in arbitral jurisprudence, the plea of abuse of process has sometimes been accepted. For example, an investment arbitral tribunal considered that the initiation of a case was abusive since the investor had changed the corporate structure in order to obtain protection under the relevant investment treaty, when a specific dispute was foreseeable.[63]

Another tribunal was prepared to accept that, under some circumstances, proceedings initiated *pari passu*, both under arbitral clauses and under municipal law, could constitute an abuse of process.[64] Further abuses of process might

[55] *Certain Phosphate Lands in Nauru (Nauru v Australia)* (Preliminary Objections, Judgment of 26 June 1992) [1992] ICJ Rep 240 paras 37–38. But see Dissenting Opinion Oda para 29.

[56] *Application of the Convention on the Prevention and Punishment of the Crime of Genocide (Bosnia and Herzegovina v Yugoslavia)* (Provisional Measures, Order of 13 September 1993) [1993] ICJ Rep 325 para 19; (Preliminary Objections, Judgment of 11 July 1996) [1996] ICJ Rep 595 para 46.

[57] *Aerial Incident of 10 August 1999 (Pakistan v India)* (Jurisdiction of the Court, Judgment of 21 June 2000) [2000] ICJ Rep 12 para 40.

[58] *Avena and Other Mexican Nationals (Mexico v United States of America)* (Judgment of 31 March 2004) [2004] ICJ Rep 12 para 44.

[59] *Immunities and Criminal Proceedings (Equatorial Guinea v France)* (Preliminary Objections, Judgment of 6 June 2018) [2018] ICJ Rep 292 paras 139ff.

[60] *Application of the Convention on the Prevention and Punishment of the Crime of Genocide (Gambia v Myanmar)* (Preliminary Objections, Judgment of 22 July 2022) (to be published) para 49 (available at www.icj-cij.org/sites/default/files/case-related/178/178-20220722-JUD-01-00-EN.pdf).

[61] At ITLOS, see, eg, *Delimitation of the Maritime Boundary Between Mauritius and Maldives in the Indian Ocean (Mauritius v Maldives) (Judgment on Preliminary Objections, Judgment of 28 January 2021)* (to be published) para 337ff (available at www.itlos.org/fileadmin/itlos/documents/cases/28/preliminary_objections/C28_Judgment_prelimobj_28.01.2021_orig.pdf). In arbitrations, see the *South China Sea Arbitration (Philippines v China)* (Award on Jurisdiction and Admissibility of 29 October 2015) 33 RIAA 1 paras 124ff.

[62] *Allegations of Genocide under the Convention on the Prevention and Punishment of the Crime of Genocide (Ukraine v Russian Federation)* (Judgment of 2 February 2024) paras 110–118 (to be reported).

[63] '*Philip Morris Asia Ltd v Australia*, Jurisdiction and Admissibility' (2015) 169 *ILR* 423 at 595ff, paras 535ff.

[64] *Waste Management v Mexico (No 2)* (Preliminary Objections, Decision of 26 June 2002) (2008) 132 ILR 145, 175–76 (NAFTA arbitration tribunal).

include an avalanche of preliminary objections or procedural arguments designed to delay the proceedings from progressing in the ordinary way; the late invocation of titles of jurisdiction, or other arguments in the hope of disrupting or prejudicing the opposing party.[65]

Conversely, some actions have not been regarded as abuse of procedure as for example the invocation of a new title of jurisdiction leading to a 'surprise attack' on the defendant. The ICJ held that state parties to the optional clause system under Article 36(2) of the ICJ Statute accepted that other states can at any time join the system by depositing a declaration, and that this deposit has immediate legal effect, creating a basis for jurisdiction.[66] What is an abuse of procedure is thus a matter to be decided according to the factual circumstances at hand, envisioning the general definition of the principle given at the beginning of this subsection.

D. Additional Considerations

Four further points need to be made on all these good faith obligations.

(a) First, the Arbitral Commission for the Former Yugoslavia (established by the European Communities) held that a state can have *recourse to countermeasures* when another state breaches its legal duties of negotiation in good faith.[67] The conclusion of the Arbitral Commission shows that these duties are giving rise to the decentralised sanctions of international law and are not mere aspirational or soft obligations. Countermeasures can indeed be taken from the legal point of view: to the extent the good faith obligations are true obligations under international law (and they are), they can be protected through countermeasures (peaceful reprisals). Such an attitude might aggravate the dispute to some extent. It could therefore be seen as contrary to the obligation not to aggravate the dispute. A distinction must be made between a situation where a tribunal is seized and other situations. In the first hypothesis, countermeasures may not be taken when the tribunal has the power to issue binding provisional measures (in this case, there is no

[65] *Legality of Use of Force (Yugoslavia v Belgium)* (Provisional Measures, Order of 2 June 1999) ICJ Rep 124ff; *Legality of Use of Force (Yugoslavia v Netherlands)* (Provisional Measures, Order of 2 June 1999) ICJ Rep 542ff. See also the Separate and Dissenting Opinion of Ansari in *Cal-Maine Foods v Iran* (1984) 6 Iran/US Claims Tribunal Reports 52, 70: 'The issue was first introduced in the Claimant's Memorial of 14 July 1983, and the raising of this new issue, which has totally altered the Claimant's grounds of action, cannot by any means be construed as constituting an amendment or supplement to the Statement of Claim … This method of changing the grounds of action is unquestionably prejudicial to the rights of the Respondents … (*Alternativa petitio non est audienda*)'.

[66] *Right of Passage over Indian Territory* [1957] ICJ Rep 125, 145–47; *Land and Maritime Boundary between Cameroon and Nigeria (Cameroon v Nigeria)* (Preliminary Objections, Judgment of 11 June 1998) [1998] ICJ Rep 275 paras 21ff. There is no duty under good faith to inform another state of the intention to subscribe to the optional clause system (para 39).

[67] *Opinion No 12* (1994) 96 ILR 723 para 2. See Buchan (ch 9 in this volume) and Wrange (ch 10 in this volume).

'necessity' to resort to countermeasures and these become unlawful).[68] In the second hypothesis, the vested right to take countermeasures to protect oneself must prevail over the general duty of non-aggravation. The latter relates only to aggravation which is avoidable and legally unsound – not to aggravation which flows from the exercise of rights or legally conceded faculties. However, when taking such countermeasures the state must take due account of the mentioned non-aggravation rule. Only strictly necessary measures must be taken. The general question remains as to what extent it is sensible to escalate the situation by taking such unilateral measures at all. This is not a legal question but pertains to the realm of legal policy.

(b) Second, apart from the negotiation phase, *specific issues of good faith can arise in other contexts*, for example, on the issue of the binding nature of provisional measures issued by a tribunal seized of an international dispute between states; in the context of estoppel or acquiescence as bases for jurisdiction of a tribunal; in the context of withdrawal of titles of jurisdiction.[69] If the title of jurisdiction contains a generic term (eg, 'military measures') or is written in subjective language (eg, 'domestic jurisdiction as determined by State X'), can one party (generally the defendant) rely on its idiosyncratic (if not abusive) interpretation of that term, to deny jurisdiction? International tribunals tend to ensure that the subjective invocation is not contrary to good faith or patently unreasonable, so as to resist a course of conduct rendering the jurisdictional ambit nugatory.[70]

(c) Third, there is a complex *duty not to aggravate the dispute* pending the decision of a tribunal (a duty which can in part be extended to the course of negotiations, as we have seen).[71] The *South China Sea* arbitration (Merits, 2016) elaborates on this.[72] The tribunal referred to Article 26 of the VCLT as well as the concept of preserving the object and purpose of the proceedings.[73]

[68] See Art 52(3)(b) of the ILC, 'Responsibility of States for Internationally Wrongful Acts' in *Yearbook of the International Law Commission. 2001, Volume II, Part Two: Report of the Commission to the General Assembly on the Work of its Fifty-Third Session* (New York, UN, 2005).

[69] Kolb (n 4) 203ff, 207ff, 231ff.

[70] ibid 223ff. In recent case law, see WTO, *Russia – Measures Concerning Traffic in Transit* (Report of the Panel, 29 April 2019) WT/DS512/R (2019) 58 ILM 899 paras 7.130–38 on the term 'national security' contained in Art XXI of the General Agreement on Tariffs and Trade (GATT) (Marrakesh, 15 April 1994).

[71] See the Introduction to this volume and Wrange (ch 10 in this volume).

[72] *South China Sea Arbitration (Philippines v China)* (Merits, Award of 12 July 2016) 33 RIAA 153 paras 1166ff.

[73] ibid para 1171: 'In the Tribunal's view, such a duty is inherent in the central role of good faith in the international legal relations between States. Article 26 of the Vienna Convention on the Law of Treaties recognises this when it provides that "[e]very treaty in force is binding upon the parties to it and must be performed by them in good faith." This obligation is no less applicable to the provisions of a treaty relating to dispute settlement. Where a treaty provides for the compulsory settlement of disputes, the good faith performance of the treaty requires the cooperation of the parties with the applicable procedure. Compulsory settlement is also premised on the notion that the final result will be binding on the parties and implemented by them as a resolution of their dispute. The very purpose of dispute settlement procedures would be frustrated by actions by any party that had the effect of aggravating or extending the dispute, thereby rendering it less amenable to settlement'.

The definition of 'aggravation of the dispute' given by the arbitral tribunal is notable:

> In the course of dispute resolution proceedings, the conduct of either party may aggravate a dispute where that party continues during the pendency of the proceedings with actions that are alleged to violate the rights of the other, in such a way as to render the alleged violation more serious. A party may also aggravate a dispute by taking actions that would frustrate the effectiveness of a potential decision or render its implementation by the parties significantly more difficult. Finally, a party may aggravate a dispute by undermining the integrity of the dispute resolution proceedings themselves, including by rendering the work of a court or tribunal significantly more onerous or taking other actions that decrease the likelihood of the proceedings in fact leading to the resolution of the parties' dispute.[74]

As to the content of the obligation, the Tribunal held that China had aggravated the dispute unlawfully in three ways: (1) by the construction of artificial islands creating a fait accompli;[75] (2) by causing irreparable harm to the marine environment, notably to the coral reefs;[76] and (3) by undermining the efficiency of the arbitral proceedings through a series of acts.[77] A dispute can therefore be unlawfully aggravated while it is pending either by acts directly related to the proper administration of justice (hampering of the proceedings) or by acts related to the subject matter in dispute (impairing the object in dispute). In other words, aggravation as to proceedings and aggravation as to subject matter can occur.

[74] *South China Sea Arbitration* (n 72) para 1176.

[75] ibid para 1177: 'The Tribunal considers that China's intensified construction of artificial islands on seven features in the Spratly Islands during the course of these proceedings has unequivocally aggravated the disputes between the Parties identified above. First, China has effectively created a *fait accompli* at Mischief Reef by constructing a large artificial island on a low-tide elevation located within the Philippines' exclusive economic zone and continental shelf, an area in which only the Philippines has sovereign rights with respect to living and non-living resources and where only the Philippines may construct or authorise artificial islands. In practical terms, the implementation of the Tribunal's decision will be significantly more difficult for the Parties, and Mischief Reef cannot be returned to its original state, before China's construction work was begun'.

[76] ibid para 1178: 'Second, China has aggravated the Parties' dispute with respect to the protection and preservation of the marine environment by causing irreparable harm to the coral reef habitat at Cuarteron Reef, Fiery Cross Reef, Gaven Reef (North), Johnson Reef, Hughes Reef, Subi Reef, and Mischief Reef. The Tribunal has already found that China has seriously violated its obligation to preserve and protect the marine environment in the South China Sea (see paragraphs 950 to 993 above) …'.

[77] ibid para 1179: 'Finally, China has undermined the integrity of these proceedings and rendered the task before the Tribunal more difficult. At the same time that the Tribunal was called upon to determine the status of features in the Spratly Islands and the entitlements that such features were capable of generating, China has permanently destroyed evidence of the natural status of those same features (see paragraphs 305 to 306, 321, 511, 541, and 578 above). The small rocks and sand cays that determine whether a feature constitutes a low-tide elevation or a high-tide feature capable of generating an entitlement to a territorial sea are now literally buried under millions of tons of sand and concrete. Despite this, the Tribunal has reached a decision on the status of features in the South China Sea using the best evidence available to it and drawing heavily on historical sources. The Tribunal is satisfied that its decisions regarding the status of features are well founded in fact, but records that they were rendered significantly more difficult by China's works at the features in question'.

It should be noted that minor, indirect or remote aggravation does not violate the principle of good faith.[78] The aggravation must have a certain gravity, and, in most cases, be done deliberately or with *dolus eventualis*. There is no general duty in international law not to do anything which could eventually prove detrimental to a settlement procedure; but there is a special duty not to perform acts which intentionally or recklessly (and sufficiently gravely) impair the efficiency of the proceedings and/or of the subject matter in dispute. A procedure before a tribunal does not freeze any action which could prove potentially and indirectly detrimental to the dispute. If that were true, there would be a powerful incentive for states to avoid committing to any judicial settlement.

(d) Finally, *duties of disclosure* exist mainly under particular international law, ie, under explicit treaty provisions. In these cases, the duty does not arise specifically from good faith but from the black letter undertaking in the applicable source. There are several such duties of information, for example in the context of nuclear non-proliferation[79] or the protection of the environment.[80] Under general international law, apart from certain circumscribed areas,[81] there are no duties of disclosure. However, in some cases, an obligation of this type could be derived directly from the principle of good faith. Thus, a tribunal could be prepared to state a duty of disclosure if for instance one party has inadvertently misled a negotiation partner and later becomes aware of the fact. In such a case the first party would have to inform the other party of the error which it has induced. The issue has been discussed mainly in the context of fraud in treaty conclusion (Article 49 of the VCLT). There is no fraud when a party merely fails to disclose crucial information; a fraud supposes active behaviour, luring the other party into an error.[82] A general duty of disclosure does not even seem to exist when certain information is exclusively accessible to one party. Moreover, in the litigation at the ICJ, there is no duty of disclosure. The Court can ask for the submission of certain documents, but

[78] In this sense, the formula of the PCIJ in *Electricity Company of Sofia and Bulgaria* (Order of 5 December 1939) [1939] PCIJ Rep Series A/B No 79, 199 is too broad: 'the parties to a case must abstain from any measure capable of exercising a prejudicial effect in regard to the execution of the decision to be given and, in general, not allow any step of any kind to be taken which might aggravate or extend the dispute'.

[79] See, eg, Art III of the Treaty on the Non-Proliferation of Nuclear Weapons signed in 1968, entered into force in 1971. Treaty on the Non-Proliferation of Nuclear Weapons' (12 June 1968) UN Doc A/RES/2373(XXII)) and the special agreements with the International Atomic Energy Agency provided for under Art III(4) of the Treaty.

[80] For example, such duties exist when an industrial project jeopardises the environment of a shared river. See *Pulp Mills on the River Uruguay (Argentina v Uruguay)* (Judgment of 20 April 2010) [2010] ICJ Rep 14 para 80, under Arts 7ff of the Statute of the River Uruguay.

[81] Particularly the duties of information and consultation under international environmental law in case of transboundary projects with potentially polluting effects. See, eg, *Certain Activities Carried Out by Nicaragua in the Border Area (Costa Rica v Nicaragua) and Construction of a Road in Costa Rica along the San Juan River (Nicaragua v Costa Rica)* (Judgment of 16 December 2015) [2015] ICJ Rep 665 paras 108 and 165ff.

[82] Rensmann (n 39) 840–41.

the concerned party may refuse to hand them over. The Court shall then draw its own conclusions from this behaviour.[83] In summary, the only exception of a general nature which would probably be admitted is that a party may not profit from its own wrong. If it has caused the error, it must remedy it by informing the other party. This is a high threshold and leaves little place for duties of disclosure under general international law.

III. The Special Law: Good Faith and Dispute Settlement in Cyberspace

Can the good faith obligations under general international law examined above be applied to cyber disputes? If so, which specific considerations apply? These questions will be discussed in this section.

Before proceeding, we should note that we will not consider all (aspects of) the obligations deriving from good faith discussed in the previous section because their character does not differ materially in cyber disputes – the obligation to accept reasonable compromise, for example, does not manifestly change in the context of disputes arising from states' conduct in cyberspace – but we recognise that the interpretation of the law of good faith in the given context of cyber disputes requires specific considerations which will be explained below.

A. Applicability of the Principle of Good Faith and of the Law of Peaceful Settlement of Disputes in Cyberspace

Although some states cautioned against presumptive, automatic application of existing rules to cyberspace,[84] general principles of international law remain central to maintaining the international order of peace and security. Following the technology-neutral interpretation of the UN Charter by the ICJ in the *Legality of the Threat or Use of Nuclear Weapons* advisory opinion, it is submitted that the UN Charter provisions on the peaceful settlement of disputes, which are to be

[83] See Art 49 of the Statute of the International Court of Justice (San Francisco, 26 June 1945).

[84] For example, Russia argued that 'given the specific legal nature of the information environment … the application of international law to the use of information and communications technologies (ICTs) should not be automatic and should not be carried out by simple extrapolation'. UNGA, 'Official Compendium of Voluntary National Contributions on the Subject of How International Law Applies to the Use of Information and Communications Technologies by States Submitted by Participating Governmental Experts in the Group of Governmental Experts on Advancing Responsible State Behaviour in Cyberspace in the Context of International Security Established Pursuant to General Assembly Resolution 73/266' (13 July 2021) UN Doc A/76/136, 80. See also R Schöndorf, 'Israel's Perspective on Key Legal and Practical Issues Concerning the Application of International Law to Cyber Operations' (2021) 97 *International Law Studies* 395–406.

fulfilled in good faith,[85] are sufficiently general in nature to apply to new phenomena including cyber disputes.

Indeed, states agreed that the UN Charter is applicable in the context of the ICT environment 'in its entirety'[86] and confirmed that the UN Charter obligations related to peaceful dispute settlement apply in the context of states' use of ICTs. The 2021 consensus report of the UN Group of Governmental Experts on Advancing Responsible State Behaviour in Cyberspace in the Context of International Security (GGE), subsequently welcomed by the UN General Assembly,[87] clearly establishes that states remain obligated to settle their disputes peacefully, even when these disputes emerge from state employment of ICTs. The report notes 'the importance of other Charter provisions relevant to the resolution of disputes by peaceful means'.[88] This includes provisions prescribing compliance in good faith. The imperative character of peaceful dispute settlement in the cyberspace context has also been widely appreciated by leading scholars[89] and individual positions of states[90] alike.

From this, one can say that there is international agreement on the application of the UN Charter and extant international law rules and principles to cyberspace which include the principle of peaceful settlement of disputes and the attached principle of good faith. Be that as it may, we will now consider how specific obligations deriving form good faith apply to cyber disputes.

B. Preservation of the Object and Purpose of the Process

Regarding the obligation to preserve the object and purpose of the dispute settlement process, two specific obligations, the obligation to ensure the confidentiality of the dispute settlement process and the obligation to refrain from aggravating the conflict, appear to be the most relevant to cyber disputes.

The obligation to preserve confidentiality is not only relevant in the peaceful settlement of cyber disputes process, but also imposes constraints on the use of ICTs in the settlement process. Concerns over the unauthorised collection and disclosure of confidential data is indeed acute and heightened in the contemporary

[85] Charter of the United Nations (San Francisco, 26 June 1945) Art 2(2).

[86] UNGA, 'Report of the Group of Governmental Experts on Advancing Responsible State Behaviour in Cyberspace in the Context of International Security' (14 July 2021) UN Doc A/76/135, para 71(e).

[87] UNGA, 'Resolution Adopted by the General Assembly: 76/19. Developments in the Field of Information and Telecommunications in the Context of International Security, and Advancing Responsible Communications Technologies' (8 December 2021) UN Doc A/RES/76/19.

[88] UNGA, 'Report of the GGE' UN Doc A/76/135, para 71(a).

[89] See, eg, DB Hollis and E Tikk, 'Peaceful Settlement in International Law' (2022) 57 *Texas International Law Journal* 1–50.

[90] See, eg, Z Jun, 'Remarks by Amb. Zhang Jun at Security Council Open Debate on Cyber Security' (*Permanent Mission of the People's Republic of China*, 29 June 2021) un.china-mission.gov.cn/eng/hyyfy/202106/t20210629_9124010.htm; UK and Japan in UNGA, 'Official Compendium' UN Doc A/76/136.

hyperconnected world. ICTs certainly allow for unprecedented data collection and disclosure or dissemination.[91] Indeed, the state practice of using ICTs for intelligence collection is now considered to be prevalent[92] and even a security necessity.[93]

The obligation to preserve confidentiality prohibits states engaged in the dispute settlement process to disclose information acquired by way of unauthorised intelligence collection to persons who may use it to gain unfair advantage in the process. The obligation has been elaborated on in the ICJ *Questions Relating to the Seizure and Detention of Certain Documents and Data* case, with *Timor-Leste* submitting that Australia's unauthorised access to data related to the dispute settlement violated good faith obligations and its right to confidentiality. The Court responded to the claim in the affirmative, arguing that parties to the conflict resolution process have the 'right to conduct arbitration proceedings or negotiations without interference by [the opposing party], including the right of confidentiality of … its communications with its legal advisers'.[94]

Two limits to the obligation can be distilled from the case mentioned above. First, as per the Court's interpretation of the good faith obligation of preserving confidentiality, sensitive, confidential data related to the ongoing or reasonably expected conflict dispute settlement[95] enjoys special legal protection. Communication between the government and its legal advisers is indeed likely to include sensitive, confidential data related to legal argumentation. Disclosure could provide unfair advantage to one of the parties in the process. However, there is no reason to limit the applicability of the obligation to this type of data only. For instance, in a dispute over cyber conduct, the disclosure of confidential technical data that supports the attribution or indicates the scope of harm done by the contentious cyber operation could work to the advantage of one of the parties in a conflict resolution process.

Second, the obligation to preserve confidentiality appears to only prohibit disclosure to a particular set of actors. In the very same case, the ICJ was adamant that preservation of confidentiality would have been violated if data relevant to the case was to be shared with 'any person or persons who could use it, or cause it to be used, to the disadvantage [of the party in a conflict resolution endeavour]'.[96]

[91] 'ICT have enabled illicit intelligence collection efforts directed and/or orchestrated by other countries at an unprecedented speed, frequency, intensity, and scale.' UNODC, 'Cyberespionage' (2022) www.unodc.org/e4j/en/cybercrime/module-14/key-issues/cyberespionage.html.

[92] See, eg, R Buchan, *Cyber Espionage and International Law* (Oxford, Hart Publishing, 2018) ch 7.

[93] 'Signals intelligence capabilities are a major reason we have been able to adapt to a dynamic and challenging security environment, and the United States must preserve and continue to develop robust and technologically advanced signals intelligence capabilities to protect our security and that of our allies and partners.' The White House, 'Executive Order on Enhancing Safeguards for United States Signals Intelligence Activities' (7 October 2022) www.whitehouse.gov/briefing-room/presidential-actions/2022/10/07/executive-order-on-enhancing-safeguards-for-united-states-signals-intelligence-activities/.

[94] *Questions Relating to the Seizure and Detention of Certain Documents and Data (Timor-Leste v Australia)* (Provisional Measures, Order of 3 March 2014) [2014] ICJ Rep 147 para 28.

[95] ibid para 51.

[96] ibid.

It can be contended that the obligation covers the leaking of confidential data to the general public,[97] giving persons an opportunity to use it in the dispute resolution process. Therefore, use of cyber tools and channels to disclose relevant data to the general public is equally prohibited.

Unauthorised data collection by itself is, generally speaking, not contradictory to the obligation to preserve confidentiality or other obligations under international law.[98] However, with the increasing use of mass data collection and data mining[99] enabled by digital technologies, a state may inadvertently collect data related to a dispute settlement belonging to the opposing party. In such a case, the good faith principle imposes a positive obligation to implement adequate protection against data being obtained by persons who could use it to the disadvantage of the opposing party in the dispute settlement. The exact modalities of compliance with this obligation are not prescribed by law. Relevant jurisprudence suggests, however, that states in possession of such sensitive data should seal it and render it inaccessible, at least until the dispute resolution process is concluded.[100] In the context of digital data, states could comply with the obligation by encrypting for example digital files relevant to the settlement process and preventing access to parties that could use it for unfair negotiation advantage.

Another highly relevant obligation in the context of cyberspace is the obligation not to aggravate the dispute. Although the definition of aggravating conduct is context-dependent,[101] we will discuss three theoretical categories of aggravating conduct distilled from international jurisprudence analysed above.[102]

First, continuance (or even intensification) of disputed conduct during the settlement proceedings may prevent the restoration of the material status before the disputed conduct occurred. It is therefore considered to be aggravating and not in line with the good faith principle. In the context of this chapter, cyber conduct utilising self-propagating ransomware[103] and wipers[104] may be particularly aggravating and deserves closer scrutiny.

[97] Not an uncommon practice, by any means. In the words of Castle and Pelc, 'leaks have become a prominent fixture of international negotiations'. M Castle and KJ Pelc, 'The Causes and Effects of Leaks in International Negotiations' (2019) 63 *International Studies Quarterly* 1147–162, 1162.

[98] '[P]eacetime cyber espionage by States does not per se violate international law.' MN Schmitt (ed), *Tallinn Manual 2.0 on the International Law Applicable to Cyber Operations*, 2nd edn (Cambridge, Cambridge University Press, 2017) Rule 32.

[99] N Pillay, 'Opening Remarks by Ms Navi Pillay, United Nations High Commissioner for Human Rights to the Side-Event at the 24th Session of the UN Human Rights Council: How to Safeguard the Right to Privacy in the Digital Age?' (*OHCHR*, 20 September 2013) www.ohchr.org/en/statements/2013/09/opening-remarks-ms-navi-pillay-united-nations-high-commissioner-human-rights?LangID=E&NewsID=13758.

[100] *Questions Relating to the Seizure and Detention of Certain Documents and Data* (n 94) para 50.

[101] SR Ratner, 'The Aggravating Duty of Non-Aggravation' (2020) 31 *European Journal of International Law* 1307–342, 1307.

[102] *South China Sea Arbitration* (2016) 33 RIAA 153.

[103] A Chernikova et al, 'Cyber Network Resilience against Self-Propagating Malware Attacks' in V Atluri et al (eds), *Computer Security – ESORICS 2022* (Cham, Springer, 2022) 531–550.

[104] D Tarakanov, 'Shamoon the Wiper in Details' (*Kaspersky*, 22 August 2012) securelist.com/shamoon-the-wiper-in-details/34369/.

Although frequently used by malicious, non-state cyber actors, it has been alleged that states are also no strangers to using ransomware.[105] The function of ransomware is to infiltrate systems, to encrypt files and to prevent the legitimate user from using the system until ransom is paid. For this reason, ransomware could be interpreted as a violation of sovereignty.[106] In a discussion on whether sovereignty is a rule or a principle in the context of state conduct in cyberspace,[107] it is not inconceivable to envision a legal dispute with ransomware at the heart of it.

Ransomware can include self-propagating mechanisms[108] and can spread without human intervention. The wider it spreads and the longer it takes before it is stopped at its source,[109] the greater the potential for irreversible consequences.[110] In the context of dispute settlement proceedings, states utilising ransomware must take actions to stop the self-propagation of malware and further system infections in order to comply with the obligation of non-aggravation.

Another type of malware with significant potential to cause irreversible damage is the type known as wipers, named after its ability to obliterate computer storage devices, causing data loss[111] and potentially rendering a system useless. Allowing a wiper to continue operating within a system while dispute settlement is underway, could prevent the restoration of the prior material situation and would be contrary to the good faith obligation not to aggravate the dispute.

Second, state conduct in violation of additional legal rights of the opposing party in a dispute resolution process can also be considered aggravating, particularly so if the conduct exhibits 'specific nexus with rights and claims making up the parties' dispute'.[112] To illustrate this, we turn our attention again to the prevalent state practice of using ICTs for unauthorised, remote intelligence collection.

In contrast to potentially unlawful disclosure, unauthorised remote intelligence collection is not contrary to the obligation to preserve confidentiality in the dispute settlement process. Acts of unauthorised intelligence collection via cyber

[105] Cybersecurity and Infrastructure Agency, 'North Korean State-Sponsored Cyber Actors Use Maui Ransomware to Target the Healthcare and Public Health Sector' (*CISA*, 7 July 2022) www.cisa.gov/news-events/cybersecurity-advisories/aa22-187a.

[106] MN Schmitt, 'Three International Law Rules for Responding Effectively to Hostile Cyber Operations' (*Just Security*, 13 July 2021) www.justsecurity.org/77402/three-international-law-rules-for-responding-effectively-to-hostile-cyber-operations/.

[107] ibid.

[108] K Baker, 'How Does Ransomware Spread? 10 Most Common Infection Methods' (*Crowdstrike*, 22 November 2022) www.crowdstrike.com/cybersecurity-101/ransomware/how-ransomware-spreads/; Anon, 'Lateral Movement' (*Crowdstrike*, 18 February 2022) www.crowdstrike.com/cybersecurity-101/lateral-movement/.

[109] A Winckles, 'Here's How the Ransomware Attack was Stopped – and Why It Could Soon Start Again' (*The Conversation*, 17 May 2017) theconversation.com/heres-how-the-ransomware-attack-was-stopped-and-why-it-could-soon-start-again-77745.

[110] See, eg, S Ghafur et al, 'A Retrospective Impact Analysis of the WannaCry Cyberattack on the NHS' (*npj Digital Medicine*, 2019) www.nature.com/articles/s41746-019-0161-6.

[111] See, eg, Editor, 'SwiftSlicer: New Destructive Wiper Malware Strikes Ukraine' (*We Live Security*, 27 January 2023) www.welivesecurity.com/2023/01/27/swiftslicer-new-destructive-wiper-malware-ukraine/.

[112] *South China Sea Arbitration* (n 72) para 1174.

means could, however, aggravate a dispute, if interpreted by a party to the dispute settlement as a violation of international law. Scholars have argued that unauthorised intelligence collection 'constitutes a violation of the territorial sovereignty of a State where information is accessed that is resident on computer networks that are supported by cyber infrastructure located on that State's territory'.[113] Importantly, a number of interpretations of international law in cyberspace by states align with this argument. Depending on the target, scale and effects, remote intelligence collection (when involving unauthorised penetration of sovereign ICT infrastructure) may be deemed internationally unlawful deprivation of sovereign rights of the targeted state[114] and, by virtue of this, constitute an aggravation of the dispute.

Given the infancy of international law in cyberspace and significant divergences in the interpretation of legal thresholds, states engaged in dispute settlement should keep abreast of interpretations ascribed to by their negotiation counterparts. States should also avoid using ICTs for any actions which may be deemed violations of international law. Indeed, as stated by the *Fisheries Jurisdiction* case of the ICJ, in the course of peaceful dispute settlement, states must 'pay reasonable regard to the legal rights of the other [State involved in the process]'.[115]

Third, conduct can be considered aggravating if it undermines the dispute settlement process. As it was established in the *South China Sea* arbitration presented above, destruction of relevant evidence (which could be achieved remotely via ICT means)[116] would make it harder for a dispute settlement intermediary to reach an objective conclusion. It is therefore unlawful. In the same vein, breach of the ICT systems of parties involved in dispute settlement – be it states or a settlement intermediary such as a tribunal – and tempering with the data related to the proceedings, would equally undermine the integrity of the proceedings and thus constitute aggravation.

The concept of aggravation is not limited to a deliberate action. Breach of the obligation may also consist of an omission.[117] Accordingly, states engaged in peaceful dispute settlement must exhibit a certain level of diligence in respect of the three acts of aggravation as discussed above. Jurisprudence confirms this, most notably in

[113] R Buchan, 'The International Legal Regulation of State-Sponsored Cyber Espionage' in AM Osula and H Rõigas (eds), *International Cyber Norms: Legal, Policy and Industry Perspectives* (Tallinn, NATO Cooperative Cyber Defence Centre of Excellence, 2016) 85. See further Buchan (n 92).

[114] For example, France, 'International Law Applied to Operations in Cyberspace: Paper Shared by France with the Open-Ended Working Group Established by Resolution 75/240' (2021) documents.unoda.org/wp-content/uploads/2021/12/French-position-on-international-law-applied-to-cyberspace.pdf para 1.1.1.

[115] *Fisheries Jurisdiction Case* [1974] ICJ Rep 3 para 78.

[116] Consider the ubiquitous type of malware known as wiper, the purpose of which is to delete computer data. Tarakanov (n 104).

[117] *Certain Activities Carried Out by Nicaragua in the Border Area* (n 81) paras 108 and 165ff; *Certain Activities Carried Out by Nicaragua in the Border Area (Costa Rica v Nicaragua); Construction of a Road in Costa Rica along the San Juan River (Nicaragua v Costa Rica)* (Provisional Measures, Order of 16 July 2013) [2013] ICJ Rep 230 para 38.

the aforementioned PCIJ *Electricity Company of Sofia and Bulgaria* case, where the Court argued that parties to the conflict resolution process must '*not allow any step of any kind to be taken* which might aggravate or extend the dispute'.[118]

As argued above, however, the PCIJ's interpretation of the obligation of non-aggravation is stretching the law too far. There are several limitations to the scope of the required diligence in the context of non-aggravation and peaceful dispute settlement.

First, applying the doctrinal understanding from analogous regimes, the required diligence is limited to prevention[119] and termination[120] of conduct that is reasonably expected to aggravate a dispute. The standard of compliance is flexible and depends on the capacity of a state.[121] In the context of this chapter and considering the language of the PCIJ's elaboration on the obligation of non-aggravation, to 'not allow' means states must employ their best efforts to prevent or to terminate potentially aggravating cyber operations. Methods of compliance in respect of cyber operations are not prescribed by law.

Second, states must only prevent or terminate aggravating conduct that is contrary to the rights of other states stemming from their territory.[122] It is commonly accepted nowadays that the cyber domain includes physical infrastructure,[123] therefore states must do their utmost to prevent or terminate aggravating conduct utilising ICT infrastructure under their territorial jurisdiction. This is an important accountability framework in the context of cyberspace where the capacities of non-state actors are formidable, including cyber operations that deprive states of their legal rights.[124] The fact that actions of non-state actors can play an important role in the aggravation of a dispute has been recognised by the ICJ in the *Certain Activities Carried Out by Nicaragua in the Border Area* case.

Third – and as noted above – aggravation can only be established in relation to deliberate conduct or conduct with *dolus eventualis*. Omission of due diligence in the context of this chapter is considered deliberate, and thus aggravating. States are guilty of such omission if they choose to forgo any attempts to terminate or prevent cyber operations stemming from their territory with an intent to facilitate

[118] *Electricity Company of Sofia and Bulgaria* [1939] PCIJ Rep Series A/B No 79, 199 [emphasis added].

[119] For example, *Alabama Claims of the United States of America against Great Britain* (Award of 14 September 1872) 29 RIAA 125, 130; *Armed Activities on the Territory of the Congo (Democratic Republic of the Congo v Uganda)* (Judgment of 19 December 2005) [2005] ICJ Rep 168, 187.

[120] *United States Diplomatic and Consular Staff in Tehran (United States of America v Iran)* (Judgment of 24 May 1980) [1980] ICJ Rep 3.

[121] '[D]iligence is proportioned to the magnitude of the subject and to the dignity and strength of the power which is to exercise it.' *The Geneva Arbitration (Alabama Claims of the United States of America against Great Britain)* in JB Moore, *History and Digest of the International Arbitrations to which the United States has been a Party* (Washington DC, Government Printing Office) vol I, 572–73.

[122] *Corfu Channel Case* (Merits, Judgment of 9 April 1949) [1949] ICJ Rep 4, 22.

[123] See, eg, N Tsagourias, 'The Legal Status of Cyberspace: Sovereignty Redux?' in N Tsagourias and R Buchan (eds), *Research Handbook on International Law and Cyberspace* (Cheltenham, Edward Elgar, 2021) 9–31.

[124] See UNGA, 'Report of the GGE' UN Doc A/76/135, s II.

the aggravating conduct to materialise. At the same time, the absence of a reasonable attempt to prevent or terminate a cyber operation is aggravating when a state consciously disregarded cyber operations stemming from its territory, knowing that they 'were most likely to lead to [aggravation] but nevertheless willingly took that risk'.[125] Related to the requirement of intent or *dolus eventualis*, lack of diligence can only be considered aggravating, and thus unlawful, when it was established that states knew or should have known of the aggravating conduct.[126]

Note that, as established above, conduct only qualifies as aggravation, and thus violation of good faith, if it is particularly grave. Gravity is evaluated on the basis of several factors, such as 'the intent to violate the norm; the scope and number of individual violations; and the gravity of their consequences for the victims'.[127]

In the context of this chapter, a discriminate cyber operation that is intended to target specific systems of a party to a dispute resolution process could be considered deliberate and intended. Stuxnet, targeting specific electronic controllers of the uranium enriching facilities in Natanz, Iran,[128] would be an example of a cyber operation exhibiting intent if there was any process of negotiations between the parties involved. The same could be claimed about the wipers targeting Ukrainian energy sector entities.[129] On the other hand, intent would be harder to prove with indiscriminate cyber operations. WannaCry ransomware, for instance, affected systems in 74 countries and had a particularly grave effect on the UK National Health Service.[130] Given its indiscriminate nature, one would be hard-pressed to establish intent on behalf of the authors of the malware to cripple the network of the UK National Health Service specifically.

Furthermore, in appraising gravity through the prism of scope and scale, indiscriminate and self-propagating cyber operations have significant potential to mushroom into a great number of separate instances of violations. They can negatively affect a significant number of systems in a given jurisdiction. Depending on the circumstances, self-propagating ransomware could thus be considered grave enough to qualify as aggravating a dispute. On the other hand, cyber operations targeting specific infrastructure, such as the Industroyer2 wiper malware 'developed specifically to target a power grid'[131] and 'scheduled to cut power for a region

[125] *Prosecutor v Dusko Tadic* (Judgment of 15 July 1999) ICTY IT-94-1-A para 220.

[126] A Kastelic, 'Due Diligence in Cyberspace: Normative Expectations of Reciprocal Protection of International Legal Rights' (*UNIDIR*, 2021) unidir.org/sites/default/files/2021-11/SecurityTechnology_DueDiligence_Report.pdf 13–14.

[127] ILC, 'Report of the Commission to the General Assembly on the Work of its Fifty-Third Session' (2001) UN Doc A/CN.4/SER.A/2001/Add.1 (Part 2) 113.

[128] 'Stuxnet is a computer worm that was designed and deployed to attack Iranian nuclear facilities.' O Buxton, 'Stuxnet: What is It and How Does It Work?' (*Avast*, 14 July 2022) www.avast.com/c-stuxnet.

[129] ESET Research, 'A Year of Wiper Attacks in Ukraine' (*We Live Security*, 24 February 2023) www.welivesecurity.com/2023/02/24/year-wiper-attacks-ukraine/.

[130] GREAT, 'WannaCry Ransomware Used in Widespread Attacks All Over the World' (*Kaspersky*, 12 May 2017) securelist.com/wannacry-ransomware-used-in-widespread-attacks-all-over-the-world/78351/.

[131] A Lameiras, 'Industroyer: A Cyber-Weapon that Brought Down a Power Grid' (*WeLiveSecurity*, 13 June 2022) www.welivesecurity.com/2022/06/13/industroyer-cyber-weapon-brought-down-power-grid/.

in Ukraine',[132] would most likely remain limited in scope and scale. They will not thus be grave enough to be considered aggravating when assessed only on the basis of their scope and scale but, as will be seen, may have grave consequences if they target specific infrastructure. The same could be argued for other types of tailored cyber operations aimed at a specific target, such as distributed-denial-of-service (DDOS) operations.

Cyber operations aimed at critical infrastructure, designed to disturb 'the backbone of a society's vital functions, services and activities'[133] are likely to be grave, and thus aggravating. This can be argued for operations developed and aimed at specific infrastructure as well as for indiscriminate malicious software such as ransomware. In evaluating the gravity of conduct from the perspective of its consequences, it matters less what type of malware was used and more what the target was.

Gravity of consequences is an equally important factor when considering due diligence in relation to aggravating conduct. This interpretation of the existing doctrine is aligned with national interpretations of law in the context of cyberspace. A number of states indicated that lack of diligence in the prevention or termination of cyber operations detrimental to the legal rights of other states – and thus aggravating an existing dispute – can only be claimed unlawful when the cyber operation in question has significant adverse consequences.[134] Taking into account the existing doctrine and evolving *opinio juris* on the application of international law in cyberspace, this may indeed emerge as *de minimis* standard in the context of due diligence expectations during the dispute settlement process.

[132] ibid.

[133] UNGA, 'Report of the GGE' UN Doc A/76/135 para 43.

[134] The Netherlands, for example, submitted that 'it is generally accepted that the due diligence principle applies only if the State whose right or rights have been violated suffers sufficiently serious adverse consequences'. The Netherlands, 'Letter to the Parliament on the International Legal Order in Cyberspace' (5 July 2019) www.government.nl/ministries/ministry-of-foreign-affairs/documents/parliamentary-documents/2019/09/26/letter-to-the-parliament-on-the-international-legal-order-in-cyberspace Appendix 1, 5. Ecuador (UNGA, 'Chair's Summary: Open-Ended Working Group on Developments in the Field of Information and Telecommunications in the Context of International Security, Third Substantive Session' (10 March 2021) UN Doc A/AC.290/2021/CRP.3) argues that states are expected to employ best efforts so that their territory is not used for 'an internationally wrongful act that is likely to produce serious adverse consequences in another State'; Finland (Finland, 'International Law and Cyberspace: Finland's National Positions' (15 October 2020) um.fi/documents/35732/0/Cyber+and+international+law%3B+Finland%27s+views.pdf/41404cbb-d300-a3b9-92e4-a7d675d5d585?t=1602758856859) argues that 'States may … not knowingly allow their territory, or cyber infrastructure within a territory under their control, to be used to cyber operations that produce serious adverse consequences for other States.' See also the positions of Canada (UNGA, 'Chair's Summary' UN Doc A/AC.290/2021/CRP.3, 10ff); Romania (UNGA, 'Official Compendium' UN Doc A/76/136, 75); and Norway (UNGA, 'Official Compendium' UN Doc A/76/136, 71).

C. Protection of Legitimate Expectations

As discussed above, legitimate expectations (LE) can be created through written or oral assurances[135] and objections,[136] which must be 'clear and specific'.[137] LE can also be deduced from state practice or conduct.[138] State conduct includes the absence of action or of an official expression of a position on the subject matter.[139] National attitudes may legitimately be presumed or discounted based on the presupposition of consistency with LE, and deeds contrary to LE may be nugatory or aggravating.

LE play an important role in the context of dispute settlement arising from state conduct in the cyber domain, particularly so in the absence of a dedicated, specific legal regime.[140] States have engaged in institutionalised multilateral discussions on the topic of international cybersecurity for more than a decade. Throughout the years, different processes (in the form of the UN GGE or the OEWG) concluded with consensus reports, later submitted to and adopted by the UN General Assembly. As indicated by the conclusions of these multilateral deliberations, the international community agreed on a number of voluntary norms of responsible state behaviour in cyberspace,[141] which may serve as a source of LE. Indeed, non-binding agreements can create indirect legal effects and form LE.[142] This, however, cannot be said for the outcomes of the aforementioned processes. First, the language of the UN General Assembly resolutions adopting norms for responsible state behaviour in cyberspace do not create direct legal obligations. They stress that these norms are 'voluntary, non-binding'.[143] The UN General Assembly resolutions also explicitly exclude indirect legal consequences of said norms. The most recent resolution states that the norms 'do not seek to limit or

[135] *Nuclear Tests (Australia v France)* (Judgment of 20 December 1974) [1974] ICJ Rep 253 para 43.

[136] *Legal Status of Eastern Greenland (Denmark v Norway)* [1933] PCIJ Rep Series A/B No 53, 56.

[137] ILC, 'Guiding Principles Applicable to Unilateral Declarations of States Capable of Creating Legal Obligations, with Commentaries Thereto' (2006) UN Doc A/CN.4/SER.A/2006/Add.l (Part 2) 377.

[138] *Temple of Preah Vihear (Cambodia v Thailand)* (Merits, Judgment of 15 June 1962) [1962] ICJ Rep 6, 40 (separate opinion of Judge Alfaro): '[I]nconsistency between claims or allegations put forward by a State, and its previous conduct in connection therewith, is not admissible.'

[139] *Arbitral Award Made by the King of Spain on 23 December 1906 (Honduras v Nicaragua)* (Judgment of 18 November 1960) [1960] ICJ Rep 192, 209.

[140] At the time of drafting this chapter, there is no dedicated legal regime or treaty dedicated to states' use of ICTs. UNGA, 'Developments in the Field of Information and Telecommunications in the Context of International Security: Note by the Secretary-General' (18 March 2021) UN Doc A/75/816, Annex I para 80: '[I]mportant proposals were put forward even though they were not necessarily agreed by all States, including the possibility of additional legally binding obligations'.

[141] UNGA, 'Report of the GGE' UN Doc A/76/135.

[142] A Zimmermann, 'Possible Indirect Legal Effects of Non-Legally Binding Instruments' (*University of Potsdam*, 26 March 2021) rm.coe.int/1-2-zimmermann-indirect-legal-effects-of-mous-statement/1680a23584.

[143] UNGA, 'Developments in the Field of Information and Telecommunications' UN Doc A/RES/76/19, 2.

prohibit action that is otherwise consistent with international law'.[144] Indeed, as eloquently put in the award in the *Chagos Marine Protected Area* arbitration, 'a State that elects to rely to its detriment upon an expressly non-binding agreement does not, by so doing, achieve a binding commitment by way of estoppel'.[145]

This conclusion corresponds to the view that LE can only be created when expressed 'with the intent to be bound'.[146] However, during the course of the multilateral deliberations on international cybersecurity, several states made oral statements or submitted written positions in relation to the normative framework. Depending on the language of these declarations, they may indeed create relevant LE in potential disputes over state conduct using ICTs. In fact, some states consider certain norms of responsible state behaviour in cyberspace to be legal obligations or reflections of customary international law. They have declared this on record,[147] and thus created LE. These LE could be reinforced when declarations are coupled with potential evidence of state practice in accordance with the norms.[148] Some states have indeed elaborated on how to implement the norms in question.[149]

For instance, in 2015, states agreed to be guided in their use of ICTs by, inter alia, norm H, according to which states should 'respond to appropriate requests to mitigate malicious ICT activity aimed at the critical infrastructure of another State emanating from their territory'.[150] Consider a situation in which a critical infrastructure asset of State A is targeted by a cyber operation stemming from the territory of State B, upon which the former issues a request, seeking assistance from the latter in mitigating the ongoing cyber operation. Suppose State B ignores the request and makes absolutely no effort to respond, despite the fact that it repeatedly voiced specific commitments to act in accordance with, inter alia, the aforementioned norm H, and issued a report detailing norm implementation efforts. Should this situation occur during an ongoing dispute settlement process, the inaction of State B could be interpreted as aggravating the dispute.

Although unilateral declarations of commitment must be specific and clear, they can be made 'to the world at large'.[151] National declarations in the context of

[144] ibid 2.

[145] *Chagos Marine Protected Area Arbitration (Mauritius v United Kingdom)* (Award of 18 March 2015) 31 RIAA 359 para 445. See also Kolb (n 4) 104: 'the law does not protect those who rely on all and believe every word'.

[146] *Nuclear Tests* (n 135) para 43.

[147] For instance, consider the position of Finland on the norm C: 'It is clear that States have an obligation not to knowingly allow their territory to be used for activities that cause serious harm to other States, whether using ICTs or otherwise.' J Taalas, 'Statement by Ambassador Janne Taalas at the Second Session of the Open-Ended Working Group (OEWG) on Developments in the Field of Information and Telecommunications in the Context of International Security, February 10 and 11' (*NATO CCD COE*, 2018) ccdcoe.org/uploads/2018/10/Statement-on-International-Law-by-Finnish-Ambassador-Janne-Taalas-at-2nd-session-of-OEWG.pdf.

[148] Zimmermann (n 142).

[149] United Kingdom of Great Britain and Northern Ireland, 'Non-Paper on Efforts to Implement Norms of Responsible State Behaviour in Cyberspace, as Agreed in UN Group of Government Expert Reports of 2010, 2013 and 2015' (September 2019) s3.amazonaws.com/unoda-web/wp-content/uploads/2019/09/uk-un-norms-non-paper-oewg-submission-final.pdf.

[150] UNGA, 'Report of the GGE' UN Doc A/76/135 para 13.

[151] *Nuclear Tests* (n 135) para 51.

UN General Assembly subsidiary bodies dedicated to the multilateral deliberations on ICTs relating to international security is an example of such declarations of commitment. Such declarations could thus create LE, to be protected in any future settlement of disputes. However, in a case of 'a unilateral declaration not directed to any particular recipient',[152] extra prudence is required in assessing its legal character and whether it formed LE. Deviation from such declarations could constitute aggravation of a conflict.

D. Prohibition of the Abuse of Rights

Prohibition of the abuse of rights during the settlement process are very relevant in the cyberspace context. Of particular significance is the prohibition of fraudulent conduct. Much as with the obligation to preserve the confidentiality of the object and the purpose of the dispute settlement process, the prohibition of fraudulent conduct during the dispute settlement process is not materially different in the context of cyberspace. But the obligation is possibly as pertinent as ever, particularly so given the significant potential of using digital technologies for falsification or outright fabrication of documents or evidence.

Several techniques utilised by malicious cyber actors support this argument and provide examples of how negotiators acting in bad faith could materialise the intent to deceive and induce the opposing party to enter a settlement through fraud. False flagging, for instance, is a group of prominent diversionary cyber techniques intended to deceive researchers 'into thinking that an operation was carried out by another party'.[153] More specifically, should the dispute originate in the cyber domain, digital evidence containing IP spoofing[154] could lure parties in the dispute resolution process into believing that an operation originated somewhere else than it actually did. IP spoofing is frequently used in DDoS operations,[155] the type of operations that targeted Estonia in 2007 and disrupted their financial as well as public sectors.[156]

Concerns over fraudulent claims through falsified evidence in the digital domain go beyond written documents meant to substantiate a claim by way of a description of a certain fact, recollection, history. Evidence, meant to mislead a party to the dispute resolution process, might come in the form of synthetic data, which could be presented during the process as genuine, representative

[152] *Frontier Dispute (Burkina Faso v Republic of Mali)* (Judgment of 22 December 1986) [1986] ICJ Rep 554 para 39.

[153] M Pihelgas (ed), 'Mitigating Risks Arising from False-Flag and No-Flag Cyber Attacks' (*NATO CCD COE*, 2018) ccdcoe.org/uploads/2018/10/False-flag-and-no-flag-20052015.pdf 6.

[154] F Ali, 'IP Spoofing' (2007) 10/4 *The Internet Protocol Journal* 2–9.

[155] AG Johansen, 'IP Spoofing: What is It and How Does It Work?' (*Norton*, 25 November 2022) us.norton.com/blog/malware/ip-spoofing-what-is-it-and-how-does-it-work.

[156] D McGuinness, 'How a Cyber Attack Transformed Estonia' (*BBC*, 27 April 2017) www.bbc.com/news/39655415.

data. Consider, for instance, synthetic media in the form of graphic, video[157] or audio[158] content created by neural networks, which could be falsely presented as a genuine reflection of the (past) reality to induce error of a party to the dispute.

None of these considerations are particularly novel. In the past, parties to a dispute tried building their legal arguments before the ICJ based on (allegedly) forged physical documentation without the apparent employment of digital technologies.[159] The critical issue, however, is that nowadays digital technologies allow for inexpensive,[160] relatively easy falsification or fabrication of material that may be intentionally used to induce error of the opposing party in the settlement process.

Note that the existence of the prohibition of fraudulent conduct does not relieve parties to a dispute resolution process of their 'duty of exercising reasonable care'[161] in relation to the representations of the opposing party, particularly so in bilateral negotiations. In light of the perils highlighted thus far, such a duty of care includes, for example, critical assessment of digital evidence by following digital forensics best practices or seeking assistance from expert non-state actors, in case the state lacks the capacity to evaluate digital evidence.[162]

E. Additional Considerations

Applying the principle of good faith to the digital domain warrants a pair of considerations that may be specific to disputes arising from cyber conduct or, more broadly, applicable to dispute settlement processes in the cyberspace context.

First, the international law of state responsibility does not prescribe the format of countermeasures.[163] It may be inferred then that a state injured by the violation of good faith obligations could take countermeasures utilising their ICT

[157] R Chesney and D Citron, 'Deepfakes and the New Disinformation War: The Coming Age of Post-Truth Geopolitics' (2019) 98 *Foreign Affairs* 147, 147; S Barari, C Lucas and K Munger, 'Political Deepfakes are as Credible as Other Fake Media and (Sometimes) Real Media' (*OSF Preprints*, 16 April 2021) osf.io/cdfh3/.

[158] N Müller, MK Markert and K Böttinger, 'Human Perception of Audio Deepfakes' (*Proceedings of the 1st International Workshop on Deepfake Detection for Audio Multimedia*, 2022) dl.acm.org/doi/pdf/10.1145/3552466.3556531.

[159] WM Reisman and C Parajon Skinner, *Fraudulent Evidence before Public International Tribunals: The Dirty Stories of International Law* (New York, Cambridge University Press, 2014) 179, 191.

[160] T Simonite, 'Cheap, Easy Deepfakes are Getting Closer to the Real Thing' (*Wired*, 5 August 2020) www.wired.com/story/cheap-easy-deepfakes-closer-real-thing/.

[161] Anon, 'Article 31. Fraud' (1935) 29 *American Journal of International Law* 1144, 1146.

[162] For instance, during the ICJ's *Maritime Delimitation and Territorial Questions (Qatar v Bahrain)* adjudication, Bahrain employed individual forensic experts to assess the evidence presented by Qatar. However, the ICJ never labelled the deeds of Bahrain as complying with their duty of exercising reasonable care in respect of evidence. Indeed, in the judicial setting this is, generally, the role of the court or other dispute settlement intermediary. See Reisman and Parajon Skinner (n 159) 179–80; *Maritime Delimitation and Territorial Questions between Qatar and Bahrain (Qatar v Bahrain)* (Merits, Judgment) ICJ Rep 2001, 40.

[163] See Buchan (ch 9 in this volume).

capabilities. This may be particularly important in the case of a dispute involving a pair of states that are not considered equal in terms of their ability to take effective measures to induce compliance with the law. Given that ICT developments democratised the ability to influence a state via cyber means,[164] cyber countermeasures could allow smaller states to take potentially effective countermeasures against, traditionally considered, more powerful states.[165]

Related to countermeasures is the difficult issue of attribution.[166] There are several public records of attribution disagreements. For example, when the US attributed Microsoft Exchange cyber operations to 'malicious cyber actors affiliated with [People's Republic of China's Ministry of State Security]',[167] the Chinese authorities dismissed the claim, labelling it 'made up out of thin air',[168] and 'unwarranted accusations'.[169] Because technical and thus legal attribution of cyber operations remains challenging,[170] it is likely that the issues related to attribution, particularly evidence and proof, will arise in an international dispute resolution process related to cyber conduct.

As in general international law, good faith does not create obligations of disclosure related to cyber attribution assertions. *Opinio juris* and state practice largely support this. In 2021, a UN General Assembly resolution welcomed the GGE report, which laid down the relevant expectations over attribution claims. It argued that 'accusations of organizing and implementing wrongful acts brought against States should be substantiated'.[171] This expectation of disclosure manifests as a voluntary, non-binding norm of state behaviour in the use of ICTs and not as an obligation.

[164] 'Some non-State actors have demonstrated ICT capabilities previously only available to States.' UNGA, 'Open-Ended Working Group on Security of and in the Use of Information and Communications Technologies 2021–2025, Draft Annual Progress Report' (28 July 2022) UN Doc A/AC.292/2022/CRP.1, 3.

[165] J Rivera, 'Achieving Cyberdeterrence and the Ability of Small States to Hold Large States at Risk' in M Maybaum, A-M Osula and L Lindström (eds), *2015 7th International Conference on Cyber Conflict: Architectures in Cyberspace* (Tallinn, NATO CCD COE, 2015) 7–24.

[166] See Tsagourias (ch 1 in this volume).

[167] The White House, 'The United States, Joined by Allies and Partners, Attributes Malicious Cyber Activity and Irresponsible State Behavior to the People's Republic of China' (19 July 2021) www.whitehouse.gov/briefing-room/statements-releases/2021/07/19/the-united-states-joined-by-allies-and-partners-attributes-malicious-cyber-activity-and-irresponsible-state-behavior-to-the-peoples-republic-of-china/.

[168] J McDonald, 'China Rejects Hacking Charges, Accuses US of Cyberspying' (*Associated Press News*, 20 July 2021) apnews.com/article/technology-business-china-hacking-6cd7d59f-1b6aa4a0539d987e5340b705.

[169] ibid.

[170] 'Due to the particularities of cyberspace, attribution – especially the attribution of malicious behavior – has always been a challenging issue for the international governance of the cyber sector.' X Manshu, 'Beyond Public Cyber Attribution: Reflections and Responses' in AE Levite et al (eds), *Managing US-China Tensions over Public Cyber Attribution* (Washington DC, Carnegie Endowment for International Peace, 2022) 31; N Tsagourias and M Farrell, 'Cyber Attribution: Technical and Legal Approaches and Challenges' (2020) 31 *European Journal of International Law* 941.

[171] UNGA, 'Report of the GGE' UN Doc A/76/135 para 71(g).

The majority of states voicing their opinion on the matter at hand, appear to support the absence of obligation of disclosure related to attribution of cyber conduct. For instance, New Zealand argued that 'States should act in good faith and take care when attributing legal responsibility to another state for malicious cyber activity. While any legal attribution should be underpinned by a sound evidential basis, there is no general obligation on the attributing State to disclose that basis.'[172] Other instances of *opinio juris*[173] support this and state practice has generally been consistent. Indeed, states publicly attributing cyber operation 'have already gone some way toward providing evidence'[174] but, predominantly, attribution evidence takes the form of circumstantial evidence.[175]

However, some states have been vocal about the fact that this norm is[176] or at least should become a legal obligation.[177] As explained above, specific and clear declarations of commitment to the implementation of norms, particularly so if coupled with related state practice, can create LE. Accordingly, states which publicly opined that disclosure of evidence in relation to the attribution of ICT operations is a legal obligation, and which have regularly substantiated their attribution claims (thus acting in accordance with the norm), must do so in the context of peaceful dispute settlement.

Given the challenges of attribution and the absence of a general duty of disclosure described above, it may be that disagreements between parties to

[172] New Zealand, 'The Application of International Law to State Activity in Cyberspace' (*Department of the Prime Minister and Cabinet*, 1 December 2020) dpmc.govt.nz/publications/application-international-law-state-activity-cyberspace.

[173] For example, according to the US, 'there is no international legal obligation to reveal evidence on which attribution is based' (UNGA, 'Official Compendium' UN Doc A/76/136, 141); '[I]nternational law does not require States to provide the evidence on which the public attribution of a cyberattack is based, though such information helps to legitimise the validity of such attribution.' (France (n 114) 11); '[T]here is no general obligation under international law as it currently stands to publicize a decision on attribution and to provide or to submit for public scrutiny detailed evidence on which an attribution is based. This generally applies also if response measures are taken.' (Germany, 'On the Application of International Law in Cyberspace: Position Paper – March 2021' (*The Federal Government*, 2021) www.auswaertiges-amt.de/blob/2446304/32e7b2498e10b74fb17204c54665bdf0/on-the-application-of-international-law-in-cyberspace-data.pdf); '[T]here is no general legal obligation requiring a State to publicly disclose any underlying information on which its decision to attribute conduct is based.' (UNGA, 'Official Compendium' UN Doc A/76/136, 117); 'The decision to attribute conduct is at the discretion of the injured state and there is no obligation under international law to disclose the information leading to such a decision.' (Switzerland, 'Switzerland's Position Paper on the Application of International Law in Cyberspace' (*Federal Department of Foreign Affairs*, 2021) www.eda.admin.ch/dam/eda/en/documents/aussenpolitik/voelkerrecht/20210527-Schweiz-Annex-UN-GGE-Cybersecurity-2019-2021_EN.pdf 6).

[174] K Eichensehr, 'Cyberattack Attribution and International Law' (*Just Security*, 24 July 2020) www.justsecurity.org/71640/cyberattack-attribution-and-international-law/.

[175] G Baram and U Sommer, 'Covert or not Covert: National Strategies During Cyber Conflict' in T Minárik et al (eds), *2019 11th International Conference on Cyber Conflict: Silent Battle* (Tallinn, NATO CCD COE, 2019) 8.

[176] According to Brazil, '[technical] difficulties must not serve as a justification to lower the bar for determinations on attribution, which must be substantiated' (UNGA, 'Official Compendium' UN Doc A/76/136, 21).

[177] The Russian Federation argues that 'it [is]increasingly relevant to formalize the norm of the 2015 GGE report stating that all accusations of organizing and implementing wrongful acts brought against States should be substantiated, as legally binding' (UNGA, 'Official Compendium' UN Doc A/76/136, 80).

a dispute settlement process will remain unsurmountable and resolution in a bilateral setting impossible. In the context of the present chapter, unsurpassable differences between parties to the dispute could arise in respect to attribution or any other technical or legal aspect of the conflict. The potential for impasse is considerable given the technically complex nature of cyberspace and divergent national positions on the application international law to cyberspace. In these instances, parties may wish to seek assistance from a third party, to act, for example, as a mediator. While there is no international obligation to do so, willingness to accept the assistance or expertise of a third party is indeed an indication of good faith.[178]

For instance, parties could entrust the dispute settlement to the ICJ. Once again, and as established in this chapter, there is no general duty of disclosure in the litigation at the ICJ. However, further analysis of examples of *opinio juris* on the applicability of the law of peaceful dispute settlement suggests potential progressive alteration of the doctrine in cyberspace. Consider the position of, for instance, Italy, arguing that transparency in making attribution claims is 'required should attribution become part of international courts and/or arbitration proceedings, with the exception of States' classified information'.[179] Furthermore, The Netherlands opined that states taking countermeasures or self-defence measures in response to unlawful cyber operation 'may eventually have to render account for its actions, for example if the matter is brought before the [ICJ, and] it must be possible to provide evidence justifying the countermeasure or the exercise of the right of self-defence'.[180] Not all states appear to agree with this interpretation.[181]

IV. Conclusions

As elaborated in this chapter, the bulk of general good faith rules can be applied to disputes in cyberspace. This hardly comes as a surprise when considering the flexibility and adaptability of the rules at stake. Indeed, states agreed that the UN Charter applies to behaviour in cyberspace in its entirety, which includes the provisions on peaceful settlement of disputes.[182]

The general conclusion is therefore that cyberspace is not so different from other spaces where human activities take place. It does not warrant a set of entirely new and specific rules. The general rules on dispute settlement apply, with some

[178] 'The readiness of the parties to accept [third party] assistance would be evidence of the good faith.' *Gabcikovo-Nagymaros Project (Hungary v Slovakia)* (Judgment of 25 September 1997) [1997] ICJ Rep 7 para 143. See Wrange (ch 10 in this volume).

[179] Italy, 'Italian Position Paper on International Law and Cyberspace' (2021) www.esteri.it/mae/resource/doc/2021/11/italian_position_paper_on_international_law_and_cyberspace.pdf. See also the position of The Netherlands (n 134).

[180] The Netherlands (n 134).

[181] See, eg, Germany (n 173).

[182] UNGA, 'Developments in the Field of Information and Telecommunications' UN Doc A/RES/76/19.

minor adjustments and adaptations. The fragmentation of international law in these areas is less than originally thought.

The specificities in the context of cyber disputes are mainly the following: the obligation to preserve confidentiality in dispute settlement prohibits states engaged in the process to disclose sensitive, confidential data to persons who could use it to the disadvantage of the opposing party. Should a state nonetheless stumble across data relevant to the dispute settlement process, it must implement adequate protections against data falling into the hands of said persons. The modality of this could, for instance, encompass encryption of digital data.

Moreover, the obligation not to aggravate the dispute prohibits continuance (or intensification) of disputed conduct. States engaged in contentious cyber activity must therefore halt potential self-propagation of malware and outright stop it. A violation of additional legal rights of an opposing party in the dispute resolution process could also constitute aggravation. Because of potentially divergent interpretations of international law in the cyber domain, states should pay due regard to the legal rights of dispute settlement counterparts in order to avoid aggravation. Further, undermining the dispute settlement process itself by way of, for example, destroying evidence, is also considered to be aggravating. This obligation is particularly relevant in the cyber domain, allowing for remote destruction of evidence. Aggravation can also consist of omission. States are thus required to exhibit a degree of diligence regarding prevention or termination of cyber acts stemming from its territory that undoubtedly will, or are most likely to, aggravate the dispute.

Good faith also imposes the obligation to protect legitimate expectations. Commitments to the implementation of voluntary norms (such as the ones agreed on by the General Assembly in 2021) coupled with proof of state practice in line with the norms, create LE. Such expectations should be respected during the dispute settlement and can result in estoppel or acquiescence.

Providing evidence with the intention to mislead a party to the conflict remains *contra* to good faith and therefore prohibited under international law in the cyberspace context. The prohibition of the abuse of rights is emphasised in this chapter, given the abundance and relative simplicity of digital tools and techniques of data manipulation and fabrication.

Finally, the chapter also considered the good faith obligation of disclosure in the context of dispute settlement. Analysing instances of *opinio juris* and international agreements on the application of international law to cyberspace, the chapter concludes that states are under no obligation to disclose evidence supporting attribution of disputed cyber conduct. However, there are two possible legal exceptions to this on the horizon. First, certain states argue that parties making attribution claims must present evidence, which creates LE that must be protected during the dispute settlement procedure. Second, *opinio juris* indicates that states might be under an obligation to disclose attribution evidence in the context of judicial dispute settlement procedure. This is particularly true when the latter is set up to determine the legality of reaction to cyber operations in the form of countermeasures or self-defence.

PART II

Institutions

3

Guarding the Gates and Shaping the Battlefield: The Role of Domestic Courts in the Settlement of International Cyber Disputes

DANIEL FRANCHINI

I. Introduction

The digital age has witnessed a dramatic rise in disputes stemming from the use of cyberspace. These disputes, encompassing issues like internet governance, privacy and surveillance, intellectual property, and online commerce, routinely find their way into domestic courtrooms.[1] However, the extent to which domestic courts engage with *international* cyber disputes – characterised by disagreements emerging primarily between sovereign states[2] – remains a complex question. While these disputes were traditionally considered beyond the purview of domestic courts, recent developments reveal a growing entanglement between their international and domestic legal dimensions.

At its core, international dispute settlement rests with dedicated international institutions, like the International Court of Justice (ICJ), or other means of dispute settlement agreed upon by states.[3] Domestic courts, as state organs whose findings are ordinarily confined within their national legal systems, seem ill-equipped

[1] See, in general, A Murray, *Information Technology Law: The Law and Society*, 5th edn (Oxford, Oxford University Press, 2023). See also Master of the Rolls, 'The Economic Value of English Law in Relation to DLT and Digital Assets' (25 July 2022) www.judiciary.uk/speech-by-the-master-of-the-rolls-the-economic-value-of-english-law-in-relation-to-dlt-and-digital-assets.

[2] See *Mavrommatis Palestine Concessions* (*Greece v Great Britain*) (Judgment of 30 August 1924) [1924] PCIJ Rep Series A No 2, 11; *Right of Passage Over Indian Territory (Portugal v India)* (Merits, Judgment) [1960] ICJ Rep 6, 34; *South West Africa Cases* (*Ethiopia v South Africa*; *Liberia v South Africa*) (Preliminary Objections, Judgment of 21 December 1962) [1962] ICJ Rep 319, 328. In line with the approach adopted by this book, the terms 'inter-state' and 'international' disputes will be used interchangeably. See Tsagourias (ch 1 in this volume) and Antonopoulos (ch 4 in this volume).

[3] On the principle of consent, see *Status of Eastern Carelia* (Advisory Opinion of 23 July 1923) [1923] PCIJ Rep Series B No 5, 27; *Fisheries Jurisdiction* (*Spain v Canada*) (Jurisdiction, Judgment of

to tackle inter-state conflicts. Principles of international law, like state immunity, further shield states from the jurisdiction of foreign courts,[4] seemingly reinforcing the divide.

However, this stark separation is increasingly challenged. The permeability of domestic legal systems to international legal norms has blurred the lines and domestic courts are increasingly tasked with interpreting and applying international law. As a result, domestic courts are vested with an 'international judicial function'.[5] They can act as 'enforcers' of international norms within their legal systems, for instance, when striking down or disapplying legislation or executive acts in violation of international law.[6] This can also occur when domestic courts do not directly apply international law but rely on domestic law provisions that reflect international legal standards.[7] In addition, although from a formal standpoint, they are 'merely facts which express the will and constitute the activities of States',[8] domestic courts' decisions can greatly impact the development of international law. They may confirm existing rules of custom through consistent application, or they may introduce novel interpretations, which in turn may spur reactions from other organs of the state or other states and ultimately shape the content of these rules.[9]

The international judicial function of domestic courts becomes particularly crucial in the context of international cyber disputes, where a tapestry of international legal norms – from human rights to international economic law – is often woven into the fabric of the conflict. Moreover, domestic courts frequently serve as the initial point of contact for individuals and corporations affected by cyber-attacks or other wrongful conduct in cyberspace – a role whose importance is heightened by the current absence of a centralised mechanism for compulsory settlement of international cyber disputes.

As a result of these dynamics, this chapter argues that domestic courts have a significant role to play in the settlement of international cyber disputes, both

4 December 1998) [1998] ICJ Rep 432 para 56; *Obligation to Negotiate Access to the Pacific Ocean (Bolivia v Chile)* (Judgment of 1 October 2018) [2018] ICJ Rep 507 para 165; UNGA, 'Declaration on Principles of International Law Concerning Friendly Relations and Cooperation among States in Accordance with the Charter of the United Nations' (24 October 1970) UN Doc A/RES/2625(XXV) (the Friendly Relations Declaration) para 5; UNGA, 'Manila Declaration on the Peaceful Settlement of International Disputes' (15 November 1982) UN Doc A/RES/37/10 (the Manila Declaration) para 3.

[4] On state immunity, see section III.A below.

[5] A Tzanakopoulos, 'Domestic Courts in International Law: The International Judicial Function of National Courts' (2011) 34 *Loyola of Los Angeles International and Comparative Law Journal* 133. See also International Law Association, 'Study Group on Principles on the Engagement of Domestic Courts with International Law: Final Report' (2016) www.ila-hq.org/en_GB/documents/conference-study-group-report-johannesburg-2016 paras 10–15; A Nollkaemper, *National Courts and the International Rule of Law* (Oxford, Oxford University Press, 2011) 6.

[6] Tzanakopoulos (n 5) 166; Nollkaemper (n 5) 6–9.

[7] Tzanakopoulos refers to these as 'consubstantial norms'; see Tzanakopoulos (n 5) 163.

[8] *Case Concerning Certain German Interests in Polish Upper Silesia (Germany v Poland)* (Merits, Judgment of 25 May 1926) [1926] PCIJ Rep Series A No 7, 19.

[9] See A Tzanakopoulos and CJ Tams, 'Introduction: Domestic Courts as Agents of Development of International Law' (2013) 26 *Leiden Journal of International Law* 531, 538–9.

'internally' with respect to the acts of the forum state and 'externally' concerning the acts of other states. Section II will focus on the internal function of domestic courts as 'guardians' of their state's international obligations in cyberspace and 'gatekeepers' with respect to international cyber disputes. In this sense, domestic courts can pre-empt international disputes by ensuring compliance with relevant international legal norms. Section III then shifts to the external function, analysing how domestic court judgments can shape international cyber disputes to which their states are parties. By contributing to articulating the legal reasoning behind the government's action, judicial pronouncements can advance claims against other states, influence diplomatic exchanges, and even, in certain instances, contribute to the settlement of international disputes. Finally, section IV will conclude by reflecting on the potential benefits and challenges of domestic courts' engagement with international cyber disputes, offering insights into the future trajectory of this evolving legal landscape.

II. Internal Engagement: Domestic Courts as 'Gatekeepers' of International Cyber Disputes of the Forum State

Domestic courts have a central role in 'moderating' international disputes that revolve around the forum state's compliance with its international obligations. This is because they represent the final avenue within a state where international law can be upheld, thus averting the engagement of the international responsibility of the state.[10] The significance of this role is further accentuated by the principle of exhaustion of local remedies, wherein individuals or entities affected by a state's internationally wrongful act must pursue all available domestic legal channels before escalating the dispute to the international legal plane.[11]

This section delves into two ways domestic courts internally engage with international cyber disputes. As reactive gatekeepers, domestic courts act as checks and balances against other state organs, reviewing and enforcing legislative and executive acts in cyberspace. Domestic courts can nip potential international disputes in the bud by ensuring these acts comply with international law. In other cases, international obligations demand proactive action by domestic courts. Failure to exercise their jurisdiction in these situations – for instance, in combating cybercrime or protecting human rights online – can trigger international responsibility for the state and risk escalating issues into full-blown disputes. Both scenarios are examined in turn.

[10] See Tzanakopoulos (n 5) 174.

[11] See Art 14 in ILC, 'Draft Articles on Diplomatic Protection, with Commentaries. UN Doc A/61/10' in *Yearbook of the International Law Commission. 2006, Volume II, Part Two: Report of the Commission to the General Assembly on the Work of its Fifty-Eighth Session* (New York, UN, 2006) 44.

A. Domestic Courts' Oversight of Legislative and Executive Acts in Cyberspace

The rise of digital technologies has significantly bolstered the capacity of government agencies to enact measures that could potentially infringe upon the rights of individuals and entities globally. The disclosure by Wikileaks in June 2013 of the involvement of the US National Security Agency (NSA) in a global surveillance program harvesting confidential online information, spotlighted this concern.[12] Domestic courts have the potential to serve as a crucial first line of defence against abuses of state power in cyberspace, although certain limitations on the courts' ability to hear these cases exist.[13] When scrutinising surveillance programs and intelligence-gathering initiatives, domestic courts should be capable – at least in principle – of ensuring their alignment with the international obligations of the forum state, especially in guaranteeing that these programs adhere to adequate international standards of ex ante and ex post oversight.[14] As examined in the next section, this type of judicial review may, in turn, be mandated by international law when human rights are at stake.[15]

Although domestic courts may not be able to review all law enforcement activities in the digital realm, they play a crucial role in defining the limits of state jurisdiction in cyberspace. The increasing fluidity and contested nature of jurisdictional boundaries are fuelled by the seamless flow of data across borders and its accessibility from anywhere in the world.[16] Traditionally, the rules of customary international law on state jurisdiction have been anchored in territoriality, granting states undisputed authority to regulate activities within their borders.[17] Furthermore, states may exercise extraterritorial jurisdiction under specific circumstances when a direct and substantial connection exists between the state and the regulated activity

[12] For an overview of Edward Snowden's revelations over the NSA programme, see E MacAskill and G Dance, 'NSA Files Decoded: Edward Snowden's Surveillance Revelations Explained' (*The Guardian*, 1 November 2013) www.theguardian.com/world/interactive/2013/nov/01/snowden-nsa-files-surveillance-revelations-decoded.

[13] See M Rumold, 'Regulating Surveillance through Litigation: Some Thoughts from the Trenches' in D Gray and SE Henderson (eds), *The Cambridge Handbook of Surveillance Law* (Cambridge, Cambridge University Press, 2017) 579.

[14] See I Brown and D Korff, 'Foreign Surveillance: Law and Practice in a Global Digital Environment' (2014) 3 *European Human Rights Law Review* 243; A Deeks, 'An International Legal Framework for Surveillance' (2015) 55 *Virginia Journal of International Law* 291; C Forcese, 'One Warrant to Rule Them All: Re-conceiving the Judicialization of Extraterritorial Intelligence Collection' (*Ottawa Faculty of Law Working Paper No 2015-41*, 2015) ssrn.com/abstract=2622606; G Malgieri and P De Hert, 'European Human Rights, Criminal Surveillance, and Intelligence Surveillance: Towards "Good Enough" Oversight, Preferably but Not Necessarily by Judges' in D Gray and SE Henderson (eds), *The Cambridge Handbook of Surveillance Law* (Cambridge, Cambridge University Press, 2017) 509.

[15] See section II.B below.

[16] U Kohl, 'Jurisdiction in Network Society' in N Tsagourias and R Buchan (eds), *Research Handbook on International Law and Cyberspace*, 2nd edn (Cheltenham, Edward Elgar, 2021) 69.

[17] See C Ryngaert, *Jurisdiction in International Law*, 2nd edn (Oxford, Oxford University Press, 2015) 42.

('prescriptive jurisdiction').[18] However, the lawful enforcement of such regulations remains confined to the state's territory ('enforcement jurisdiction').[19]

Applying the principle of territoriality to online activities raises considerable difficulties.[20] Algorithms often determine the location of data stored by multinational cloud service providers, meaning the location of the data can be uncertain. Solely relying on server location to determine jurisdictional entitlements could be overly restrictive and potentially arbitrary.[21] Indeed, states have consistently rejected this approach.[22] Significantly, however, though free to assert prescriptive jurisdiction based on factors other than territory, states have continued to rely on some forms of territoriality to justify jurisdiction in cyberspace.[23]

In particular, states have frequently advanced regulatory claims over cyber activities based on what Kohl has defined as the 'destination approach'.[24] According to this approach, jurisdiction is claimed based on the impact or effect of the online activity. However, there is some disagreement regarding the extent to which these effects must be felt within the state's territory.[25] The interesting aspect of the dynamics by which this practice is emerging is that, for the most part, it has been spearheaded by decisions of domestic courts.

The landmark *LICRA v Yahoo!* case, one of the earliest high-profile cases to adopt the destination approach, exemplifies this.[26] A French court held that France was entitled to apply its laws prohibiting the sales of Nazi memorabilia to Yahoo!'s .com site, even though it was hosted in the USA, simply by virtue that the site was accessible in France and caused harm there. Recent years have seen a parallel trend in US courts. In a trademark infringement case, the Court of Appeals for the First Circuit, overturning the district court's decision, asserted jurisdiction over Scrutinizer, a German company, citing its global web-based services that attracted numerous US customers.[27] Similarly, the Court of Appeals for the Fourth Circuit established jurisdiction over Russian music piracy websites, considering

[18] Alongside territoriality, other principles of jurisdiction include nationality, passive personality, universality, and the protective principle; see Ryngaert (n 17) 85ff. See also B Oxman, 'Jurisdiction of States' in *Max Planck Encyclopedia of Public International Law* (Oxford, Oxford University Press, 2007) [10]; J Crawford, *Brownlie's Principles of Public International Law*, 9th edn (Oxford, Oxford University Press, 2019) 442.

[19] See *Case of the SS 'Lotus' (France v Turkey)* (Judgment of 7 September 1927) [1927] PCIJ Rep Series A No 10, 18–19; Crawford (n 18) 462.

[20] See DJB Svantesson, 'A New Jurisprudential Framework for Jurisdiction: Beyond the Harvard Draft' (2015) 109 *American Journal of International Law Unbound* 69, 70.

[21] C Ryngaert, 'Extraterritorial Enforcement Jurisdiction in Cyberspace: Normative Shifts' (2023) 24 *German Law Journal* 537, 548.

[22] Kohl (n 16) 89.

[23] See Ryngaert (n 21) 538.

[24] Kohl (n 16) 78.

[25] For instance, whether mere accessibility of online content from within the state is sufficient; see Kohl (n 16) 78.

[26] *LICRA v Yahoo! Inc & Yahoo France* (Tribunal de Grande Instance de Paris, 22 May 2000).

[27] *Plixer Int'l, Inc v Scrutinizer GmbH* 905 F 3d 1, 4 (1st Cir 2018).

the significant number of US visitors and personalised advertisements targeting US customers on the sites.[28]

These cases underscore the pivotal role of domestic courts in scrutinising and enforcing claims of jurisdiction in cyberspace. Domestic legislation, such as French laws against the promotion of Nazism or US trademark laws, is typically drafted in broad terms without specific provisions regarding its application to cyberspace. Consequently, domestic courts often grapple with defining the precise scope of these laws, thereby clarifying the jurisdictional claims of one state in relation to the conflicting claims of others. Depending on the type of remedy they issue – for instance, takedown or search orders – domestic courts' pronouncements may also include a component of enforcement jurisdiction, which has proven especially contentious when applied to the internet.[29] Thus, domestic courts' decisions frequently become critical milestones in either sparking or preventing international disputes concerning jurisdiction in cyberspace.[30]

The *Microsoft Ireland* case showcases the diverse roles domestic courts may play in this regard.[31] In the context of a US drug enforcement investigation, a warrant compelled Microsoft to disclose a customer's electronic communications stored on servers outside the US. Microsoft contested the warrant, arguing that, as the data was stored in Ireland, it fell outside the scope of the Stored Communications Act (SCA), the statute underlying the warrant. Prior to this dispute reaching US courts, there was uncertainty about the application of the SCA to data stored beyond US borders. A district court judge initially ruled against Microsoft,[32] precipitating a jurisdictional conflict between the US and the state where the data was located (Ireland) and potentially triggering a bilateral (cyber) dispute between the two states.[33] On appeal, however, the Court for the Second Circuit reversed the district court's decision, finding that the SCA did not have extraterritorial application.[34] This decision 'rectified' the previous assertion

[28] *UMG Recordings, Inc v Kurbanov* 963 F 3d 344 (4th Cir 2020).

[29] See Ryngaert (n 21) 539. For the idea that adjudicative jurisdiction may include the exercise of enforcement jurisdiction, see ST Mouland, 'Rethinking Adjudicative Jurisdiction in International Law' (2019) 29 *Washington International Law Journal* 173, 184.

[30] This divergence in outcomes can also be attributed to the fact that different domestic courts may reach varying conclusions on the same international law issues. For instance, following the French judgment in the *Yahoo!* case, a US district court determined it could not be enforced in the US due to its inconsistency with the First Amendment to the US Constitution regarding freedom of expression; see *Yahoo! Inc v La Ligue Contre le Racisme et l'Antisemitisme* 145 F Supp 2d 1168, 1180 (ND Cal 2001). This decision was later reversed by the Appeal Court; see *Yahoo! Inc v La Ligue Contre le Racisme et L'Antisemitisme* 433 F 3d 1199 (9th Cir 2006).

[31] *Matter of Warrant to Search a Certain E-Mail Acct Controlled & Maintained by Microsoft Corp* 829 F 3d 197 (2d Cir 2016), vacated and remanded sub nom. *United States v Microsoft Corp* 138 S Ct 1186, 200 L Ed 2d 610 (2018).

[32] *In re Warrant to Search a Certain E-Mail Acct Controlled & Maintained by Microsoft Corp* 15 F Supp 3d 466, 471 (SDNY 2014).

[33] *cf* Tzanakopoulos (n 5) 168.

[34] *Matter of Warrant to Search a Certain E-Mail Acct Controlled & Maintained by Microsoft Corp* 829 F 3d 197, 222 (2d Cir 2016).

of jurisdiction by limiting its extraterritorial reach, thereby preventing the escalation of the international dispute.[35]

Both rulings were based on divergent interpretations of domestic law. However, the presence of an international dispute became apparent following the Appeal Court's decision. As the case advanced to the Supreme Court, third parties, including Ireland and other foreign states affected by the litigation, submitted amici curiae briefs. Ireland expressed concerns about potential infringements on its sovereign rights in its submission. It argued that data stored on Irish servers should be accessed through the proceedings prescribed under the Ireland-US Mutual Legal Assistance Treaty (MLAT).[36] Conversely, the UK filed a brief arguing that the geographic storage location of data should not be the primary factor when determining whether a state should gain access to communications located abroad but accessible domestically.[37] The EU, in its submission, emphasised that, in any event, comity considerations would necessitate an analysis of potential conflicts with foreign laws, including the General Data Protection Regulation.[38]

Under these circumstances, the US Supreme Court was tasked with a dual role: interpreting the SCA domestically while considering its impact on the international legal plane. Depending on its interpretation, the Court could either exacerbate or prevent a dispute with other states. Although not bound to align with foreign states' claims, the Supreme Court had interpretative tools such as the presumption against extraterritoriality, the principle of comity, and the *Charming Betsy* doctrine to ensure that its interpretation of domestic law remained consistent with international law and minimised conflict with other states.[39] Ultimately, the case was withdrawn before the Supreme Court reached a verdict. However, this case illustrates how, in certain situations, domestic courts may function akin to international dispute settlement bodies, crafting interpretations that balance competing sovereign interests.

Beyond the specific dispute at hand, domestic litigation can also stimulate initiatives to settle future disputes arising from similar facts, especially when legislative and executive organs are better placed to offer these. The *Microsoft Ireland* case was crucial in prompting the US Congress to enact the Clarifying Lawful Overseas Use of Data (CLOUD) Act of 2018.[40] This legislation overhauled

[35] In a similar way, see more recently T Cochrane, '*KBR v SFO*: the United Kingdom's Microsoft Ireland?' (*Just Security*, 25 February 2021) www.justsecurity.org/74875/kbr-v-sfo-the-united-kingdoms-microsoft-ireland.

[36] *United States of America v Microsoft Corporation*, Brief for Ireland as Amicus Curiae in Support of Neither Party (13 December 2017) 2017 WL 6492481.

[37] *In re Microsoft Corporation*, Brief of the Government of the United Kingdom of Great Britain and Northern Ireland as Amicus Curiae in Support of Neither Party (13 December 2017) 2017 WL 6398769.

[38] *In re Microsoft Corporation*, Brief of the European Commission on Behalf of the European Union as Amicus Curiae in Support of Neither Party (13 December 2017) WL 6383224.

[39] CA Bradley, *International Law in the US Legal System*, 2nd edn (Oxford, Oxford University Press, 2015) 10–20.

[40] See US Department of Justice (DOJ), 'CLOUD Act Resources' (24 October 2023) www.justice.gov/criminal/cloud-act-resources.

the system for accessing electronic information held by US-based global internet providers, clarifying rules for US law enforcement while authorising bilateral executive agreements to streamline cross-border data access for foreign governments. The CLOUD Act can thus be seen as key in pre-empting the emergence of future international cyber disputes on this matter, with the US having already concluded agreements with the UK[41] and Australia,[42] and other states expected to follow suit.[43]

In sum, domestic courts play a critical role as gatekeepers of legality in cyberspace, acting against state overreach, defining jurisdictional boundaries, and even facilitating international dispute settlement. By interpreting domestic law with international considerations in mind and encouraging further solutions, domestic courts can help promote the rule of law in cyberspace and prevent the escalation of conflicts between states.

B. Domestic Courts' Role in Fulfilling International Law Obligations in Cyberspace

Some obligations that states are subject to when operating in cyberspace necessitate active involvement from domestic courts for their fulfilment. Notably, domestic courts play a central role in realising obligations related to suppressing certain malicious cyber operations. Failure to exercise adjudicative jurisdiction in these circumstances will trigger the international responsibility of the forum state and is bound to generate international disputes.

The rise in criminal activities through information and communications technology (ICT) has led to the establishment of several international legal instruments to suppress 'cybercrime'.[44] Chief among them is the 2001 Convention on Cybercrime (Budapest Convention), drafted under the auspices of the Council of

[41] US DOJ, 'Cloud Act Agreement between the Governments of the US, United Kingdom of Great Britain and Northern Ireland' (3 October 2019) www.justice.gov/criminal/criminal-oia/cloud-act-agreement-between-governments-us-united-kingdom-great-britain-and-northern. See J Daskal and P Swire, 'The UK-US CLOUD Act Agreement is Finally Here, Containing New Safeguards' (*Just Security*, 8 October 2019) www.justsecurity.org/66507/the-uk-us-cloud-act-agreement-is-finally-here-containing-new-safeguards.

[42] US DOJ, 'Cloud Act Agreement between the Governments of the US and Australia' (15 December 2021) www.justice.gov/criminal/criminal-oia/cloud-act-agreement-between-governments-us-and-australia.

[43] See, eg, US DOJ, 'United States and Canada Welcome Negotiations of a CLOUD Act Agreement' (22 March 2022) www.justice.gov/opa/pr/united-states-and-canada-welcome-negotiations-cloud-act-agreement. These agreements can be seen as an alternative to regulations arising from EU law; see M Rojszczak, 'CLOUD Act Agreements from an EU Perspective' (2020) 38 *Computer Law and Security Review* 1.

[44] See United Nations Office on Drugs and Crime, *Comprehensive Study on Cybercrime* (Vienna, UN, 2013); P Kastner and F Mégret, 'International Legal Dimension of Cybercrime' in N Tsagourias and R Buchan (eds), *Research Handbook on International Law and Cyberspace*, 2nd edn (Cheltenham, Edward Elgar, 2021) 254.

Europe but open to virtually all states.[45] Under this and other conventions that follow the same structure, State Parties are obligated to 'adopt such legislative and other measures as may be necessary to establish jurisdiction' over a number of cyber-offences.[46] In certain circumstances, they are also obligated to exercise adjudicative jurisdiction for the purpose of prosecuting an alleged offender. According to Article 24(6):

> If extradition for a criminal offence … is refused solely on the basis of the nationality of the person sought, or because the requested Party deems that it has jurisdiction over the offence, the requested Party shall submit the case at the request of the requesting Party to its competent authorities for the purpose of prosecution and shall report the final outcome to the requesting Party in due course. Those authorities shall take their decision and conduct their investigations and proceedings in the same manner as for any other offence of a comparable nature under the law of that Party.[47]

In other words, State Parties where the accused is found have a choice between submitting the case to their prosecuting authorities or extraditing the individual to a state willing to prosecute.[48] However, as the ICJ clarified, extradition is an option, while prosecution remains an international obligation whose violation constitutes a wrongful act engaging the responsibility of the state.[49] Thus, in conventions using this language, State Parties have a primary duty to prosecute, involving the exercise of domestic court jurisdiction.

Given the transnational nature of cybercrime, international legal instruments dedicated to its suppression also impose obligations concerning inter-state cooperation.[50] Article 25(1) of the Budapest Convention, for instance, mandates State Parties to provide mutual assistance for investigations or proceedings related

[45] Convention on Cybercrime (Budapest, 23 November 2001) ('Budapest Convention'). As of December 2023, the Budapest Convention has 68 Parties and 23 states have signed it or been invited to accede.

[46] See Budapest Convention, Art 22; Arab Convention on Combating Information Technology Offences (Cairo, 21 December 2010), Art 5 ('Arab Convention'); Directive 2013/40/EU of the European Parliament and of the Council of 12 August 2013 on attacks against information systems and replacing Council Framework Decision 2005/222/JHA [2013] OJ L218/8, Arts 3–8.

[47] See also Budapest Convention, Art 22(3); Arab Convention, Art 30(2).

[48] See K Kittichaisaree, *The Obligation to Extradite or Prosecute* (Oxford, Oxford University Press, 2018) 179.

[49] *Questions Relating to the Obligation to Prosecute or Extradite (Belgium v Senegal)* (Judgment of 20 July 2012) [2012] ICJ Rep 422 para 95.

[50] See, eg, Budapest Convention, Arts 23, 25, 27; Arab Convention, Arts 32, 34–35; Commonwealth of Independent States' Agreement on Cooperation in Combating Offences Related to Computer Information (Minsk, 1 June 2001) Arts 5–6; Agreement among the Governments of the Shanghai Cooperation Organization's Member States on Cooperation in the Field of Ensuring International Information Security (Yekaterinburg, 16 June 2009). Cooperation duties can also derive from agreements concerning the suppression of other offences; see, eg, International Convention for the Suppression of Terrorist Bombings (New York, 15 December 1997) Art 10. Several states have also concluded mutual legal assistance treaties (MLATs), making assistance between two states in criminal matters obligatory under international law; see B Zagarism, 'United States Treaties on Mutual Assistance in Criminal Matters' in M Cherif Bassiouni (ed), *International Criminal Law, Volume 2: Multilateral and Bilateral Enforcement Mechanisms* (Brill, Nijhoff, 2008) 385.

to criminal offences in cyberspace. This cooperation extends to the judicial authorities of the relevant states, particularly when judicial pronouncements are required for evidence production or the seizure and forfeiture of criminal assets.[51] When judicial cooperation forms part of the international obligations of a state, failure by its domestic courts to exercise jurisdiction – for instance, failure to respond to a request for mutual legal assistance under MLAT[52] – will once again engage the international responsibility of the state and likely lead to the emergence of international disputes.

Beyond specific treaty obligations, the question arises as to whether the exercise of domestic court jurisdiction for the suppression of cybercrime may be compelled by a general rule of custom, particularly in the context of a broader discussion on the existence of a duty of 'cyber due diligence' under international law.[53]

According to the *Tallinn Manual 2.0*, '[a] State must exercise due diligence in not allowing its territory, or territory or cyber infrastructure under its governmental control, to be used for cyber operations that affect the rights of, and produce serious adverse consequences for, other States'.[54] This perspective aligns with the views of several states and scholars, arguing in support of the existence of binding due diligence obligations in cyberspace.[55] However, the acceptance of this stance is not universal and remains a subject of ongoing debate.

In its 2021 Report, the UN Group of Governmental Experts on Advancing Responsible State Behaviour in Cyberspace in the Context of International Security identified due diligence as part of a set of 'voluntary, non-binding norms

[51] For an example of a complex transnational operation to take down the infrastructure of malware and a botnet involving the judicial authorities of several states, see US DOJ, 'Emotet Botnet Disrupted in International Cyber Operation' (28 January 2021) www.justice.gov/opa/pr/emotet-botnet-disrupted-international-cyber-operation.

[52] For a discussion of the current MLAT system and the potential scope of proposed reforms, see J Daskal, 'Law Enforcement Access to Data Across Borders: The Evolving Security and Rights Issues' (2015) 8 *Journal of National Security Law and Policy* 473; P Swire, 'Why Cross-Border Government Requests for Data Will Keep Becoming More Important' (*Lawfare*, 23 May 2017) www.lawfaremedia.org/article/why-cross-border-government-requests-data-will-keep-becoming-more-important.

[53] See K Bannelier-Christakis, 'Cyber Diligence: A Low-Intensity Due Diligence Principle for Low-Intensity Cyber Operations' (2014) 14 *Baltic Yearbook of International Law* 23, 23; MN Schmitt, 'In Defense of Due Diligence in Cyberspace' (2015) *The Yale Law Journal Forum* 68; R Buchan, 'Cyberspace, Non-State Actors and the Obligation to Prevent Transboundary Harm' (2016) 21 *Journal of Conflict and Security Law* 429; J Kulesza, *Due Diligence in International Law* (Leiden, Brill Nijhoff, 2016); A Coco and T De Souza Dias, '"Cyber Due Diligence": A Patchwork of Protective Obligations in International Law' (2021) 32 *European Journal of International Law* 771; J Kenny, 'Cyber Operations and the Status of Due Diligence Obligations in International Law' (2023) 73 *International and Comparative Law Quarterly* 135.

[54] Rule 6, in MN Schmitt (ed), *Tallinn Manual 2.0 on the International Law Applicable to Cyber Operations*, 2nd edn (Cambridge, Cambridge University Press, 2017) 30.

[55] See, among others, Ministry of Armed Forces of France, 'Droit International Appliqué aux Opérations dans le Cyberspace' (2019) www.defense.gouv.fr/sites/default/files/ministere-armees/Droit%20international%20appliqu%C3%A9%20aux%20op%C3%A9rations%20dans%20le%20cyberespace.pdf 6–7; Federal Government of Germany, 'On the Application of International Law in Cyberspace. Position Paper' (March 2021) www.auswaertiges-amt.de/blob/2446304/32e7b2498e10b74fb17204c54665bdf0/on-the-application-of-international-law-in-cyberspace-data.pdf 3; Italian Ministry for Foreign Affairs and International Cooperation, 'Italian Position Paper on International

of responsible State behaviour', stating that 'States *should* not knowingly allow their territory to be used for internationally wrongful acts using ICTs'.[56] Similarly, despite extensive discussion on the topic, the 2021 Final Report of the UN Open-Ended Working Group on Developments in the Field of Information and Telecommunications in the Context of International Security failed to include any language on due diligence obligations due to the lack of consensus among states.[57] These, among other factors, have raised doubts about the existence of a customary duty of cyber due diligence under international law.[58]

Even if one accepts the existence of a customary international obligation of due diligence in cyberspace, there is ambiguity about its content. The *Tallinn Manual 2.0* states that compliance with the due diligence principle requires a state to take feasible measures to end cyber operations on its territory that adversely affect another state's rights.[59] According to the Manual, however, this duty does not extend to preventative measures,[60] '[n]or is there any obligation under the due diligence principle for the State to prosecute those engaging in the underlying cyber operations; rather, the obligation is limited to taking feasible measures to terminate the operations'.[61]

Divergent opinions exist among scholars on this matter. According to Buchan, the principle of cyber due diligence includes not only an obligation to prevent, but also 'a duty to investigate and, where appropriate, punish those responsible because such conduct serves "a critical preventative function by reinforcing the state's prohibitory measures and deterring other potential wrongdoers"'.[62] Similarly, Bannelier-Christakis found that measures to prevent and punish cyber

Law and Cyberspace' (2021) www.esteri.it/mae/resource/doc/2021/11/italian_position_paper_on_international_law_and_cyberspace.pdf 6–7. For a full list, see NATO Cooperative Cyber Defence Centre of Excellence et al, 'International Cyber Law: Interactive Toolkit. Due Diligence' cyberlaw.ccdcoe.org/wiki/Due_diligence. In the literature, see Schmitt (n 53) 80; Buchan (n 53) 451; Kulesza (n 53) 300–02; Coco and De Souza Dias (n 53) 774.

[56] UNGA, 'Report of the Group of Governmental Experts on Advancing Responsible State Behaviour in Cyberspace in the Context of International Security' (14 July 2021) UN Doc A/76/135 (2021 GGE Report) 10, 17. See also Schmitt (n 53) 73.

[57] UNGA, 'Final Substantive Report of the Open-Ended Working Group on Developments in the Field of Information and Telecommunications in the Context of International Security' (10 March 2021) UN Doc A/AC.290/2021/CRP.2.

[58] See, eg, UK Foreign, Commonwealth and Development Office, 'Application of International Law to States' Conduct in Cyberspace: UK Statement' (3 June 2021) www.gov.uk/government/publications/application-of-international-law-to-states-conduct-in-cyberspace-uk-statement/application-of-international-law-to-states-conduct-in-cyberspace-uk-statement para 12; Government of Canada, 'International Law Applicable in Cyberspace' (April 2022) www.international.gc.ca/world-monde/issues_development-enjeux_developpement/peace_security-paix_securite/cyberspace_law-cyberespace_droit.aspx para 26; R Schöndorf, 'Israel's Perspective on Key Legal and Practical Issues Concerning the Application of International Law to Cyber Operations' (2021) 97 *International Law Studies* 395, 403–44. See also Kenny (n 53) 156.

[59] Schmitt (n 54) 43.

[60] ibid 44–45.

[61] ibid 48.

[62] Buchan (n 53) 442, citing *Pulp Mills on the River Uruguay (Argentina v Uruguay)* (Judgment of 20 April 2010) [2010] ICJ Rep 14 para 158.

acts contrary to the rights of other states are '*one of the best ways* to implement the "due diligence" obligation'.[63]

This conclusion gains further weight when considering malicious cyber activities with harmful effects on specific human rights, such as cyberbullying, defamation, and hate speech.[64] International human rights law imposes both negative and positive duties on states, requiring them not only to refrain from violating human rights but also to take reasonable measures to protect individuals from threats posed by various entities according to a due diligence standard.[65] Even if a general due diligence obligation remains disputed, specific human rights obligations often imply due diligence requirements to prevent, halt, and remedy harms in cyberspace.[66] These may involve providing civil remedies and criminal provisions to facilitate effective investigations and prosecutions of human rights violations.[67]

In *KU v Finland*,[68] the European Court of Human Rights (ECtHR) exemplified this with respect to the right to private and family life under Article 8 of the European Convention on Human Rights. The case involved a false online advertisement using a child's name on a dating site. When Finnish courts failed to compel the internet service provider to disclose the perpetrator's identity, the ECtHR found a violation of the petitioner's rights, emphasising:

> States have a positive obligation inherent in Article 8 of the Convention to criminalise offences against the person, including attempted offences, and to reinforce the deterrent effect of criminalisation by applying criminal-law provisions in practice through effective investigation and prosecution.[69]

In essence, when confronted with malicious cyber activities prohibited under certain treaties or at least when these activities have detrimental effects on certain human rights, the involvement of domestic courts extends beyond being an opportunity for states to rectify wrongful acts; it becomes a substantive step

[63] Bannelier-Christakis (n 53) 35, drawing support for this duty from *Corfu Channel* (*United Kingdom of Great Britain and Northern Ireland v Albania*) (Merits, Judgment of 9 April 1949) [1949] ICJ Rep 4, 19–20.

[64] Coco and De Souza Dias (n 53) 795–97.

[65] See UN Human Rights Committee, 'General Comment No 31 [80]: The Nature of the General Legal Obligation Imposed on States Parties to the Covenant' (26 May 2004) UN Doc CCPR/C/21/Rev.1/Add.13 para 8; S Besson, 'Due Diligence and Extraterritorial Human Rights Obligations – Mind the Gap!' (2020) 9 *ESIL Reflections* 1, 2.

[66] See G Rona and L Aarons, 'State Responsibility to Respect, Protect and Fulfill Human Rights Obligations in Cyberspace' (2016) 8 *Journal of National Security Law and Policy* 503, 516–22; Coco and De Souza Dias (n 53) 796.

[67] See, eg, UN Human Rights Committee, 'General Comment No 31 [80]' UN Doc CCPR/C/21/Rev.1/Add.13 paras 15, 18; UN Human Rights Committee, 'General Comment No 36. Article 6: Right to Life' (3 September 2019) UN Doc CCPR/C/GC/35 paras 27–28.

[68] *KU v Finland* App No 2872/02 (ECtHR, 2 March 2009).

[69] ibid para 46, citing *MC v Bulgaria* App No 39272/98 (ECtHR, 4 December 2003) para 150.

mandated to comply with international law. Domestic courts, therefore, play a crucial role in minimising the risk of international disputes across a diverse range of circumstances.

III. External Engagement: Domestic Courts' Contribution to Shaping International Cyber Disputes with Other States

Alongside their role as 'gatekeepers' of international cyber disputes, domestic courts may also shape international cyber disputes between their state and other states. Their direct involvement in international cyber disputes is, however, complex due to two sets of constraints: one imposed by international law and the other arising from considerations of comity and judicial propriety.

International law purports to set clear boundaries for the permissible actions of states, including limitations on their jurisdiction over matters affecting other sovereign entities. Principles like state jurisdiction and state immunity play a fundamental role in shielding states from unilateral actions by other states' domestic courts. Additionally, domestic courts often employ various 'avoidance techniques' to avoid potentially contentious inter-state issues.[70] These techniques, such as the act of state doctrine and the political question doctrine, act as procedural shields, deflecting the need for domestic courts to engage with international disputes.

However, when domestic courts are able to engage with inter-state cyber disputes, their action can be transformative. By articulating the state's claims concerning the legal qualifications of the relevant cyber activity, they effectively define the national position on the matter. These claims, in turn, can be 'positively opposed' by other states, laying the groundwork for a formal dispute.[71] In this sense, domestic courts can be seen as catalysts, allowing nascent international cyber disagreements to 'mature' into fully-fledged disputes between sovereign states.[72] Moreover, the pressure exerted through domestic litigation can serve as an incentive for negotiated settlements, encouraging states to resolve the dispute through one of the available means of dispute settlement.

Examples of this dynamic can be observed in two scenarios: the US 'indictment strategy' against foreign state actors involved in alleged cyberattacks, and domestic legal proceedings against private contractors accused of participating in such operations. Both examples will be examined in turn.

[70] See E Benvenisti, 'Judicial Misgivings Regarding the Application of International Law: An Analysis of Attitudes of National Courts' (1993) 4 *European Journal of International Law* 159.

[71] See *South West Africa Cases* (n 2) 328.

[72] See Tzanakopoulos (n 5) 168.

A. The US Indictment Strategy as a Tool for Domestic Courts' Engagement with International Cyber Disputes

Since 2014, the US Department of Justice (DOJ) has employed an 'all-tool approach' to counter cyberattacks allegedly perpetrated by foreign state actors.[73] This approach includes issuing indictments against individual hackers and officials allegedly affiliated with foreign governments, often as part of a broader strategy to pressure and engage with those states on cyber issues.[74] This 'indictment strategy' was first employed against five members of the Chinese People's Liberation Army (PLA), accused of hacking into the computer systems of American corporations and stealing trade secrets.[75] Subsequently, the number of indictments issued by the DOJ against alleged state-sponsored hackers has surged, covering a spectrum of malicious cyber activities globally.[76]

The indictments themselves rarely lead to actual prosecutions in US courts, as the targeted individuals are often beyond the reach of US enforcement agencies. Instead, they act primarily as 'speaking indictments', revealing important

[73] J Carlin, 'Remarks at the National Cyber-Forensics and Training Alliance' (23 September 2015) www.justice.gov/opa/speech/assistant-attorney-general-john-carlin-delivers-remarks-national-cyber-forensics-and.

[74] See CI Keitner, 'Attribution by Indictment' (2019) 113 *American Journal of International Law Unbound* 207; G Hinck and T Maurer, 'Persistent Enforcement: Criminal Charges as a Response to Nation-State Malicious Cyber Activity' (2020) 10 *Journal of National Security Law and Policy* 525, 525; H Lee, 'Public Attribution in the US Government: Implications for Diplomacy and Norms in Cyberspace' (2023) 6 *Policy Design and Practice* 198, 204–05.

[75] US DOJ, 'US Charges Five Chinese Military Hackers for Cyber Espionage Against US Corporations and a Labor Organization for Commercial Advantage' (19 May 2014) www.justice.gov/opa/pr/us-charges-five-chinese-military-hackers-cyber-espionage-against-us-corporations-and-labor. See J Goldsmith and RD Williams, 'The Failure of the United States' Chinese-Hacking Indictment Strategy' (*Lawfare*, 28 December 2018) www.lawfaremedia.org/article/failure-united-states-chinese-hacking-indictment-strategy.

[76] See C Cimpanu, 'DOJ Explains Recent Wave of Cyber-Espionage-Related Indictments' (*ZDNet*, 5 October 2018) www.zdnet.com/article/doj-explains-recent-wave-of-cyber-espionage-related-indictments/. Recent examples include: US DOJ, 'Two Chinese Hackers Working with the Ministry of State Security Charged with Global Computer Intrusion Campaign Targeting Intellectual Property and Confidential Business Information, Including COVID-19 Research' (21 July 2020) www.justice.gov/opa/pr/two-chinese-hackers-working-ministry-state-security-charged-global-computer-intrusion; US DOJ, 'Six Russian GRU Officers Charged in Connection with Worldwide Deployment of Destructive Malware and Other Disruptive Actions in Cyberspace' (19 October 2020) www.justice.gov/opa/pr/six-russian-gru-officers-charged-connection-worldwide-deployment-destructive-malware-and; US DOJ, 'Three North Korean Military Hackers Indicted in Wide-Ranging Scheme to Commit Cyberattacks and Financial Crimes Across the Globe' (17 February 2021) www.justice.gov/opa/pr/three-north-korean-military-hackers-indicted-wide-ranging-scheme-commit-cyberattacks-and; US DOJ, 'Four Chinese Nationals Working with the Ministry of State Security Charged with Global Computer Intrusion Campaign Targeting Intellectual Property and Confidential Business Information, Including Infectious Disease Research' (19 July 2021) www.justice.gov/opa/pr/four-chinese-nationals-working-ministry-state-security-charged-global-computer-intrusion; US DOJ, 'Four Russian Government Employees Charged in Two Historical Hacking Campaigns Targeting Critical Infrastructure Worldwide' (24 March 2022) www.justice.gov/opa/pr/four-russian-government-employees-charged-two-historical-hacking-campaigns-targeting-critical.

details of the malicious cyber operations to the public.[77] As argued by Hinck and Maurer, these serve multiple purposes, including attributing malicious activity to specific actors, disrupting hacker networks, coordinating with other US government agencies, providing restitution to victims and defenders, pressuring states to cease future attacks, and supporting the development of robust cyber norms.[78] Similarly, Keitner identified three functions served by the US indictment strategy. First, these indictments have a coercive function, as information gleaned through forensic investigations may form the basis for other governmental actions, such as the imposition of economic sanctions.[79] Second, they serve as a deterrent purpose by showcasing US capabilities in detecting potential cyber wrongdoers.[80] Third, these indictments possess an expressive function, enabling the USA to define and communicate standards of behaviour in cyberspace.[81]

The effectiveness of the indictment strategy as a tool for confronting international cyber threats remains a matter of debate. Critics argue its impact is limited, citing examples of Chinese state-affiliated hackers being charged without leading to any meaningful deterrence of cyber theft.[82] Some suggest alternative methods, such as disruption and sanctions, may be more effective.[83] Proponents, including former US Assistant Attorney General John Carlin, contend that the indictment strategy, as part of a comprehensive approach, is vital for disrupting and deterring state-sponsored hacking.[84]

Be that as it may, the decision to address malicious cyber operations through domestic criminal law proceedings, as opposed to or in conjunction with diplomatic demarches, sanctions, or other avenues,[85] holds significant weight. Criminal charges demand a high standard of evidence, requiring federal prosecutors to convince a grand jury or a federal judge of probable cause and later prove guilt 'beyond a reasonable doubt' before a jury.[86] Moreover, criminal charges focus on individuals rather than states, providing prosecutors with the option, when

[77] M Chalfant, 'Mueller's "Speaking Indictments" Offer Clues to Strategy' (*The Hill*, 24 August 2018) thehill.com/policy/national-security/402902-muellers-speaking-indictments-offer-clues-to-strategy.

[78] G Hinck and T Maurer, 'What's the Point of Charging Foreign State-Linked Hackers?' (*Lawfare*, 24 May 2019) www.lawfaremedia.org/article/whats-point-charging-foreign-state-linked-hackers.

[79] Keitner (n 74) 210–11.

[80] ibid 211.

[81] ibid. While these indictments are typically framed under US law, they may offer insights into the United States' stance on applicable international law in cyberspace. Indeed, some accompanying statements explicitly reference 'international norms'; see, eg, US DOJ, 'Two Chinese Hackers Working with the Ministry of State Security' (n 76).

[82] Goldsmith and Williams (n 75).

[83] P Machtiger, 'Disrupt, Don't Indict: Why the United States Should Stop Indicting Foreign State Actor Hackers' (*Just Security*, 3 April 2020) www.justsecurity.org/69104/disrupt-dont-indict-why-the-united-states-should-stop-indicting-foreign-state-actor-hackers.

[84] JP Carlin, 'Detect, Disrupt, Deter: A Whole-of-Government Approach to National Security Cyber Threats' (2016) 7 *Harvard National Security Journal* 391, 418.

[85] Lee found that US government actors publicly attribute cyber incidents through four distinct 'channels': criminal, technical, official policy, and unofficial policy; see Lee (n 74) 202.

[86] Hinck and Maurer (n 74) 529.

unveiling charges against proxy hackers, to decide whether to allege state sponsorship, influencing the impact of the accusations.[87]

Crucially for the current discussion, this strategy grants domestic courts a prominent role in any international dispute arising from these malicious cyber activities. By scrutinising the evidence presented by prosecuting authorities, domestic courts can offer a more detailed legal analysis of the cyber activities in question and their attribution to foreign states. This can contribute to articulating the government's claims and strengthening its position in the dispute with the relevant foreign state. Whether or not the perpetrators can be brought to justice, the mere act of issuing the indictment and potentially hearing the claims may already provide victims of cyber offences with a form of satisfaction for the harm suffered. It can also serve as the foundation for further reparation schemes.[88] Finally, domestic court proceedings may heighten the pressure on the offending state to cease wrongful acts and refrain from future malicious cyber activities.

Addressing cyber threats through domestic criminal law proceedings can be a significant factor in pushing relevant states to resolve disputes through available means of dispute settlement. Supporters of this strategy point to the 2014 PLA indictment as an example, suggesting its role in prompting a bilateral agreement between the US and China on curbing cyber-enabled economic espionage in 2015.[89] However, the success of the indictment strategy as a negotiation gambit has been inconsistent. Subsequent indictments have not yielded similar results, and the US-China trade war that began in 2018 witnessed a resurgence of Chinese cyber activities,[90] highlighting the limitations of relying solely on the indictment strategy.[91]

Another layer of complexity surrounding the indictment strategy involves the issue of functional immunity, which shields foreign state officials from prosecution in domestic courts for acts committed in their official capacity.[92] Herein lies

[87] ibid 530.

[88] On satisfaction as a form of reparation, see C Hoss, 'Satisfaction' in A Peters (ed), *Max Planck Encyclopedia of Public International Law* (Oxford, Oxford University Press, 2011).

[89] B Wittes, 'James Lewis on the China Cyber Deal' (*Lawfare*, 5 October 2015) www.lawfaremedia.org/article/james-lewis-china-cyber-deal.

[90] See DQ Wilber, 'China "Has Taken the Gloves Off" in Its Thefts of US Technology Secrets' (*Los Angeles Times*, 16 November 2018) www.latimes.com/politics/la-na-pol-china-economic-espionage-20181116-story.html.

[91] The USA responded with a series of criminal charges to put increased pressure on China, all of which have been part of the DOJ's 'China Initiative'; see US DOJ, 'Attorney General Jeff Sessions Announces New Initiative to Combat Chinese Economic Espionage' (1 November 2018) www.justice.gov/opa/speech/attorney-general-jeff-sessions-announces-new-initiative-combat-chinese-economic-espionage.

[92] Alongside functional immunity, which applies to acts performed in an official capacity by all state officials, international law also provides for personal immunity, which is granted to a limited group of high-ranking officials, protecting them from foreign court jurisdiction for all acts while in office; see UNGA, 'Immunity of State Officials from Foreign Criminal Jurisdiction: Memorandum by the Secretariat' (31 March 2008) UN Doc A/CN.4/596 paras 88–89; UNGA, 'Preliminary Report on Immunity of State Officials from Foreign Criminal Jurisdiction, by Roman Anatolevich Kolodkin, Special Rapporteur' (29 May 2008) UN Doc A/CN.4/601, 177; R Van Alebeek, *The Immunity of States and Their Officials in International Criminal Law and International Human Rights Law* (Oxford, Oxford

the conundrum of associating accused foreign hackers with a foreign state. On the one hand, establishing a connection between the malicious cyber operation and a state agent simplifies the attribution of said activity to the foreign state.[93] This is particularly important when, as mentioned earlier, indictments serve purposes beyond domestic court prosecution, such as providing the basis for issuing economic sanctions against the allegedly responsible state.[94] On the other hand, attributing the relevant activity to the state implies that the underlying acts were likely 'performed in an official capacity', preventing the individual state agent from standing trial before foreign domestic courts.[95]

The basis for functional immunity is typically found in the fact that, under international law, official acts of state representatives are imputable to the state.[96] In this sense, functional immunity operates as 'a mechanism for diverting responsibility to the state',[97] which is the actual defendant in the proceedings.[98] However, in similar circumstances, proceedings against the state would, in turn, be barred by the rules of state immunity, as malicious cyber operations ordinarily amount to 'sovereign activities' excluded from the jurisdiction of foreign domestic courts under the dominant theory of state immunity.[99] None of the existing immunity codifications contains an exception for malicious cyber operations, although certain activities may fall under other immunity exceptions in specific circumstances.[100]

University Press, 2008) 8; R Pedretti, *Immunity of Heads of State and State Officials for International Crimes* (Leiden, Brill Nijhoff, 2015) 2.

93 Under Art 4 of the International Law Commission's Articles on State Responsibility, the conduct of 'any state organ' is attributable to a state, even if it 'exceeded its competence under internal law'; see ILC, 'Draft Articles on Responsibility of States for Internationally Wrongful Acts, with Commentaries' in *Yearbook of the International Law Commission. 2001, Volume II, Part Two: Report of the Commission to the General Assembly on the Work of its Fifty-Third Session, as Corrected* (New York, UN, 2008) 40. See also *Application of the Convention on the Prevention and Punishment of the Crime of Genocide* (*Bosnia and Herzegovina v Serbia and Montenegro*) (Judgment of 26 February 2007) [2007] ICJ Rep 43 para 385.

94 See text at nn 78–9 above.

95 However, debate exists as to the exact scope of functional immunity; see CI Keitner, 'Foreign Official Immunity and the Baseline Problem' (2011) 80 *Fordham Law Review* 605, 614; Z Douglas, 'State Immunity for the Acts of State Officials' (2012) 82 *British Yearbook of International Law* 281, 296; R Van Alebeek, 'Functional Immunity of State Officials from the Criminal Jurisdiction of Foreign National Courts' in T Ruys, N Angelet and L Ferro (eds), *The Cambridge Handbook of Immunities and International Law* (Cambridge, Cambridge University Press, 2019) 499.

96 See D Akande and S Shah, 'Immunities of State Officials, International Crimes, and Foreign Domestic Courts' (2010) 21 *European Journal of International Law* 815, 826; Douglas (n 95) 322–23; *Prosecutor v Blaškić* (Judgment (on the Request for Review of the Decision of 18 July 1997) of 29 October 1997) ICTY IT-95-14 para 38; *Re Rissmann* (1973) 71 ILR 577, 581 (Italy). It is also possible that the conduct may be attributable to the individual state official; see UNGA, 'Preliminary Report on Immunity of State Officials' UN Doc A/CN.4/601, 179–80.

97 Akande and Shah (n 96) 826.

98 See Douglas (n 95) 287.

99 The 'restrictive theory' of state immunity distinguishes between immune sovereign acts and non-immune private acts, and is today the most widely adopted approach among states; see P-H Verdier and E Voeten, 'How Does Customary International Law Change? The Case of State Immunity' (2015) 59 *International Studies Quarterly* 209; Crawford (n 18) 472–73.

100 In a recent lawsuit concerning the alleged use of Pegasus spyware, the English High Court ruled that the exception for injuries sustained within UK territory precluded Saudi Arabia's claim of state

Others have proposed that amending immunity legislation, such as the US Foreign Sovereign Immunities Act (FSIA), by creating a new and tailored cyber exception, may be the best way to ensure accountability for states that threaten human rights with cyber tools and conduct cyber economic espionage.[101]

To date, the DOJ has largely downplayed these concerns. In a statement accompanying the 2014 PLA indictment, the then Assistant Attorney General for National Security, John Carlin, asserted:

> State actors engaged in cyber espionage for economic advantage are not immune from the law just because they hack under the shadow of their country's flag. Cyber theft is real theft and we will hold state sponsored cyber thieves accountable as we would any other transnational criminal organization that steals our goods and breaks our laws.[102]

This stance, however, remains untested in both domestic and international courts, potentially paving the way for future disputes regarding the scope of state immunity in cyberspace. These challenges may also account for some recent developments explored in the following section.

B. Engagement through Proceedings against Private Cyber Contractors

While directly holding foreign states accountable for malicious cyber operations through domestic courts faces hurdles due to state immunity, a novel approach has emerged in light of governments' increasing reliance on external experts to design, construct, or execute malicious cyber operations.[103] Instead of targeting foreign sovereign states, recent cases have seen lawsuits brought against private contractors allegedly involved in hacking on behalf of these states.

immunity; see *Al-Masarir v Saudi Arabia*, [2023] QB 475. In the US, some argue that certain cyber operations may fall under the terrorism exceptions contained in the Foreign Sovereign Immunities Act of 1976 (FSIA); see JS Goldman and B Strong, 'Overcoming Immunity of Foreign Gov't Cyberattack Sponsors' (*Anderson Kill*, 2 December 2020) www.andersonkill.com/Publications/Overcoming-Immunity-of-Foreign-Govt-Cyberattack-Sponsors; JJ Martin, 'Hacks Dangerous to Human Life: Using JASTA to Overcome Foreign Sovereign Immunity in State-Sponsored Cyberattack Cases' (2021) 121 *Columbia Law Review* 119.

[101] See S Kleiner and L Wolosky, 'Time for a Cyber-Attack Exception to the Foreign Sovereign Immunities Act' (*Just Security*, 14 August 2019) www.justsecurity.org/65809/time-for-a-cyber-attack-exception-to-the-foreign-sovereign-immunities-act/; AL Silow, 'Bubbles over Barriers: Amending the Foreign Sovereign Immunities Act for Cyber Accountability' (2021) 12 *Journal of National Security Law and Policy* 659.

[102] US DOJ, 'US Charges Five Chinese Military Hackers' (n 75).

[103] See Silow (n 101) 660–61; JH Dwan, TP Paige and R McLaughlin, 'Pirates of the Cyber Seas: Are State-Sponsored Hackers Modern-Day Privateers?' (2022) 4 *Law, Technology and Humans* 49; S Feldstein and B (Chun Hey) Kot, 'Why Does the Global Spyware Industry Continue to Thrive? Trends, Explanations, and Responses' (*Carnegie Endowment*, 14 March 2023) carnegieendowment.org/2023/03/14/why-does-global-spyware-industry-continue-to-thrive-trends-explanations-and-responses-pub-89229.

In October 2019, WhatsApp, an online messaging platform owned by Facebook Inc (now Meta), filed a lawsuit against NSO Group (NSO) before the district court for the Northern District of California.[104] NSO, an Israeli company specialising in surveillance technology, developed the Pegasus spyware, enabling remote intelligence extraction from mobile devices. While NSO claims to sell its software to government agencies exclusively for law enforcement operations, investigative reports have revealed numerous instances of misuse against journalists, lawyers, and activists.[105] In its complaint, WhatsApp alleged that NSO used its servers without authorisation to transmit malicious code to around 1,400 users, aiming to infect their devices for surveillance, in breach of the Computer Fraud and Abuse Act and other US statutes.[106]

NSO moved to dismiss the case, claiming 'derivative immunity' because foreign governments used its spyware technology for law enforcement activities ordinarily covered by immunity.[107] The district court rejected this plea, finding that state immunity had no bearing on this case given that the lawsuit targeted the company and its agents in their individual capacities, not their sovereign customers:

> defendants have not argued that any of their foreign sovereign customers would be forced to pay a judgment against defendants if plaintiffs were to prevail in this lawsuit. … [T]he court can craft injunctive relief that does not require a foreign sovereign to take an affirmative action. Thus, plaintiffs do not seek to enforce a rule of law against defendants' customers.[108]

This decision is in line with customary international law, according to which non-state entities do not enjoy state immunity simply by being complicit in the wrongful acts of foreign states.[109] This holds true even when domestic courts must assess the legal position of said states to decide the case.[110] On appeal, the Court for the Ninth Circuit affirmed the district court's decision, holding that entities like NSO, which do not qualify as foreign states, cannot claim foreign sovereign immunity under the FSIA.[111] This precedent will likely have a bearing on another suit against NSO, filed by Apple, accusing NSO of enabling clients to hack into Apple users' devices through its spyware.[112]

[104] *WhatsApp Inc et al NSO Group Techs Ltd et al* No 3:19-cv-07123 (ND Cal, 29 October 2019) Complaint.

[105] See S Kirchgaessner et al, 'Revealed: Leak Uncovers Global Abuse of Cyber-Surveillance Weapon' (*The Guardian*, 18 July 2021) www.theguardian.com/world/2021/jul/18/revealed-leak-uncovers-global-abuse-of-cyber-surveillance-weapon-nso-group-pegasus.

[106] *WhatsApp Inc et al* (n 104) 809.

[107] ibid. See R Buchan and D Franchini, '*WhatsApp v NSO Group*: State Immunity and Cyber Spying' (*Just Security*, 16 April 2020) www.justsecurity.org/69684/whatsapp-v-nso-group-state-immunity-and-cyber-spying.

[108] *WhatsApp Inc NSO Group Techs Ltd* 472 F Supp 3d 649, 665 (ND Cal 2020).

[109] See D Franchini, 'State Immunity and Third-Party Limits on the Jurisdiction of Domestic Courts' (2023) 72 *International and Comparative Law Quarterly* 819, 825–26.

[110] ibid.

[111] *WhatsApp Inc NSO Group Techs Ltd* 17 F 4th 930, 937 (9th Cir 2021).

[112] *Apple Inc NSO Group Techs Ltd et al* No 5:21-cv-09078 (ND Cal, 23 November 2021) Complaint.

The differentiation between domestic proceedings targeting foreign states involved in malicious cyber operations and those focusing on their private contractors opens new avenues for domestic courts' involvement in international cyber disputes. Even if direct legal action against states remains shielded by immunity, the process of evidence gathering and judicial review in cases against private contractors offers crucial insights into the 'what' and 'how' of malicious cyber operations. This contributes to establishing findings related to attribution and the application of relevant international legal rules, which government agencies may utilise for executive action. In a notable example, in November 2021, the Biden administration added surveillance technology companies, including NSO Group, to the Commerce Department's list of sanctioned entities, citing reports of misuse originating partly from domestic court litigation.[113]

Engaging in international cyber disputes through litigation against private contractors may also enable domestic courts to contribute to the development of the international legal framework governing cyberspace. By clarifying key concepts and legal qualifications applicable to malicious cyber activities, these cases set important precedents for future disputes and contribute to cross-fertilisation in cyber law-making.[114] Some domestic courts may also consider and incorporate relevant international legal principles, such as the principle of 'territorial sovereignty',[115] into their decisions. Integrating international norms into domestic legal proceedings further contributes to their development and solidifies their acceptance among states.

IV. Conclusion

Far from having a limited role in settling international cyber disputes, domestic courts emerge as pivotal actors, wielding influence both within and beyond their borders. This chapter has identified two crucial roles played by these courts: an 'internal' gatekeeping function concerning the forum state and an 'external' shaping function vis-à-vis other states.

Internally, domestic courts can scrutinise cyber-related activities of their own legislatures and executives. This may ensure alignment with international law

[113] See Anon, 'United States Makes Efforts to Curb Misuse of Surveillance Technology' (2022) 116 *American Journal of International Law* 426.

[114] This may help alleviate concerns about the perceived overreliance on self-regulation within the private tech sector; refer to I Kilovaty, 'Privatized Cybersecurity Law' (2020) 10 *UC Irvine Law Review* 1181.

[115] For instance, in the *Tidal* case, the Norwegian Supreme Court found that a search against the music streaming company carried out within the country using access credentials provided by its employees did not violate the principle of territorial sovereignty; see *Tidal Music AS v The Public Prosecution Authority* (28 March 2019) HR-2019-610-A (case no 19-010640STR-HRET) para 71. In an earlier case, a Canadian judge found that extraterritorial intrusive surveillance presumptively impinged on the territorial sovereignty of foreign states; see *Re Canadian Security Intelligence Service*

obligations and prevent potential violations, which is vital in pre-empting the emergence of international cyber disputes. In some circumstances, particularly with respect to suppressing certain cyber offences and cyber activities harming human rights, exercising domestic court jurisdiction may itself form part of the state's international obligations.

Externally, domestic courts can actively shape international cyber disputes between sovereign states. When capable of exercising jurisdiction over malicious cyber activities of state-sponsored foreign actors, such as in the case of recent US indictments, domestic courts can contribute to articulating the government's claims and strengthening the state's position in the dispute. The pressure generated by domestic litigation can also nudge states towards negotiation and settlement of cyber disputes through one of the available means. Finally, domestic courts, through their judicial pronouncements, can contribute to the development of international legal norms and principles governing cyberspace.

While the increasing involvement of domestic courts in international cyber disputes holds tremendous potential, it also raises concerns about politicisation. Their participation in politically sensitive matters may expose them to geopolitical pressures, potentially compromising their impartiality. Safeguarding judicial independence, upholding the rule of law, and ensuring transparent processes are, therefore, crucial to maintaining the integrity of domestic courts. Striking a balance between addressing cybersecurity threats and preventing undue interference can be achieved by developing international legal frameworks that specify circumstances requiring domestic court action. Instruments such as the Budapest Convention and mutual legal assistance treaties can be seen as meaningful steps towards minimising these risks.[116]

While international judicial cooperation is undoubtedly crucial in combating cyber threats, any legal instruments aimed at promoting this must tread a delicate tightrope. The Budapest Convention, for instance, has been long criticised for its potential to be misused by governments seeking to limit the enjoyment of fundamental rights online.[117] Similarly, the ongoing initiative within the UN General Assembly to formulate a Comprehensive Cybercrime Convention has come under scrutiny for comparable reasons.[118]

Act [2008] SCRS-10-07, 2008 CF 301 para 50. See generally S Watts and T Richard, 'Baseline Territorial Sovereignty and Cyberspace' (2018) 22 *Lewis and Clark Law Review* 771.

[116] See section II.B above.

[117] See Council of Europe Commissioner for Human Rights, *The Rule of Law on the Internet and in the Wider Digital World* (*COE*, 2014) rm.coe.int/the-rule-of-law-on-the-internet-and-in-the-wider-digital-world-issue-p/16806da51c, 17.

[118] UNGA, 'Resolution Adopted by the General Assembly on 27 December 2019: 74/247. Countering the Use of Information and Communications Technologies for Criminal Purposes' (20 January 2020) UN Doc A/RES/74/247. See D Brown, 'Cybercrime is Dangerous, but a New UN Treaty Could be Worse for Rights' (*Just Security*, 13 August 2021) www.justsecurity.org/77756/cybercrime-is-dangerous-but-a-new-un-treaty-could-be-worse-for-rights; C Ohanian, 'The UN Cybercrime Treaty has a Cybersecurity Problem in It' (*Just Security*, 17 October 2022) www.justsecurity.org/83582/the-un-cybercrime-treaty-has-a-cybersecurity-problem-in-it.

However, abandoning efforts at developing a comprehensive legal framework for international judicial cooperation may not be the ideal answer. A more effective path forward may lie in crafting international legal agreements that empower domestic courts to strike a balance between competing interests in this area. These agreements should enable a measured degree of executive action to address legitimate cybersecurity concerns while safeguarding respect for all relevant human rights obligations, providing vital checks and balances against potential abuses.

Only through such carefully constructed legal frameworks can domestic courts be empowered to navigate this complex and ever-evolving legal landscape effectively. This, in turn, will enable them to play a central role in promoting the rule of law in cyberspace.

4

Cyber Disputes Before the ICJ: Issues of Jurisdiction and Admissibility

CONSTANTINE ANTONOPOULOS

I. Introduction

Cyberspace is a domain consisting of information and communication technology infrastructures.[1] It is not a physical but a virtual space[2] where individuals, corporations and states pursue their various activities with ever-increasing frequency.[3] At the same time, cyberspace is a domain where malicious acts are committed by both governments and private persons,[4] giving rise to disputes. Because cyberspace is an intangible domain, dividing it into areas of exclusive sovereignty or sovereign rights is difficult. The celebrated statement in the *Island of Palmas* arbitration – 'Sovereignty in the relations between States signifies independence. Independence in regard to a portion of the globe is to exercise therein, to the exclusion of any other State, the functions of a State'[5] – appears to have no application to cyberspace at first reading. However, this is not absolutely true. The United Nations (UN)

[1] MN Schmitt, 'Introduction' in N Tsagourias and R Buchan (eds), *Research Handbook on International Law and Cyberspace*, 2nd edn (Cheltenham, Edward Elgar, 2021) 1.

[2] Rule 1, MN Schmitt (ed), *Tallinn Manual 2.0 on the International Law Applicable to Cyber Operations*, 2nd edn (Cambridge, Cambridge University Press, 2017) 12. According to the USA, Department of Defense, *Dictionary of Military and Associated Terms JP 1-02* (Washington DC, United States Government Printing Office, 12 April 2001, as amended through 31 August 2005) 139, cyberspace refers to the 'notional environment in which digitized information is communicated over computer networks'.

[3] Schmitt (n 1) 1, states that during the Covid-19 pandemic, cyberspace has become virtually the only medium for conducting many essential activities online and that 'as of October 2020, 63.2 per cent of the world's population used the Internet (with usage in Europe being 87.2 per cent and in North America 90.3 per cent), an increase of 1.266 per cent since 2000' (footnote omitted).

[4] UNGA, 'Report of the Group of Governmental Experts on Developments in the Field of Information and Telecommunications in the Context of International Security' (24 June 2013) UN Doc A/68/98 para 5: 'ICTs are dual-use technologies and can be used for both legitimate and malicious purposes. Any ICT device can be the source or the target of misuse. … The combination of global connectivity, vulnerable technologies and anonymity facilitates the use of ICTs for disruptive activities.'

[5] *Island of Palmas (Netherlands v USA)* (1928) 2 RIAA 829, 838.

Group of Governmental Experts on Advancing Responsible State Behaviour in Cyberspace in the Context of International Security has acknowledged that 'State sovereignty and international norms and principles that flow from sovereignty apply to State conduct of ICT-related activities, and to their jurisdiction over ICT infrastructure within their territory.'[6] Even though there is no cyber equivalent to territory, air space, territorial sea, or Exclusive Economic Zone (EEZ), cyberinfrastructure is either situated or crosses state territory. By virtue of this fact, it is subject to the jurisdiction of states. Moreover, individuals or corporations operating in or through cyberspace reside in states and, therefore, are under their jurisdiction. In addition, cyberspace is a domain where acts that violate state sovereignty can take place – such as use of force, unlawful intervention, and the seizure of data that are protected by official secrets legislation or are kept confidential on particular grounds (for instance data constituting legal advice or other material that support a state's case before an international tribunal).[7]

Cyber disputes are increasingly becoming the object of corporate, commercial or criminal litigation before municipal courts.[8] Acts such as corporate espionage and cyber fraud that often result in extensive financial loss for the victims are committed by skilled hackers who very often succeed in maintaining their anonymity.[9] The novelty of this conduct poses a challenge to the law and procedure of municipal dispute settlement institutions. Still, it is a challenge the domestic law and domestic institutions of several states have successfully overcome by showing resourcefulness in applying existing laws and procedures to the particularities of cyberspace.[10] Equally, cyber disputes may involve states either as perpetrators or victims of malicious uses of cyberspace.

Inter-state cyber disputes may arise because of the hostile use of cyberspace attributable to a state.[11] Disputes may also arise in the context of bilateral relations concerning cooperation in cyber matters such as the acquisition of cyber technology, the shared use of cyber infrastructure, or the exercise of jurisdiction.

[6] UNGA, 'Report of the GGE' UN Doc A/68/98 para 20; UNGA, 'Report of the Group of Governmental Experts on Developments in the Field of Information and Telecommunications in the Context of International Security' (22 July 2015) UN Doc A/70/174 paras 26–28; UNGA, 'Report of the Group of Governmental Experts on Advancing Responsible State Behaviour in Cyberspace in the Context of International Security' (14 July 2021) UN Doc A/76/135 paras 70–71; R Buchan, *Cyber Espionage and International Law* (Oxford, Hart Publishing, 2018) ch 3; *cf* WH von Heinegg, 'Territorial Sovereignty and Neutrality in Cyberspace' (2013) 89 *International Law Studies* 123, 126–127.

[7] Rules 1–5, Schmitt (n 2) 11 et seq; *Questions Relating to the Seizure and Detention of Certain Documents and Data (Timor-Leste v Australia)* (Provisional Measures, Order of 3 March 2014) [2014] ICJ Rep 147 paras 27–28, 42–48; Buchan (n 6) ch 3. See also Kolb and Kastelic (ch 2 in this volume).

[8] For UK courts, see C Weston-Simmons and R Mansigani, 'Cyber Litigation: The New Frontier' (2018) December *Corporate and Commercial Disputes Review. Norton Rose Fulbright* 10–11. See also Franchini (ch 3 in this volume).

[9] ME O'Connell, 'Cyber Security without Cyber War' (2012) 17 *Journal of Conflict and Security Law* 187, 190.

[10] Weston-Simmons and Mansigani (n 8) 10–11.

[11] See Tsagourias (ch 1 in this volume) on the definition of cyber disputes as international legal disputes.

The subject matter of this type of dispute may raise questions of state responsibility for violations of international law or responsibility for the performance of treaty obligations. If a dispute arises, states are under a treaty and customary law obligation to settle it by peaceful means[12] of their choice[13] regardless of whether the dispute is one involving acts (or omissions) occurring in cyberspace or related to cyberspace. One such means of dispute settlement is submitting a cyber dispute to judicial settlement, particularly to the International Court of Justice (ICJ).

The ICJ is the principal judicial organ of the UN.[14] It is governed by the UN Charter,[15] the Statute of the ICJ that constitutes an integral part of the UN Charter,[16] and the ICJ Rules of Procedure that the judges of the Court have drafted.[17] According to Article 34 of the ICJ Statute, 'only States may be parties in cases before the Court'.[18] It follows that the ICJ is *ipso facto* 'open' to (to wit, it may be used by) all UN Member States to settle their disputes.[19] The Court has the competence to settle disputes on any issue of international law that may arise concerning any part of the globe. This may include cyberspace as a domain, part of which falls under the jurisdiction of states because, as was said, its infrastructure has a territorial basis within states. Moreover, to the extent that cyber disputes may involve questions of state responsibility or performance of treaty obligations, they are classical categories of disputes submitted for settlement to the ICJ. That being said, the particularities of cyberspace as a domain may have some consequences for the exercise of jurisdiction by the Court, the admissibility of an application, and the production and probative value of evidence.

The chapter will thus deal, first, with the issue of objections to the existence of a dispute, which is the prerequisite for the exercise of jurisdiction by the

[12] Art 2(3) of the Charter of the United Nations (San Francisco, 26 June 1945); UNGA, 'Declaration on Principles of International Law Concerning Friendly Relations and Co-operation among States in Accordance with the Charter of the United Nations' (24 October 1970) UN Doc A/RES/2625(XXV); UNGA, 'Report of the GGE' UN Doc A/70/174 para 26; UNGA, 'Report of the GGE' UN Doc A/76/135 para 71(a); UNGA, 'Final Substantive Report of the Open-Ended Working Group on Developments in the Field of Information and Telecommunications in the Context of International Security' (10 March 2021) UN Doc A/AC.290/2021/CRP.2 para 35; Rule 65, Schmitt (n 2) 303–11.

[13] Art 33 of the UN Charter; UNGA, 'Report of the GGE' UN Doc A/76/135 para 71(a); UNGA, 'Final Substantive Report of the OEWG' UN Doc A/AC.290/2021/CRP.2 para 35.

[14] Arts 7(1) and 92 of the UN Charter.

[15] Arts 92–96, ch XIV of the UN Charter.

[16] Art 92 of the UN Charter provides that the ICJ 'shall function in accordance with the annexed Statute, which … forms an integral part of the present Charter'. Statute of the International Court of Justice (San Francisco, 26 June 1945).

[17] Art 30(1) of the ICJ Statute. The Rules of the Court currently in force were drafted in 1978 with a number of amendments of specific provisions that have occurred ever since (International Court of Justice Rules of Court (The Hague, 14 April 1978)).

[18] Art 34(1) of the ICJ Statute.

[19] Art 93(1) of the UN Charter. According to Art 93(2) states that are not members of the UN may become contracting parties to the ICJ Statute on conditions determined on a case-by-case basis by the UN General Assembly on the recommendation of the Security Council. See UNSC 'Resolution 9 (1946) Adopted by the Security Council at Its 76th Meeting, on 15 October 1946' (15 October 1946) UN Doc S/RES/9(1946).

Court (section II). Second, it will consider two grounds of admissibility of an application regarding cyber disputes: the position of third parties in relation to the settlement of a cyber dispute between two litigants by the Court in the light of the *Monetary Gold* principle, and the existence of legal interest (*locus standi*) of either of the litigants (section III). Third, it will discuss the possibility of a joinder of cases given the involvement of a plurality of states, either applicant or respondent, in disputes with the same subject matter (section IV). Fourth, it will examine the question of the type and probative value of evidence taken into account by the Court for the resolution of cyber disputes (section V). Finally, it will conclude based on the discussion in sections II to V (section VI).

II. Issues of Jurisdiction: The Existence of a Cyber Dispute

Although all Member States of the UN are automatically contracting parties to the ICJ Statute, the Court does not automatically possess jurisdiction to settle disputes between UN Member States. The jurisdiction of the ICJ is based on state consent expressed by additional, formal, or informal means. As the Court ruled in the *Corfu Channel* case, '[w]hile the consent of the parties confers jurisdiction on the Court, neither the Statute nor the Rules require that this consent should be expressed in any particular form'.[20] The bases for establishing consent to the jurisdiction of the Court are prescribed in the ICJ Statute and the Rules of Procedure. These are: (i) a special bilateral agreement (*compromis*) by which a specific dispute is submitted to the Court by states (Article 36(1) of the ICJ Statute); (ii) a compromissory clause in a treaty in force designating the ICJ as the forum for the resolution of disputes, the subject of which is the application or interpretation of the specific treaty (Articles 36(1) and 37 of the ICJ Statute); (iii) a declaration under the Optional Clause accepting the compulsory jurisdiction of the Court (Article 36(2) and (5) of the ICJ Statute); and (iv) the principle of *forum prorogatum* (Article 38(5) of the Rules of the Court).

Consent to the jurisdiction of the Court has as its object the settlement of a dispute.[21] The existence of a dispute is thus a prerequisite for the exercise of jurisdiction by the Court. It follows from this that a ground on which a party to a dispute may object to the jurisdiction of the Court is the non-existence of a dispute. Although logic dictates that two states do not submit a matter to the ICJ unless it constitutes a dispute, this is not self-evident.[22] As was said, there are various ways

[20] *The Corfu Channel Case (UK v Albania)* (Preliminary Objection, Judgment of 25 March 1948) [1948] ICJ Rep 15, 27.

[21] Arts 36 and 38 of the ICJ Statute.

[22] The existence of a dispute is not a matter of contention when two states submit a case by special agreement in which they specify the subject matter of the dispute and state what they wish the Court to adjudge and declare. See X Hanquin (ed), *Jurisdiction of the International Court of Justice, Collected Courses of the Xiamen Academy of International Law*, V 10 (Leiden, Brill Nijhoff, 2017) 109.

of consenting to the jurisdiction of the Court, some of which are general. The respondent state may thus deny the existence of a dispute altogether, or the dispute as presented to the Court by the applicant state, or claim that the applicant is in dispute with another state.[23]

The ICJ and its predecessor, the Permanent Court of International Justice (PCIJ), have adopted a definition of 'dispute' that is straightforward and commonsense at its core. In *Mavromatis Palestine Concessions*, the PCIJ ruled that 'a dispute is a disagreement on a point of law or fact, a conflict of legal views or interests between two persons'.[24] Moreover, as the ICJ ruled in the *South West Africa Cases* (Preliminary Objections), this disagreement or conflict should be established as a direct exchange of claims in which 'the claim of one party is positively opposed by the other'.[25] The combined effect of these two rulings has set a precedent that still remains valid.[26] In other cases, the Court has elaborated on this definition and clarified its content further. Thus, in the *Interpretation of Peace Treaties* (Advisory Opinion)[27] and the *Alleged Violation of Sovereign Rights* case,[28] the Court ruled that the parties must 'hold clearly opposite views concerning the question of the performance or non-performance of certain international obligations'. In addition, the Court has stated in *Application of the Convention on the Elimination of All Forms of Racial Discrimination* that the existence of a dispute is a matter of substance and not form[29] and that it is a question of objective determination based on facts.[30] In this respect, facts attesting to the existence of a dispute may constitute government or other officials' statements, diplomatic documents and exchanges in bilateral or multilateral settings, the failure to respond to a claim by a state when it finds itself in circumstances where a response is called for,[31] or a state becoming aware that another state has expressed an opposite claim relating to claims, acts

[23] H Thirlway, *The International Court of Justice* (Oxford, Oxford University Press, 2016) 53.

[24] *The Mavromatis Palestine Concessions* (Jurisdiction, Judgment of 30 August 1924) [1924] PCIJ Rep Series A No 2, 6, 11.

[25] *South West Africa Cases (Ethiopia v South Africa; Liberia v South Africa)* (Preliminary Objections, Judgment of 21 December 1962) [1962] ICJ Rep 319, 328: 'it is not sufficient for one party to a contentious case to assert that a dispute exists with the other party. A mere assertion is not sufficient to prove the existence of a dispute any more than a mere denial of the existence of the dispute proves its non-existence. Nor is it adequate to show that the interests of the two parties to such a case are in conflict. It must be shown that the claim of one party is positively opposed by the other'.

[26] A Zimmermann et al (eds), *The Statute of the International Court of Justice: A Commentary*, 3rd edn (Oxford, Oxford University Press, 2019) 721.

[27] *Interpretation of Peace Treaties with Bulgaria Hungary and Romania (First Phase)*, Advisory Opinion of 30 March 1950) [1950] ICJ Rep 65, 74.

[28] *Alleged Violations of Sovereign Rights and Maritime Spaces in the Caribbean Sea (Nicaragua v Colombia)* (Preliminary Objections, Judgment of 17 March 2016) [2016] ICJ Rep 3 para 50.

[29] *Application of the Convention on the Elimination of All Forms of Racial Discrimination (Georgia v Russian Federation)* (Preliminary Objections, Judgment of 1 April 2011) [2011] ICJ Rep 70 para 30; *Alleged Violations of Sovereign Rights* [2016] ICJ Rep 3 para 50.

[30] ibid. *Interpretation of Peace Treaties* [1950] ICJ Rep 65, 74; *Application of the Convention on the Elimination of All Forms of Racial Discrimination* (n 29) para 30; *Alleged Violations of Sovereign Rights* (n 29) para 50.

[31] *Application of the Convention on the Elimination of All Forms of Racial Discrimination* (n 29) para 30.

or omissions of the former. It is 'awareness' that has been elevated by the Court from a question of fact to a substantive or formal requirement for the existence of a dispute.

In the *Marshall Islands* case, the Court rejected the application of the plaintiff state because, in its view, no dispute existed with the respondent states. The Court ruled that the existence of a disagreement on issues of law or fact that materialised as a claim by one party positively opposed by the other was not sufficient for the existence of a dispute. It required, in addition, as a matter of substance that the respondent had been aware or 'could not have been unaware' that its position met with the clear and positive opposition of the plaintiff. As the Court explained,

> [t]he evidence must show that the parties 'hold clearly opposite views' with respect to the issue brought before the Court … As reflected in previous decisions of the Court in which the existence of a dispute was under consideration, a dispute exists when it is demonstrated, on the basis of the evidence, that the respondent was aware, or could not have been unaware, that its views were "positively opposed" by the applicant …[32]

This finding was adopted by eight votes to eight with the casting vote of the President and has been the subject of authoritative criticism. In particular, the late Judge Crawford, in his Dissenting Opinion, stated that an 'objective awareness' test in relation to the existence or not of a dispute had not been supported by previous judgments of the Court, and it would, in effect, amount to a requirement of formal notification which the Court had not upheld in previous jurisprudence.[33] Its adoption by a borderline majority may cast doubt about the authority of the Court's finding that awareness of the existence of a dispute is required and even render its application in future cases quite unlikely.[34]

This actually appears to be the case in subsequent cases when the respondent state attempted to advance an expanded version of 'awareness' as a substantive requirement for the existence of a dispute. In *Genocide Convention (The Gambia v Myanmar)*, the respondent state (Myanmar), in its fourth preliminary objection, requested the Court to reject the application of The Gambia, claiming the non-existence of a dispute between the parties under the Genocide Convention. In the opinion of Myanmar, the existence of a dispute depended on 'mutual awareness of the opposing views of the parties' in the sense that not only did the respondent need to be aware of the claims of the applicant, but the applicant also had to be

[32] *Obligations Concerning Negotiations Relating to Cessation of the Nuclear Arms Race and to Nuclear Disarmament (Marshall Islands v United Kingdom)* (Preliminary Objections, Judgment of 5 October 2016) [2016] ICJ Rep 833 para 41. See also *Obligations Concerning Negotiations relating to Cessation of the Nuclear Arms Race and to Nuclear Disarmament (Marshall Islands v India)* (Jurisdiction and Admissibility, Judgment of 5 October 2016) [2016] ICJ Rep 255 para 38; *Obligations Concerning Negotiations Relating to Cessation of the Nuclear Arms Race and to Nuclear Disarmament (Marshall Islands v Pakistan)* (Jurisdiction and Admissibility, Judgment of 5 October 2016) [2016] ICJ Rep 552 para 38.

[33] *Obligations Concerning Negotiations Relating to Cessation of the Nuclear Arms Race* (n 32) paras 3–19.

[34] Zimmermann et al (n 26) 722–23.

aware of the opposing views of the respondent to its initial claims.[35] The Court rejected the double awareness argument asserted by Myanmar. It is, however, interesting to note that the Court did not include the awareness on the part of the respondent as a substantive requirement for the existence of a dispute. Its review of previous rulings on the parameters of the concept of dispute, starting with the *Mavromatis* case and extending to its most recent judgment, omits any reference to the *Marshall Islands* Judgment on Jurisdiction and Admissibility even though it does constitute the most recent and supposedly important contribution to the substantive definition of the concept of dispute.[36] Furthermore, in *Marshall Islands*, the Court ruled that the critical date for establishing the existence of a dispute is the date of the application instituting proceedings. The Court appeared to deviate from past jurisprudence and denied any material or formative effect on the crystallisation of a dispute to subsequent procedural acts of the parties.[37] Whereas a dispute must exist, as a matter of principle, on the date of the seisin of the Court, the possibility of its crystallisation at a subsequent stage must not be excluded.[38]

The next question to consider is how the Court's aforementioned definitions of dispute can apply to cyber disputes.[39] Cyberspace is a domain where malicious cyber operations are often covert, and denying unlawful acts is extremely easy. In this setting, the requirement of awareness on the part of the respondent as an indispensable prerequisite for the existence of a dispute, as opined in the *Marshall Islands* case, will exclude most cyber disputes from the docket; this is unless a prospective applicant expressly asserts that a breach of international law has occurred in cyberspace, it is attributed to a specific state, and the latter becomes aware of it. If the Court does not abandon the requirement of unequivocal 'awareness' of the applicant's claim by the respondent as a formal constitutive element of dispute, very few cyber disputes will likely be entertained by the ICJ. Indeed, this would be the case regarding most malicious cyber operations. It appears that for an assertion by State B that State A has infected its cyber network by implanting a virus, has acquired confidential data by hacking government networks, or has caused denial of service by setting up botnets on the territory or jurisdiction of another state, State A must have positive knowledge of the claims by State B. In a cyber setting, this appears to require not just knowledge of the alleged breach but also of the proof that the breach is attributed to it. 'Awareness' of a breach of the territorial sovereignty of State B can, for example, be established if a suspect is arrested by the police of State A, in which case the factual context of the alleged breach will become known and communicated. But sending a virus, hacking,

[35] *Application of the Convention on the Prevention and Punishment of the Crime of Genocide (Gambia v Myanmar)* (Preliminary Objections, Judgment of 22 July 2022) (to be published) (available at www.icj-cij.org/sites/default/files/case-related/178/178-20220722-JUD-01-00-EN.pdf) para 52.

[36] ibid paras 63–64.

[37] *Obligations Concerning Negotiations Relating to Cessation of the Nuclear Arms Race* (n 32) paras 42–43.

[38] Zimmermann et al (n 26) 723.

[39] See Tsagourias (ch 1 in this volume).

or setting up botnets would not constitute in themselves communication of a breach because they may be anonymous, covert, or just not detected.[40] Additional compelling evidence of the involvement of State A would be required to become 'aware' of the facts that underlie the dispute. This implies that merely strong indicators of State A's involvement and its denial would not suffice to establish the existence of a dispute. However, this would conflate the question of the existence of a cyber dispute as the basis of instituting proceedings for its settlement with the actual resolution of the merits of the dispute. Thus, denying the existence of the dispute for lack of 'awareness' would amount to excluding judicial settlement of the merits of a dispute by the Court not as a matter of choice by states but as an inescapable fact. Judge Crawford persuasively argued in his dissenting opinion in *Marshall Islands* that the Court and its predecessor have steadily maintained a lower threshold and demonstrated flexibility on the question of the existence of a dispute in order to facilitate their settlement.[41] Only by remaining consistent with this approach is there a credible prospect that the Court shall become a regular forum for the settlement of cyber disputes.

The judgment in the *Genocide Convention (Gambia v Myanmar)* (Preliminary Objections) case, in which the Court discussed the requirements of the existence of a dispute, is promising in this respect. In this case, Myanmar argued that a dispute under the Genocide Convention did not exist between it and The Gambia because of a lack of 'mutual awareness' by both parties of 'their respective positively opposed positions'. In other words, Myanmar appears to have argued that its 'awareness' of The Gambia's claims was not adequate for the dispute to exist, but it also required its own express opposition to these claims. The Court rejected the argument and found that a dispute existed between the parties because there was no requirement that the respondent expressly oppose the applicant's claims. This would provide the respondent with the means to prevent a finding on the existence of a dispute by remaining silent.[42] In the context of cyber disputes, the mere denial by the respondent in general terms (and not by specific evidence to the contrary) of the claims of the applicant could be equivalent to silence if the claim of hostile cyber acts by the applicant was not based on irrefutable evidence of the respondent's responsibility and the respondent did not oppose it expressly. Thus, the mere denial by Russia of Estonia's claims that it was responsible for the 2007 incapacitation of its entire cyber network, Germany's claims that Russia was responsible for obtaining data by hacking the German Federal Parliament computer network in 2015, or the US claims that confidential data was obtained by hacking government networks in 2020 would suffice to prevent a finding on the existence of a dispute by the Court had the injured states seized it. The clarity with which a claim of a wrongful cyber act must be raised to establish the existence of a dispute need not

[40] See Tsagourias (ch 1 in this volume).

[41] *Obligations Concerning Negotiations Relating to Cessation of the Nuclear Arms Race* (n 32) Judge Crawford Dissenting Opinion at 1093, paras 7–9.

[42] *Application of the Convention on the Prevention and Punishment of the Crime of Genocide* (to be published) para 71. On silence and disputes see Tsagourias (ch 1 in this volume).

constitute certainty beyond reasonable doubt about the identity of the responsible state. A strong probability of this identity would suffice even without opposition from the alleged wrongdoing state.

It is noteworthy that the *Tallinn Manual 2.0* defines the concept of dispute in cyberspace by adopting the basic requirements of the *Mavromatis* and *South West Africa* judgments, namely the disagreement between two states on a point of fact or law and that a claim of one party is positively opposed by the other.[43] Anything more in terms of requirements for the existence of a dispute in the particular context of cyberspace (such as the 'awareness' or 'mutual awareness' of each party's claim by the other) would make establishing the existence of a dispute nearly impossible. In this respect, a cyber dispute between two states needs not to have fully crystallised on the date of the filing of the application instituting proceedings; rather, it will be sufficient to have a disagreement on fact or law and an assertion merely denied by the alleged responsible state.

III. Issues of Admissibility: The *Monetary Gold* Principle and *Locus Standi*

The admissibility of applications concerning cyber disputes of state responsibility may be the subject of preliminary objections on two grounds: first, the *Monetary Gold* principle, and second, the question of legal interest or *locus standi*.

A. The Monetary Gold Principle

The Court introduced the *Monetary Gold* principle in the *Case of the Monetary Gold Removed from Rome in 1943.*[44] In this case, the Court ruled that Italy, the plaintiff, could not claim Albanian Monetary Gold as reparation for the damage allegedly suffered by Italian nationals unless it was first established that Albania had incurred international responsibility for the nationalisation by the Albanian government of the assets of the Central Bank of Albania. In other words, the determination of the responsibility of Albania was a prerequisite for deciding Italy's claim. Therefore, the interests of Albania constituted the subject matter of the case, and given the absence of Albania from the proceedings, the Court declined to exercise jurisdiction. The Court ruled that

> [t]o adjudicate upon the international responsibility of Albania without her consent would run counter to a well-established principle of international law embodied in the Court's Statute, namely, that the Court can only exercise jurisdiction over a State with its consent. … In the present case, Albania's legal interests would not only be affected by

[43] Rule 65, Schmitt (n 2) 304.

[44] *Case of the Monetary Gold Removed from Rome in 1943 (Italy v France, UK, USA)* (Preliminary Question, Judgment of 15 June 1954) [1954] ICJ Rep 19, 32.

> a decision, but would form the very subject-matter of the decision. In such a case, the Statute cannot be regarded, by implication, as authorizing proceedings to be continued in the absence of Albania.[45]

The principle articulated by the Court was applied 40 years later in the *East Timor* case. Portugal requested the Court to adjudge that a treaty concluded between Australia and Indonesia concerning the joint exploration and exploitation of the Timor continental shelf violated the right of self-determination of the people of East Timor. The Court ruled that Australia's conduct could not be assessed without determining the grounds on which Indonesia could not have concluded the 1989 treaty:

> [T]he very subject-matter of the Court's decision would necessarily be a determination whether, having regard to the circumstances in which Indonesia entered and remained in East Timor, it could or could not have acquired the power to enter into treaties on behalf of East Timor relating to the resources of the continental shelf. The Court could not make such a determination in the absence of the consent of Indonesia.[46]

The Court has generally approached the *Monetary Gold* principle with considerable circumspection by adopting a rather strict view concerning the circumstances allegedly requiring its application. In *Nicaragua* (Jurisdiction and Admissibility), the USA asserted that the Court could not decide on Nicaragua's claim without adjudicating on the rights and obligations of other states, in particular Honduras, in the absence of their consent to the jurisdiction of the Court.[47] The Court rejected the US contention by ruling that Nicaragua's claim against the USA constituted an autonomous claim on its merits, in the sense of not being dependent on the prior determination of a third state's claim. Moreover, the Court ruled that there was, in principle, no 'indispensable parties rule' that was admissible under its Statute. The Court stated that Honduras and other neighbouring states of Nicaragua did not have the position of Albania in the *Monetary Gold* case so as to be truly indispensable in the proceedings before the Court.[48] In the *Nauru* case, the Court outlined a narrow framework within which it would apply the *Monetary Gold* principle. It ruled that although the administration of Nauru had been entrusted jointly to Australia, New Zealand and the UK, the determination of the responsibility of Australia did not require the prior determination, as a logical prerequisite, of the responsibility of either New Zealand or the UK.[49]

[45] ibid.

[46] *Case Concerning East Timor (Portugal v Australia)* (Judgment of 30 June 1995) [1995] ICJ Rep 90 paras 28–29.

[47] *Case Concerning Military and Paramilitary Activities in and against Nicaragua (Nicaragua v USA)* (Jurisdiction and Admissibility, Judgment of 26 November 1984) [1984] ICJ Rep 392 para 86.

[48] ibid, para 88.

[49] *Case Concerning Certain Phosphate Lands in Nauru (Nauru v Australia)* (Preliminary Objections, Judgment of 26 June 1992) [1992] ICJ Rep 240 para 55. Contra 301–02 (per Judge Jennings); 326–28 (per Judge Ago); 329–43 (per Judge Schwebel). The Court admitted that implications for the legal situations of third parties may arise but ruled that Art 59 of the ICJ Statute sufficiently guarantees the

The *Monetary Gold* principle is not expressly provided in the Statute or the Rules of the Court. It has been argued that the Court must abandon it altogether as incompatible with the object and purpose of the Statute and, in particular, with the settlement of disputes between two states, the consent of whom to the jurisdiction of the Court is not disputed. The deference to the absence of consent of a third state that is an outsider in relations to the proceedings in progress has been considered as contrary to Articles 36, 38 and 59 of the ICJ Statute and sound legal policy on the grounds of compliance, due process and legitimacy.[50] However, even though this is a compelling view, it is not supported either by state practice or the Court because the principle of consent to the jurisdiction of the Court is premised on the sovereign equality of states, and the interpretation of the ICJ Statute is in accordance with general international law.[51] Moreover, the *Monetary Gold* principle has been applied by the Court in relation to the *exercise* of its jurisdiction concerning *particular claims* and not generally concerning its jurisdiction to settle the dispute between the original parties.[52] The *Monetary Gold* principle may indeed impede the settlement of disputes that are not strictly bilateral but involve multilateral rights or obligations that concern the international community at large – such as peremptory norms of international law that create obligations *erga omnes*. However, the Court is not insensitive to this contingency. It has applied the principle with great circumspection, and it may circumvent it by adopting the approach of other international tribunals that have decided claims involving the rights and obligations of third states because they constitute 'givens' in the sense of being matters already settled by past decisions of other international institutions.[53] In the *Marshall Islands* case, the UK invoked the *Monetary Gold* principle in a preliminary objection to the admissibility of the plaintiff's (the Marshall Islands') application, arguing that if the Court adjudicated on the UK's rights and obligations under the Nuclear Non-Proliferation Treaty, it would also adjudicate on the rights and obligations of other states possessing nuclear weapons that were absent and had not consented to the jurisdiction of the Court. While the Court did not deal with this preliminary objection, having found that a dispute had not existed between the parties, Judge Crawford, in his Dissenting Opinion, did. He expressed a succinct view on the issue that merits to be quoted at length:

protection of third parties' interests that may be affected by litigation. Art 59 of the ICJ Statute provides that 'The decision of the Court has no binding force except between the parties and in respect of the particular case.'

[50] Z Mollengarden and N Zamir, 'The *Monetary Gold* Principle: Back to Basics' (2021) 115 *American Journal of International Law* 41–77.

[51] D Akande, 'Introduction to the Symposium on Zachary Mollengarden & Noam Zamir "The *Monetary Gold* Principle: Back to Basics"' (2021) 115 *American Journal of International Law Unbound* 140, 141–42. Also see Zimmermann et al (n 26) 729–32; O Pomson, 'Does the *Monetary Gold* Principle Apply to International Courts and Tribunals Generally?' (2019) 10 *Journal of International Dispute Settlement* 88–125.

[52] P d'Argent, 'The *Monetary Gold* Principle: A Matter of Submissions' (2021) 115 *American Journal of International Law Unbound* 149–53.

[53] M Paparinskis, 'Long Live *Monetary Gold* *Terms and Conditions Apply' (2021) 115 *American Journal of International Law Unbound* 154–59.

> The case law has however set firm limits to the *Monetary Gold* principle. It applies only where a determination of the legal position of a third State is a necessary prerequisite to the determination of the case before the Court. … An inference or implication as to the legal position of that third State is not enough: its position is protected by Article 59 of the Statute … The *Monetary Gold* ground of inadmissibility is particularly sensitive to the precise basis of the Applicant's claim. The decision of a given case may or may not rest on a prior determination of the legal position of a third State depending on how the case is put. In the present case, *Monetary Gold* may well impose limits on the consequences that can be drawn from the Respondent's conduct, if indeed it is held to involve a breach of international law. But precisely what those limits are will depend on the ground of decision. It is true, for example, that the Court cannot order third States to enter into negotiations, and that one cannot negotiate alone. But a third State could breach an obligation to negotiate by its own conduct and the Court could determine as much. Everything depends on what the precise scope and application of Article VI of the NPT, or any parallel customary international law obligation, entail. This is at the heart of the dispute in the present case. But these are all issues for the merits.[54]

Regarding cyber disputes, responsibility may lie with the perpetrator state and other third states; the former for its acts or omissions constituting internationally wrongful acts and the latter for violating their duty of due diligence. If the Court is seized of the dispute between the victim state and the perpetrator state, the latter may object based on the *Monetary Gold* principle. The respondent may thus contend that in adjudicating on its responsibility, the Court will also rule on the responsibility of other states without their consent. In a context such as the Stuxnet attack against the Iranian nuclear program, where there were allegedly two perpetrator states (US and Israel), the institution of proceedings against one of them would probably give rise to the objection that the other perpetrator state is an indispensable party in the proceedings. It would be argued that any finding concerning the responsibility of the respondent state would also be a finding on the responsibility of the state which is not present in the proceedings without its consent. Moreover, in the context of the use of a botnet involving the territories of several states, bringing a claim against one of these states concerning its responsibility for breaching its obligation of due diligence would raise the same objection, namely, that a finding on the responsibility of the respondent would constitute a finding on the responsibility of the other states that do not participate in the proceedings. The critical question is whether a finding on the responsibility of the states absent from the proceedings constitutes a logical prerequisite for establishing the responsibility of the respondent state. It is submitted that it does not. That said, the contrary argument may also be plausible due to the interconnectedness of cyberspace that appears to deny a purely bilateral character to

[54] *Obligations Concerning Negotiations Relating to Cessation of the Nuclear Arms Race* (n 32) Judge Crawford Dissenting Opinion at 1093, paras 32–33. Also see BI Bonafé, 'Adjudicative Bilateralism and Community Interests' (2021) 115 *American Journal of International Law Unbound* 164–69.

cyber disputes.[55] However, this would raise an insurmountable barrier that would make the settlement of cyber disputes by the ICJ impossible. By contrast, the application of the *Monetary Gold* principle is to be expected in the case where, by virtue of a treaty between States A, B and C, confidential data of State C are stored in government computers of State B and the maintenance of the network is entrusted exclusively to expert technicians of State A. The data is destroyed because the government information technology network of State B breaks down. State C claims that State B is responsible because it failed to prevent the breakdown of the system. However, this cannot be established without evaluating as a prerequisite the responsibility of State A for breach of its due diligence obligation to carry out network maintenance. It is, therefore, submitted that the *Monetary Gold* principle must be upheld but applied on a case-by-case basis in accordance with the relevant facts.

B. Legal Interest (Locus Standi)

Legal interest or *locus standi* before the Court is premised on the capacity of a state to be a litigant because it is the 'injured state' or the 'specially affected state' by the unlawful acts that are the subject matter of the dispute. It is at present admissible that a non-specially affected state may invoke the responsibility of the state that violated international customary law obligations *erga omnes* or obligations *erga omnes partes* in the context of a multilateral treaty – viz Article 48 of the International Law Commission's Articles on State Responsibility (2001).[56] However, whether such a state has the right to institute proceedings and have this claim adjudicated before the ICJ is controversial. In the *South West Africa* cases, the Court, by a borderline majority (by the casting vote of the President), rejected the applications of the plaintiff states (Liberia and Ethiopia) by dismissing them as an inadmissible *actio popularis* for lack of specific legal interest as injured states.[57] But in *Obligation to Prosecute or Extradite*[58] and *The Gambia v Myanmar*[59] cases, the Court upheld the legal interest of, respectively, Belgium and The Gambia to institute proceedings as a contracting party to the Torture and Genocide Conventions in view of alleged violations of the *erga omnes partes* obligations under these Conventions. In both cases, the Court stated that every

[55] *cf Obligations Concerning Negotiations Relating to Cessation of the Nuclear Arms Race* (n 32) Judge Tomka Separate Opinion at 885, para 40.

[56] J Crawford, *The International Law Commission's Articles on State Responsibility. Introduction, Text and Commentaries* (Cambridge, Cambridge University Press, 2002) 276–80.

[57] *South West Africa Cases (Ethiopia v South Africa; Liberia v South Africa)* (Second Phase), Judgment of 18 July 1966) [1966] ICJ Rep 6 paras 88, 99.

[58] *Questions relating to the Obligation to Prosecute or Extradite (Belgium v Senegal)* (Judgment of 20 July 2012) [2012] ICJ Rep 422 paras 68–70.

[59] *Application of the Convention on the Prevention and Punishment of the Crime of Genocide* (n 35) paras 108–09, 112–14.

contracting party under either the Torture or the Genocide Convention had legal standing to bring a claim for its breach by another contracting party, irrespective of the fact that the victims of this breach were its nationals. Having said this, there appears to be a clear tendency to move away from the very conservative ruling in the *South West Africa* cases relating to legal interest in case of a violation of an obligation owed *erga omnes partes* under a multilateral treaty or an *erga omnes* obligation under customary law.[60]

Many states may raise allegations of violations of international legal obligations in cyberspace. In most cases, all of them are injured states as they suffer interference or damage in relation to their cyber networks. An illustration is the NotPetya virus that infected computer networks in many states across Europe, Asia and the Americas in 2017.[61] Clearly, these states would have *locus standi* before the Court provided that they established a jurisdictional link with the respondent. The question, however, is whether *any* state has the legal interest to bring a cyber claim before the Court. The invocation of responsibility in this context has been value-centred. It concerns violations of customary law obligations, the subject of which are values that are important to the international community as a whole (eg, international peace and security, self-determination, the prevention of genocide, slavery and racial discrimination).[62] The question is whether the use of cyberspace is such a value. I submit that despite the importance of cyberspace in every aspect of public and private life, it does not constitute a value per se. Yet, it is a domain where human activity may violate values protected by obligations *erga omnes*. Viewed in this light, state responsibility for cyber breach of customary law obligations owed to the international community as a whole may be invoked by any state and the institution of proceedings on this basis is a logical consequence. Indeed, the insistence upon the strict bilateral nature of state responsibility and the admissibility of the institution of proceedings exclusively by the state affected by the cyber breach does not seem consonant with either the global nature of cyberspace as a domain or the very substance of obligations owed to the international community as a whole.

IV. Joinder of Cases

Cyber disputes, whether their subject matter is state responsibility or breach of a rule of a peremptory nature (such as the rule of the prohibition of the use of force), have both bilateral and multilateral dimensions due to the normative character of the right or obligation in question. But in addition to this, they always have a

[60] *Case Concerning the Barcelona Traction, Light and Power Company, Limited (Belgium v Spain)* (Second Phase, Judgment of 5 February 1970) [1970] ICJ Rep 3 para 33.

[61] For the facts of this incident, see n 64 below and C Antonopoulos, 'State Responsibility in Cyberspace' in N Tsagourias and R Buchan (eds), *International Law and Cyberspace*, 2nd edn (Cheltenham, Edward Elgar, 2021) 113–14.

[62] *Case Concerning the Barcelona Traction, Light and Power Company* (n 60) para 33.

factual multilateral dimension because of the nature of cyberspace. An illustration is the cyberattack against Iran's nuclear program using the Stuxnet virus in 2010. The virus infected many computers, 60 per cent of which were in Iran and the remaining 40 per cent in other states, mainly Indonesia, India, Azerbaijan and Pakistan. The USA and Israel allegedly perpetrated the Stuxnet attack, but both states denied any involvement. In this incident, there has been a plurality of states either as perpetrators or as victims.[63] Another illustration is gaining access to a network in one state and hacking networks in other states. As a result, the perpetrator's wrongful act has many victims. That was the case with the NotPetya incident in 2017[64] and the SolarWinds hacking in 2020.[65] In both cases, the Russian Federation was held responsible but denied the allegation. If a dispute were to arise, the perpetrator will be a single state but the victims multiple. In other cases, there can be more than one source of the injurious act situated in the territories of a plurality of states as in the case of botnets. An illustration of this scenario is the DDoS (Distributed Denial of Service) committed against Estonia in 2007 through the use of botnets or hijacked computers in several states that targeted Estonia's governmental and commercial websites. Again, Russia allegedly committed this cyberattack, but it denied any involvement.[66]

From the examples mentioned above, it transpires that a truly multilateral dispute may arise where several applicants institute proceedings before the ICJ against a single (and the same) state or where a single applicant seizes the Court against a plurality of respondent states. What are the effects of this state of affairs on the admissibility of a case?

First, there is the possibility of joining cases before the ICJ. Whereas it is theoretically possible that proceedings may be instituted jointly by two or more states against a single respondent or by a single applicant against two or more respondents together, in practice, it is more common for injured states to institute separate proceedings against the same respondent or for a single state to start parallel proceedings against two or more states. That said, by virtue of Article 47 of the Rules, the Court has the discretion to join the proceedings. A joinder means that two or more cases are heard and decided together. This happened in the *South West Africa* cases *(Liberia and Ethiopia v South Africa)* and the *North Sea Continental*

[63] P Ilevicius, 'Stuxnet Explained – The Worm that Went Nuclear' (*NordVPN*, 10 March 2022) nordvpn.com/blog/stuxnet-virus/.

[64] NotPetya is a data encrypting malware that was used to infect the network of a Ukrainian Tax Preparation provider used by many Ukrainian businesses. As a result, the networks of many multinational corporations in the USA, the UK, France, Germany, Italy and Poland were infected through their Ukrainian subsidiaries. HYPR, 'NotPetya. Five Facts to Know About History's Most Destructive Cyberattack' (*Security Encyclopedia*) www.hypr.com/security-encyclopedia/notpetya.

[65] From March to December 2020, the SVR hackers from the Russian Federation penetrated the Orion cybersecurity software provided by SolarWinds, and through this, it gained access to the networks of a number of US government agencies, such as five branches of the US military, the US State Department, the US Treasury and homeland security. B Schneier, 'The US has Suffered a Massive Cyberbreach. It's Hard to Overstate How Bad it is' (*The Guardian*, 23 December 2020) www.theguardian.com/commentisfree/2020/dec/23/cyber-attack-us-security-protocols.

[66] Council on Foreign Relations, 'Estonian Denial of Service Incident' (May 2007) www.cfr.org/cyber-operations/estonian-denial-service-incident.

Shelf cases (*The Netherlands and Denmark v Germany*).[67] Moreover, a joinder may be decided when two states bring proceedings against each other that relate to the same (or closely related) matters; this happened in *Certain Activities Carried out by Nicaragua in the Border Area (Costa Rica v Nicaragua)*[68] and *Construction of a Road Along the San Juan River (Nicaragua v Costa Rica)*.[69] However, a joinder is a matter that falls within the discretion of the Court, and the practice of the Court does not offer grounds for predictability. Thus, there was no joinder in the *Fisheries Jurisdiction* cases (*UK v Iceland, FR Germany v Iceland*), the *Nuclear Tests* cases (*Australia v France, New Zealand v France*) and the *Application of the International Convention on the Elimination of All Forms of Racial Discrimination* cases (*Armenia v Azerbaijan, Azerbaijan v Armenia*). Moreover, when a single applicant instituted proceedings against two or more states, this has never occurred against all respondents jointly. In *Lockerbie* and *Legality of the Use of Force*, the applicants (respectively, Libya and Yugoslavia) brought parallel cases against a plurality of respondents (respectively, the USA/UK and ten NATO Member States). In both cases, the Court did not see fit to order a joinder. It appears that the Court may take into account the wishes of the applicants as well as their positions and submissions when deciding to order a joinder or not, but its practice cannot be predicted with any degree of certainty.[70] It is submitted that a joinder is the best course of action the Court may take if it is called to settle a cyber dispute involving (as it is most likely) a plurality of states. This type of dispute will concern the same domain, it will be based on the same facts, its object will be the harmful effects of the use of cyberspace, and all parties will contribute to the identification of the real perpetrator of the cyber breach. Thus, in contexts such as the NotPetya incident, all or at least two victim states may bring a case against the alleged perpetrator, produce a single body of evidence, and help decisively overcome deniability by establishing the perpetrator's identity.

V. Evidence

The subject of evidence in proceedings before the Court[71] is very briefly and generally dealt with in the ICJ Statute (Articles 48–52), while its regulation is more

[67] *North Sea Continental Shelf Cases (Denmark/Federal Republic of Germany, Federal Republic of Germany/Netherlands)* (Order of 26 April 1968) [1968] ICJ Rep 9.

[68] *Certain Activities Carried Out by Nicaragua in the Border Area (Costa Rica v Nicaragua)* (Order of 17 April 2013) [2013] ICJ Rep 166.

[69] *Construction of a Road Along the San Juan River (Nicaragua v Costa Rica)* (Order of 17 April 2013) [2013] ICJ Rep 184.

[70] Thirlway (n 23) 80.

[71] See generally, Zimmermann et al (n 26) 1371 et seq; R Kolb, *The International Court of Justice* (Oxford, Hart Publishing, 2013) 928 et seq; M Roscini, 'Digital Evidence as a Means of Proof before the International Court of Justice' (2016) 21 *Journal of Conflict and Security Law* 541–54; N Tsagourias and M Farrell, 'Cyber Attribution: Technical and Legal Approaches and Challenges' (2020) 31 *European Journal of International Law* 941–67.

detailed in the Rules of the Court (adopted in 1978) and the non-binding Practice Directions that were adopted between 2001 and 2009.[72] The ICJ Statute provides that documents support written pleadings[73] and that the Court may request the parties to produce documents and supply any explanation before the opening of the oral pleadings.[74] Further, the Court admits witness, expert witness and expert evidence.[75] The importance of having a consistent and developed legal framework of evidence has been stressed by former President of the Court Judge Tomka: 'In many ways, the production and management of evidence constitute the most crucial building blocks in ensuring a just and well-reasoned judicial outcome in a dispute between sovereign States.'[76]

In general, the Court relies on the evidence that the parties produce in support of their claims concerning questions of fact. It does not search for facts beyond what the parties allege.[77] Moreover, the parties may produce any form or type of evidence, and the Court has wide discretion to evaluate it freely.[78] The Court appears to set as a standard of proof that the evidence furnished is clear and convincing. At the same time, it requires evidence to be 'fully conclusive' (equivalent to 'beyond reasonable doubt') in cases where the subject of claims are charges of grave breaches of international law.[79] Moreover, the Court gives much importance to the source of evidence (whether it has been an impartial, independent and disinterested agency that conducted the investigation), its character (as first-hand and contemporaneous), and its corroboration.[80] A further question relates to the inadmissibility of certain evidence. The Court has consistently refused to admit as evidence statements of the parties made during negotiations when the specific negotiations have not led to an agreement.[81] By contrast, the Court appears not to disapprove of a party's refusal to produce evidence containing sensitive information on national security matters.[82] At the same time, the Court has not rejected

[72] Thirlway (n 23) 99; Roscini (n 71) 543–44.

[73] Art 43 of the ICJ Statute; Arts 50 and 56 of the ICJ Rules of Court.

[74] Art 49 of the ICJ Statute.

[75] Art 51 of the ICJ Statute; Arts 63–65 of the ICJ Rules of Court.

[76] P Tomka, 'Speech by HE Judge Peter Tomka, President of the International Court of Justice, to the Sixty-Ninth Session of the General Assembly of the United Nations' (*ICJ*, 30 October 2014) www.icj-cij.org/public/files/press-releases/8/18388.pdf.

[77] Zimmermann et al (n 26) 1376. The parties to a dispute are under no obligation to prove the existence of rules of international law by virtue of the general principle of law *jura novit curia*. This, however, does not absolve parties that claim the existence of rules of customary international law from producing evidence of the two elements of state practice and *opinio juris*; see Zimmermann et al (n 26) 1377.

[78] Tomka (n 76) 3.

[79] *Application of the Convention on the Prevention and Punishment of the Crime Genocide (Bosnia and Herzegovina v Serbia and Montenegro)* (Merits, Judgment of 26 February 2007) [2007] ICJ Rep 43 para 209; Zimmermann et al (n 26) 1402–05.

[80] Tsagourias and Farrell (n 71) 956.

[81] Zimmermann et al (n 26) 1379, fn 54.

[82] *cf* ibid 1380. Thus, the ICJ has not adopted the firm position of the International Criminal Tribunal for the former Yugoslavia in the *Blaskic* case that the refusal of Croatia to produce evidence on grounds of national security would 'defeat the essential object and purpose' of the tribunal. See *Prosecutor v*

as inadmissible evidence obtained unlawfully even though it has ruled that the act of securing the evidence in question constituted a breach of the law. In the *Corfu Channel* case, the Court found that the minesweeping operation, 'Retail', of the UK Royal Navy inside the territorial sea of Albania without its consent to secure sea mines as evidence of Albania's responsibility was a violation of the latter's territorial sovereignty; nevertheless, it did not rule that the evidence was inadmissible.[83] That said, it is doubtful that the Court will admit evidence obtained as a result of a breach of a rule of *jus cogens*, such as the prohibition of torture.[84]

The Governmental Group of Experts has stressed the importance of evidence relating to cyber disputes.[85] The special nature of cyberspace makes identifying perpetrators of unlawful acts and their attribution to states extremely difficult. Therefore, the standard of proof and the probative value of evidence is an extremely challenging issue in the context of cyber disputes. The evidence which the Court shall be called to evaluate is primarily digital evidence and cyber data. This kind of evidence appears to pose no difficulty for the Court, even though the only reference made to digital evidence is in Practice Direction IX bis (adopted in 2006).[86] It concerns documents and whether they are 'readily available' so as to be produced after the conclusion of written proceedings dispensing with the consent of the other litigant.[87] The difficulty concerns, first, access to the evidence; second, their authenticity; and third, their probative value. As to the first question, cyber evidence consisting of government reports and investigation data are kept secret or are confidential on grounds of national security, and a party to a dispute is very likely to decline to produce it if the Court makes an order under Article 49 of the Statute. In this case, the Court may note the refusal or not react at all. This leaves a litigant with the option to obtain this evidence by having access to the cyber network of the other party with its consent or without it. In the former instance, the acquisition of evidence is lawful, but in the latter, it is not because it would violate the other party's territorial sovereignty.[88] The evidence, however, would be admissible unless their acquisition constitutes a breach of a peremptory norm.[89] The second question is particularly important because digital data may be interfered with and falsified. It is in this context where the power of the Court to

Timohir Blaskic Decision on the Objection of the Republic of Croatia to the Issuance of Subpoena Duces Tecum, 18 July 1997, IT-95-14, paras 115, 131–134. See also *Corfu Channel Case* (Merits, Judgment of 9 April 1949) [1949] ICJ Rep 4, 32; *Application of the Convention on the Prevention and Punishment of the Crime Genocide* (n 79) para 205.

[83] *Corfu Channel Case* (n 82) 34. *cf* Tomka (n 76) 3.

[84] Zimmermann et al (n 26) 1381.

[85] UNGA, 'Report of the GGE' UN Doc A/70/174 para 28(f).

[86] www.icj-cij.org/practice-directions#fn8.

[87] Roscini (n 71) 546. See also AS Serrano, 'International Dispute Settlement Digital Evidence and Online Dispute Resolution' in Buchan, Franchini and Tsagourias (eds), *The Changing Character of International Dispute Settlement: Challenges and Prospects* (Cambridge, Cambridge University Press, 2023) 467ff.

[88] Rule 11, Schmitt (n 2) 66–71; von Heinegg (n 5) 129.

[89] Roscini (n 71) 553; Tsagourias and Farrell (n 71) 957.

appoint its own cyber expert under Article 50 of the Statute must be more extensively and systematically used.[90] It appears to be the best approach to establish the authenticity of digital evidence as such a person would be impartial and independent compared to experts appointed by the parties, and her findings would be more readily considered credible. Moreover, the appointment of an expert by the Court would bypass the fact that a refusal of the other party to disclose cyber data is not grounds for adverse inference.[91] The third question concerns the lack of impartiality and independence of either government or private security companies' data concerning attribution or other aspects of malicious use of cyberspace. Moreover, it is not always certain whether governments adopt the findings of private companies. This may leave the Court with no other option than to rely heavily on circumstantial evidence as it has done in the *Corfu Channel* case.[92] The difficulty of obtaining evidence, because it is on networks situated in the territory of the other litigant, appears to make recourse to circumstantial evidence the only feasible option. However, it is not always a sufficient basis to establish all facts of a cyber dispute without any reference to primary evidence.[93]

VI. Conclusion

The question of settlement of cyber disputes before the ICJ has an element of speculation at first sight. At the same time, the Court is competent to hear disputes involving any issue concerning any area of international law. Thus, cyber disputes may form part of the docket in the not-too-distant future, given the reality of cyberspace and its frequent hostile use. A state that seizes the Court concerning a dispute with another state, the subject matter of which relates to cyberspace, may expect preliminary objections to the Court's jurisdiction and the application's admissibility. The most likely objection to jurisdiction appears to concern the existence of a dispute between the parties. This is to be resolved on the basis of consistent jurisprudence that a dispute is a disagreement on questions of law and fact that is established when one state positively opposes the claims of the other while the awareness by the respondent of this opposition is merely a question of fact and not a formal requirement for the existence of a dispute. As to objections to admissibility, they are expected to consist of the invocation of the *Monetary Gold* principle and the lack of legal interest (or *locus standi*) on the part of the respondent. As the use of cyberspace involves and affects a plurality of states, the application

[90] The Court has been very reluctant to appoint its own experts and prefers to rely on expert witnesses appointed by the parties. Zimmermann et al (n 26) 1393–97; Tomka (n 76) 2.

[91] Tsagourias and Farrell (n 71) 957–58.

[92] UNGA, 'Report of the Group of Governmental Experts on Developments in the Field of Information and Telecommunications in the Context of International Security' (30 July 2010) UN Doc A/65/201, 2.

[93] Tsagourias and Farrell (n 71) 958.

of the *Monetary Gold* principle appears to be contingent on how a specific claim is formulated. The Court shall evaluate on this basis whether the rights and obligations of a third state form the subject matter of the dispute as a prerequisite for the settlement of the dispute between the initial parties. If this is the case, the Court shall discontinue the proceedings because consent to its jurisdiction is central to its jurisprudence and not a matter to tamper with. On the other hand, it shall proceed if it establishes either that the rights and obligations of the third state are not a prerequisite to resolving the dispute before it or if they constitute a 'given' as a result of a decision by another international institution. Turning to legal standing, it is the victim of a hostile use of cyberspace that primarily has an interest in bringing a claim before the ICJ. Be that as it may, the interconnectedness of cyberspace may give rise to an interest shared by the international community relating to its principled use that may constitute the basis of *erga omnes* obligations to this end. This, in turn, would offer every state the legal standing to seize the Court. Once a cyber dispute is submitted to the ICJ, it may be corroborated by evidence that is to be freely and flexibly evaluated by the Court, considering the particularities of cyberspace as a domain. As the prospect of submitting cyber disputes to the ICJ looms, the Court is expected to rise to the challenge, given its long tradition and experience as a forum for the settlement of inter-state disputes.

5

The EU and the Peaceful Settlement of Cyber Disputes: The Goals, Tools and Normative Framework of EU Cyber Policy

ANNEGRET BENDIEK, MARTIN MÜLLER AND MATTHIAS C KETTEMANN

I. Introduction

In 2022, the Council of Foreign Ministers commissioned Josep Borrell, the European Union's (EU's) foreign affairs representative, and the European Commission to bring together the bloc's various strands of foreign, security, and defence policy in order 'to ensure complementarity and coherence of external digital policy initiatives'.[1] Indeed, the challenge of an EU cyber foreign and security policy lies in effectively assembling and streamlining the numerous EU and Member States' initiatives and legal and policy instruments.

The focus of our investigation in this chapter is the question of how the EU's approach to cyber policy is normatively framed and practically implemented internally and externally and how this contributes to the peaceful settlement of disputes. In particular the external implementation of the EU's cyber policies produces a cyber 'Brussels Effect'.[2] As Anu Bradford noted, the EU's normative 'primers' such as the General Data Protection Regulation (GDPR)[3] and, more recently, platform

[1] Council of the EU, Council Conclusions on EU Digital Diplomacy [2022] 11406/22.

[2] A Bradford, *The Brussels Effect: How the European Union Rules the World* (New York, Oxford University Press, 2020).

[3] Regulation (EU) 2016/679 of the European Parliament and of the Council of 27 April 2016 on the protection of natural persons with regard to the processing of personal data and on the free movement of such data, and repealing Directive 95/46/EC (General Data Protection Regulation) [2016] OJ L119/1.

regulation through the Digital Services Act[4] and the Digital Markets Act[5] echo loudly beyond the EU's borders due to the Union's market power.[6]

We will argue that the existing legal framework can be used more effectively to bolster the EU's cyber policy. By strengthening cyber resilience, enhancing cyber diplomacy, and developing cyber defence, the EU can – based on existing rules – formulate and implement a more effective cyber policy, which can also contribute to dispute resolution internally and externally.

In section II, we set out to define the concept of EU digital sovereignty with its internal and external dimensions. Section III lays out the key elements of the EU's Cybersecurity Strategy, which include cyber resilience (preparing for threats), cyber diplomacy (defusing and responding to threats), and cyber defence (defending against threats). Section IV will analyse the treaty framework applicable to the EU cyber policy and how the EU has revised its approach to cyber policy. Section V will consider the external perspective of the EU's cyber policy and look at the Brussels Effect's potential reach in the global cybersecurity realm. In doing this, we aspire to provide an outlook for future developments in cybersecurity and map out how the EU can support dispute settlement initiatives on a global level.

II. The EU's Approach to Digital Sovereignty

It is broadly accepted that international norm processes can dissuade state actors from attacking critical infrastructure and prevent disputes from arising. For example, the norms for responsible state behaviour in cyberspace[7] adopted by the United Nations (UN) Group of Governmental Experts (GGE) set international standards for state behaviour in cyberspace. The mandate of the Open-Ended Working Group (OEWG) covers confidence-building measures as well as other thematic strands (threats, norms, international law, capacity building, and regular institutional dialogue). The UN General Assembly negotiations demonstrate that, despite political differences, work is underway to agree on common norms for responsible state behaviour in cyberspace.

In the EU, the notion of digital sovereignty is critical and underpins its far-reaching cybersecurity policies, which we will examine in section III. A significant

[4] Regulation (EU) 2022/2065 of the European Parliament and of the Council of 19 October 2022 on a single market for digital services and amending Directive 2000/31/EC (Digital Services Act) [2022] OJ L277/1.

[5] Regulation (EU) 2022/1925 of the European Parliament and of the Council of 14 September 2022 on contestable and fair markets in the digital sector and amending Directives (EU) 2019/1937 and (EU) 2020/1828 (Digital Markets Act) [2022] OJ L265/1.

[6] On the role of negotiations as consensus-building phases, see A Bendiek and I Stuerzer, 'The Brussels Effect, European Regulatory Power and Political Capital: Evidence for Mutually Reinforcing Internal and External Dimensions of the Brussels Effect from the European Digital Policy Debate' (2023) 2 *Digital Society* 1–25 (doi.org/10.1007/s44206-022-00031-1).

[7] UNGA, 'Report of the Group of Governmental Experts on Advancing Responsible State Behaviour in Cyberspace in the Context of International Security' (14 July 2021) UN Doc A/76/135.

aspect of the EU's ambition for digital sovereignty is the settlement of cyber disputes and a rule-based international order based on the due diligence principle. Seeking digital sovereignty has an internal and external dimension. For this reason, EU cyber diplomacy seeks to foster cybersecurity and trust-building internally between Member States and globally between the EU and the rest of the world. Only a digital foreign policy based on the principle of due diligence, democratic multilateralism, and a parliamentary multi-stakeholder approach is in line with Europe's own values and norms and, by extension, consistent with the functional requirements of global politics regarding the digital environment.

As the EU lacks sovereignty per se, it has been argued that the EU has 'pooled' or 'collective' sovereignty in areas where integration has proceeded the furthest, such as the internal market.[8] That said, the EU must completely rethink its approach to sovereignty to overcome conflict in the digital sphere.[9] The EU cannot remain content with the outdated notion of popular sovereignty (*la volontée générale*) or its character of a rule-making authority, nor with Carl Schmitt's pretence of ultimate power. Sovereignty should be explained as a multi-level political practice in Europe.

An appropriate understanding of 'European' sovereignty under the conditions of digitisation requires the development of a complex concept of sovereignty that incorporates the aforementioned understandings. Complex sovereignty, above all, includes a legal dimension of formal internal and external competence. Politics in Europe is politics within the community of law – and thus hardly possible beyond legal procedures. The low effectiveness of intergovernmental policies, such as the Common Foreign and Security Policy (CFSP), clearly underlines such dependence. Europe's participation in political processes in the International Telecommunication Union (ITU) or other international bodies also becomes legally relevant when actors such as the European Commission implement their formal internal and external competences against other actors or in interaction with them. This includes both negotiating power vis-à-vis other states and the intra-European ability to establish agreements among Member States. The past has clearly shown that the latter is critical. Other states easily exploit Member State disagreement to play one against another and block common European policies. Thus, complex sovereignty refers to the EU's internal and external ability to effectively exercise legal competences within Europe and internationally based on law-based European decision-making processes.[10]

[8] C Beaucillon, 'Strategic Autonomy: A New Identity for the EU as a Global Actor' (2023) 8 *European Papers* 417, 422; D Broeders, F Christiano and M Kaminska, 'In Search of Digital Sovereignty and Strategic Autonomy: Normative Power Europe to the Test of Its Geopolitical Ambitions' (2023) 61 *Journal of Common Market Studies* 1261, 1264.

[9] Broeders, Christiano and Kaminska (n 8) 1265; for a French perspective, see G Klossa, 'Opinion: Pas de souveraineté numérique pour l'Europe sans souveraineté médiatique' (*Les Echos*, 29 December 2020) www.lesechos.fr/idees-debats/cercle/opinion-pas-de-souverainete-numerique-pour-leurope-sans-souverainete-mediatique-1276866.

[10] *cf* A Bendiek and J Neyer, 'Europas digitale Souveränität. Bedingungen und Herausforderungen internationaler politischer Handlungsfähigkeit' in M Oswald and I Borucki (eds), *Demokratietheorie im Zeitalter der Frühdigitalisierung* (Wiesbaden, Springer VS, 2020) 103–25.

The growing number of international conflicts intensifies demands for the establishment of 'digital sovereignty'[11] and 'strategic autonomy of the EU'.[12] The old idea of a global liberal order based on consensual values and norms is increasingly receding, eclipsed by calls for the EU to maintain a more self-confident posture by, for example, tapping into ideas of 'technological'[13] or 'data' sovereignty[14] that focus more narrowly on technological leadership or, respectively, localisation of European data. The EU is built on traditions of thought to which protectionist and compartmentalisation-oriented ideas are first and foremost alien. For this reason, economic cooperation in the internal market is central to the EU, but it is coupled with the understanding that fundamental rights and the rule of law in the Union and abroad must be protected.[15]

In Articles 3 and 10 of the Treaty on European Union (TEU),[16] the EU emphasises the individual self-determination of European citizens through its commitment to market freedom and democracy. It realises a political order that takes a stand on fundamental ethical questions without claiming universal truth. This ethically based understanding of society can also be found in current position papers of the European institutions on the opportunities and challenges of the digital society. The Council of Europe,[17] the European Council,[18] and the European Commission[19] have all adopted a series of declarations and position papers expressing the idea of a democratic digital society that is both socially and individually centred. In each of these papers, technological progress is seen as a man-made opportunity that is fundamentally open and adept at improving society. New technologies must not only be efficient but also contribute to democracy and human rights.

[11] B Becker, 'Your Tax Lady' (*Politico*, 6 November 2018) www.politico.com/newsletters/morning-tax/2018/06/11/your-tax-lady-248338.

[12] Strategic autonomy means 'the ability, in terms of capacity and capabilities, to decide and act upon essential aspects of one's longer-term future in the economy, society and their institutions'. P Timmers, 'Ethics of AI and Cybersecurity When Sovereignty is at Stake' (2019) 29 *Minds and Machines* 635, 635.

[13] S Poli, 'Reinforcing Europe's Technological Sovereignty through Trade Measures: The EU and Member States' Shared Sovereignty' (2023) 8 *European Papers* 429, 432.

[14] T Christakis, 'European Digital Sovereignty. Successfully Navigating between the "Brussels Effect" and Europe's Quest for Strategic Autonomy' (*SSRN*, December 2020) ssrn.com/abstract=3748098, 66, 98–99; more general, B Ferrand and H Carrapico, 'Digital Sovereignty and Taking Back Control: From Regulatory Capitalism to Regulatory Mercantilism in EU Cybersecurity' (2022) 31 *European Security* 435, 444.

[15] A von Bogdandy, 'The European Union as a Human Rights Organization? Human Rights and the Core of the European Union' (2000) 37 *Common Market Law Review* 1307, 1307.

[16] Treaty on European Union (Maastricht, 7 February 1992).

[17] Council of Europe, 'Unboxing Artificial Intelligence: 10 Steps to Protect Human Rights' (May 2019) rm.coe.int/unboxing-artificial-intelligence-10-steps-to-protect-human-rights-reco/1680946e64; Council of Europe, 'Declaration by the Committee of Ministers on the Manipulative Capabilities of Algorithmic Processes. Decl(13/02/2019)1' (13 February 2019) search.coe.int/cm/pages/result_details.aspx?objectid=090000168092dd4b.

[18] European Council, 'European Council Meeting (19 October 2017) – Conclusions' [2017] EUCO 14/17.

[19] European Commission, 'Communication from the Commission Artificial Intelligence for Europe' [2018] COM 2018/237 final.

To summarise what was hitherto said, the first point we made is that the EU has sovereignty, which provides it with normative powers, although it is 'pooled sovereignty' derived from its Member States. Second, in the digital sphere, where sovereignty in the sense of *territorial* sovereignty loses meaning, normative power to act remains and gains significance by grounding the terms 'digital sovereignty' and the inter-related term of 'strategic autonomy'.

This raises the next question: How can the EU achieve digital sovereignty by acting normatively? As was said, there is a normative order in cyberspace whose normativity is based not only on laws but also on institutions with a normative effect, ie, a regulative one.[20] With this in mind, we will discuss the EU's various legal and institutional cyber initiatives.

III. Key Elements of the EU's Cybersecurity Strategy

The current 'EU Cybersecurity Strategy for the Digital Decade'[21] was presented in December 2020 by the European Commission and the High Representative for Foreign Affairs and Security Policy, Josep Borrell. It is closely linked to other Union initiatives, such as the Digital Single Market Strategy,[22] the Commission's Economic Recovery Plan,[23] and the Security Union Strategy 2020–2025.[24] The 2020 EU Cybersecurity Strategy includes the establishment of a 'Joint Cyber Unit' in the EU Commission that will be tasked with strengthening the information technology (IT) capabilities of defence communities in the field of cybersecurity and of law enforcement agencies in cooperation with civilian and diplomatic communities. According to the strategy, the EU will also draw upon the work of the European Defence Agency and promote cooperation in the military domain of operation, drawing on the newly created European Defence Fund. Furthermore, the EU will be given a 'cybersecurity shield' to identify threats early and take countermeasures before damage is done.

The three key elements of the EU's Cybersecurity Strategy are measures targeted at cyber resilience to build up capacities against attacks (II.A), cyber diplomacy to navigate cyber conflicts so lawful measures can be taken against attackers (III.B), and cyber defence to counter attacks and defend against them (III.C).

[20] MC Kettemann, *The Normative Order of the Internet* (Oxford, Oxford University Press, 2020) 242.

[21] European Commission, 'Joint Communication to the European Parliament and the Council. The EU's Cybersecurity Strategy for the Digital Decade' [2020] JOIN 2020/18 final.

[22] European Commission, 'Communication from the Commission to the European Parliament, the Council, the European Economic and Social Committee and the Committee of the Regions. A Digital Single Market Strategy for Europe' [2015] COM 2015/192 final.

[23] Council Regulation (EU) 2020/2094 of 14 December 2020 establishing a European Union Recovery Instrument to support the recovery in the aftermath of the COVID-19 crisis [2020] OJ L433/23.

[24] European Commission, 'Communication from the Commission to the European Parliament, the Council, the European Economic and Social Committee and the Committee of the Regions on the EU Security Union Strategy' [2020] COM 2020/605 final.

A. Cyber Resilience

Resilience can only be achieved as a pan-European and pan-societal task through close coordination at the EU level and with other democratic partners by including economic policy and technological expertise. This means that EU cyber diplomacy must set the framework for these aims, as individual countries' competencies or borders do not bind the cyber and information space. Public institutions, business, the scientific community, and civil society at the European level must collaborate much more intensively than they have done to date. Establishing a European Cybersecurity Industrial, Technology and Research Competence Centre and a network of national coordination centres is a good first step. Cyber diplomacy can create supranational, democratic, economic, and technological conditions, both internally and externally, to provide the necessary infrastructure, know-how, and cutting-edge technology.

These goals are served by the EU's recently planned and implemented legal acts and strategies on data, markets, services, and algorithms in Europe and, most recently, on cybersecurity. This would at least be the logical consequence. Essential legal acts for resilience building to protect critical infrastructure in Europe have also been adopted by the EU institutions at a brisk pace in recent months. They have reshaped the EU's cyber diplomacy stance, which so far has been characterised by defensive measures at the technical level but lacked broader norm-building initiatives.[25] A revised network and information security directive (NIS2 Directive) has entered into force in January 2023 to be implemented by Member States by October 2024.[26] The scope of addressees and minimum standards for infrastructure operators' implementation and reporting obligations have been significantly expanded. These legislative initiatives are essential building blocks for securing the digital single market. The proposals also extend to the cybersecurity of the single market, which forms the basic protection for EU cyber defence. With the Strategic Compass in March 2022,[27] the Council Conclusions on the elaboration of an EU Cyber Posture in May 2022,[28] and the Joint Communication of the Commission and the High Representative for Foreign Affairs and Security Policy on Cyber Defence,[29] the spill-over effects from sectoral, ie, cybersecurity of critical infrastructures, to hard security of Europe, can be observed.

[25] A Bendiek and MC Kettemann, 'Revisiting the EU Cybersecurity Strategy: A Call for EU Cyber Diplomacy' (2021) 16 *SWP Comment* 1, 2.

[26] Directive (EU) 2022/2555 of the European Parliament and of the Council of 14 December 2022 on measures for a high common level of cybersecurity across the Union [2022] OJ L333/80 (NIS2 Directive).

[27] European Commission, 'A Strategic Compass for Security and Defence' www.eeas.europa.eu/sites/default/files/documents/strategic_compass_en3_web.pdf.

[28] Council of the European Union, 'A Strategic Compass for Security and Defence – For a European Union that Protects its Citizens, Values and Interests and Contributes to International Peace and Security' [2022] 7371/22.

[29] European Commission, 'JOINT Communication to the European Parliament and the Council: EU Policy on Cyber Defence' [2022] JOIN 2022/49 final.

All these policies are financially underpinned by the generously endowed 'Digital Europe', 'Horizon 2030', 'Defence Fund', and 'Peace Facility' budgets. Foremost among these are legislative acts such as the Cyber Resilience Act,[30] which introduces cybersecurity requirements for all products connected to other devices and networks.[31] Additionally, the pooling of information on situational awareness in the cyber and information space at the EU level – whether in the EU Intelligence and Situation Centre (EU-INTCEN), the Single Intelligence Analysis Capacity (SIAC), or the EU Joint Cyber Unit – is considered an expanding priority.

Since 2013, the EU has been working on its options for response to attacks from – and conflicts in – the cyber and information space.[32] Existing EU law and the 2016 EU Network and Information Security Directive (NIS Directive)[33] have been revised to protect critical infrastructures. Critical infrastructure is a particularly attractive target for cyberattacks[34] because the consequences for the EU can be far-reaching. Cyberattacks can be used as leverage for extortion or as a launching point for military operations. While not used as a term in the first version, the NIS framework as a whole can be considered to form the 'cyber resilience' element of the EU's cyber strategy.[35]

B. Cyber Diplomacy

It is only since 2018 that the EU has had the Cyber Diplomacy Toolbox[36] at its disposal to counter serious cyberattacks.[37] It has designed its own sanctions regime against IT attacks that was deployed in July 2020 during the technical and legal handling of the 2015 hacker attacks on the German Parliament. Beyond the Diplomatic Response Framework (Cyber Diplomacy Toolbox), it is worth mentioning the Cyber Defence Policy Framework (2018);[38]

[30] European Commission, 'Proposal for a Regulation on Horizontal Cybersecurity Requirements for Products with Digital Elements and Amending Regulation (EU) 2019/1020' [2022] COM 2022/454 final. The regulation has not yet been passed at the time of writing.

[31] European Commission, 'Europe's Internet of Things Policy' (updated 12 July 2023) digital-strategy.ec.europa.eu/en/policies/internet-things-policy.

[32] This part draws partly from Bendiek and Kettemann (n 25).

[33] Directive (EU) 2022/2555 of the European Parliament and of the Council of 6 July 2016 concerning measures for a high common level of security of network and information systems across the Union.

[34] ENISA, 'ENISA Threat Landscape 2022' (October 2022) www.enisa.europa.eu/publications/enisa-threat-landscape-2022/@@download/fullReport 24.

[35] Recitals 2 and 5 of the NIS2 Directive mention 'cyber resilience' explicitly.

[36] Council of the European Union, 'Council Conclusions on a Framework for a Joint EU Diplomatic Response to Malicious Cyber Activities ("Cyber Diplomacy Toolbox")' [2017] ST 10474/17.

[37] *cf* A Bendiek, 'The EU as a Force for Peace in International Cyber Diplomacy' (2018) 19 *SWP Comment* 1–8.

[38] Council of the European Union, 'EU Cyber Defence Policy Framework (2018 Update)' [2018] 14413/18.

the EU Cybersecurity Act[39] and Screening of (Digital) Investment (both 2019)[40] as well as the EU toolbox for 5G security[41] and the EU Security Union Strategy (both 2020).[42] In addition, the EU-US Trade and Technology Council has emphasised transatlantic cooperation for this purpose, particularly regarding a common China policy. At the same time, further digital partnerships were launched with Singapore and Japan, as well as a 'Trade and Technology Council' with India. Last but not least, a 'Declaration for the Future of the Internet'[43] was supported by 60 countries to promote the importance of freedom of expression and human rights online.

C. Cyber Defence

Since 2020, the EU has focused its activities – jointly with the Member States – on building operational capacity to prevent, deter, and respond to serious cyber incidents in Europe. The Strategic Compass on Security and Defence of March 2022 includes numerous defensive measures to counter hybrid threats, illegitimate influence, and disinformation more effectively in the future. The Defence package also provides for developing critical technologies central to the EU's cybersecurity and defence capabilities. With the Space package, the EU wants to enable its satellite-based information and communications capability. The EU Council adopted conclusions on developing a fully-fledged EU cyber posture in May 2022 and asked the Commission to formulate an EU cyber defence policy. In a joint communication with the High Representative of the Union, the Commission then proposed to establish an 'EU Cyber Defence Coordination Centre (EUCDCC)'.[44] The Centre is to serve as a cooperation platform for the civilian and military authorities of the Union and its Member States. It will be responsible for cybersecurity and for improving situational awareness and coordination in the event of major attacks. However, it remains to be seen whether these can be understood as major steps towards a cyber defence policy that is committed to serving different objectives simultaneously, including the achievement of security and trust-building goals in the context of the Organization for Security and Co-operation in Europe (OSCE), 'strategic autonomy', and 'digital sovereignty'.

[39] Regulation (EU) 2019/881 of the European Parliament and the Council of 17 April 2019 on ENISA (the European Union Agency for Cybersecurity) and on information and communications technology cybersecurity certification and repealing Regulation (EU) No 526/2013 (Cybersecurity Act) [2019] OJ L151/15.

[40] Regulation (EU) 2019/452 of the European Parliament and the Council of 19 March 2019 establishing a framework for the screening of foreign direct investments into the Union [2019] OJ L79 I/1.

[41] European Commission, 'Secure 5G deployment in the EU – Implementing the EU toolbox' [2020] COM 2020/50 final.

[42] European Commission, 'Communication from the Commission on the EU Security Union Strategy' [2020] COM 2020/605 final.

[43] European Commission, 'Declaration for the Future of Internet' (28 April 2022) digital-strategy.ec.europa.eu/en/library/declaration-future-internet.

[44] European Commission, 'EU Policy on Cyber Defence' [2022] JOIN 2022/49, 3.

To implement the Cybersecurity Strategy, proposals will be made under the Common Foreign and Security Policy to expand the EU Cyber Diplomacy Toolbox to effectively counter attacks on critical infrastructure, supply chains, and democratic institutions and processes. Although there are references to EU initiatives such as those to combat hybrid threats, the deepening of confidence, and security-building measures of EU cyber diplomacy toward third countries remains largely underexplored. The need for such actions has been noted, but no concrete examples or institutional venues to implement them have been provided. Cyber diplomacy and trust-building measures in cybersecurity continue to be politically contested and conceptually underdeveloped. We will now discuss how such a development based on the EU competences could look.

IV. The Normative Framing of EU Cyber Policy

A. Developing Cyber Policy Norms

The one-sidedness of the EU Cybersecurity Strategy inherent in excluding diplomatic tools such as confidence-building measures remains problematic because international norm-building is still a key element for trust and security in the cyber and information space.[45] The European External Action Service (EEAS) needs to be adequately empowered to take on the task of cyber diplomacy by aligning its mandate accordingly. The current strategy neglects the important lesson of the nuclear age: disarmament and trust-building actions lead to generally enhanced security. Joseph Nye argues that contrary to popular belief, deterrence in cyberspace can work.[46] He is convinced that the development of international norms, which has so far been very limited, can positively affect security in the cyber and information space. For this, he argues, it is essential not to limit the principle of deterrence to classic territorial defence and immediate retaliation. Rather, he perceives a cost-benefit analysis of unintended consequential effects as an approach better suited to deter potential intruders from launching attacks.

The EU Policy on Cyber Defence is, first of all, an instrument for security and trust-building among the EU Member States. The Communication of the Commission and the High Representative for Foreign Affairs and Security Policy already outlines the possible foundations for these measures to be taken further within the EU: the EU cyber posture shall initially build on existing institutions such as the Permanent Structured Cooperation (PESCO) and Cyber Rapid Response Teams (CRRT). The basis at the level of primary law shall be Article 42(7)

[45] We argue that the EU Cybersecurity Strategy must be discussed alongside other external measures. Therefore, *cf* section IV.A for a detailed critique.

[46] JS Nye, 'Deterrence and Dissuasion in Cyberspace' (2017) 41 *International Security* 44, 44.

of the TEU and Article 222 of the Treaty on the Functioning of the European Union (TFEU).[47] In the following section, the competences of the Union institutions resulting from the EU treaties are outlined and evaluated.

B. Legal Basis

The solidarity clause of Article 222 of the TFEU is a special form of the solidarity principle that characterises the Union as a whole.[48] By decision of the Council under Article 222(3) of the TFEU, the Union may use 'all the instruments at its disposal, including the military resources made available to it by the Member States' in cases of terrorist threats or acts,[49] natural disasters or those caused by man.[50] Article 222 of the TFEU does not establish any competence of the Union in defence and security matters but contains an allocation of tasks for coordination purposes.[51] At the level of secondary law, Article 222 of the TFEU is significantly shaped by Council Decision 2014/415/EU[52] of 24 June 2014.

However, Article 222 of the TFEU only applies to cyber incidents committed by non-state actors; for those committed by state actors Article 42(7) of the TEU applies. At the level of international law, terrorist attacks have been defined as 'armed attacks' by Security Council Resolutions 1368 (2001) and 1373 (2001). They can thus trigger the right of self-defence according to Article 51 of the UN Charter,[53] reiterated in Article 42(7) of the TEU. In summary, it can be stated that cyberattacks by non-state actors, provided they fulfil the criteria of a 'terrorist offence', already permit the use of the solidarity clause and coordinating action by the Union.[54] However, this leaves so-called cyber proxies out of the equation, ie, groups that are officially non-state actors but are in fact supported or encouraged by state actors who are beneficiaries.[55] As such, they will often be subject to (indirect) responsibility under international customary law as substantiated in Articles 5 and 8 of the Articles of State Responsibility (ASR).[56] Yet, there is

[47] Treaty on the Functioning of the European Union (Rome, 25 March 1957).

[48] C Calliess, 'EUV/AEUV' in C Calliess and M Ruffert (eds), *AEUV/EUV*, 6th edn (München, CH Beck, 2022) Art 222 Recital 10.

[49] Art 222(1) lit a of the TFEU.

[50] Art 222(1) lit b of the TFEU.

[51] D Thym, 'Art 222 [Gegenseitige Unterstützung bei Terroranschlägen und Katastrophen]' in E Grabitz, M Hilf and M Nettesheim (eds), *Das Recht der Europäischen Union* (München, CH Beck, 2012) Recital 25.

[52] Council of the European Union, 'Council Decision of 24 June 2014 on the Arrangements for the Implementation by the Union of the Solidarity Clause' [2014] OJ L192/53.

[53] Charter of the United Nations (San Francisco, 26 June 1945).

[54] See also RA Wessel, 'Cybersecurity in the European Union' in E Conde, ZV Yaneva and M Scopelliti (eds), *The Routledge Handbook of European Security and Policy* (Milton, Routledge, 2019) 283–300.

[55] *cf* T Maurer, '"Proxies' and Cyberspace' (2016) 21 *Journal of Conflict & Security Law* 383, 390–399; different conceptions summarised by K Zettl-Schabath, 'Staatliche Cyberkonflikte. Proxy-Strategien von Autokratien und Demokratien im Vergleich' (Bielefeld, Transcript Verlag, 2023) 19–25.

[56] United Nations, 'Responsibility of States for Internationally Wrongful Acts' legal.un.org/ilc/texts/instruments/english/draft_articles/9_6_2001.pdf.

currently uncertainty about the state or non-state involvement in cyber incidents as the attribution of cyber incidents is rather difficult, as pointed out elsewhere.[57]

Furthermore, cyber incidents could be understood as a 'disaster'. This only covers 'man-made disasters' which are exceptional events such as a chemical plant explosion or a nuclear reactor accident, but also epidemics such as COVID-19 (Recital 20).[58]

In conclusion, although using Article 222 of the TFEU seems convincing in the current state of cyber affairs, we suggest updating the Council Decision 2014/415/EU for cyber incidents to institutionalise the use of Article 222 of the TFEU. It is also advisable that the Commission's capabilities in cyberspace are strengthened through secondary legislation, as has been done with the Cybersecurity Act in the past, using Article 114 of the TFEU.

C. Foreign and Defence Policy

The Policy on Cyber Defence takes up several EU defence initiatives, which, from their basis in the CFSP, are articulated more precisely in Articles 42 and 46 of the TEU. What is supposed to follow is a further development of existing projects in PESCO. This shall be done explicitly through the newly created EUCDCC modelled on the Cyber and Information Domain Coordination Centre (CIDDC), including the EU-INTCEN, as well as a network of military and civilian Computer Security Incident Response Teams of the Member States and the Computer Emergency Response Team of the EU institutions (CERT-EU).[59] These plans could be realised within the framework of PESCO under the existing rules.

However, the communication of the Commission and the High Representative also envisions the creation of a Cyber Situation and Analysis Centre at the Commission, to be supported by the European Union Agency for Cybersecurity (ENISA) and CERT-EU. Neither Article 42 nor Article 47 allow for such a permanent authority to be placed at the Commission. This would require a change of the treaties, which seems unrealistic in the current political situation and too time-consuming, given the current cyberspace threat levels.

D. Capacity Building Among Member States

The Cybersecurity Strategy also mentions jointly coordinated NATO-EU situational awareness in the cyber and information space but remains nonspecific about its implementation. The potential of the Helsinki-based European Centre of

[57] L Finlay and C Payne, 'The Attribution Problem and Cyber Armed Attacks' (2019) 113 *American Journal of International Law Unbound* 202, 202; H Lahmann, *Unilateral Remedies to Cyber Operations* (Cambridge, Cambridge University Press, 2020) 65–108.

[58] Thym (n 51) Recital 20.

[59] European Commission, 'EU Policy on Cyber Defence' [2022] JOIN 2022/49.

Excellence for Countering Hybrid Threats to build 'legal resilience' in relation to state interference is equally under-utilised in EU-NATO cooperation discourse. Some governments advocate active countermeasures similar to the USA and its demonstration of supremacy in cyberspace. Others, however, argue for developing a consensual frame of reference that assigns accountability to states according to their resilience measures to prevent conflict escalation in the cyber and information spaces.

The EU strategy seeks to integrate both approaches more effectively than in the past. To realise this ambition, the EEAS must be given stronger mandates regarding personnel, funding, and legal competence.

A pan-European and pan-societal approach to cybersecurity means formalising knowledge exchange between institutions, security authorities, academia, and industry. Defence and diplomacy in the cyber and information spaces remain sovereign tasks. However, these tasks are guided by principles of international law.[60] As established by the European Court of Human Rights (ECtHR) in a series of judgments starting with the *Loizidou v Turkey* judgment,[61] civil and political human rights must be protected in extraterritorial contexts by member states to the ECtHR and thus EU Member States. For the 'second generation of human rights', namely social, economic and cultural human rights, such jurisprudence does not exist. More refinement can be practised through the *Maastricht Principles*[62] as states are obliged to respect human rights first, protect them second (eg, through impact assessments), and last, fulfil them by keeping ICTs secure. These positive, extraterritorial human rights obligations shape an EU Member State's precautionary or 'due diligence' obligation.

V. The External Effects of EU Cyber Policy

As the Union moves forward in fostering digital sovereignty internally, Member States should also be prepared to update Europe's narrative as a force for peace in the digital age through more robust and coordinated foreign, security, and defence policies and by honouring their strategic orientation and institutional anchoring in EU cyber diplomacy. Based on this hypothesis, we develop in this section what a future cyber doctrine might look like along the lines of the EU's current 'external reaching' efforts.

[60] *cf* MC Kettemann and AS Tiedeke, 'Cybersecurity and Extraterritorial Obligations of States' in M Gibney et al (eds), *The Routledge Handbook on Extraterritorial Human Rights Obligations* (London, Routledge, 2021) 404–18.

[61] *Loizidou v Turkey* App No 15318/89 (ECtHR, 18 December 1996).

[62] International Court of Justice, 'Maastricht Principles on Extraterritorial Obligations of States in the Area of Economic, Social and Cultural Rights' (29 February 2012) www.icj.org/wp-content/uploads/2012/12/Maastricht-ETO-Principles-ENG-booklet.pdf.

A. EU Step-by-Step Approach to Cyber Diplomacy

In its cyber diplomacy efforts, the EU relies on CFSP Toolbox.[63] Its measures can be divided into preventative, cooperative, stabilising and restrictive, in addition to Member States' lawful responses by way of self-defence. Political measures are agreed upon in the EU Council with the assistance of the EEAS. In grave instances, malicious cyber activities could amount to the use of force or an armed attack. In the latter case, Member States can take a sovereign decision to exercise individual or collective self-defence as recognised in Article 51 of the UN Charter and in accordance with international and humanitarian law.

Regarding the EU's political dialogues with third states, it has developed cyber dialogues that aim to influence the behaviour and attitude of its dialogue partners. The EU also supports confidence-building measures (CBMs) such as those developed by the OSCE. Dialogues with regional organisations such as the African Union or the Association of Southeast Asian Nations (ASEAN) are particularly important. The EU and the respective regional body can define how to build the region's capacities for using cyberspace (known as 'cyber capacity building') in association, partnership or cooperation agreements, or even through the Instrument contributing to Stability and Peace (IcSP).

To facilitate the repression of an ongoing incident in a cooperative manner, an EU delegation in a host country can transmit a diplomatic note (*démarche*) to that country's government. This requires an instruction from the High Representative of the Union for Foreign Affairs and Security Policy. In a conflict situation, the delegation head can deliver a proposal to conduct comprehensive talks or merely convey key messages. *Démarches* can also be formulated and delivered together with third states. Where the EU delegation head has been recalled due to conflict, this type of cooperative solution is no longer possible.

Stability measures serve a signalling function by strategically communicating to a potential aggressor to refrain from engaging in malicious cyber activities. The European Council can adopt an EU act or position in this respect, but only unanimously. It can also pass a resolution to implement such an act. In that case, qualified-majority voting applies, except for acts of implementation concerning military affairs or defence.[64] The High Representative of the Union for Foreign Affairs and Security Policy can also make a declaration 'in the name of the EU'. However, this has to be agreed beforehand with all EU states. It is usually employed if there is no need for an immediate response, the EU has to work out its position vis-à-vis a new situation, or has modified an established position. However, the High Representative can also make a declaration under their own responsibility if a quick reaction is required but it is not possible to seek agreement from the EU 27.

[63] See generally, A Bendiek, 'The European Union's Foreign Policy Toolbox in International Cyber Diplomacy' (2018) 3 *Cyber, Intelligence, and Security* 57–71.

[64] Art 31(2) of the TEU.

The EU can impose restrictive measures (sanctions) if it intends to push through political objectives following serious cyberattacks.[65] These measures tend to target government officials of third states but also state companies or other legal or natural persons. Sanctions must be voted for unanimously in the Council and conform to the CFSP's objectives under Article 24 of the TEU. Sanctions can be divided into two main categories: those decided autonomously by the EU and those that the EU is obliged to impose following a resolution by the UN Security Council.[66] Under EU law, sanctions must be targeted. For instance, specific persons or companies may be put on a sanctions list in order to block their bank accounts as long as minimum rule-of-law standards are met. Until now, the EU has issued sanctions for a few incidents by introducing and amending Council Decision (CFSP) 2019/797.[67]

In this established system of diplomatic measures at the EU level, activating Article 222 of the TFEU can be seen as the fifth step between stability measures and sanctions. Regarding the specific threats in cyberspace, Article 222 of the TFEU can contribute to the emergence of a common understanding and uniform approach within the Member States and European institutions.

B. Filling-In the Vacuum between Cyber Diplomacy and Cyber Defence

As was said, by the end of 2022, EU Member States have adopted a Cyber Posture and a Cyber Defence Policy. So far, the main focus has been on interoperability and information sharing among military computer emergency response teams.[68] The EU Cyber Posture paves the way for closing the gap between cyber diplomacy and cyber defence (see Table 5.1 below).

Table 5.1 EU Cyber Posture[69] (Bendiek 2023)

Peace (prevent)	Peace (discourage)	Hybrid (deter)	War (respond)
Defensive (resilience)	Investigative (rule of law enforcement, mutual legal assistance, extradition)	Active Defence (restrictive measures, 'danger ahead')	Offensive defence ('electronic combat', 'hackbacks')

(continued)

[65] See chapters by Buchan (ch 9 in this volume) and Wrange (ch 10 in this volume).

[66] See chapter by Mikanagi (ch 6 in this volume).

[67] Council Decision (CFSP) 2019/797 of 17 May 2019 concerning restrictive measures against cyberattacks threatening the Union or its Member States [2019] OJ L129, 13. For a closer examination, *cf* A Bendiek and M Schulze, 'Attribution: A Major Challenge for EU Cyber Sanctions. SWP Research Paper 11' (*Stiftung Wissenschaft und Politik*, December 2021) www.swp-berlin.org/publications/products/research_papers/2021RP11_EU_CyberSanctions.pdf 20–33. The decision has recently been updated, *cf* https://eur-lex.europa.eu/legal-content/EN/ALL/?uri=CELEX:32024D1779.

[68] A Bendiek, 'Deutsche Cybersicherheit in Europa. Parliamentary Hearing' (*Deutscher Bundestag*, 25 January 2023) www.bundestag.de/resource/blob/930592/83771a56c9163cef28c5da493828f026/Stellungnahme-Bendiek-data.pdf.

[69] ibid 11.

Table 5.1 ***(Continued)***

Peace (prevent)	Peace (discourage)	Hybrid (deter)	War (respond)
Joint Cyber Unit, CSIRTs-EU, EU CyCLONe, EU INTCEN	Europol, Regulation (EU) 2022/991	ENISA, EU INTCEN, EUMS INTEL, Art 222 TFEU	Cyber Defence Force (Art 42(6) and (7) TEU, Art 4, 5 NATO Treaty)
Vulnerability remediation	Localisation	Attribution	Defence

The interplay between proportional deterrence and resilience by denial are critical elements of cybersecurity. According to ENISA, energy infrastructure is a particularly attractive target for cyberattacks,[70] as the consequences can be far-reaching and can be used as leverage for blackmail or as a starting point for military operations.

For this reason, the guidelines for companies in the energy sector have also included electrical power charging equipment. They complement the generation and transport infrastructures of the energy sub-sectors of natural gas, district heating, petroleum, electricity and hydrogen, which are classified as critical sectors. These measures implement individual due diligence obligations for IT security in peacetime. This is one of numerous strategies designed to build resilience.

For self-defence and risk management, governments also resort to intelligence, scan vulnerabilities, and, if necessary, use Trojans for prosecution (threat hunting).

Cyberattacks are classified as hybrid in the continuum between peace and war when cyber attacks on state infrastructure are launched with the malicious intent to manipulate or disrupt. These broad-based pinprick attacks are carried out by hacker groups acting on behalf of or tolerated by states. The distributed denial-of-service (DDoS) attacks by 'Killnet', a pro-Russian hacker group, have so far been comparatively harmless disruptive attacks that only restrict the web presence of western governments.[71] In 2022, 'Killnet' hackers published a list of German 'target' web addresses on their Telegram channel, presumably to inform their followers about their plans and to encourage them to participate. The websites of the Postbank and the Wiesbaden-based Areal Bank were listed, as well as hospitals and universities. Policy-makers must question whether such actions can be classified as a hybrid threat.

Theories about the potential impact of cyberattacks are currently being tested in reality. Ukraine experienced massive attacks on the country's digital infrastructure, individual websites, banks, and government and military offices before Russia's invasion. Since then, according to open-source information, there have been no new widespread or severe cyberattacks, or the ones launched by Russia were unsuccessful. One possible exception was the attack on the satellite link (ViaSat), which Ukraine used, among other purposes, for target acquisition and

[70] European Union Agency for Cybersecurity, 'Energy Sector' (*ENISA*) www.enisa.europa.eu/topics/critical-information-infrastructures-and-services/energy-sector.

[71] *cf* European Repository of Cyber Incidents, 'Table View' https://eurepoc.eu/table-view/ with Initator name 'KillNet'.

guidance of its artillery. This cyberattack caused failures in the control of wind turbines in Germany at the beginning of March.[72] Another one was a disruptive attack on Ukraine's largest telecommunications provider, Kyivstar, in December 2023.[73] However, Elon Musk's provision of an alternative communication network via Star Link ultimately thwarted the strategic aim of the attack.

Possible lessons from such cyberattacks, including for the EU's own information and communication infrastructures, have yet to be systematically evaluated. The EU is a potential target for hacking attacks pursuing tactical interests in the context of geostrategic conflicts. It was reported for example that the Dutch military intelligence service MIVD has uncovered in 2022 a network of routers of small and medium-sized businesses under the control of Sandworm, a Russian cyber unit that also caused the 2016 blackout in Ukraine.[74] Like sleeper cells in the Cold War, the routers could have been activated and used unnoticed by their controllers for espionage or sabotage.

The question to be asked is when is the threshold of the mutual assistance clause in the EU or the self-defence clause in NATO crossed? The political intention is to remain deliberately unclear about what constitutes an armed attack in cyberspace. For example, NATO has stipulated that a hacker attack can trigger Article 5 of the NATO Treaty[75] but – as in the case of conventional attacks – has left open exactly when this occurs. The intention is to keep the adversary in the dark so that it is not encouraged to test a defined threshold that could trigger a counteraction. However, this is problematic because it does not contribute to the expectation of reliability of actor behaviour, which, in principle, defuses conflict. Moreover, this logic fails to recognise that there is no need for a 'major cyberattack' to trigger Article 5 to the extent that many small cyberattacks or 'pinprick' attacks can cumulatively have sufficient impact. Furthermore, Russia and China do not conceptually separate war from peace as western democracies do. For them, hybrid war is a 'total war' countered by 'total defence'. Total war is not upstream of conventional uses of force; instead, the use of military force can but does not need to be part of a hybrid warfare strategy. It should be added that all levels of state power are used to influence and weaken strategic rivals in the West. This includes instrumentalising commodities such as gas, physical infrastructures and sea cables and conducting low-level cyber operations.

As far as the EU is concerned, it must determine which response to cyberattacks below the threshold of force is appropriate. Another course of action would be to supra-nationalise the EU cybersecurity agency ENISA and empower it with

[72] *cf* European Repository of Cyber Incidents, 'Viasat Hack: Russian Military Intelligence Disrupted Ukrainian Satellite Broadband Services' (February 2022) eurepoc.eu/table-view/?cyber_incident=1514.

[73] European Repository of Cyber Incidents, 'Presumed Russian Sandworm Hackers infiltrated Networks Of Ukrainian Telecommunications Provider Kyivstar As Early As May 2023 And Caused Massive Disruption On 12 December 2023' eurepoc.eu/table-view/?cyber_incident=2897.

[74] Russian state hacker target Dutch routers: Volkskrant, 3 March 2022: www.dutchnews.nl/2022/03/russian-state-hackers-target-dutch-routers-volkskrant/.

[75] North Atlantic Treaty (Washington DC, 4 April 1949).

an active operational defence capability in an emergency. In the meantime, tougher punitive measures could be enabled by activating Article 222 of the TFEU but not the military assistance clause, as discussed above.

VI. Concluding Thoughts on the EU's Contribution to Dispute Settlement

Since 2013, the EU has worked steadily to build a comprehensive cybersecurity policy, but only recently has it developed a cyber defence strategy. The EU has not yet been empowered to respond to large-scale cyber threats and to provide defence capabilities. A possible solution could be a solidarity commitment at the EU level by developing a common EU cyber doctrine under the head goal of 'digital sovereignty' and 'strategic autonomy'. More than ever, the EU is faced with the proposition that individual Member States are too small to hold their own in the competition between China, the USA and Russia, and the multitude of hybrid threats and cyberattacks. That said, the path to a Common Foreign and Security Policy has been largely unsuccessful.

Looking into the future, it is not only the Strategic and Digital Compasses that need to be interlinked but also 'internal measures' such as technical 'standardisation' through the Cyber Resilience Act and the NIS2 Directive or cyber diplomacy efforts. These (soft) laws – or rather the process of their genesis – should be at the core of a modern understanding of European digital sovereignty in its manifold dimensions. As was said, the concept of digital sovereignty is complex and is nowadays better understood as a process, not a status quo. Put differently, sovereignty no longer refers to a legally defined (territorial) status; instead, it needs to be understood in the context of EU actors' moderating capacity of legitimising their positions through transparent, internal opinion-forming processes and effectively exercising them internationally in multi-stakeholder bodies and institutions.[76] EU debates on norm harmonisation and subsequent standardisation contribute to deepening integration and advance internal re-sovereignisation. At the same time, EU norms and standards backed by all Member States carry significant political capital, which can be transformed into their successful externalisation, even leading to the exercise of a certain degree of regulatory power over foreign (and bigger) markets.[77] In this way, the internal re-sovereignisation process can strengthen European external re-sovereignisation. The so-called 'Brussels Effect' is essentially based on the reinforcement of European norms internally and externally.

[76] A Bendiek, 'The Impact of the Digital Service Act (DSA) and Digital Markets Act (DMA) on European Integration Policy. SWP Working Paper 02' (*Stiftung Wissenschaft und Politik*, April 2021) www.swp-berlin.org/publications/products/arbeitspapiere/WP0121_Bendiek_Digital_Service_Act_and_Digital_Markets_Act.pdf 5.

[77] A Bendiek and I Stürzer, 'Advancing European Internal and External Digital Sovereignty. SWP Comment No 20' (*Stiftung Wissenschaft und Politik*, March 2022) www.swp-berlin.org/publikation/advancing-european-internal-and-external-digital-sovereignty.

Although the EU is well aware of a looming geopolitical conflict in the digital sphere, as indicated in the Strategic Compass,[78] it is insufficiently prepared for such conflict. In addition to the designation of cyberspace as a domain of military operations (eg, the NATO declaration in 2016),[79] the capacity to develop, produce, and operate new and emerging technologies is increasingly discussed from a geopolitical perspective. Burrows et al point out that 'high tech has come to signify high politics', meaning that digital and technological sovereignty are no longer limited to the topic of trade conflicts but are fuel to the fire of actual international conflict – not least great power conflict.[80]

As a result, great power conflict driven by technological competition is already emerging between the USA and China. The EU is striving to avoid becoming the scene of a technological proxy war between the USA and China[81] by forming the EU-US Trade and Technology Council and introducing certification regimes and toolboxes, with the latter also included in the Strategic Compass. However, while these measures in themselves are insufficient to prevent such conflict due to a lack of coherent understanding of hybrid threats and corresponding counterstrategy, let alone political responsibility scattered across institutions, the EU lacks an understanding of security that is equivalent to concepts of 'sustainability' or 'resilience'.[82] The EU pursues digitalisation and connectivity across sectors and realises its economic potential while also increasing vulnerabilities, yet it remains unprepared to protect itself against these vulnerabilities' exploitation.

To support dispute settlement on an international level, the EU must walk a fine line by building resilience to deter attacks while not encouraging the further militarisation of cyberspace. Internal measures to deter cyberattacks can support a change in adversaries' behaviour. It is thus evident that the cyber resilience and cyber defence aspects of the bloc's cybersecurity strategy are interlinked with its cyber diplomacy.

With this in mind, EU cyber diplomacy is linked to its strategic capacity to act. It presupposes that the Union can also assert its ideas on data protection and cybersecurity internationally. A European 're-sovereignisation' of cyber diplomacy in the digital age means realising that a minimum degree of dominance or control by the EU over the necessary technological resources – from Internet nodes through cloud infrastructure to international standard-setting – is what

[78] European Commission (n 27).

[79] GA Crowther, 'The Cyber Domain' [2017] Fall *The Cyber Defense Review* 63–78.

[80] M Burrows et al, 'Unpacking the Geopolitics of Technology' (*Atlantic Council*, 8 December 2021) www.atlanticcouncil.org/in-depth-research-reports/report/unpacking-the-geopolitics-of-technology/.

[81] A Bendiek, N Godehardt and D Schulze, 'The Age of Digital Geopolitics' (*IPS*, 11 July 2019) www.ips-journal.eu/in-focus/chinas-new-power/the-age-of-digital-geopolitics-3593/.

[82] A Bendiek and R Bossong, '"Hybride Bedrohungen": Vom Strategischen Kompass zur Nationalen Sicherheitsstrategoe. SWP-Aktuell Nr 40' (*Stiftung Wissenschaft und Politik*, 23 June 2022) www.swp-berlin.org/publikation/hybride-bedrohungen-vom-strategischen-kompass-zur-nationalen-sicherheitsstrategie.

makes digital sovereignty possible in the first place, even though digital sovereignty is also central to maintaining the internal market to counter the sirens of isolationism and territorial sovereignty. The maxim of such 'strategic openness' in its institutional, democratic, and economic dimensions can ensure that the post-war era will not evolve into a digital prewar era. Cooperation between the EU and democracies such as the USA and Canada and harmonisation of IT security legislation might promote these value-based ambitions before a multilateral framework achieving dispute settlement is reached.

6

The Role of the Security Council in Addressing Malicious Cyber Operations that Threaten International Peace and Security

TOMOHIRO MIKANAGI*

I. Introduction

In recent years states have attributed malicious cyber operations to other states[1] and have instituted criminal proceedings or imposed sanctions on those allegedly involved in these operations.[2] If a state accuses another state of being involved in malicious cyber operations and the accused state denies the allegation, a dispute emerges. This dispute is likely to be centred around the issue of attribution, but there is no established international mechanism to resolve attribution disputes.[3] Although there have been various proposals for the establishment of international attribution mechanisms, none have materialised.[4] The United Nations (UN) General Assembly (GA) also established processes for discussing the application of international law to cyber operations such as the UN Group of Governmental

* The views expressed here are presented in his personal capacity and do not represent the official position of the Japanese Government.

[1] FJ Egloff and A Wenger, 'Public Attribution of Cyber Incidents' (2019) 244 *Center for Security Studies Analyses in Security Policy* 1, 1.

[2] For examples of US criminal investigations relating to cyber operations, see CI Keitner, 'Symposium on Cyber Attribution: Attribution by Indictment' (2019) 113 *American Journal of International Law Unbound* 207. For examples of national sanction regimes against malicious cyber operations, see MV Callo-Müller and I Bogdanova, 'Unilateral Cyber Sanctions and Global Cybersecurity Law-Making' (*OpinioJuris*, 24 January 2022) opiniojuris.org/author/maria-vasquez-callo-muller-and-iryna-bogdanova/.

[3] See Tsagourias (ch 1 in this volume). Also see N Tsagourias and F Middleton, 'Fact-Finding and Cyber Attribution' in R Buchan, D Franchini and N Tsagourias (eds), *The Changing Character of International Dispute Settlement: Challenges and Prospects* (Cambridge, Cambridge University Press, 2023) 439–466.

[4] Y Shany and MN Schmitt, 'An International Attribution Mechanism for Hostile Cyber Operations' (2020) 96 *International Law Studies* 196; N Tsagourias and M Farrell, 'Cyber attribution: technical and legal approaches and challenges' (2020) 31 *European Journal of International Law* (2020), 941.

Experts (GGE)[5] and the Open-Ended Working Group (OEWG).[6] However, their reports do not reveal any progress on how attribution disputes can be resolved. In any case, the success of an international attribution mechanism would depend on the willingness of states to provide evidence but, so far, attribution statements have not been accompanied by evidence supporting the attribution claims.[7] If states making attribution claims are reluctant to release evidence, it is difficult for any mechanism to make meaningful judgments on attribution. The reluctance of states to reveal and share evidence also seems to militate – at least for the time being – against the establishment of such a mechanism under UN auspices.[8] That said, the truth of the matter is that the increase in the number of malicious cyber operations and their seriousness, as well as the ensuing attribution disputes, can endanger international peace and security.

The 2015 GGE report pointed out:

> There are [...] disturbing trends in the global ICT environment, including a dramatic increase in incidents involving the malicious use of ICTs by State and non-State actors. These trends create risks for all States, and the misuse of ICTs *may harm international peace and security.*[9]

Faced with an operation that constitutes a threat to international peace and security and in the absence of an international attribution mechanism to identify the perpetrator, what can the victim state do to rally international action? The first option is to bring the matter before the Security Council (SC). As is well known, the SC has primary responsibility for the maintenance of international peace and security under Article 24 of the Charter, and Chapter VII endows it with broad mandatory powers. In this chapter, I will thus examine the role of the SC in the settlement of inter-state cyber disputes by looking at its powers under Chapter VII of the UN Charter.

If a cyber dispute is brought to the attention of the SC, it can determine that it constitutes a threat to international peace and security and take the necessary measures in order to maintain international peace and security.

The SC can for example condemn malicious cyber operations. The Council can also take particular measures in the form of sanctions under Article 41 of the UN Charter to suppress malicious cyber operations. In the following section, these possibilities are examined in more detail.

[5] See UNGA, 'Report of the Group of Governmental Experts on Advancing Responsible State Behaviour in Cyberspace in the Context of International Security' (14 July 2021) UN Doc A/76/135.

[6] See UNGA, 'Final Substantive Report of the Open-Ended Working Group on Developments in the Field of Information and Telecommunications in the Context of International Security' (10 March 2021) UN Doc A/AC.290/2021/CRP.2.

[7] Shany and Schmitt (n 4) 217.

[8] ibid 196, 213 and 221. See also T Mikanagi and K Mačák, 'Attribution of Cyber Operations: An International Law Perspective on the Park Jin Hyok Case' (2020) 9 *Cambridge International Law Journal* 51, 68–71.

[9] UNGA, 'Reports of the Group of Governmental Experts on Developments in the Field of Information and Telecommunications in the Context of International Security' (22 July 2015) UN Doc A/70/174 para 3 (emphasis added).

II. Condemn Malicious Cyber Operations

A. Threat to International Peace and Security

The 2015 GGE report has pointed out that the misuse of information and communications technologies (ICTs) may harm international peace and security. Paragraph 13(a) of the 2015 GGE report reads:

> Consistent with the purposes of the United Nations, including to maintain international peace and security, States should cooperate in developing and applying measures to increase stability and security in the use of ICTs and to prevent ICT practices that are acknowledged to be harmful or that *may pose threats to international peace and security.*[10]

The 2021 GGE report also stressed that 'incidents involving the malicious use of ICTs by States and non-State actors have increased in scope, scale, severity and sophistication'.[11]

To give an example of the scale of malicious cyber operation, in a 172-page-long affidavit published in June 2018,[12] a special agent of the Federal Bureau of Investigation (FBI) argued that Mr Park Jin Hyok, an alleged North Korean hacker, was a member of the conspiracy behind many cyber incidents, including the 2014 operation against Sony Pictures Entertainment (SPE), the 2016 operation against the Bangladesh Bank, and the 2017 WannaCry incident. According to the affidavit, the operation against SPE rendered thousands of SPE computer terminals inoperable, and the operation against a Bangladesh Bank caused a loss of approximately US$81 million. Concerning WannaCry, on 19 December 2017, the UK Foreign Office Minister Lord Ahmad of Wimbledon attributed the WannaCry incident to the so-called Lazarus Group, an actor linked to North Korea. According to Minister Ahmad, the WannaCry incident impacted 300,000 computers in 150 countries, including 48 National Health Service trusts.[13]

It follows that if the scope, scale, severity and sophistication of malicious cyber operations are increasing, the SC may qualify certain malicious cyber operations as a threat to international peace and security according to Article 39 of the UN Charter.

Even if individual operations may not amount to a threat to international peace and security, if a series of large-scale malicious cyber operations are bundled together, the aggregated harm caused by them to public and private assets and human health in various countries can be considerable. They might thus reach the

[10] UNGA, 'Reports of the GGE' UN Doc A/70/174 para 13(a) (emphasis added).

[11] UNGA, 'Report of the GGE', UN Doc A/76/135 para 6.

[12] US District Court for the Central District of California, *United States of America v Park Jin Hyok* (Case No MJ 18-1479, Criminal Complaint of 8 June 2018) Annex. See Mikanagi and Mačák (n 8).

[13] Foreign and Commonwealth Office, 'Press Release: Foreign Office Minister Condemns North Korean Actor for WannaCry Attacks' (*Government of the UK*, 19 December 2017) www.gov.uk/government/news/foreign-office-minister-condemns-north-korean-actor-for-wannacry-attacks.

threshold of a threat to international peace and security. In this respect, it should be recalled that the SC enjoys considerable discretion when determining a threat to international peace and security and it may take into account qualitative and quantitative criteria when making such determinations, and may also take into account other variables such as the risk of possible conflict.

B. Condemnation by the Security Council

If the SC determines that a particular malicious cyber operation constitutes a threat to international peace and security, it has the power to take necessary and appropriate measures to maintain or restore international peace and security.[14] Condemning states for threatening international peace and security is one such measure. For the SC to adopt a resolution condemning a state for being responsible for malicious cyber operations, it must garner nine affirmative votes, including the five permanent members (P5) (or at least secure their abstention).[15] This however means that, if the state alleged to be behind the malicious cyber operations is one of the P5 or a state aligned to one or more of the P5, it will be difficult to achieve the required support.

The SC has not passed yet any such resolution mainly due to the antagonism that exists between its members and the difficulties in attribution. However, issues of cyber security have been discussed by the SC.

On 21 February 2020, Georgia sent a letter to the Secretary-General and the President of the SC regarding alleged large-scale cyber operations launched against various targets in Georgia on 28 October 2019. The letter was circulated as a UN document[16] and, on 5 March 2020, the United States of America (US), the UK and Estonia raised this issue in the SC under 'Any Other Business'. They argued that Russia's military intelligence service, the GRU, conducted these operations, but no action was taken by the Council on this matter.

On 29 June 2021, under the presidency of Estonia, the Council addressed cyber threats to international peace and security in the first high-level open debate on cybersecurity in a formal setting. Following the open debate, Estonia circulated a draft presidential statement (PRST) on cybersecurity to Council members, but it was not adopted.[17]

[14] Art 24 of the UN Charter.

[15] Art 27 of the UN Charter.

[16] UNGA and UNSC, 'Protracted Conflicts in the GUAM Area and Their Implications for International Peace, Security and Development: Identical Letters dated 21 February 2020 from the Permanent Representative of Georgia to the United Nations Addressed to the Secretary-General and the President of the Security Council' (24 February 2020) UN Doc A/74/714-S/2020/135.

[17] Security Council Report, February 2022 Monthly Forecast, 'In Hindsight: The Security Council and Cyber Threats, an Update' (*February 2022 Monthly Forecast*, 31 January 2022) www.securitycouncilreport.org/monthly-forecast/2022-02/in-hindsight-the-security-council-and-cyber-threats-an-update.php.

Malicious cyber operations were also discussed by the SC in the context of sanctions against North Korea (the Democratic People's Republic of Korea or DPRK). The SC adopted resolutions imposing sanctions against the DPRK's nuclear and missile developments. On 26 May 2022, a draft resolution proposed by the USA for strengthening sanctions against the DPRK in response to the ballistic missile launch of 24 March 2022 and other repeated missile launches was debated by the SC. The draft resolution contained several paragraphs relating to malicious cyber activities, inter alia:

> Malicious Cyber Activity
>
> 21. *Expresses deep concern over the DPRK's pattern of malicious activity using ICT* against other Member States and individuals and entities subject to their jurisdiction, including financial institutions, for the purpose of evading sanctions and contributing to its nuclear and ballistic missile programs, and calls upon all Member States to take appropriate measures within their own jurisdictions, and in accordance with their respective legal processes, to prevent the DPRK and its nationals from using their territories to conduct or facilitate such malicious ICT activity, and clarifies that such measures could include but are not limited to, repatriating to the DPRK any DPRK national conducting malicious activities using ICT-enabled devices or networks and closing businesses associated with any such DPRK national.[18]

Annex II of the draft resolution contains a detailed description of malicious cyber activities by the Lazarus Group and explains its connection to the DPRK as follows:

> The Lazarus Group targets institutions such as government, military, financial, manufacturing, publishing, media, entertainment, and international shipping companies, as well as critical infrastructure, using tactics such as cyberespionage, data theft, monetary heists, and destructive malware operations. *Created by the Democratic People's Republic of Korea (DPRK) as early as 2007, this malicious cyber group is subordinate to the 110th Research Center, 3rd Bureau of the Reconnaissance General Bureau (RGB)* [KPe031]. The 3rd Bureau is also known as the 3rd Technical Surveillance Bureau and is responsible for many of the DPRK's cyber operations. In addition to the RGB's role as the main entity responsible for DPRK's malicious cyber activities, the RGB also continues to be the principal DPRK intelligence agency and is involved in the trade of DPRK arms.[19]

Draft Annex II also contains a detailed description of the malicious cyber operations conducted by the Lazarus Group, and the relevant part reads as follows:

> In 2020, the Lazarus group targeted critical infrastructure in India, a part of targeting aeronautics and defence sectors using 'DTrack' malware. Furthermore in 2020, the Lazarus Group conducted cyber operations against German and Russian defence companies as well as Russian energy and information technology sectors, which was a part of a cybercampaign called 'ThreatNeedle'.[20]

[18] UNSC, 'United States of America: Draft Resolution' (26 May 2022) UN Doc S/2022/431 para 21 (emphasis added).

[19] ibid Annex II 2(a) (emphasis added).

[20] ibid.

This detailed description of malicious cyber activities by the Lazarus Group and its connection to the DPRK is preceded by repeated references to the Lazarus Group's cyber activities and its relationship with the Reconnaissance General Bureau (RGB) in the reports of the Panel of Experts established pursuant to resolution 1874 (2009). Paragraph 26 of resolution 1874 (2009) reads:

> 26. Requests the Secretary-General to create for an initial period of one year, in consultation with the Committee, *a group of up to seven experts ('Panel of Experts')*, acting under the direction of the Committee to carry out the following tasks: (a) assist the Committee in carrying out its mandate as specified in resolution 1718 (2006) and the functions specified in paragraph 25 of this resolution; (b) *gather, examine and analyze information from States, relevant United Nations bodies and other interested parties* regarding the implementation of the measures imposed in resolution 1718 (2006) and in this resolution, in particular incidents of non-compliance; (c) *make recommendations on actions* the Council, or the Committee or Member States, may consider to improve implementation of the measures imposed in resolution 1718 (2006) and in this resolution; and (d) provide an interim report on its work to the Council no later than 90 days after adoption of this resolution, and a final report to the Council no later than 30 days prior to termination of its mandate with its findings and recommendations.[21]

In its report submitted to the SC Committee established under resolution 1718 (2006) (the 1718 Committee) on 1 February 2018, the Panel noted a trend in the DPRK's evasion of financial sanctions through cyber operations illegally forcing the transfer of funds from financial institutions and cryptocurrency exchanges.[22] It referred to the USA, the Republic of Korea and other Member States' view that the Lazarus Group and the RGB were involved in these activities.[23] The Panel also recommended to the 1718 Committee that '[i]nformation about cyberattacks conducted by the Reconnaissance General Bureau as a means to evade financial sanctions and to gain foreign currency should be added to the Reconnaissance General Bureau's entry on the 1718 sanctions list'.[24] The Panel published follow-up reports in 2019,[25] 2020,[26] 2021[27] and 2022.[28] It is interesting to note that

[21] UNSC, 'Resolution 1874 (2009) Adopted by the Security Council at its 6141st meeting, on 12 June 2009' (12 June 2009) UN Doc S/RES/1874 (2009) (emphasis added).

[22] UNSC, 'Resolution 1718 (2006) Adopted by the Security Council at Its 5551st Meeting, on 14 October 2006' (14 October 2006) UN Doc S/RES/1718 (2006).

[23] UN Doc S/2019/171 paras 109–14.

[24] ibid para 118.

[25] UNSC, 'Midterm Report of the Panel of Experts Submitted Pursuant to Resolution 2464 (2019)' (30 August 2019) UN Doc S/2019/691 paras 57–76.

[26] UNSC, 'Final Report of the Panel of Experts Submitted Pursuant to Resolution 2464 (2019)' (2 March 2020) UN Doc S/2020/151 paras 115–19 and 179–88; UNSC, 'Midterm Report of the Panel of Experts Submitted Pursuant to Resolution 2515 (2020)' (28 August 2020) UN Doc S/2020/840 paras 116–21 and 144–49.

[27] UNSC, 'Final Report of the Panel of Experts Submitted Pursuant to Resolution 2515 (2020)' (4 March 2021) UN Doc S/2021/211 paras 125–29, 156–61 and 164; UNSC, 'Midterm Report of the Panel of Experts Submitted Pursuant to Resolution 2569 (2021)' (8 September 2021) UN Doc S/2021/777 paras 153–55.

[28] UNSC, 'Final Report of the Panel of Experts Submitted Pursuant to Resolution 2569 (2021)' (1 March 2022) UN Doc S/2022/132 paras 154–61 and 182–84.

attribution was made by the Panel of Experts based on information gathered through its own research and information submitted by member states. The draft resolution was supported by 13 out of 15 members of the Council but was vetoed by China and Russia.[29]

Although malicious cyber operations were mentioned in the SC debates concerning North Korea, they were parasitic to the sanctions imposed against North Korea's nuclear and missile development. This means that malicious cyber activities were not the main concern of the SC and, in fact, cyber activities were examined in the context of the DPRK's evasion of financial sanctions and not as a threat in themselves.

The SC can further adopt a resolution condemning non-state actors involved in malicious cyber operations. This pertains in particular to operations with serious effects on economic activities, human lives or critical infrastructures in multiple states. By 'naming and shaming' them, the SC can prevent threats to international peace and security by putting states on alert.

The SC can also condemn states for allowing non-state actors to operate from their territory or infrastructure if strong evidence exists that the host state supported or acquiesced to such activities. The SC can thus mitigate disputes between states over the activities of non-state actors by putting pressure on them to suppress such activities.

If the Council is provided with sufficient evidence to attribute malicious cyber operations to a non-state actor but lacks sufficient evidence to prove a state's support or acquiescence, it can condemn the non-state actor without condemning a particular state. Even in this case, the state involved will probably feel political pressure to stop supporting or acquiescing to the activities of the non-state actor. This can mitigate disputes because, without the host state's support, it will be more difficult for the non-state actor to engage in malicious cyber operations against other states. The host state may also feel obliged to actively suppress the activities of non-state actors in its territory.

Although there is no relevant SC practice yet, an example from inter-state relations can be instructive. In the case of the Colonial Pipeline Incident in May 2021, President Biden stated:

> We do not believe – I emphasize, we do not believe the Russian government was involved in this attack. But we do have strong reason to believe that criminals who did the attack are living in Russia. That's where it came from – were from Russia.
>
> We have been in direct communication with Moscow about the imperative for responsible countries to take decisive action against these ransomware networks.[30]

[29] UNSC, 'Non-Proliferation/Democratic People's Republic of Korea' (26 May 2022) UN Doc S/PV.9048. In their statements immediately after the vote, China and Russia did not mention the references to cyber activity in the draft resolution as their reason for exercising their veto power.

[30] The White House, 'Remarks by President Biden on the Colonial Pipeline Incident' (13 May 2021) www.whitehouse.gov/briefing-room/speeches-remarks/2021/05/13/remarks-by-president-biden-on-the-colonial-pipeline-incident/.

Russia did not openly challenge these findings. Reports exist that Russia possibly took some measures to address the US's concerns.[31] This case shows that states may find it difficult to ignore calls for action if faced with strong evidence showing the existence of malicious cyber activities by non-state actors within their territory.

Alternatively, the SC can condemn malicious cyber operations without attributing them to or condemning any particular actor. In this case, members of the SC should have less reason to oppose the resolution. The SC's reaction to terrorism provides a good example. The SC adopted resolution 1368 immediately after the 9/11 terrorist attacks. It states that the SC is '[d]etermined to combat by all means threats to international peace and security caused by terrorist acts'[32] and '[un]equivocally condemns in the strongest terms the horrifying terrorist attacks which took place on 11 September 2001 in New York, Washington, DC and Pennsylvania and regards such acts, like any act of international terrorism, as a threat to international peace and security'.[33] It also '[c]alls on all States to work together urgently to bring to justice the perpetrators, organizers and sponsors of these terrorist attacks and stresses that those responsible for aiding, supporting or harbouring the perpetrators, organizers and sponsors of these acts will be held accountable'[34] and '[ca]lls also on the international community to redouble their efforts to prevent and suppress terrorist acts including by increased cooperation and full implementation of the relevant international anti-terrorist conventions and Security Council resolutions'.[35]

This resolution did not attribute the attack to a particular actor and did not condemn any particular actor, but it strongly condemned the '9/11' attacks themselves and called for cooperation against the attacks. Similar condemnation and calls for cooperation are made in many PRSTs and press statements.[36] For example, in PRST/2007/26: 'The Security Council *unequivocally condemns the terrorist attack that took place in Marib*, Republic of Yemen, on 2 July 2007' and 'urges all States, in accordance with their obligations under international law and resolution 1373 (2001), 1566 (2004) and 1624 (2005), to *cooperate with and provide support and assistance*, as appropriate, to the Government of Yemen in this regard. It also reaffirms that terrorism in all its forms and manifestations constitutes one of the most serious *threats to international peace and security*'.[37]

[31] S Lyngaas, 'US Officials Believe Russia Arrested Hacker Responsible for Colonial Pipeline Attack' (*CNN Politics*, 14 January 2022) edition.cnn.com/2022/01/14/politics/us-russia-colonial-pipeline-hack-arrest/index.html.

[32] UNSC, 'Resolution 1368 (2001) Adopted by the Security Council at Its 4370th Meeting, on 12 September 2001)' (12 September 2001) UN Doc S/RES/1368 (2001).

[33] UNSC, 'Resolution 1368' UN Doc S/RES/1368 para 1.

[34] ibid para 3.

[35] ibid para 4.

[36] For the rules adopting different types of outcomes, please refer to the Permanent Mission of Japan to the United Nations, 'Handbook on the Working Methods of the Security Council' (January 2021) www.un.org/securitycouncil/sites/www.un.org.securitycouncil/files/handbook_on_the_working_methods_of_the_security_council.pdf 77 (the annex on Major Types of Outcomes of the Security Council).

[37] UNSC, 'Statement by the President of the Security Council' (9 July 2007) UN Doc S/PRST/2007/26 (emphasis added). There are also other examples of PRSTs condemning terrorist attacks such as UNSC,

As an example of press statements condemning terrorist attacks without attribution, the press statement issued on the Manchester terrorist attack on 22 May 2017: '*condemned in the strongest terms the barbaric and cowardly terrorist attack which took place in Manchester*, United Kingdom'; 'reaffirmed that *terrorism in all its forms and manifestations constitutes one of the most serious threats to international peace and security*' and '*urged all States*, in accordance with their obligations under international law and relevant Security Council resolutions, *to cooperate actively* with the Government of United Kingdom and all other relevant authorities in this regard'.[38]

These statements take different forms, but they have similar content: they condemn terrorist acts and call for cooperation without actually naming the perpetrators of the acts.[39]

In the same vein, the SC can condemn certain types of malicious cyber operations as a threat to international peace and security, in particular those affecting critical state infrastructure such as medical facilities, financial services, energy, water, transportation and sanitation.[40] The SC can also call upon states to cooperate. Paragraph 51 of the 2021 GGE report refers to paragraph 13(h) of the 2015 GGE report, which calls for cooperation against malicious cyber operations aimed at the critical infrastructure of a state, and it states that such cooperation is particularly important when dealing with those operations that have the potential to threaten international peace and security.[41]

The SC has not as yet passed any resolution condemning malicious cyber operations, but the benefits of such practice should not be underestimated. By condemning malicious cyber operations, the SC clarifies which cyber activities are unacceptable from the perspective of the maintenance of international peace and security. Consequently, it would be politically more difficult for states or non-state actors to engage in or support such cyber activities. This, in turn, will contribute to the prevention and de-escalation of disputes among states. Moreover,

'Statement by the President of the Security Council' (27 December 2007) UN Doc S/PRST/2007/50; UNSC, 'Statement by the President of the Security Council' (2 June 2008) UN Doc S/PRST/2008/19; UNSC, 'Statement by the President of the Security Council' (21 August 2008) UN Doc S/PRST/2008/32; UNSC, 'Statement by the President of the Security Council' (22 September 2008) UN Doc S/PRST/2008/35; and UNSC, 'Statement by the President of the Security Council' (17 July 2009) UN Doc S/PRST/2009/22.

[38] UN Press release SC/12833, 23 May 2017 (emphasis added).

[39] For examples of numerous press statements condemning terrorist attacks, see Security Council Report, 'UN Documents for Counter-Terrorism' www.securitycouncilreport.org/un-documents/counter-terrorism/.

[40] Paragraph 18 of the UNGA, 'Final Substantive Report of the OEWG', UN Doc A/AC.290/2021/CRP.2 reads: 'While it is each State's prerogative to determine which infrastructures it designates as critical, such infrastructure may include medical facilities, financial services, energy, water, transportation and sanitation.'

[41] For various possibilities of triggering Chs VI and VII of the Charter in the ICT environment, see T de Souza Dias, *Applying Chapters VI and VII of the Charter of the United Nations in the Cyber Context: the Challenges And Opportunities of Information and Communications Technologies* (Geneva, Switzerland: UNIDIR, 2021) unidir.org/wp-content/uploads/2023/05/UNIDIR_UN_Charter_in_Cyber_Context.pdf.

condemnation of a malicious cyber operation and a call for cooperation may assist states affected by such operations to demand their suppression whereas states from whose territory the malicious cyber operations emanate are put on notice to supress them.

C. The Uniting for Peace Procedure

What happens if a state launches a malicious cyber operation against another state causing very serious damage but because of the veto, the SC fails to respond? In such a case the GA may make recommendations to Member States for the maintenance of international peace and security according to the procedure under the 1950 *Uniting for Peace* resolution.[42] The GA cannot adopt legally binding resolutions as the SC can do under Article 25 of the UN Charter, but if a resolution is adopted with an overwhelming majority[43] condemning a state for its involvement in a malicious cyber operation against another state, it carries significant political weight which may lead to strong political pressure on the addressee of the resolution. For this to happen, there must be convincing evidence showing the attribution of the cyber operations to the state so that the overwhelming majority of Member States are persuaded to vote for the resolution.

III. Imposition of Sanctions against Individuals and Entities Involved in Malicious Cyber Operations

A. Targeted Sanctions

If there are malicious cyber operations with serious effects on economic activities, human lives or critical infrastructures in multiple states and the SC adopts a resolution determining that they amount to a threat to international peace and security under Article 39 of the UN Charter, it can consider the adoption of sanctions under Article 41.

It is true that certain states have already introduced laws authorising economic restrictions on actors responsible for malicious cyber activities.[44] However, without the cooperation of the states whose territories are used by these actors, their effectiveness is limited. The role of the SC is thus critical because of the universal scope and binding effect of its sanctions. The SC can impose sanctions, including

[42] UNGA, 'Resolution Adopted by the General Assembly. 377(V). Uniting for Peace' (3 November 1950) UN Doc A/RES/5/377.

[43] See, eg, the General Assembly resolutions on Ukraine UN Doc A/RES/ES-11/1 and UN Doc A/RES/ES-11/4.

[44] Callo-Müller and Bogdanova (n 2).

an asset freeze and travel ban for the individuals and entities involved in such operations. Even if the host state denies its support or knowledge of the activities of said actors, it will be difficult to oppose the implementation of the SC-mandated measures if the financial assets of the individuals or entities listed in the resolution are in that state's territory or the listed individuals travel to or from that state. Such a resolution may not directly resolve the dispute between states over allegations of support or acquiescence to malicious cyber operations by non-state actors, but if it is implemented correctly, it can assist in the prevention or non-aggravation of the dispute between the accusing and accused state, because it will make the activities of the non-state actor more difficult or suppress them entirely. To date, the SC has not adopted any resolution imposing targeted sanctions on individuals or entities for their malicious cyber activities.

An example of an attempt to do this was the vetoed draft resolution on North Korea mentioned above.[45] In paragraph 5, the drafters intended to add the Lazarus Group to the sanction list and impose the measures specified in paragraph 8(d) of resolution 1718 (2006) based on the work of the Panel of Experts established by resolution 1874. Resolution 1718 imposes asset freeze as follows:

> (d) All Member States shall, in accordance with their respective legal processes, *freeze immediately the funds, other financial assets and economic resources which are on their territories* at the date of the adoption of this resolution or at any time thereafter, that are *owned or controlled, directly or indirectly, by the persons or entities designated* by the Committee or by the Security Council as being engaged in or providing support for, including through other illicit means, DPRK's nuclear-related, other weapons of mass destruction-related and ballistic missile-related programmes, or *by persons or entities acting on their behalf or at their direction*, and ensure that any funds, financial assets or economic resources are prevented from being made available by their nationals or by any persons or entities within their territories, to or for the benefit of such persons or entities.[46]

It should be noted that the effectiveness of targeted sanctions depends on their implementation by states whose territories are used for the activities of the listed entity or individual whereas their effective monitoring by the SC and its subsidiary bodies is essential.

B. Measures Other than Asset Freezes and Travel Bans

Malicious cyber actors may use illicit online financial transactions not only to gain profit, but also to fund their activities. Therefore, in addition to the asset freeze and travel ban, the SC can adopt a resolution imposing strict control and increased vigilance over illicit financial transactions relating to malicious cyber operations. This includes transactions of virtual assets and virtual asset service providers (VASPs).

[45] UNSC, 'United States of America: Draft Resolution' (26 May 2022) UN Doc S/2022/431.
[46] UNSC, 'Resolution 1718 (2006)' UN Doc S/RES/1718 para 8(d) (emphasis added).

The Panel of Experts established by resolution 1874 (2009) made several recommendations relating to the strengthening of the regulatory frameworks for virtual assets and VASPs.[47] In this area, the Financial Action Task Force (FATF) has been adopting new recommendations. In June 2019, the FATF revised its Recommendation 15 and included reference to VASPs as underlined below:

> Recommendation 15 – New Technologies
>
> Countries and financial institutions should identify and assess the money laundering or terrorist financing risks that may arise in relation to (a) the development of new products and new business practices, including new delivery mechanisms, and (b) the use of new or developing technologies for both new and pre-existing products. In the case of financial institutions, such a risk assessment should take place prior to the launch of the new products, business practices or the use of new or developing technologies. They should take appropriate measures to manage and mitigate those risks. To manage and mitigate the risks emerging from virtual assets, *countries should ensure that virtual asset service providers are regulated for AML/CFT purposes, and licensed or registered and subject to effective systems for monitoring and ensuring compliance with the relevant measures called for in the FATF Recommendations.*[48]

In July 2021, it adopted the 'Second 12-Month Review of the Revised FATF Standards on Virtual Assets and Virtual Asset Service Providers' and published the following findings in the report:

> 71. The types of offences involving virtual assets include ML, the sale of controlled substances and other illegal items (including firearms), fraud, tax evasion, sanctions evasion, *computer crimes (e.g. cyberattacks resulting in thefts or ransomware)*, child exploitation, human trafficking and TF. Among these, narcotics-related and fraud offences (e.g. investment scams and swindling, blackmail, and extortion) are the most prevalent. *There has been a large increase in the value of virtual assets collected as ransomware payments and in the use of virtual assets to commit and launder the proceeds of fraud in the last year, which is consistent with the general pattern of misuse of online financial services as a result of COVID-19-related confinement measures.* In particular, the pace and sophistication of *ransomware* attacks continued to increase in 2021 rapidly, victimizing, notably, governments, schools, hospitals, and other critical infrastructure providers all over the world. The proceeds of such ransomware attacks are often moved via unhosted or privacy wallets and/or other anonymity-enhancing tools and methods to VASPs, where they are exchanged for other virtual assets or fiat currency and can be used by illicit actors *to pay for their criminal enterprises*. Separately, sophisticated illicit activity by state actors using virtual assets for *sanctions evasion* has also been observed.[49]

[47] UNSC, 'Midterm Report (2019)' UN Doc S/2019/691 paras 73–75; UNSC, 'Final Report (2019)' UN Doc S/2020/151 para 186.

[48] Public Statement on Virtual Assets and Related Providers (21 June 2019) www.fatf-gafi.org/en/publications/Fatfrecommendations/Public-statement-virtual-assets.html; 'The FATF Recommendations' www.fatf-gafi.org/en/publications/Fatfrecommendations/Fatf-recommendations.html (emphasis added).

[49] FATF, 'Second 12-Month Review of Revised FATF Standards – Virtual Assets and VASPs' (5 July 2021) www.fatf-gafi.org/en/publications/fatfrecommendations/documents/second-12-month-review-virtual-assets-vasps.html (emphasis added).

These measures aim to strengthen the regulation of money laundering (ML) and terrorist financing (TF). They should also be useful to suppress malicious cyber activities – not necessarily relating to terrorism – that increasingly involve the use of virtual assets.

By doing so, malicious cyber activities, including ransomware attacks, can at least be made more difficult. These measures can also contribute to the prevention of further malicious operations which might cause disputes or escalate tensions between states. This kind of recommendation might require technical and other assistance to be provided to certain Member States. In the area of counterterrorism cooperation, after the 9/11 attacks the SC unanimously adopted resolution 1373 (2001),[50] establishing a Counter-Terrorism Committee (CTC) assisted by an Executive Directorate (CTED). The CTC and CTED have been carrying out expert assessments of Member States' implementation of relevant resolutions. There is no subsidiary body relating to cybersecurity established under the SC. Other UN organs such as UNODA and UNODC can, within their respective mandates and resources, be tasked by the SC or GA to assist Member States in strengthening control over illicit online financial transactions and increasing vigilance over such transactions for the prevention of their involvement in malicious cyber operations. Alternatively, even though it is not foreseeable now, a subsidiary body like the CTC and CTED can be theoretically established by the SC for cybersecurity if it can gain sufficient support among Council members.

IV. Strengthen Cooperation Mechanisms Among States

Cyber operations can be implemented through proxies and multiple aliases operating from within multiple states. This increases the risk of disputes, but the suppression of malicious cyber operations requires collective and coordinated action. This raises the issue of cooperation between states to prevent unnecessary disputes and suppress malicious cyber operations.

This issue was addressed in the 2015 GGE Report,[51] whereas the 2021 Report states that:

> A State receiving a request for assistance needs to determine, in as transparent and timely a fashion as possible and respecting the urgency and sensitivity of the request, whether it has the capabilities, capacity and resources to provide the assistance requested. States from which the assistance is requested are not expected to ensure a particular result or outcome.[52]

[50] UNSC, 'Resolution 1373 (2001) Adopted by the Security Council at Its 4385th Meeting, on 28 September 2001' (28 September 2001) UN Doc S/RES/1373 (2001).

[51] UNGA, 'Reports of the GGE', UN Doc A/70/174 para 13(h).

[52] UNGA, 'Report of the GGE', UN Doc A/76/135 para 53.

The UN can facilitate cooperation by assisting communication among states. The GGE reports addressed confidence-building measures and called for the appointment of Points of Contacts (PoCs).[53] In 2021, the OEWG report pointed out that:

> States concluded that establishing national Points of Contact (PoCs) is a CBM in itself, but is also a helpful measure for the implementation of many other CBMs, and is invaluable in times of crisis. States may find it useful to have PoCs for, inter alia, diplomatic, policy, legal and technical exchanges, as well as incident reporting and response.[54]

It also recommended that:

> 51. States, which have not yet done so, consider nominating a national Point of Contact, inter alia, at the technical, policy and diplomatic levels, taking into account differentiated capacities. States are also encouraged to continue to consider the modalities of establishing a directory of such Points of Contact at the global level.[55]

Regarding the role that the UN can play in this regard, the 2021 GGE Report reads:

> 78. Addressing global ICT security threats also requires global approaches that are both inclusive and universal. *States could invite the United Nations Secretary-General* to facilitate voluntary exchanges between all Member States on lessons, good practices and guidance relevant to PoC networks that are already in place at the regional and subregional levels. Such work could contribute to discussions relevant to the establishment of a *directory of such PoCs* at the global level.[56]

The SC or GA may adopt a resolution requesting the UN Secretary-General to facilitate voluntary exchanges among Member States. This can be done in response to a particular cyber incident or as a standing request applicable to future incidents.

Alternatively, cooperation among states can be promoted through multilateral treaties. On 27 December 2019, the GA adopted resolution 74/247 and decided to establish

> an open-ended ad hoc intergovernmental committee of experts, representative of all regions, to elaborate a comprehensive international convention on countering the use of information and communications technologies for criminal purposes, taking into full consideration existing international instruments and efforts at the national, regional and international levels on combating the use of information and communications technologies for criminal purposes.[57]

In May 2021, the Ad Hoc Committee convened a three-day organisational session in New York. On 26 May 2021, the GA adopted resolution 75/282, entitled 'Countering the use of information and communications technologies for

[53] UNGA, 'Reports of the GGE', UN Doc A/70/174 para 16(a).
[54] UNGA, 'Final Substantive Report of the OEWG', UN Doc A/AC.290/2021/CRP.2 para 47.
[55] ibid para 51.
[56] UNGA, 'Report of the GGE', UN Doc A/76/135 para 78 (emphasis added).
[57] UNGA, 'Resolution Adopted by the General Assembly on 27 December 2019: 74/247. Countering the Use of Information and Communications Technologies for Criminal Purposes' (20 January 2020) UN Doc A/RES/74/247 para 2.

criminal purposes', and decided that the Ad Hoc Committee 'shall convene for at least six sessions of 10 days each, to commence in January 2022, and conclude its work to provide a draft convention to the GA at its 78th session'.[58] The Ad Hoc Committee held its first session from 28 February to 11 March 2022 and approved the roadmap and mode of work for the Committee.[59] The revised draft text of the convention presented by the Ad Hoc Committee in early 2024 includes provisions on issues such as criminalisation, jurisdiction, international cooperation, preventive measures, technical assistance and information exchange.[60] If the convention is adopted[61] and strengthens communication and cooperation between criminal law enforcement authorities, this will may eventually contribute to the avoidance of misunderstandings that could lead to disputes among states.

V. Conclusion

Malicious cyber operations such as ransomware have imposed heavy costs on our societies but can also threaten international peace and security. The SC can play an important role in this regard because it has primary responsibility for the maintenance of international peace and security. If malicious cyber operations, which pose a threat to international peace and security, occur and a dispute arises among states, the SC should make efforts to find out who the perpetrator of the operations is and examine the claims relating to the possible involvement of states or non-state actors. If the SC is not able to condemn those involved in such malicious cyber operations or impose sanctions, it can still condemn certain cyber activities as unacceptable for the maintenance of international peace and security. The GGE and OEWG have already contributed to the clarification of unacceptable cyber operations and indicated that malicious cyber operations with a serious impact on critical infrastructure could amount to a threat to international peace and security.

In the area of counterterrorism, the 9/11 attacks in 2001 seemed to be a watershed moment for the SC to become active in taking measures to suppress terrorism and maintain international peace and security. However, concerning cybersecurity, will there be a watershed moment for the SC to become more active in this area?

[58] UNGA, 'Resolution Adopted by the General Assembly on 26 May 2021: 75/282. Countering the Use of Information and Communications Technologies for Criminal Purposes' (1 June 2021) UN Doc A/RES/75/282 para 4.

[59] UNGA, 'Report of the Ad Hoc Committee to Elaborate a Comprehensive International Convention on Countering the Use of Information and Communications Technologies for Criminal Purposes on Its First Session' (24 March 2022) UN Doc A/AC.291/7.

[60] UNGA, 'Further revised draft text of the Convention' (6 February 2024) UN Doc A/AC.291/22/Rev.2. See also chapter by Iakovidis (Chapter 7 in this volume).

[61] UNGA 'Report of the Ad Hoc Committee to Elaborate a Comprehensive International Convention on Countering the Use of Information and Communications Technologies for Criminal Purposes on its concluding session' (23 February 2024) UN Doc A/AC.291/26.

PART III

Methods

7

The Brave New World of Cyberspace: Do Traditional Diplomatic Tools Apply to Cyber?

IAKOVOS V IAKOVIDIS*

I. Introduction

In his dystopian 1932 novel, *Brave New World*, Aldous Huxley describes a future where technical progress seems to guarantee an effortless and pain-free life for the citizens of the World State.[1] The emergence of new technologies, or the Fourth Industrial Revolution,[2] has brought reality a step closer to the book's plot. Quantum computing, the Internet of Things, neurotechnology, machine-to-human interaction, and the World Wide Web laid the foundation for a new international space: cyberspace. But as in Huxley's vision, the future was not immune from turbulence, so the new cyber world is still facing some of the scourges of the old era, both domestic and transboundary. Organised crime, ransomware, election meddling, human rights violations, threats to international peace and security,[3] encroachments on sovereignty, and terrorist attacks are only a few of the challenges that the new system and its actors are facing. Cyber attacks are the main instrument through which these activities are carried out. Given the international character of these attacks, one may legitimately wonder whether a traditional tool of international relations, namely diplomacy, plays a role in cyberspace and whether established diplomatic tools of dispute settlement apply to cyberspace.

According to a traditional definition, 'diplomacy is the application of intelligence and tact to the conduct of official relations between the governments of

* The views and opinions expressed in this chapter are the author's, writing in his personal capacity, and do not necessarily reflect the views or positions of any entity he represents.

[1] A Huxley, *Brave New World* (London, Chatto and Windus, 1932).

[2] K Schwab, *The Fourth Industrial Revolution* (New York, Crown Business, 2016) 1.

[3] UNGA, 'Open-Ended Working Group on Developments in the Field of Information and Telecommunications in the Context of International Security, Chair's Summary' (10 March 2021) UN Doc A/AC.290/2021/CRP.3, 7.

independent states …, and between governments within international institutions; or, more briefly, the conduct of business between states by peaceful means'.[4] Diplomacy underpins state interaction through peaceful means and the use of peaceful means also underpins the settlement of inter-state disputes. More specifically, the interdiction of the use of force in the relations between states formulated in the United Nations (UN) Charter[5] has its corollary in the duty to settle their disputes peacefully.[6] This customary rule is enshrined in Articles 2(3) and 33 of the UN Charter. The latter reflects previous formulations of this duty, as in the 1899 and 1907 Hague Conventions for the Pacific Settlement of International Disputes,[7] the 1919 Covenant of the League of Nations,[8] and the 1928 Briand-Kellogg Pact.[9] It contains a non-exhaustive list of means for the peaceful settlement of disputes, such as mediation, conciliation, enquiry, arbitration, recourse to the courts, and negotiation.[10]

The reference to 'any dispute' in Article 33 discards any claim that there is differentiation between disputes. We should thus adopt the broadest definition of a dispute,[11] as defined by the Permanent Court of International Justice in the case of *Mavrommatis Concessions in Palestine*: 'A dispute is a disagreement on a point of law or fact, a conflict of legal views or of interests between two persons.'[12] Moreover, Article 33 is a 'hinge provision' between the articles in the Charter which establish substantive rights and obligations to guide state behaviour, and rules governing the functions of UN organs concerning the peaceful settlement of disputes.[13] As Article 33 explains, the dispute needs to be one 'the continuance

[4] I Roberts (ed), *Satow's Diplomatic Practice*, 7th edn (Oxford, Oxford University Press, 2017) 1.1.

[5] Art 2(4) of the Charter of the United Nations (San Francisco, 26 June 1945) (UN Charter).

[6] Art 2(3) of the UN Charter. See also *Case Concerning Military and Paramilitary Activities in and against Nicaragua (Nicaragua v United States of America)* (Merits, Judgment of 27 June 1986) [1986] ICJ Rep 14, 145 para 290. See also UNGA, 'Manila Declaration on the Peaceful Settlement of International Disputes' (15 November 1982) UN Doc A/RES/37/10 Annex, para 2. For an analysis of the Declaration, see C Economidès, 'La Déclaration de Manille sur le Règlement Pacifique des Différends Internationaux' (1982) *Annuaire Français de Droit International* 613.

[7] Art 1 in the Convention for the Pacific Settlement of International Disputes (The Hague, 29 July 1899), and the Convention for the Pacific Settlement of International Disputes (The Hague, 18 October 1907).

[8] 'Pacte de la Société des Nations' (1920) 1 *League of Nations Official Journal* 3.

[9] General Treaty for Renunciation of War as an Instrument of National Policy (Paris, 27 August 1928).

[10] Art 33 of the UN Charter. '1. The parties to any dispute, the continuance of which is likely to endanger the maintenance of international peace and security, shall, first of all, seek a solution by negotiation, enquiry, mediation, conciliation, arbitration, judicial settlement, resort to regional agencies or arrangements, or other peaceful means of their own choice. 2. The Security Council shall, when it deems necessary, call upon the parties to settle their dispute by such means.'

[11] H Ascensio, 'Chapitre VI Règlement pacifique des différends – Article 33' in JP Cot and A Pellet (eds), *La Charte des Nations Unies, Commentaire article par article*, 3rd edn (Paris, Economica, 2005) 1047–1060, 1049.

[12] *The Mavrommatis Palestine Concessions* (Judgment of 30 August 1924) PCIJ Rep Series A No 2, 11. See also chapters by Tsagourias (ch 1 in this volume) and Antonopoulos (ch 4 in this volume).

[13] JP Queneudec (ed), *La Charte des Nations Unies, Commentaire article par article*, 2nd edn (Paris, Economica, 1991) 566.

of which is likely to endanger the maintenance of international peace and security' which practically means that the obligation not to use force to settle disputes and the obligation to settle disputes peacefully cover situations just below those covered by Chapter VII of the UN Charter.[14]

Leaving aside mediation, arbitration, and litigation,[15] this chapter focuses on inter-state diplomacy, specifically on bilateral, regional and multilateral engagement, as a mechanism for the settlement of cyber disputes.[16] Diplomacy lies at the heart of Article 33 and revolves mostly around one of the means provided in Article 33 (which is often confused with diplomacy itself), namely, negotiation. Negotiation in a diplomatic context can be perceived as the political pursuit of an agreed outcome through consultation with other parties. In a dispute context, diplomatic negotiations constitute the most common way of dispute settlement.[17] Whether in a global, regional, or bilateral framework, diplomacy brings opposing parties to the table. It creates channels of communication where information is exchanged and the main parameters of the dispute to be solved are identified. It helps to build trust – through, among other means, confidence-building measures – between the actors involved in the dispute. It establishes an enabling environment for a long-lasting commitment to a peaceful solution.

Within the context of a 'hybrid and networked rule of law' in cyberspace, which corresponds to its interconnectedness and multi-agency,[18] I posit that diplomacy is a pertinent means of settling cyber disputes and can also be an effective means. I will evidence this by explaining how diplomacy adjusts its traditional tools in the cyber context to support and promote the peaceful settlement of cyber disputes. With this in mind, I will consider how diplomacy unfolds its potential in various political contexts (section II), and in particular in the bilateral (section III), regional (section IV) and global circles (section V) to resolve disputes arising from the malicious use of information and communications technologies (ICTs).

II. Diplomacy and Dispute Settlement

Modern diplomacy, and its instantiation as negotiation, can be perceived as a system articulated within three concentric circles, each of which addresses the

[14] Ascensio (n 11) 1051.

[15] F Sander and L Rozdeiczer, 'Selecting an Appropriate Dispute Resolution Procedure: Detailed Analysis and Simplified Solution' in M Moffitt and R Bodrone (eds), *Handbook of Dispute Resolution* (San Francisco, Jossey-Bass, 2005) 386.

[16] John Merills distinguishes diplomatic/political from legal means of dispute settlement. While negotiation, mediation, enquiry, and conciliation belong to the former, arbitration and judicial settlement belong to the latter. Analysing the trends and prospects of the peaceful settlement of disputes, the author notes that negotiation remains the basic means of resolving disputes peacefully. JG Merills, *International Dispute Settlement*, 5th edn (Cambridge, Cambridge University Press, 2011) 284.

[17] Roberts (n 4) 24.13.

[18] N Tsagourias, 'The Rule of Law in Cyberspace: A Hybrid and Networked Concept?' (2020) 80 *Zeitschrift fur Auslandisches Offentliches Recht und Volkerrecht* 433, 434.

peaceful settlement of disputes in its own unique and complementary way. The first is the bilateral circle, which comprises the entire spectrum of state-to-state relations. Whether between neighbouring states or states located afar, friends or foes, bilateral diplomacy is the cornerstone of the international system regarding inter-state relations and disputes. The proverbial 'diplomatic channel' is activated, and bilateral meetings are held between parties while holding Ariadne's thread, which will lead them out of the dispute maze. Moving outwards, the second circle is the regional circle, which consists mainly of alliances of states based on ideological, military, economic, or other affinities. The Organization of American States (OAS), the Economic Community of West African States (ECOWAS) and the Association of Southeast Asian Nations (ASEAN) are just some indicative paradigms of this circle of diplomacy. The emergence of these groupings can be traced back to amphictyonies in Ancient Greece, where city-states were coalescing around a holy shrine to weave political and military bonds.[19] In this circle, dispute settlement is more often than not assisted by the regional organisation itself and aided by participating states, as well as by guidelines, confidence-building and other measures. The role and importance of regional organisations in cyber dispute settlement cannot be stressed enough, particularly in encouraging states to act responsibly in cyberspace.[20] Finally, the external circle is the global circle, where intergovernmental organisations attempt to devise global solutions through multilateral cooperation. Dispute settlement acquires a global dimension since the issue to be resolved is brought to the international community's attention, and appropriate procedures can be used to achieve a negotiated outcome. As will be seen below, the UN, the global institution par excellence, is elaborating both voluntary norms and binding rules to enable, among others, the peaceful settlement of cyber disputes. And though one can justifiably question the effectiveness of international law,[21] at the same time, a rule-based negotiation can yield significant results and underline the pacifying role of international law.[22]

Trying to depict these three diplomatic circles, we could imagine their centre to comprise the dispute to be solved. The radius from the centre refers to the political distance between involved parties, shorter in the bilateral circle, longer in the

[19] See Thucydides, 'The Peloponnesian War' in M Hammond and PJ Rhodes (eds), *Oxford World's Classics* (Oxford, Oxford University Press, 2009).

[20] Additionally, among other functions, regional organisations are useful fora to discuss ICT issues and facilitate the implementation of cyber norms. UK Foreign, Commonwealth and Development Office, 'Acting Responsibly in Cyberspace, Summary Report: Wilton Park Conference WP3146' (November 2022) www.wiltonpark.org.uk/app/uploads/2023/01/WP3146-Summary-Report-Acting-Responsibly-in-Cyberspace-Nov-2022-1.pdf 2.

[21] See, eg, BA Simmons and DJ Hopkins, 'The Constraining Power of International Treaties: Theories and Methods' (2005) 99 *American Political Science Review* 623. See also J von Stein, 'Do Treaties Constrain or Screen? Selection Bias and Treaty Compliance' (2005) 99 *American Political Science Review* 611.

[22] P Huth, SE Croco and B Appel, 'Does International Law Promote the Peaceful Settlement of International Disputes? Evidence from the Study of Territorial Conflicts Since 1945' (2011) 105 *American Political Science Review* 415.

global circle, whereas the circumference indicates the increasing – as it gets larger – number of participating states in the regional and global circle. Of course, sovereignty is the ineluctable canvass behind all three concentric circles, either assumed and exercised by states themselves or by regional and international organisations exercising some element of transferred competencies.

These three concentric circles can all contribute to the peaceful settlement of cyber disputes. As the 2021 Report of the Group of Governmental Experts on Advancing Responsible State Behaviour in Cyberspace in the Context of International Security acknowledged:

> [C]ontinued discussion and exchanges of views by States, collectively at the United Nations … is essential for deepening common understandings, avoiding misunderstandings, and increasing predictability and stability. Such discussions could be informed and supported by regional and bilateral exchanges of views between States.[23]

UN reports have also stressed the application of the obligation to settle cyber disputes peacefully[24] and confirmed the application of international law, including the UN Charter, to cyberspace.[25] In such an environment, cyber diplomacy[26] has been taking its embryonic steps. However, the question that can be asked is whether it can still be effective to settle cyber disputes. This question must be answered against the background of a non-traditional environment, where states, private actors, digital platforms, non-state actors and individuals interact.

III. Bilateral Circle and Cyber Disputes

In its 2015 report, the UN Group on Government Experts recommended eleven non-binding norms, rules, or principles for responsible state behaviour in the ICT

[23] UNGA, 'Report of the Group of Governmental Experts on Advancing Responsible State Behaviour in Cyberspace in the Context of International Security' (14 July 2021) UN Doc A/76/135 para 72.

[24] J Kulesza, 'Peaceful Settlement of Interstate Online Disputes', in 'Special Issue: International Law as a Driver of Internet Governance' (2022) 11 *Laws* 1.

[25] 'International law, particularly the Charter of the United Nations, is applicable and essential to maintaining peace, security and stability in the Information, Communication and Technology Environment'. UNGA, 'Report of the Open-ended Working Group on Security of and in the Use of Information and Communications Technologies 2021–2025' (8 August 2022) UN Doc A/77/275, Annex, para 2. See also UNGA, 'Report of the Group of Governmental Experts on Developments in the Field of Information and Telecommunications in the Context of International Security' (24 June 2013) UN Doc A/68/98, para 19; UNGA, 'Report of the Group of Governmental Experts on Developments in the Field of Information and Telecommunications in the Context of International Security' (22 July 2015) UN Doc A/70/174, paras 24 and 25; UNGA, 'Developments in the Field of Information and Telecommunications in the Context of International Security' (30 December 2015) UN Doc A/RES/70/237.

[26] Cyber diplomacy can be defined as the conduct of diplomacy concerning a state's interests in cyberspace. SB Psaila, 'Improving the Practice of Cyber Diplomacy: Training, Tools, and Other Resources' (*Diplo*, September 2021) www.diplomacy.edu/wp-content/uploads/2021/10/Cyber-diplomacy-study-Diplo-Phase-I.pdf. Basically, it is traditional diplomacy applied to cyber issues, that needs to be disassociated from practising diplomacy through cyber tools. However, it shouldn't be excluded that gradually, over time, the latter comes to complement the former.

environment to states.[27] By embracing traditional diplomatic methods, such as cooperation between states, exchange of information, assistance, and other cooperative measures, the report underlines the value of diplomatic negotiations when malicious cyber incidents occur.

Over the last 20 years, diplomatic services responded to the new cyber reality by increasing, for example, diplomatic assignments and positions related to cyber issues. Most foreign affairs ministries worldwide contain cybersecurity bureaus, departments, and experts. At the same time, many diplomatic missions abroad include at least a digital attaché or cyber counsellor in their staff. The existence of experienced and trained cyber diplomats contributes to the prevention of disputes and their settlement, once they emerge, through traditional diplomatic methods. This surge in the number of cyber diplomats ineluctably led to the development of policy initiatives. Counter Ransomware Initiatives,[28] Cyber Defense Pledge Conferences,[29] and Cyber Policy Consultations are only some of the tools traditional diplomacy devised to shape cyber reality and address cyber disputes. In this sense, diplomacy seems to adapt itself efficiently to cyber needs. Another novel diplomatic tool is bilateral cyber dialogues or consultations.

For example, Switzerland and the United States of America (US) initiated their first-ever bilateral cyber dialogue in July 2020. According to the Swiss Federal Department of Foreign Affairs press release,[30] international cooperation is central to making Switzerland's cyberspace more secure, preserving the Internet's openness, and exploiting Switzerland's economic potential. In addition, 'bilateral cyber dialogues are an integral part of Switzerland's National Strategy for Protection against Cyber Risks, which was adopted by the Federal Council in 2018'.[31] At the same time, the USA is engaging in cyber consultations with many states, such as Mexico,[32] Singapore,[33] and Korea,[34] to mention a few.

[27] UNGA, 'Report of the GGE' UN Doc A/70/174 para 13.

[28] The Second International Counter Ransomware Initiative Summit took place in Washington, DC, in November 2021, reuniting 36 countries and the EU. The White House, 'Fact Sheet: The Second International Counter Ransomware Initiative Summit' www.whitehouse.gov/briefing-room/statements-releases/2022/11/01/fact-sheet-the-second-international-counter-ransomware-initiative-summit/.

[29] In November 2022, the NATO Cyber Defense Pledge Conference took place in Rome. Italian Government, 'NATO Cyber Defense Pledge Conference 2022' (20 November 2022) www.esteri.it/en/sala_stampa/archivionotizie/approfondimenti/2022/11/segui-la-diretta-nato-cyber-defense-pledge-conference-2022/.

[30] Switzerland, Federal Department of Foreign Affairs, 'Cyber Dialogue: Switzerland and the US Join Forces for an Open and Secure Digital Space' (9 July 2020) www.eda.admin.ch/eda/en/fdfa/fdfa/aktuell/news.html/content/eda/en/meta/news/2020/7/9/79810.html.

[31] ibid.

[32] US Department of State, 'Joint Statement on U.S.–Mexico Working Group on Cyber Issues' (18 August 2022) www.state.gov/joint-statement-on-u-s-mexico-working-group-on-cyber-issues/.

[33] Cyber Security Agency of Singapore, 'Singapore and United States Expand Existing Cooperation on Cybersecurity: Joint Media Release by Cybersecurity Agency of Singapore and Cybersecurity and Infrastructure Security Agency' (23 August 2022) www.csa.gov.sg/News-Events/Press-Releases/2021/singapore-and-united-states-expand-existing-cooperation-on-cybersecurity.

[34] The 6th US–Republic of Korea Cyber Policy Consultations was held in December 2022. US Department of State, 'The 6th U.S.–Republic of Korea Cyber Policy Consultations: Media Note' (15 December 2022) www.state.gov/the-6th-u-s-republic-of-korea-cyber-policy-consultations/.

One of the most sought-after achievements of these cyber consultations is maximising transparency and building trust through creating diplomatic grids of communication, particularly when the parties involved do not traditionally belong to the same political, military, or ideological camp. For instance, the Netherlands inaugurated their initial round of cyber consultations with the Russian Federation in September 2021 in the Hague. According to an ensuing statement from the Russian Foreign Ministry, the agenda included a wide array of security-related issues on the use of information technology (IT) on global and regional platforms, as well as on the bilateral track.[35] It is of interest for this chapter to note that both parties underlined 'the necessity to prevent conflicts and any kind of confrontation in the IT sphere, to use IT for peaceful ends, and strengthened the international cooperation in countering informational crimes'.[36] In the case of the emergence of a cyber dispute, pre-established diplomatic communication channels – including designated points of contact – and agreed-upon procedures to handle incidents may render efforts to peacefully settle a dispute more effectively. Hence, state actors tend to confirm through their practice that diplomacy and bilateral cyber talks constitute a valuable means to prevent conflicts and confrontation in cyberspace and create an enabling environment for the peaceful settlement of a dispute.

When Presidents Biden and Putin met in Geneva on 2 June 2021, this summit drew the world's attention due mainly to increasing tension between the two superpowers over various issues and the short-lived Strategic Stability Dialogue it established. What went mostly unnoticed is that one of the few things that the American and the Russian negotiating teams were able to agree on was the establishment of a bilateral task force/committee to address cyber disputes.[37] Regrettably, the Russian invasion of Ukraine in February 2022 and the subsequent severing of diplomatic ties between Moscow and Washington did not allow us to see whether this agreement would have been instrumental in resolving new cyber disputes.

Similarly, China engaged with various actors in bilateral cyber dialogues during the past five years.[38] An interesting format of cyber dialogue was launched

[35] Tass, 'First Russian–Dutch Consultations on Cybersecurity Take Place in The Hague' (17 September 2021) www.tass.com/politics/1339323.

[36] ibid.

[37] The White House, 'Remarks by President Biden in Press Conference' (16 June 2021) www.whitehouse.gov/briefing-room/speeches-remarks/2021/06/16/remarks-by-president-biden-in-press-conference-4/.

[38] Indicatively, we can refer to the First US–China Law Enforcement and Cybersecurity Dialogue (US Department of Justice, 'First U.S.–China Law Enforcement and Cybersecurity Dialogue: Summary of Outcomes' (6 October 2017) www.justice.gov/opa/pr/first-us-china-law-enforcement-and-cybersecurity-dialogue); the 4th China–France Cyber Dialogue which took place virtually in June 2022 (People's Republic of China, Ministry of Foreign Affairs, 'China and France Hold 4th China–France Cyber Dialogue' (17 June 2022) www.fmprc.gov.cn/mfa_eng/wjb_663304/zzjg_663340/jks_665232/jkxw_665234/202206/t20220617_10704811.html); and the 8th EU–China Task Force Meeting which was held in November 2021 (People's Republic of China, Ministry of Foreign Affairs, 'The 8th Meeting of China–EU Cyber Taskforce was Held' (26 November 2021) www.fmprc.gov.cn/mfa_eng/wjb_663304/zzjg_663340/jks_665232/jkxw_665234/202111/t20211126_10453799.html).

between the United Kingdom (UK) and China. In March and September 2022, Chatham House and the China Institute of Contemporary International Relations convened two 1.5 Track Cyber Dialogues between China and the UK. While Track I Diplomacy is traditional intergovernmental diplomacy, Track II diplomacy is a term coined to portray contacts and consultations – often discreetly organised by one or more states – between non-state actors, civil society organisations, and private individuals.[39] It is a path usually taken when diplomatic channels cannot provide the necessary framework to appropriately approach a topic, dispute, or other delicate issue. Track 1.5, as in the case of the cyber dialogue between London and Beijing, is a hybrid situation where, on the one hand, think tanks, academics, and experts engage in consultations and, on the other, government officials participate in negotiations and exchange views on issues of mutual interest and concern.[40]

According to the Chatham House website, participants in this Track 1.5 Cyber Dialogue discussed

> UK and China's high level national approaches to cyberspace, views on international cyber governance, harnessing the potential of emerging technologies and mitigating the risks, … international rules for responsible state behaviour in cyberspace, approaches to data governance, security and emerging technologies, and views on public attribution.[41]

This 1.5 diplomatic track can be an extremely useful communication channel in many diplomatic contexts, particularly where existing geopolitical tensions do not encourage a rapprochement and discussions between state actors.

States also enter into cyber dialogues with international organisations. For instance, in December 2022, the USA held their 8th Cyber Dialogue with the European Union (EU), where the building of cyber capabilities and the enhancement of cyber resilience were discussed.[42] Identifying key areas of policy convergence and deepening common understanding enhances the possibility of a peaceful settlement should a dispute arise. In another geographic context, the second ASEAN–China Cyber Dialogue was held in October 2022 in Singapore, where there was an exchange of views on protecting critical infrastructure in cyberspace, among other topics.[43]

[39] See generally, P Jones, *Track Two Diplomacy in Theory and Practice* (Stanford, Stanford University Press, 2015). See also JV Montville, 'Track Two Diplomacy: The Work of Healing History' (2006) 7 *The Whitehead Journal of Diplomacy and International Relations* 15.

[40] J Mapendere, 'Track One and a Half Diplomacy, and the Complementarity of Tracks' (2000) 2 *Culture of Peace Online Journal* 66, 70.

[41] Chatham House, 'UK–China Track 1.5 Cyber Dialogue' www.chathamhouse.org/about-us/our-departments/international-security-programme/uk-china-track-15-cyber-dialogue.

[42] European Commission, 'Cybersecurity: EU Holds 8th Security Dialogue with the United States' (16 December 2022) digital-strategy.ec.europa.eu/en/news/cybersecurity-eu-holds-8th-dialogue-united-states.

[43] People's Republic of China, Ministry of Foreign Affairs, 'The Second ASEAN–China Cyber Dialogue was Held in Singapore' (21 October 2022) www.fmprc.gov.cn/mfa_eng/wjdt_665385/wshd_665389/202210/t20221021_10789736.html.

Diplomatic talks are not always successful. When cyber dialogues do not seem to deliver the anticipated results, another traditional tool of bilateral diplomacy, namely, public statements naming adverse parties or criticising their conduct, can be used. Though it is still debatable whether naming and shaming are efficient in a diplomatic world used to handling issues with discretion and prudence, public statements present some serious advantages, particularly in the case of public attribution. First, when the attribution of a cyber incident becomes public, the perpetrator of a malicious cyber operation, which in most cases is clandestine, is revealed and exposed. This is true both in cases where the cyber attack is attributed to a third state or a non-state actor operating from the territory of a third state. Second, the alleged perpetrator usually denies all accusations and, at the same time, affirms their respect for the rules and norms of responsible state behaviour in cyberspace, upholding – at least on a rhetorical level – their commitment to international law and a secure cyberspace. Third, a public statement can, under certain conditions, serve as a preventive measure for future attacks.[44] As is well known in diplomatic practice, in most cases, there is also an in-person démarche to substantiate the allegations contained in the statement. However, public statements can equally present disadvantages, especially when the culprit state denies its involvement, in which case official exchanges may lead to the straining of bilateral relations.

To conclude this section, the main advantages of the first circle are the directness of exchanges between the states involved, the non-interference of third parties, and the possibility of integrating dispute settlement in a wider grid of bilateral relations. However, empirical evidence is needed to substantiate the effectiveness of diplomacy in cases where cyber disputes are part of, or constitute the mere reflection of, entrenched geopolitical disagreements. Yet, in this case, states involved can move to the second diplomatic circle, the regional circle. The latter, without being mutually exclusive with the first circle, is complementary and can run in parallel with bilateral diplomacy.

IV. Regional Circle and Cyber Disputes

Regional organisations can provide an ideal hub for resolving disputes between their members. Though not always unchallenged, there is convincing evidence

[44] See statements by the High Representative of the EU on cyber attacks against Ukraine (Council of the EU, 'Declaration by the High Representative on Behalf of the European Union on Malicious Cyber Activities Conducted by Hackers and Hacker Groups in the Context of Russia's Aggression against Ukraine' (19 July 2022) www.consilium.europa.eu/en/press/press-releases/2022/07/19/declaration-by-the-high-representative-on-behalf-of-the-european-union-on-malicious-cyber-activities-conducted-by-hackers-and-hacker-groups-in-the-context-of-russia-s-aggression-against-ukraine/) and on the Microsoft Exchange Server data breach (Council of the EU, 'China: Declaration by the High Representative on Behalf of the European Union Urging Chinese Authorities to Take Action against Malicious Cyber Activities Undertaken from Its Territory' (19 July 2021) www.consilium.europa.eu/en/press/press-releases/2021/07/19/declaration-by-the-high-representative-on-behalf-of-the-eu-urging-china-to-take-action-against-malicious-cyber-activities-undertaken-from-its-territory/).

that intergovernmental regional organisations demonstrate increased effectiveness when assisting their members to settle their disputes peacefully.[45] There are several reasons for this.

First, regional organisations, as was seen, promote the peaceful settlement of disputes and occasionally also set a framework for their resolution.[46] Second, as the UN Charter provides, these organisations have primary responsibility for the pacific settlement of local disputes.[47] Last but not least, membership rules may contain incentives for the peaceful settlement of disputes or deterrents to recourse to force.[48]

In the cyber context, many regional organisations have raised their cyber awareness over the last two decades. The OAS, Organization for Security and Co-operation in Europe (OSCE), and ASEAN are some of the organisations that have developed cyber working groups and mechanisms to facilitate the peaceful settlement of disputes, to further regional coordination, and to advance cyber multilateralism.

The OAS established a Cybersecurity Program focusing on policy development, capacity building, and research.[49] It also facilitated the implementation of confidence-building measures (CBMs) by supporting its Member States in developing national cybersecurity strategies. In parallel, the Working Group on Co-operation and Confidence-Building Measures in Cyberspace developed Regional Confidence Building Measures to Promote Trust and Cooperation in Cyberspace, which were adopted during the second meeting of the Working Group in Santiago, Chile, in April 2019.[50] In its preamble, the American States recognise that:

> MFAs and diplomacy are powerful and important tools when it comes to generating not just 'cooperation bridges', but also discussion, work, and negotiations on international norms and CBMs, among others. Cyber diplomacy, then, is a crucial dimension for the international discussion of cybersecurity and cyberspace.[51]

[45] P Quayle and X Gao (eds), *International Organisations and the Promotion of Effective Dispute Resolution, AIIB Yearbook of International Law* (Leiden, Brill/Nijhoff, 2019) 1–3, 77–89, 103–20.

[46] The Council of Europe and the European Court of Human Rights are examples of regional intergovernmental organisations settling human rights disputes.

[47] Art 52 of the UN Charter.

[48] On 16 March 2022, the Committee of Ministers of the Council of Europe voted in favour of the expulsion of the Russian Federation from the CoE with immediate effect because of the war of aggression and its invasion of Ukraine. This decision occurred after 26 years of Russian membership of the CoE. CoE, 'Resolution CM/Res(2022)2 on the Cessation of Membership of the Russian Federation to the Council of Europe'(16 March 2022) search.coe.int/cm/Pages/result_details.aspx?ObjectID=0900001680a5da51; CoE, 'Newsroom: The Russian Federation is Excluded from the Council of Europe' (16 March 2022) www.coe.int/en/web/portal/-/the-russian-federation-is-excluded-from-the-council-of-europe.

[49] The OAS Cybersecurity Program is implemented by the Inter-American Committee against Terrorism (CICTE). See OAS, 'Cybersecurity Program' www.oas.org/ext/en/security/prog-cyber.

[50] OAS CICTE, 'Draft Regional Confidence Building Measures to Promote Cooperation and Trust in Cyberspace, OAS/Ser.L/X.5, CICTE/GT/MFCC/doc.12/19 rev 2, Santiago, Chile' (24 April 2019) www.oas.org/en/sms/cicte/cybersecurity/sessions/regular/2019/.

[51] ibid.

Designation of points of contact, development and strengthening of capacity building, mainstreaming cybersecurity training, and fostering cooperation and exchanging best practices are the four proposed voluntary cyber CBMs. To further disseminate the content of the measures, the Working Group set up its own website,[52] which presents its activities and is where members can access the entirety of cyber CBMs. The third and fourth meetings of the Working Group – which took place in 2021 in Washington, DC, USA, and in 2022 in Ciudad de Mexico, Mexico – dealt extensively with the issues of cooperation and confidence-building measures, as it has been reflected in the reports and documents of these meetings.[53]

The OSCE, a collective security intergovernmental organisation of 57 participating states, has developed two sets of cyber CBMs since 2012. In the first set, adopted by the Permanent Council in December 2013, the OSCE participating states were invited to 'hold consultations in order to reduce the risks of misperception, and of possible emergence of political or military tension or conflict that may stem from the use of Information and Communication Technology (ICT)'.[54] This CBM hints directly at the peaceful settlement of disputes, given that misperception can be easily classified as one of the initial reasons for a dispute and, almost ineluctably, political and military tension. Therefore, urging states to hold consultations in times of crisis clearly positions diplomacy as the first dispute settlement channel.

OSCE CBM 8 calls upon participating states to nominate contact points to 'facilitate pertinent communication and dialogue on security of and in the use of ICTs'.[55] In 2016, the Permanent Council adopted five additional cyber CBMs, bringing the OSCE CBMS to 16 by emphasising the exchange of information, resilience building, and cyber readiness. In the five additional CBMs, participating states are encouraged to facilitate inter-state exchanges to enhance transparency, predictability, and stability.[56] CBM 15 invites participating states to collaborate in developing 'shared responses to common challenges including crisis management procedures in case of widespread or transnational disruption of ICT-enabled critical infrastructure'.[57] Within the above framework, the EU, along with Switzerland

[52] Working Group on Cooperation and Confidence-Building Measures in Cyberspace, 'About Us' www.oascybercbms.info.

[53] The documents of the third and fourth meetings can be retrieved at OAS CICTE, 'Third Meeting for the Working Group on Cooperation and Confidence-Buildings Measures in Cyberspace' (27 July 2021) www.oas.org/en/sms/cicte/cybersecurity/sessions/regular/2021/ and OAS CICTE, 'Fourth Meeting for the Working Group on Cooperation and Confidence-Buildings Measures in Cyberspace' (26–27 October 2022) www.oas.org/ext/en/main/calendar/event/id/63.

[54] OSCE, 'Decision No 1106, Initial Set of OSCE Confidence-Building Measures to Reduce the Risks of Conflict Stemming from the Use of Information and Communication Technologies' (3 December 2013) PC.DEC/1106, CBM 3.

[55] ibid CBM 8.

[56] OSCE, 'Decision No 1202, OSCE Confidence Building Measures to Reduce the Risks of Conflict Stemming from the Use of Information and Communication Technologies' (10 March 2016) PC. DEC/1202.

[57] ibid CBM 15.

and North Macedonia, decided in September 2022 to adopt CBM 12, which consists of 'facilitating inter-state exchanges in different formats, including on regional and subregional level, engaging private sector, academia and civil society'.[58]

Over the last two decades, the EU has done tremendous cybersecurity work.[59] The creation of ENISA,[60] the elaboration of an EU Cybersecurity Strategy,[61] and the development of public-private partnerships[62] are just some of the initiatives undertaken to increase preparedness and resilience. Within the EU, the Cyber Crisis Liaison Organisation Network (CyCLONe) brings together agencies in charge of cyber crisis management of the 27 EU Member States at technical (Computer Security Incident Response Team – CSIRT) and political (Integrated Political Crisis Response – IPCR) levels. These platforms enable real-time exchange of information and create a favourable environment for exchanges on technical and operational levels. In the same context, in a working paper[63] presented by a group of countries[64] during the informal inter-sessional meeting of the 2021–2025 UN Open-Ended Working Group (OEWG) that took place between 5 and 9 December 2022, it was proposed that emphasis should be laid on the interplay between regional Points of Contact (PoC) directories and the UN PoC directory.

Reference should also be made to the ASEAN Regional Forum Points of Contact directory, set up in 2020, where senior and working-level contacts have been nominated and updated biannually. The ASEAN Regional Forum (ARF) is a multilateral dialogue Asia–Pacific forum created by ASEAN in 1993. It has 27 participants.[65] In 2020, the ARF established the PoC Directory on Security of and in the Use of Information and Communication Technologies for prevention

[58] ibid CBM 12.

[59] See chapter by Bendiek et al (ch 5 in this volume).

[60] The European Network and Information Security Agency (ENISA) was created by Regulation (EC) No 460/2004 of the European Parliament and of the Council of 10 March 2004 establishing the European Network and Information Security Agency [2004] OJ L77/1. Subsequent regulations have modified its mandate, the last being Regulation (EU) 2019/881 of the European Parliament and the Council of 17 April 2019 on ENISA (the European Union Agency for Cybersecurity) and on information and communications technology cybersecurity certification and repealing Regulation (EU) No 526/2013 (Cybersecurity Act) [2019] OJ L151/15.

[61] European Commission, 'Press Release: New EU Cybersecurity Strategy and New Rules to Make Physical and Digital Critical Entities More Resilient' (16 December 2020) ec.europa.eu/commission/presscorner/api/files/document/print/en/ip_20_2391/IP_20_2391_EN.pdf.

[62] The European Cybersecurity Organisation (ECSO, 'Home' ecs-org.eu/) is one of the major players that brings together private and public partnerships within the European context, thus contributing to developing a more robust cybersecurity community.

[63] Australia et al, 'Implementing Cyber Confidence Measures Globally: Towards the UN Point of Contact Directory, Working Paper' (25 November 2022) docs-library.unoda.org/Open-Ended_Working_Group_on_Information_and_Communication_Technologies_-_(2021)/Joint_Working_Paper_-_Next_steps_to_a_UN_PoC_Directory.pdf.

[64] Australia, Brazil, Canada, Chile, Fiji, Germany, Israel, the Republic of Korea, Mexico, the Netherlands, Singapore, and Uruguay.

[65] The participants in the ARF are Australia, Bangladesh, Brunei Darussalam, Cambodia, Canada, China, Democratic People's Republic of Korea, European Union, India, Indonesia, Japan, Lao People's Democratic Republic, Malaysia, Mongolia, Myanmar, New Zealand, Pakistan, Papua New Guinea, Philippines, Republic of Korea, Russia, Singapore, Sri Lanka, Thailand, Timor-Leste, US, and Vietnam.

and response purposes. In parallel, ASEAN strengthened cooperation on cybersecurity among its ten Member States.[66] As the ASEAN 2021–2025 Cybersecurity Cooperation Strategy highlights, policy coordination, incident response, and capacity building have been some of its achievements to date.[67] The creation of the ASEAN Cybersecurity Coordination Committee, set up in 2020 to strengthen cross-sectoral coordination on cybersecurity,[68] is a remarkable policy achievement since it allows further policy coordination enhancement.

It appears that the regional circle presents a well-suited framework for promoting international inter-state cooperation in cyberspace, particularly through developing CBMs and facilitating inter-state cooperation. There are three basic advantages of the regional circle: trust building among members of the organisation, interaction with third states, and the existence of established methods, procedures, and guidelines for dispute resolution. However, given the intrinsically global nature of cyberspace, multilateral diplomacy may achieve better results in global fora, such as the UN, when it comes to identifying rules and norms of responsible state behaviour and codifying international law.

V. Global Circle and Cyber Disputes

The global circle of diplomacy refers mainly to international intergovernmental institutions such as the International Telecommunication Union (ITU) or UN. The UN is the most comprehensive institution with a global mandate, among others, to maintain international peace.

Within the global circle, the ITU, which prides itself on being the oldest UN agency, created in 1865,[69] attempts to position itself as the cybersecurity and internet governance leader. Besides the 193 Member States, the ITU has a multistakeholder approach, with over 900 ITU members coming from the private sector and academia. Its remit expanded to include the entire field of ICTs. However, it has not gone unchallenged since most developed countries believe this is not the appropriate forum to deal with cybersecurity.[70] The ITU's Global Cybersecurity

[66] Brunei Darussalam, Cambodia, Thailand, Singapore, Indonesia, Vietnam, Lao People's Democratic Republic, Myanmar, Philippines, and Malaysia.

[67] ASEAN, 'ASEAN Cybersecurity Cooperation Strategy (2021-2025)' www.asean.org/wp-content/uploads/2022/02/01-ASEAN-Cybersecurity-Cooperation-Paper-2021-2025_final-23-0122.pdf.

[68] ibid.

[69] ITU, 'About International Telecommunication Union (ITU)' www.itu.int/en/about/Pages/default.aspx. On 15 November 1947, an agreement between ITU and the newly created UN recognised ITU as the specialised agency for telecommunications. The agreement formally entered into force on 1 January 1949. ITU, 'Overview of ITU's History (3)' www.itu.int/en/history/Pages/ITUsHistory-page-3.aspx.

[70] I Foulkes, 'What's the ITU and Why is It Important?' (*swissinfo.ch*, 20 September 2022) www.swissinfo.ch/eng/business/what-s-the-itu-and-why-is-it-important-/47914594. The recent interest of countries in expanding the cyber agenda to technical organisations is demonstrated by the interest shown in the directorial positions of these bodies, as was the case for the position of the Director-General of the ITU. The position of the outgoing Chinese Secretary-General, Houlin Zhao, was claimed by candidates

Agenda[71] consists of five pillars: legal measures, technical and procedural measures, organisational structures, capacity building, and international cooperation. In the Guidelines for Utilization of the Global Cybersecurity Agenda by the ITU,[72] international cooperation is dealt with in section VI, which stresses the importance of the UN in fostering cooperation and the role of the ITU in facilitating capacity building and security in the use of ICTs.

The role of the UN regarding cyber disputes is manifold. Over the last two decades, the UN has provided the institutional and normative framework to establish and promote rules and norms in cyberspace.

In 2004, the UN, following UNGA Resolution 58/32,[73] created a 20-member strong Group of Governmental Experts (GGE) on Developments in the Field of Information and Telecommunications in the Context of International Security. From 2004 to 2017, there were five successive Groups of Governmental Experts. Their reports affirmed the application of international law and the UN Charter to cyber operations, including the peaceful settlement of cyber disputes. Disagreements prevented the adoption of a report by the fifth GGE in June 2017. Still, the sixth and final GGE (2019–2021)[74] endorsed a report[75] focusing on existing and emerging threats, rules and norms of responsible state behaviour, international law and confidence-building measures. Although some criticism was raised about its under-representative character (25 members[76] out of 193 UN Member States), the truth is that the formation of this group of experts simply followed the current UN practice in similar cases. UNGA Resolution 68/243 called in its operative paragraph 4 for an equitable geographic distribution, a formulation often used in UN texts when a smaller group needs to be established.[77] For instance, UNGA Resolution 60/251, which created the 47-member strong Human Rights Council in 2006, underlines in its operative paragraph 7 that 'membership shall be based on equitable geographic distribution'.[78]

from the Russian Federation and the USA, with the latter having elected Ms Doreen Bogdan-Martin as the incumbent Secretary-General of the ITU at the Plenipotentiary Conference that took place in Bucharest in September 2022. ITU, 'Member States Elect Doreen Bogdan-Martin as ITU Secretary-General' (29 September 2022) www.itu.int/en/mediacentre/Pages/PR-2022-09-29-ITU-SG-elected-Doreen-Bogdan-Martin.aspx.

[71] ITU, 'Global Cybersecurity Agenda (GCA)' www.itu.int/en/action/cybersecurity/Pages/gca.aspx.

[72] ITU, 'Guidelines for Utilization of the Global Cybersecurity Agenda by the ITU' www.itu.int/en/action/cybersecurity/Documents/Guidelines%20for%20utilization%20of%20the%20GCA.pdf.

[73] UNGA, 'Resolution Adopted by the General Assembly: 58/32. Developments in the Field of Information and Telecommunication in the Context of International Security' (18 December 2003) UN Doc A/RES/58/32.

[74] Created by UNGA, 'Resolution Adopted by the General Assembly on 5 December 2018: 73/27. Developments in the Field of Information and Telecommunications in the Context of International Security' (11 December 2018) UN Doc A/RES/73/27.

[75] UNGA, 'Report of the GGE' UN Doc A/76/135.

[76] Australia, Brazil, China, Estonia, France, Germany, India, Indonesia, Japan, Jordan, Kazakhstan, Kenya, Mauritius, Mexico, Morocco, Netherlands, Norway, Romania, Russian Federation, Singapore, South Africa, Switzerland, United Kingdom, United States, Uruguay.

[77] UNGA, 'Resolution 68/243' UN Doc A/RES/68/243 para 4.

[78] UNGA, 'Resolution Adopted by the General Assembly: 60/251. Human Rights Council' (3 April 2006) UN Doc A/RES/60/251, 3.

The GGE addressed the diplomatic dimension of cyber disputes and set the rails upon which effective cyber diplomacy can operate.[79] In its fourth report,[80] the Group focused on threats from using ICT and actions to counter them, including norms, legal rules, and confidence-building measures. The Group noted that 'common understandings on how international law applies to State use of ICTs are important for promoting an open, secure, stable, accessible and peaceful ICT environment'.[81]

However, the most important assertion the GGE made in the context of the diplomatic settlement of disputes is the affirmation that 'States must observe, among other principles of international law, State sovereignty, sovereign equality, the settlement of disputes by peaceful means and non-intervention in the internal affairs of other States'.[82] The inclusion of the principle of peaceful settlement of disputes is important, with diplomatic negotiations being the most used process in a bilateral and multilateral context regarding cyber disputes. In its 2021 report,[83] the GGE stressed the significance of diplomacy in the cyber context and dedicated many parts to the necessity of cyber diplomatic activities to guarantee security in cyberspace. In particular, paragraph 70 of the report reiterates the commitment of states to the settlement of international disputes by peaceful means, while the very next paragraph[84] states that:

> in accordance with their obligations under Article 2(3) and Chapter VI of the Charter of the United Nations, States party to any international dispute, including those involving the use of ICTs, the continuance of which is likely to endanger the maintenance of international peace and security, shall, first of all, seek a solution by such means as described in Article 33 of the Charter, namely negotiation, enquiry, mediation, conciliation, arbitration, judicial settlement, resort to regional agencies or arrangements, or other peaceful means of their own choice.

Currently, there are two processes running parallel to each other: a five-year (2021–2025) Open-Ended Working Group on the security of and the use of information and communication technologies, which was created by UN General Assembly Resolution 75/240,[85] and the Ad Hoc Committee created by UN General Assembly Resolution 74/247[86] to elaborate a comprehensive international

[79] CyberPeace Institute, 'The UN GGE Final Report: A Milestone in Cyber Diplomacy, but Where is the Accountability?' (9 June 2021) www.cyberpeaceinstitute.org/news/the-un-gge-final-report-a-milestone-in-cyber-diplomacy-but-where-is-the-accountability/.

[80] UNGA, 'Report of the GGE' UN Doc A/70/174.

[81] ibid para 29.

[82] ibid para 28b.

[83] UNGA, 'Report of the GGE' UN Doc A/76/135.

[84] ibid para 71(a).

[85] UNGA, 'Resolution Adopted by the General Assembly: 75/240. Developments in the Field of Information and Telecommunications in the Context of International Security' (4 January 2021) UN Doc A/RES/75/240.

[86] UNGA, 'Resolution Adopted by the General Assembly: 74/247. Countering the Use of Information and Communications Technologies for Criminal Purposes' (20 January 2020) UN Doc A/RES/74/247.

convention on countering the use of information and communications technologies for criminal purposes. Within the context of the OEWG,[87] which is open to all states, the creation of a Global PoC Directory is a tangible example of practical and result-oriented diplomacy: a mechanism for collecting good practices and experiences. This directory aims to create lines of communication to coordinate efforts in the event of significant cyber incidents. It is to be noted that this type of directory is not meant to be simple focal points; they tend to create communities of cyber experts and policymakers, which shape attitudinal approaches and become the driving force of efforts to create safer cyber environments. This directory is a natural follow-up to similar efforts undertaken on a regional level, particularly the Transnational Threats Department of the OSCE Secretariat and the EU CyCLONe mentioned above.

As the OEWG's first report suggests,[88] the PoC Directory falls under the spectrum of CBMs. These refer to tools traditionally used in diplomacy to ease tensions between two or more parties, prevent further escalation, and facilitate the return to normalcy. CBMs also decrease the risk of misunderstanding and confusion through communication channels. In this framework, cyber confidence measures can be agreed upon and can act as stepping stones towards better comprehension and global cooperation among state actors. Their implementation is instrumental in enhancing existing synergies between the UN system and regional capacity-building initiatives. For instance, Recommendation 5 under Section E (Confidence Building Measures) of the OEWG's Annual Progress Report[89] encourages states to disseminate information on developments in the field of ICTs in the context of international security through the reports of the Secretary-General as well as through the UN Institute for Disarmament Research (UNIDIR) Cyber Portal.

In the context of increasing transparency, the OEWG also invites states to proceed with surveys of national implementation of rules, norms and principles. It encourages states to assist each other in developing common understanding and to facilitate the implementation of rules, norms and principles of responsible state behaviour in the use of ICTs.[90] In parallel, the adoption by the First Committee of the General Assembly of the 'Programme of Action to Advance Responsible State Behaviour in the Use of Information and Communications Technologies in the Context of International Security'[91] takes the discussion a step further by allowing states to strengthen their capacities in the cyber domain.

[87] The United Nations Office for Disarmament Affairs hosts the website of the Open-Ended Working Group. UN Office for Disarmament Affairs, 'Open-Ended Working Group on Information and Communication Technologies' meetings.unoda.org/open-ended-working-group-on-information-and-communication-technologies-2021.

[88] UNGA, 'Report of the OEWG' UN Doc A/77/275 Annex, para 16.

[89] ibid para 16(e), 5.

[90] ibid 9.

[91] UNGA, 'Programme of Action to Advance Responsible State Behaviour in the Use of Information and Communications Technologies in the Context of International Security' (13 October 2022) UN Doc A/C.1/77/L.73.

While UN efforts highlight the value of international intergovernmental diplomatic cooperation, they also underscore disagreements in the interpretation and implementation of international law. That being said, diplomacy can help to identify and mitigate existing differences. In 2019, the General Assembly adopted Resolution 74/247,[92] establishing upon the initiative of the Russian Federation, an Ad Hoc Committee[93] aimed at initiating the process for a Comprehensive International Convention on Countering the Use of Information and Communication Technologies for Criminal Purposes (the cybercrime draft convention).[94] UNGA Resolution 75/282[95] set the work program for the Ad Hoc Committee, and a draft Convention was submitted to the Ad Hoc Committee on 27 July 2021.[96] However, although this process is open to all UN Member States, international organisations, and accredited non-governmental organisations (NGOs), elaborating a new set of international rules through a treaty did not spark the expected enthusiasm and consensus.[97] One might be surprised to see traditional proponents of a rule-based order reluctant to endorse such codification initiatives. However, the cyber field is not the only domain where such an attitude transpires.[98] This can have a two-fold explanation: on the one hand,

[92] UNGA, 'Resolution 74/247' UN Doc A/RES/74/247. The General Assembly adopted the Resolution with 79 yes votes, 60 no votes, and 34 abstentions, and 21 states did not participate in the vote. Among the opponents of the Resolution were the EU Member States, the USA, and the UK, while Russia and China were among the proponents.

[93] The work of the Ad Hoc Committee is steered by elected officers from the following countries: Algeria (Chair), Indonesia (Rapporteur), Australia, China, Dominican Republic, Egypt, Estonia, Japan, Nicaragua, Nigeria, Poland, Portugal, Russian Federation, Suriname, and the US as Vice-Chairs (UNGA, 'Resolution Adopted by the General Assembly: 75/282. Countering the Use of Information and Communications Technologies for Criminal Purposes' (1 June 2021) UN Doc A/RES/75/282, 1, fn 1). The United Nations Office on Drugs and Crime, based in Vienna, serves as the Secretariat of the Ad Hoc Committee (UNGA, 'Resolution 75/282' UN Doc A/RES/75/282, 2, para 2) and the scheduled sessions of the Ad Hoc Committee are being held alternatively in New York and Vienna.

[94] It should be noted in this regard that there is already in force an international instrument on cybercrime, the Budapest Convention by the Council of Europe (CoE), which has been ratified by 69 states, with Russia being the only Member State of the CoE not having signed it. See Convention on Cybercrime (Budapest, 23 November 2001). Many state parties are not European states or in the Council of Europe. See CoE, 'The Budapest Convention (ETS No. 185) and its Protocols' www.coe.int/en/web/cybercrime/the-budapest-convention The competing instruments have been perceived by some as a fundamental confrontation between liberal and authoritarian visions of the global digital order. V Stanzel and D Voelsen, 'Diplomacy and Artificial Intelligence, SWP Research Paper 1' (*Stiftung Wissenschaft und Politik*, January 2022) www.swp-berlin.org/publications/products/research_papers/2022RP01_Diplomacy_and_AI.pdf.

[95] UNGA, 'Resolution 75/282' UN Doc A/RES/75/282.

[96] UNGA, 'Ad Hoc Committee to Elaborate a Comprehensive International Convention on Countering the Use of Information and Communication Technologies for Criminal Purposes: Consolidated Negotiating Document' (19 December 2022) UN Doc A/AC.291/19; UN Office on Drugs and Crime, 'Fifth Session of the Ad Hoc Committee' www.unodc.org/unodc/en/cybercrime/ad_hoc_committee/ahc_fifth_session/main.

[97] J Hakmeh, 'Can a Cybercrime Convention for All Be Achieved?' (*Chatham House*, 31 March 2022) www.chathamhouse.org/2022/03/can-cybercrime-convention-all-be-achieved.

[98] For instance, a typical example of the ambivalence that can accompany the proposal for an international instrument was reflected in the proposal supported by Latin American countries in a binding treaty on the rights of older persons. UNGA, 'Resolution Adopted by the General Assembly: 67/139.

there is a belief that existing international legal instruments provide a sufficient legal framework as long as their full implementation can be ensured and properly put into practice. On the other, there is fear that any new instrument may not achieve the highest desired human rights protection and, even worse, water down the content of legal provisions, mainly due to the opposing views of participating states. In this respect, the contribution of the Office of the High Commissioner for Human Rights (OHCHR) at the First Session of the Ad Hoc Committee mirrors these concerns.[99] In its comments, the Office underscores that:

> [P]rovisions regulating cybercrimes and their application may pose significant human rights risks, as evidenced by the common use at national levels of cybercrime laws and policies to restrict freedom of expression, target dissenting voices, justify Internet shutdowns, interfere with privacy and anonymity of communications, and limit the rights to freedom of association and peaceful assembly.[100]

The above two reasons explaining treaty scepticism help to reveal a third one, namely that treaties require state consent, whereas soft law is quasi-binding without formal state consent and may evolve into customary law. This means that the process of elaborating the new cybercrime convention, compared to the report steered by the OEWG (2021–2026), presents the disadvantage of the need for many ratifications/accessions. Without passing further comment on the acceptance of the cybercrime convention, it is worth examining some of its provisions relevant to this chapter.

The Ad Hoc Committee held its Concluding Session in New York on 9 February 2024. Although no consensus has been reached[101] and most provisions have been agreed *ad referendum*, there are some very interesting lessons on cyber diplomacy to draw from the work carried out during the first Organisational Session of the Ad Hoc Committee in May 2021 at the UN headquarters. First, the quasi-universal participation of the states in the process demonstrates their interest in the topic and their desire to regulate activities in cyberspace, as well as their preference for negotiation as the most appropriate means to address these issues. Second, the 'further revised draft of the Convention'[102] constitutes a compromise between various positions expressed during the negotiations by UN Member States. It became clear that some diverging views were imported from outside

Towards a Comprehensive and Integral International Legal Instrument to Promote and Protect the Rights and Dignity of Older Persons' (20 December 2012) UN Doc A/RES/67/139, introduced by El Salvador, was adopted with 54 positive votes, 5 negative votes and a record number of 118 abstentions, demonstrating the perplexity with which the majority of the international community, including western states, received this proposal for a new international convention.

[99] OHCHR, 'OHCHR Key-Messages Relating to a Possible Comprehensive International Convention on Countering the Use of Information and Communications Technologies for Criminal Purposes' (17 January 2022) www.unodc.org/documents/Cybercrime/AdHocCommittee/First_session/OHCHR_17_Jan.pdf.

[100] ibid 1.

[101] At the last meeting of the Concluding Session, Member States agreed to extend the session at a date to be determined later.

[102] UNGA, 'Further revised draft text of the Convention' (6 February 2024) UN Doc A/AC.291/22/Rev.2.

the cyber field,[103] such as discussions on gender, preserving human rights, and criminalisation of some offences. This observation confirms the permeability of the cyber and non-cyber worlds. Third, the principle of the peaceful settlement of disputes in cyberspace has been reaffirmed.

Regarding diplomacy, the preamble, which usually contains the general principles upon which a treaty is built, is unequivocal on the necessity of cyber diplomacy given that it emphasises enhancing coordination, international cooperation and capacity-building to deal with the scourge of cybercrime.[104] Furthermore, Chapter V[105] of the draft Convention is entitled 'International cooperation'. Beyond the general principles of international cooperation (Article 32), it contains useful provisions on mutual legal assistance (Articles 40–46), law enforcement cooperation and joint investigations. However, perhaps the most important provision is Article 62[106] in Chapter IX ('Final provisions'). It reads:

> State Parties shall endeavour to settle disputes concerning the interpretation or application of this Convention through negotiation or any other peaceful means of their own choice.

It follows that diplomacy and its main tool, negotiation, is the first option available to states whenever a dispute arises related to the interpretation or application of the Convention. And, in an indirect nod to Article 33 of the UN Charter, should negotiation not succeed, other peaceful means can be used. If these means fail to resolve the dispute, a recourse to adjudicatory methods is foreseen. Article 62, paragraph 2 foresees the possibility of arbitration, and if this proves equally inconclusive, a recourse to the International Court of Justice is envisaged.[107] However, the implementation level of this Article remains to be seen once this instrument enters into force.

The preceding discussion has shown that the global circle of diplomacy complements the bilateral and regional circles. Global codification initiatives, inter-state cooperation, and the elaboration of norms, rules and principles highlight the benefits of diplomacy and the laying of political and legal foundations for the peaceful settlement of disputes. Adding to bilateral and regional initiatives, diplomatic activity at the global level seems to take the lead in preserving international peace and settling disputes peacefully. Yet, no matter how well it adapts to cyberspace, diplomacy also has limits.

[103] For instance, there was an exchange of views on the draft Arts 13 and 15 on the definition of sexual offences and criminalisation of other behaviours, as well as the overall debate on the terminology of the Convention. See Global Initiative against Transnational Organised Crime, 'Cyber Convention Check-in' (26 January 2024) globalinitiative.net/announcements/cyber-convention-check-in/.

[104] UNGA, 'Further revised draft text' UN Doc A/AC.291/22/Rev.2, preambular paras 6, 8 and 9.

[105] ibid Arts 35–52.

[106] ibid Art 62.

[107] 'If, six months after the date of the request for arbitration, those States Parties are unable to agree on the organisation of the arbitration, any one of those States Parties may refer the dispute to the International Court of Justice by request in accordance with the Statute of the Court'. UNGA, 'Further revised draft text' UN Doc A/AC.291/22/Rev.2 Art 62, para 2.

VI. Conclusion

While international law is furthering its rule-based grip on cyberspace,[108] cyber threats and attacks continue their unrelenting spike in scale and sophistication.[109] In its 2024 predictions, Diplo, a Geneva-based Swiss-Maltese NGO specialising in internet governance, foresees that there will be more threats to submarine cables, internet exchange points, and other parts of critical internet infrastructure. The efforts to secure a free cyberspace will be an uphill struggle due to the existing trends of deterioration of the geopolitical environment[110] and the emergence of new vulnerabilities, mainly because of our increasing dependency on complex new technologies.[111]

In this chapter, I explained how diplomacy, through its three concentric circles – bilateral, regional, and global – adjusted its traditional methods to the peaceful settlement of cyber disputes. That said, one must be aware of the limits of cyber diplomacy that coincide with those of traditional diplomacy. Deep-rooted geopolitical conflicts can spill over to cyberspace without a realistic prospect of settlement. Paraphrasing Von Clausewitz,[112] cyberspace can be a place for the continuation of the physical world tensions with other means. Cyber incidents, malicious activities, and ICT attacks can just be the reflection or continuation of real-world tensions or hostilities. Moreover, further research is needed to establish the working relationship between diplomacy and other methods of peaceful settlement of disputes, in particular, adjudication. In the meantime, cyber diplomacy needs to be more attuned to technological developments and become better equipped to face the challenges that the ever-changing environment of cyberspace

[108] Recently, a Council of Advisers composed of 11 states parties to the ICC Rome Statute (Rome Statute of the International Criminal Court (Rome, 17 July 1998)) was created to explore whether the ICC can prosecute cybercrimes without a statutory amendment. These countries are Argentina, Austria, Belgium, Costa Rica, Czechia, Estonia, Liechtenstein, Luxembourg, Portugal, Spain, and Switzerland. The Global Campaign for Ratification and Implementation of the Kampala Amendments on the Crime of Aggression, 'The Council of Advisers on the Application of the Rome Statute to Cyberwarfare' www.crimeofaggression.info/the-campaign/the-council-of-advisers-on-the-application-of-the-rome-statute-to-cyberwarfare/.

[109] D Sabbagh, 'Cyber-Attacks Have Tripled in Past Year, Says Ukraine's Cybersecurity Agency' (*The Guardian*, 19 January 2023) www.theguardian.com/world/2023/jan/19/cyber-attacks-have-tripled-in-past-year-says-ukraine-cybersecurity-agency.

[110] Diplo, '12 AI and Digital Predictions for 2024' www.diplomacy.edu/blog/12-ai-and-digital-predictions-for-2024#Security. The Geneva Internet Platform account on the state of offensive cyber capabilities notes indications or evidence that over 57 states already dispose of or build offensive cyber capabilities. Digital Watch, 'Cyberconflict and Warfare – The State of Offensive Cyber Capabilities' www.dig.watch/topics/cyberconflict.

[111] J Kurbalija, 'Tracking the Pulse of Digital Governance and Diplomacy in 2023: A Quarterly Progress Report – Cybersecurity: Preserving the Internet in Difficult Times' (*Diplo*, 6 January 2023) www.diplomacy.edu/blog/2023-digital-governance-predictions/#7_Cybersecurity_Preserving_the_internet_in_difficult_times.

[112] Prussian General Carl von Clausewitz was an early 19th-century warfare theorist known for his unfinished work *Vom Kriege* (On War). One of his most famous quotes is that 'War is the continuation of the politics of definite classes and states by other means'. C von Clausewitz (M Howard and P Paret (eds)), *On War* (Princeton, Princeton University Press, 1976) 44.

is posing. Further interaction with non-state actors, particularly the private sector and NGOs, is also needed. In a cyber diplomacy White Paper published in 2021,[113] the authors suggested that the first step for effective cyber diplomacy is governments' awareness of how cyber issues affect states' domestic and foreign policy agendas. Cyber diplomacy can assist in capacity building through training and exchange of information, developing CBMs, and adapting policy measures to cyber needs. It also stressed that national cyber diplomacies must identify a focal point, influence regional bodies, and align national legislation to international commitments.[114] As it has often been highlighted, the diplomatic effort to counter cyber threats needs to be cross-cutting, given that sovereignty, human rights, and business are interdependent.[115] Finally, mainstreaming cyber issues in national policies and devising strategies for increasing cyber resilience is equally essential for cyber diplomacy to succeed in its mission.

The effort to determine how the principle of peaceful settlement of disputes can be implemented in cyberspace will continue. In a concept paper[116] submitted by Canada and Switzerland in November 2022 to the 2021–2025 OEWG regarding the topics to be included in the Programme of Work for 2023, peaceful settlement of disputes was among the four topics proposed along with the UN Charter, international humanitarian law, and state responsibility. In explaining their choice, the two states argued that Articles 2(3) and 33 of the UN Charter have been of 'continuous importance' since the framework for responsible state behaviour was agreed upon in the 2015 GGE Report. However, they add that now is the time to discuss 'how these rules could contribute to peace and security by providing both an obligation on States and a tool for de-escalation', reminding all that the topic aligns with the work of the UN Secretary-General on a New Agenda for Peace[117] where some countries have already highlighted the importance of the peaceful settlement of disputes.[118]

[113] Cybersecurity Tech Accord, 'Effective Cyber Diplomacy White Paper: A Guide to Countries' Engagement in International Security Dialogues' (25 October 2021) www.cybertechaccord.org/effective-cyber-diplomacy-white-paper-a-guide-to-countries-engagement-in-international-security-dialogues/.

[114] ibid.

[115] C Painter, 'Diplomacy in Cyberspace: The Rise of the Internet and Cyber Technologies Constitutes One of the Central Foreign Policy Issues of the 21st Century' (2018) 95(5) *The Foreign Service Journal* 26.

[116] Anon, 'A Practical Approach to International Law in the 2021-2025 OEWG: Updated Concept Paper by Canada and Switzerland' (18 November 2022) docs-library.unoda.org/Open-Ended_Working_Group_on_Information_and_Communication_Technologies_-_(2021)/Updated_-_A_Practical_Approach_to_International_Law_in_the_OEWG_-_Canada-Switzerland_Concept_Paper_Nov_18_2022.pdf.

[117] UN Department of Political and Peacebuilding Affairs, 'New Agenda for Peace' dppa.un.org/en/new-agenda-for-peace#_ftn1, fn 1.

[118] Among others, see Greece's submission on the New Agenda for Peace, where the peaceful settlement of disputes is mentioned as one of the principles that form the bedrock of the UN. UN Department of Political and Peacebuilding Affairs, 'Our Common Agenda: Greece's Priorities and Proposals on New Agenda for Peace' dppa.un.org/sites/default/files/greece.pdf.

In *Brave New World Revisited*,[119] written over 35 years after his first title, Aldous Huxley lamented some of the failures of this brave new world while also pointing to future dangers. 'This blind biological enemy of freedom is allied with immensely powerful forces generated by the very advances in technology of which we are most proud.'[120] In this struggle, the millennia-old practice of diplomacy, appropriately adapted to the demands of our time, can and should serve as a torch to elucidate the dark corners of this brave new world of cyberspace.

[119] A Huxley, *Brave New World Revisited* (New York, Harper & Brothers, 1962).
[120] ibid 9.

8

Settlement of Inter-State Data Disputes

JOANNA KULESZA

I. Introduction

This chapter provides an analysis of the scope and limits of potential inter-state disputes involving data. It covers recent European Union (EU) policies aimed at protecting the digital single market, such as the General Data Protection Regulation (GDPR), and their transboundary effects. Section II defines the notion of data, distinguishing between personal and non-personal information, with due regard to diverging regional approaches to data governance and management. Section III looks at data as a privacy protection vehicle with references to the EU's approach to personal data protection and the GDPR, as well as their universal impact. The United States (US)' framing of the GDPR as an international trade barrier as well as the Chinese attempts to accommodate the GDPR criteria in their consumer protection and export policies are the key points of analysis. This section also examines the reflexive policies adopted by states such as Russia and China, aimed at ensuring national data management and cyber-sovereignty. Section III covers the human rights dimension of data, deriving from the personal vs non-personal distinction made in section II. Analysing personal data processing principles and their international impact, the author goes on to discuss the impact of the transatlantic data divide on inter-state disputes. This is done with references to recent case law in the two leading cases filed by Maximilian Schrems and the potential impact of the Artificial Intelligence (AI) Act of 2021. International transfers of personal data are analysed as examples of inter-state data disputes, with judicial and diplomatic solutions applied thereto serving as case study examples. Section III concludes these human rights considerations with a reflection on the fundamental link between personal data protection and security with the Snowden revelations serving as an example of an inter-state dispute regarding data. Section IV explores the potential for inter-state disputes deriving from differing approaches to free expression. These result in potential dilemmas in identifying and implementing laws on hate speech or disinformation. A brief review of strategies for social media networks' self- and co-regulation, geo-blocking, and content filtering is provided.[1] The author also points to the recent European code of practice on disinformation as a potential non-judicial, multistakeholder solution to pressing data transfer issues. Section V reviews international norms imposing an obligation to settle inter-state disputes peacefully. This is done by considering their suitability to address cyber disputes over the free flow of data while taking into account the constraints identified in previous sections. It also covers conflict resolution measures included in contemporary international law and discusses their application to transboundary data flows. While mediation mechanisms are readily available in certain areas of international trade law, states are yet to develop mediation mechanisms for cybersecurity-related data disputes. In Section VI the chapter concludes with recommendations on appropriate measures for the settlement of cybersecurity-related disputes, based on current challenges and recent advancements in the relevant domains.

II. Defining Data in Cyberspace: Personal and Non-Personal Data

The information society runs on data: whatever services companies offer or processes they perform, data is the oil of the information society. The all-encompassing notion of 'data' can mean all transmitted or processed digitalised information. It covers any transfer between and among devices based on the Internet Protocol.[2]

If the above were a comprehensive and sufficient definition of data, solving inter-state data disputes would be easier – we would be dealing with one coherent category of data. Unfortunately, this is not the case. The diversity of data means that international disputes relating to data may cover a broad range of issues, cases, and incidents, ranging from commercial disputes, through disinformation and cybercrime, all the way to critical infrastructure protection. This is why, for analytical purposes, it is useful to refer to a well-established dichotomy between personal and non-personal data. This distinction will allow us to further categorise potential inter-state data disputes and to seek solutions specific to a given data category. Many jurisdictions recognise data either as personal or non-personal. The latter category is relatively open to processing and dissemination, provided that cybersecurity or intellectual property issues are duly addressed. The personal data category, however, operates under strict legislative scrutiny, requiring controllers and processors to comply with a complex matrix of norms, principles, and obligations, as will be discussed below.

[1] M Finnemore and DB Hollis, 'Constructing Norms for Global Cybersecurity' (2016) 110 *American Journal of International Law* 425.

[2] IETF, 'RFC 791 Internet Protocol, DARPA Internet Program, Protocol Specification' (September 1981) www.rfc-editor.org/rfc/rfc791.

In jurisdictions that legally recognise this distinction, personal data protection is a measure to protect privacy. This is done through a detailed, public law framework, dating back to the early 1980s. It can be traced back to the 1980 OECD privacy protection framework[3] and the 1981 Council of Europe Convention 108,[4] both of which have been recently updated (in 2013 and 2018 respectively). The aforementioned instruments, which enjoyed broad adoption and implementation as legal obligations or good practices, allowed for personal data protection to become a distinct legal category, applicable to all online policy processes.[5] It includes, for example, the right to deletion, labelled as the right to be forgotten, granting each individual (data subject) an enforceable right to decide how long, by whom, and for what purpose information about them is to be stored and processed.[6] This individual prerogative, viewed as an element of the human right to privacy, imposes positive and negative obligations on states. States must refrain from unjustified interference with the right to privacy and must ensure that one's information is protected against unlawful access by third parties, for example through surveillance. Their positive obligations imply the duty to act with utmost care to ensure that no other party violates the rights of individuals. The practical application of this duty has encountered serious challenges, starting with that of an applicable definition of what is to be protected, ie, 'personal data'.

Personal data has been consistently defined in numerous legal documents as 'any data relating to an identified or identifiable individual'.[7] This definition has proven persistently challenging for policymakers, academics, and practitioners alike. It is a very flexible definition, intentionally drafted as such to be 'timeproof' against unpredictable technological advancements. The drafters were convinced that whatever new technological challenges arise, the brief definition would always protect individuals against the use of their data without explicit consent or a specific provision of law. This was a lesson European states have learnt all too well

[3] OECD, 'Recommendation of the Council Concerning Guidelines Governing the Protection of Privacy and Transborder Flows of Personal Data' (23 September 1980) [C(80)58/FINAL]; OECD, 'Recommendation of the Council Concerning Guidelines Governing the Protection of Privacy and Transborder Flows of Personal Data' (2013) [C(80)58/FINAL, as amended on 11 July 2013 by C(2013)79].

[4] Council of Europe, Convention for the Protection of Individuals with Regard to Automatic Processing of Personal Data (Strasbourg, 28 January 1981) CETS No 108; Council of Europe, Protocol Amending the Convention for the Protection of Individuals with Regard to Automatic Processing of Personal Data (Strasbourg, 10 October 2018) CETS No 223.

[5] G Greenleaf, 'Balancing Globalisation's Benefits and Commitments: Accession to Data Protection Convention 108 by Countries Outside Europe' (*University of New South Wales Law Research Paper No 16*, June 2016) papers.ssrn.com/sol3/papers.cfm?abstract_id=2801054; G Greenleaf, 'Global Data Privacy Laws' (2017) 145 *Privacy Laws and Business International Report* 10–13; Y McDermott, 'Conceptualising the Right to Data Protection in an Era of Big Data' (2017) 4 *Big Data and Society* doi.org/10.1177/2053951716686.

[6] V Mayer-Schonberger, *Delete: The Virtue of Forgetting in the Digital Age* (Princeton, Princeton University Press, 2009).

[7] Eg, the OECD defines personal data as 'any information relating to an identified or identifiable individual (data subject)'; OECD, 'Recommendation of the Council' [C(80)58/FINAL, as amended by C(2013)79] Annex 1, para 1.

during World War II and were committed not to repeat. They agreed that regardless of what future power shifts in individual European countries might bring, all European citizens' data would be protected against racial, religious, or social bias and discrimination. States are therefore under a positive obligation to take all necessary measures, legal or non-legal, to ensure the personal data of individuals within their effective jurisdiction is protected from collection and processing without specific legal authorisation or explicit consent. This obligation covers state agents and third parties, including private companies.

As will be explained below, this approach is, however, neither universally adopted nor broadly shared despite proving perpetually popular in Europe.[8] So much so, that the EU decided to exert a universal 'Brussels effect' based on an Act that regulates online communications through personal data policies – the General Data Protection Regulation (GDPR). The same regulatory approach seems to be taken with the newly (at the time of writing) drafted AI Act,[9] fully aligned with the personal data approach of the GDPR.[10]

International adoption of this personal data protection standard could be used as an example of a universal, effective legal standard in the contemporary globalised data economy. In Europe and like-minded countries, it has been perceived as an operational, effective way to ensure individual privacy. Outside Europe, however, there are states and transnational corporations which view it as a significant constraint to innovation and free data flows across globalised markets.[11] This is why 'data disputes' offer an interesting example of how they can become inter-state disputes and how they could be settled amicably.[12] To address this challenge, both aspects of 'data' must be covered. We shall start with the privacy perspective, which will then be compared and analysed within the national security context.

III. Privacy and Personal Data

When inter-state data flows are analysed from a human rights perspective, two aspects are most important: privacy and freedom of expression. Personal data

[8] PM Schwartz and DJ Solove, 'Reconciling Personal Information in the United States and European Union' (2014) 102 *California Law Review* 877; M Tzanou, 'European Union Regulation of Transatlantic Data Transfers and Online Surveillance' (2017) 17 *Human Rights Law Review* 545; M Tzanou, 'Schrems I and Schrems II: Assessing the Case for the Extraterritoriality of EU Fundamental Rights' in F Fabbrini, E Celeste and J Quinn (eds), *Data Protection Beyond Borders: Transatlantic Perspectives on Extraterritoriality and Sovereignty* (Oxford, Hart Publishing, 2021).

[9] European Commission (2016) 'Proposal for a Regulation of The European Parliament and of the Council Laying Down Harmonised Rules on Artificial Intelligence (Artificial Intelligence Act) and Amending Certain Union Legislative Acts', COM/2021/206 final, 2021/0106(COD).

[10] See generally, A Bradford, *The Brussels Effect: How the European Union Rules the World* (Oxford, Oxford University Press, 2020).

[11] See, eg, MF Ferracane, 'The Costs of Data Protectionism' in M Burri (ed), *Big Data and Global Trade Law* (Cambridge, Cambridge University Press, 2021) 76ff.

[12] See also J Kulesza, 'Peaceful Settlement of Interstate Online Disputes' (2022) 11 *Laws* 49 doi.org/10.3390/laws11030049.

protection is a measure to protect the privacy of the individual and must be balanced against the rights and interests of others. Another necessary balancing exercise is between the protection of specific categories of information and free expression. Both are discussed in the following sections to better identify the scope of potential inter-state data disputes they may give rise to and the ways of mitigating them.[13]

The right to privacy is well-established in human rights law, supplemented by the protection of one's reputation, home, and correspondence.[14] Its formulation in national legal systems differs significantly, with distinct civil law approaches recognising privacy as a human right entrenched in dignity, or else as a consumer protection measure aimed at facilitating trade and trust.[15] Criminal law protection of privacy, if it exists, is usually limited to the protection of one's correspondence and communications, with exceptions restricted to court-mandated surveillance, searches, or seizures.[16] Despite international consensus on the right to privacy as demonstrated by the International Covenant on Civil and Political Rights, states have been unable to agree on and enforce a uniform and universal working consensus on the protection of individual privacy as the ICCPR drafters phrased it.[17] It is because of this practical challenge that a principles-based system of data protection law emerged.[18] The complementary nature of these two rights – a right safeguarding the protection of individual privacy and the complementary right to personal data protection – is reflected, for example, in the EU Charter of Fundamental Rights,[19] where two separate provisions, Articles 7 and 8 respectively, reinstate privacy and personal data. In contrast to privacy, the processing of personal data comes with a range of detailed guiding principles, discussed in section III.A below.

[13] Additionally, one could also investigate the protection of property, particularly intellectual property rights, and the mitigation of international trade disputes. They will only be signalled in this chapter, but not covered in detail because they are too far-reaching.

[14] International Covenant on Civil and Political Rights (New York, 16 December 1966) (ICCPR) Art 17 confirms that 'No one shall be subjected to arbitrary or unlawful interference with his privacy, family, home, or correspondence, nor to unlawful attacks on his honour and reputation. Everyone has the right to the protection of the law against such interference or attacks.' The preamble states that 'Considering that, in accordance with the principles proclaimed in the Charter of the United Nations, recognition of the inherent dignity and of the equal and inalienable rights of all members of the human family is the foundation of freedom, justice and peace in the world, … and Considering the obligation of States under the Charter of the United Nations to promote universal respect for, and observance of, human rights and freedoms …'.

[15] PM Schwartz and K-N Peifer, 'Structuring International Data Privacy Law' (2019) www.law.berkeley.edu/wp-content/uploads/2019/10/Schwartz-Intl-Data-Privacy-Law-21.pdf 21.

[16] One should note, however, the growing practical significance of these exceptions with the use of electronic surveillance means similar to the Pegasus software. See European Parliament, 'PEGA – Committee to Investigate the Use of Pegasus Surveillance Spyware' (2022) multimedia.europarl.europa.eu/pl/package/pega-committee-to-investigate-use-of-pegasus-surveillance-spyware_22903.

[17] ICCPR Art 17.

[18] O Lynskey, *The Foundations of EU Data Protection Law* (Oxford, Oxford University Press, 2015).

[19] Charter of Fundamental Rights of the European Union [2012] OJ C326/391.

Their implementation is balanced and counterweighted. One the one hand, there is the passive obligation of a state to refrain from interference with individual rights and liberties and on the other, the positive obligation to ensure effective legal and practical tools to safeguard them. It is in this latter context that we would expect states to ensure appropriate laws and regulations protecting individual privacy. Since the early 1980s, good international practice in this regard amounted to the approval and implementation of comprehensive data protection laws. These cover a uniform, universal definition of personal data, a clear understanding of specific roles granted to data processors and controllers, as well as a comprehensive set of detailed data protection principles. While their scope and meaning are settled, their practical implications have given rise to inter-state disputes as discussed below.

A. Processing Personal Data

The set of specific obligations data processors and controllers must follow are based on the assumption that data about an individual is the object of their prerogative. This is why all data processing norms include seven principles of personal data protection.[20] The most fundamental principle is that of lawfulness, fairness, and transparency in personal data processing. It requires state agencies and businesses to only collect personal data when there is a specific purpose laid down in law. The complementary commitment to fairness implies that all other principles be implemented with due care and in line with other human rights provisions. Transparency gives individual data subjects the right to obtain information about who is collecting and processing their data and how it is done, as well as for what purposes. A data subject also has the right to intervene in such processing and collection, for example by exercising their right to deletion ('to be forgotten'). The second principle of personal data protection is purpose limitation: third parties may only collect and process personal data for specific purposes identified in law or based on consent. No one may process personal data without specifying such purpose. The data minimalisation principle implies that data controllers and processors are to obtain the least amount of data necessary to meet their aims. They must refrain from collecting and processing more data than is strictly necessary for the specified purpose. Data controllers and processors are also under an obligation to ensure that the data which is being processed is accurate, current, and linked to an

[20] See ch 2 of the General Data Protection Regulation (EU) 2016/679 [2016] OJ L119/1; or [2018] OJ L127/2 (GDPR) on Principles, which includes: Art 5 referencing the principles relating to processing of personal data; Art 6 reinstating the principle of lawfulness of processing; and Art 7 reiterating the conditions for consent. These provisions introduce seven data protection principles which are: 1. the principle of lawfulness, fairness, and transparency; 2. purpose limitation principle; 3. data minimisation principle; 4. accuracy principle; 5. storage limitation principle; 6. the principle of data integrity and confidentiality; and 7. accountability principle.

identified or identifiable individual. The principle of storage limitation implies that data may only be held for a time that is required by law and necessary for obtaining a given aim. All data controllers and processors are under direct obligation to ensure that the data they collect and process are stored securely. Most recently, as per the GDPR, fines for failing to show due care in protecting personal data have significantly increased.[21] This development reflects the last and seventh principle of personal data processing, which is accountability. This principle means that data controllers and processors must be held accountable for any violations of the norms and principles described briefly above.

I will now explain the scope of any potential inter-state data dispute that may arise from these principles, since states' approaches may differ. More specifically, expectations of data collection, storage, and processing differ even among states that recognise data protection as a measure to protect privacy. The differences are even more pronounced among those who view data collection and processing as a consumer protection or national security issue.

B. Transatlantic Data Divide

This divergence of approaches has been particularly visible in the free data flow dispute between the EU and the US since the early 2000s. It was the expansion of the Internet that caused the EU and the US to engage in discussions about the desired shape of transboundary data flows between them.

EU states have held the consistent view that the 1995 Personal Data Protection Directive applied to cyberspace.[22] This is a measure to protect EU citizens' rights also beyond the EU borders. Its provisions prohibit exporting personal data to third countries have proven particularly challenging when applied to states not recognised by the European Commission as compliant with the data processing rules described above. The US is one of those states that had a valid interest in compliance with European data protection laws, yet it was not in a position to impose any kind of data protection law upon states and individual actors within its jurisdiction, because these categories were alien to the US' legal system. This is not to say that the US never recognised the right to privacy – quite the contrary. It is a constitutional principle included in the Bill of Rights. The scope and meaning of privacy in the Fourth Amendment are quite different, however, from those reflected in

[21] Recently (2022) the French data protection authority (Commission nationale de l'informatique et des libertés, CNIL) fined a US company, Clearview AI, with €20 million for failing to comply with its notice to cease collection and use of personal data on French territory, noting absence of a legal basis for processing. CNIL, 'Délibération de la formation restreinte n° SAN-2022-019 du 17 octobre 2022 concernant la société CLEARVIEW AI' (*Légifrance*, 17 October 2022) www.legifrance.gouv.fr/cnil/id/CNILTEXT000046444859?isSuggest=true.

[22] Directive 95/46/EC of the European Parliament and of the Council of 24 October 1995 on the protection of individuals about the processing of personal data and on the free movement of such data (Data Protection Directive) [1995] OJ L281/31, 31–50.

EU laws. In the US, the right to privacy protects US persons (and US persons only) against interference from the government without a valid legal ground and a court order.[23] These provisions are not aimed at or applicable to private parties, including business enterprises. Any data collection constraints imposed on businesses in the US originate from consumer protection laws. They are comprehensive and effective but do not reflect the need to protect 'personal data' of individuals.

Despite this, the US and the EU found a fragile compromise, allowing European companies to share personal data with their American counterparts. An adequacy decision was issued by the European Commission in 2001, based on a so-called Safe Harbour Agreement.[24] The Agreement reflected a selection of the seven data processing principles and a vague promise that US companies would aim to comply with them. The US Department of Trade was authorised to ensure that the US indeed is a 'safe harbour' for Europeans' data, but this proved not to be the case. The Safe Harbour Agreement did not place any legal obligations on US companies to adhere to European data protection standards as a necessary precondition for access to the European Market. The US Department of Trade merely encouraged and supported those US companies who wished to follow the European data protection rules. It was, however, in no position to punish those who did not. Despite independent and European Commission reviews and attempts at improving the status quo, the Safe Harbour Agreement remained a declaration of intent rather than an enforceable legal framework.[25] Most US companies did not see the added value of complying with European standards and decided against the additional investment in development and enforcement of personal data protection policies. Despite the European Commission's adequacy decision and the US declaration of compliance, diverging understandings of privacy and data protection resulted in an unbridgeable transatlantic divide for the free and secure flow of data.

This is reflected in a sequence of Court of Justice of the European Union (CJEU) cases brought by Max Schrems.[26] In his complaint to the CJEU, he reflected on the concerns referenced above and requested the Court to review the legality of the adequacy decision.[27] The Court shared Schrems' concerns and invalidated

[23] The phrase 'US persons' is derived from the US Constitution Amendment 14 and its s 1 on the Citizenship Clause Doctrine to reference US citizens.

[24] European Commission, '2000/520/EC: Commission Decision of 26 July 2000 pursuant to Directive 95/46/EC of the European Parliament and of the Council on the adequacy of the protection provided by the safe harbour privacy principles and related frequently asked questions issued by the US Department of Commerce' [2000] OJ L215/7, 7–47.

[25] R Gellman and P Dixon, 'Failures of Privacy Self-Regulation in the United States' in D Wright and P De Hert (eds), *Enforcing Privacy: Regulatory, Legal and Technological Approaches* (Cham, Springer, 2016) 65. See also European Commission, 'Communication from the Commission to the European Parliament and the Council on the Functioning of the Safe Harbour from the Perspective of EU Citizens and Companies Established in the EU, COM/2013/0847 final' (2013) eur-lex.europa.eu/legal-content/EN/TXT/?uri=CELEX%3A52013DC0847.

[26] Judgment in Case C-362/14 *Maximillian Schrems v Data Protection Commissioner* ECLI:EU:C:2015:650 (*Schrems I*); Judgment in Case C-311/18 *Data Protection Commissioner v Facebook Ireland Limited and Maximillian Schrems* ECLI:EU:C:2020:559 (*Schrems II*).

[27] European Commission, '2000/520/EC: Commission Decision of 26 July 2000' (notified under document number C(2000) 2441).

the transatlantic US-EU Safe Harbour Agreement. It confirmed that neither the Department of Trade nor US companies were protecting Europeans' data 'adequately'. It determined that, even if the US companies involved took adequate security precautions, US public authorities were not subject to the Safe Harbour guidelines, putting European citizens' data and privacy at risk of US government surveillance.[28] The decision sealed the fate of transatlantic data flows and could, potentially, have halted all e-commerce between the two sides of the Atlantic. This scenario needed to be mitigated quickly. The EU and the US quickly amended their data arrangement to ensure a continuous flow of transatlantic data. Yet the newly established 'Privacy Shield' arrangement proved to be as flawed and ineffective as its predecessor. It was only a matter of time before the CJEU again found it inconsistent with the EU's provisions on fundamental rights, privacy, and data protection.[29]

Thus far, the challenge of halting transatlantic data flows has been mitigated because US companies decided to comply with the GDPR and the CJEU judgments. It transpires that the transboundary GDPR effect and pending financial liability worked, although the issue of international consensus on transboundary data flows remains.

EU countries view GDPR and its transboundary effect as an achievement, pointing to the 'Brussels effect' as a paradigm of globally effective regulation of online activities.[30] Some authors praised the Council of Europe for a similar effect (the 'Strasbourg' effect) through its Convention 108, as updated in 2018 (Convention 108+).[31] The EU seems determined to repeat this formula with a series of upcoming legislative proposals, including a regulation encompassing

[28] See, eg, R Gellman and P Dixon, 'Failures of Privacy Self-Regulation in the United States' in D Wright and P De Hert (eds), *Enforcing Privacy: Regulatory, Legal and Technological Approaches* (Cham, Springer, 2016) 65.

[29] C Kuner, 'The Schrems II Judgment of the Court of Justice and the Future of Data Transfer Regulation' (*European Law Blog*, 17 July 2020) europeanlawblog.eu/2020/07/17/the-schrems-ii-judgment-of-the-court-of-justice-and-the-future-of-data-transfer-regulation/; T Christakis, K Propp and P Swire, 'The Redress Mechanism in the Privacy Shield Successor: On the Independence and Effective Powers of the DPRC' (*Cross-Border Data Forum*, 24 October 2022) www.crossborderdataforum.org/the-redress-mechanism-in-the-privacy-shield-successor-on-the-independence-and-effective-powers-of-the-dprc; Case C-362/14, *Maximillian Schrems v Data Protection Commissioner* ECLI:EU:C:2015:650, paras 73, 75, 76, 78, p. 22; Case C-311/18 *Data Protection Commissioner v Facebook Ireland Limited and Maximillian Schrems*, Judgment of the Court (Grand Chamber) of 16 July 2020, ECLI:EU:C:2020:559, paras 101, 104, p. 5; M Tzanou, 'Schrems I and Schrems II: Assessing the Case for the Extraterritoriality of EU Fundamental Rights' in F Fabbrini, E Celeste and J Quinn (eds), *Data Protection Beyond Borders: Transatlantic Perspectives on Extraterritoriality and Sovereignty* (Oxford, Hart Publishing, 2021) 5 ff.

[30] See, eg, A Bendiek and I Stuerzer, 'The Brussels Effect, European Regulatory Power and Political Capital: Evidence for Mutually Reinforcing Internal and External Dimensions of the Brussels Effect from the European Digital Policy Debate' (2023) 2 *Digital Society* 1. See also chapter by Bendiek et al (ch 5 in this volume).

[31] LA Bygrave, 'The "Strasbourg Effect" on Data Protection in Light of the "Brussels Effect": Logic, Mechanics and Prospects' (2020) 38 *Computer Law and Security Review* 105460 doi.org/10.1016/j.clsr.2020.105460; Council of Europe, Modernised Convention for the Protection of Individuals with Regard to the Processing of Personal Data, adopted by the Committee of Ministers at its 128th Session of the Committee of Ministers (Elsinore, 18 May 2018) as per the Decision of the Committee of Ministers 128th session of the Committee of Ministers (Elsinore, 18 May 2018).

'digital services' – the Digital Services Act – as well as the dedicated AI Act.[32] These plans are to confirm Europe's role as a data regulatory superpower.[33]

Europe indeed offers a unique approach to ensuring human rights protection across jurisdictions, including the online environment. It built its contemporary international standing on an elaborate regulatory scheme. Within the 46 states of the Council of Europe or the 27 members of the EU, human rights served as the common denominator for ensuring policy compliance. This is not to say that such compliance has been ideal – far from it. Both the Council of Europe and the EU strive to ensure the rule of law and respect for human rights in the small, yet diverse, continent.

Although parties thus far refrained from declaring the existence of a data dispute, the divergence of opinions on the need to ensure the protection of data, particularly personal data, is a useful example of a potential transnational data dispute, a focal interest of this chapter. The EU determination to enforce compliance with the GDPR, particularly through a judicial dispute settlement mechanism, is of paramount importance in this respect. The CJEU helped to identify the scope of the dispute, determine the applicable law to the dispute parties, and advance the international debate over the applicable legal framework to transboundary data flows. It can be viewed as a prime example of judicial settlement of disputes over transboundary data flows.

C. Personal Data Transfers under EU Law

Article 45 of the GDPR covers the principles for transnational transfers of personal data based on an adequacy decision. According to its stipulations, a third country, a territory, or one or more designated sectors within that third country, or the international organisation in question, may receive personal data transfers if the Commission specifies that the recipient offers an adequate level of protection. Specific authorisation is not necessary for such a transfer.[34]

In determining whether the level of protection is adequate, the Commission will, in particular, consider the following factors: the rule of law; respect for human rights and fundamental freedoms; applicable legislation, both general and sectoral, including those of public security, defence, national security, and criminal law, as well as the implementation of such legislation; data protection rules;

[32] European Commission, 'Proposal for a Regulation of the European Parliament and of the Council Laying Down Harmonised Rules on Artificial Intelligence (Artificial Intelligence Act) and Amending Certain Union Legislative Acts, COM/2021/206 final' (2021) eur-lex.europa.eu/legal-content/EN/TXT/?uri=CELEX:52021PC0206.

[33] For a detailed analysis see, eg, M Cremona and J Scott, *EU Law Beyond EU Borders: The Extraterritorial Reach of EU Law* (Oxford, Oxford University Press, 2019).

[34] C Kuner, 'Article 45: Transfers on the Basis of an Adequacy Decision' in C Kuner et al (eds), *The EU General Data Protection Regulation (GDPR): A Commentary* (Oxford, Oxford University Press, 2020) 774.

professional rules and security measures; case law; effective and enforceable data subject rights, and effective administrative and judicial redress for the data subjects whose personal data are being transferred are among the requirements for the forward transfer of personal data to another third country or international organisation. Moreover, the Commission will assess the presence and proper operation of one or more independent supervisory authorities in charge of overseeing compliance with data protection laws in the third country or under the jurisdiction of an international organisation. This authority must have the power to assist and advise data subjects in the exercise of their rights and collaborate with supervisory authorities in the Member States. Obligations imposed by legally binding conventions or instruments, as well as those resulting from the third country's or international organisation's participation in multilateral or regional systems, particularly concerning the protection of personal data, will be considered in the assessment. Initially the Commission is to determine whether the level of protection in a third country, a territory, one or more designated sectors within a third country, or an international organisation, provides an adequate level of protection following these provisions. The effective implementation legislation must include a mechanism for periodic reviews that occur at least every four years. The Commission must also continually follow up on advancements in third countries and international organisations that may have an impact on how decisions are implemented. Should disputes over the interpretation of these provisions or their application arise, the Commission must consult with a third country or international organisation.

These provisions reiterate the overall principle of Recitals 103 through 106, explicitly authorising the Commission to decide that a third country, a territory, a specific sector within a third country, or an international organisation, offers an adequate level of data protection. By making this decision with immediate effect for the entire Union, the Commission creates legal certainty and uniformity regarding the third country or international organisation that is thought to provide such a level of protection. In these situations, personal data transfers to the relevant third country or international organisation are permitted without the need for additional authorisation. The Commission may also decide to revoke such a decision after providing the third country or international organisation with notice and a thorough statement outlining the reasons.

According to Article 46 of the GDPR, a controller or processor may transfer personal data to a third country or an international organisation in the absence of a decision made under Article 45, but only under the following circumstances: if they implemented appropriate safeguards; if there are enforceable data subject rights; and if there are effective legal remedies available to data subjects. A legally binding and enforceable agreement between public authorities or bodies may be used to provide these appropriate safeguards, without needing any special authorisation from a supervisory authority. Moreover, and interesting for this discussion, binding corporate rules introduced per Article 47 of the GDPR may also serve this purpose, similar to standard data protection clauses adopted by the Commission or a supervisory authority and approved by the Commission. When a code of conduct that has been approved under Article 40 combined with legally binding and enforceable commitments from the controller or processor in the third country to implement the necessary safeguards (including those on data subjects' rights), these requirements are also considered to be met.

Most significantly, these provisions were verified when the Commission Decision 2016/1250 on the EU-US Privacy Shield was invalidated by CJEU judgment C-311/18 (*Schrems II*). Interestingly though, the CJEU upheld the validity of standard contractual clauses (SCCs), provided that they contain effective mechanisms to ensure practical compliance with the 'essentially equivalent' level of protection promised to EU citizens by the GDPR. Following the adoption of an adequacy decision, the Commission was required by Article 45(4) of the GDPR to periodically assess whether the decision's operation is still appropriate, legally and pragmatically. When there are questions in that regard, another examination is required. Additionally, communication with the relevant third country's authorities is necessary for this ongoing adequacy monitoring. Following Article 70(1)(b) if the GDPR, the Commission may seek assistance in this process from the European Data Protection Board.[35]

Data flows are crucial to national security, just as personal data protection is fundamental to the effective protection of individual privacy. As challenging as it is for lawmakers, this junction gives fertile ground for legal interpretations and analysis. National security viewed from a data collection and processing perspective is usually reflected in surveillance and state security laws. This is no different in the US, with a key national security act dating back to the 1970s. The Foreign Intelligence Surveillance Act of 1978 (FISA)[36] was amended by the US Patriot Act in the aftermath of the 9/11 attacks.[37] It was one of the responses in the global 'war on terror' that the US declared shortly thereafter. In 2013, the *New Yorker* in the US and *The Guardian* in the UK simultaneously published a report on mass surveillance performed by the US National Security Agency (NSA). A top-secret FISA court order mandated Verizon Business Network Services to provide a daily feed to the NSA containing 'telephony metadata' ie, complete records of call details, including location data of all calls in its system, also those that are carried out entirely on the Internet 'within the United States, including local telephone calls'.[38] These provisions allowed for the execution of a dedicated PRISM program, a comprehensive

[35] See also D Korff and I Brown, *Exchanges of Personal Data after the Schrems II Judgment* (Brussels, European Parliament, 2021).

[36] Foreign Intelligence Surveillance Act of 1978, 50 USC 1801 §§ 1801–811, 1821–829, 1841–846, 1861–862, 1871.

[37] US Congress, 'Uniting and Strengthening America by Providing Appropriate Tools Required to Intercept and Obstruct Terrorism (USA Patriot Act) Act Of 2001', *Public Law* 107–56.

[38] Anon, 'Verizon Forced to Hand Over Telephone Data – Full Court Ruling' (*The Guardian*, 6 June 2013) www.theguardian.com/world/interactive/2013/jun/06/verizon-telephone-data-court-order.

intelligence operation comprising mass data collection, algorithm-based analysis, and dedicated backdoors installed on US-manufactured devices.[39] The publications provoked global outrage. International partners and local NGOs accused the US government of violating the Fourth Amendment to the US Constitution and having grave disregard for binding international law treaties, including the ICCPR. The case laid the heaviest burden on international trust and security, with allies in Europe and beyond outraged at the scale of mass surveillance that the US had also conducted on its allies, following the Snowden revelations.

This is why the GDPR can be seen as a direct reaction to the urgent need for advancing global privacy protections. While, again, no international legal dispute between parties was declared, the political tension thickened. This time it was the interest of national security in the US that justified mass data interception, prioritising national security concerns over the individual privacy of non-US persons. Existing international arrangements proved vastly futile.

The debate that followed focused on the limits of national data control, including mandating back doors on equipment, the security of supply chains for chips, and software manufactured in each jurisdiction. The result was the discussion on supply chain security and the war on tariffs between China and the US. In 2015, China announced its 'Made in China 2025' program, claiming technological independence from foreign suppliers. In 2016, Beijing promulgated its national cybersecurity law, similar in its effect to the FISA Act,[40] to be followed in 2021 with a Data Security Law of the People's Republic of China.[41]

States did not claim that data is a reason for international disputes, but their behaviour spoke louder than their diplomatic words and demonstrated that such a dispute exists indirectly.[42] The most recent example of such a dispute is the trade-related disagreement between the US and China.[43]

[39] For a comprehensive review and implications, see T Christakis, 'Squaring the Circle? International Surveillance, Underwater Cables, and EU-US Adequacy Negotiations (Part 1)' (*Cross-Border Data Forum*, 26 April 2021) www.crossborderdataforum.org/squaring-the-circle-international-surveillance-underwater-cables-and-eu-us-adequacy-negotiations-part-1.

[40] Cybersecurity Law of the People's Republic of China, Order No 53 of the President (11 July 2016). The Bill covers the Chinese understanding of the principle of cyberspace sovereignty while identifying security obligations relevant for internet services providers, software and hardware producers, personal information protection and key information infrastructure.

[41] Bloomberg News, 'China's New Data Law Gives Xi the Power to Shut Down Tech Firms' (*Bloomberg*, 11 June 2021) www.bloomberg.com/news/articles/2021-06-10/china-passes-law-to-strengthen-control-over-tech-firms-data; National People's Congress of the People's Republic of China; Order of the President of the People's Republic of China No. 84; The Data Security Law of the People's Republic of China, adopted at the 29th Meeting of the Standing Committee of the Thirteenth National People's Congress of the People's Republic of China on 10 June 2021.

[42] T Christakis, K Propp and P Swire, 'Towards OECD Principles for Government Access to Data' (*Lawfare*, 20 December 2021) www.lawfareblog.com/towards-oecd-principles-government-access-data.

[43] For recent reference, see, eg, R Reich, 'Data, not Arms, the Key Driver in Emerging US-China Cold War' (*The Guardian*, 10 July 2021) www.theguardian.com/world/2021/jul/10/china-us-cold-war-data-markets-national-security.

IV. Free Expression, Hate Speech, and Disinformation

Inter-state data disputes, as they currently unfold, are no longer only about the status of personal and non-personal data. When attempting to identify the scope of online data disputes, one should also look at the limits of free data flow that originate from legally protected interests other than privacy. Freedom of expression, like privacy, is a fundamental human right, reflected in all human rights treaties and national laws.[44] Just as privacy, it is not absolute and can be restricted through legal provisions to protect the legitimate collective or individual interests of others. In a careful legal balancing act, freedom of expression may need to give way to the protection of reputation, public safety, prevention of crime, or protection of morals.[45] National and regional legal systems usually frame freedom of expression and the free flow of data in the context of protecting the rights and interests of others. Yet recent developments bring a new perspective to these old debates with an alleged right to be truthfully informed, or alternatively, a right to freedom from disinformation. No specific provision on any of these rights can be explicitly found in the law. However, states, international organisations, and private companies alike go to great lengths to protect the average internet user from being misled, falsely or inaccurately informed, or bluntly lied to. And they do so following a public expectation for them to act as unique 'Ministries of Truth', halting harmful data.

Where does the free flow of information end and 'disinformation' begin? Who should make the distinction and impose a restriction on the public's right to be informed? Technically the answer is simple: it is up to media companies, particularly the big social media ones, to keep us safe from disinformation. They do claim to act with due care to make sure that this is the case. Meta advances its algorithms and AI to detect and deter 'fake news and viral disinformation'.[46] This is done not only with tacit consent, but with eager support from states and civil society. States encourage and support private companies in doing so, while all parties concerned realise that there is no legal red line for determining truths, half-truths, lies, and confusion. Legal due care obligations do exist, but these rest upon a selected group of individuals acting in a specific context, for example, media editors, investment advisors, banking executives, and doctors, who are expected not to deceive their patients. National criminal laws provide for the liability of professionals who fail to act with due care. But this is by far not the standard for average internet users. They have a right to share their ideas and opinions without limitation and restraint if they do not infringe on the abovementioned rights of others. There is no right to

[44] See, eg, A Koltay, *Freedom of Speech: The Unreachable Mirage* (Budapest, CompLex, 2013).

[45] European Convention on Human Rights (Rome, 4 November 1950) Art 10(2).

[46] P Monteiro Borges and R Rampazzo Gambarato, 'The Role of Beliefs and Behavior on Facebook: A Semiotic Approach to Algorithms, Fake News, and Transmedia Journalism' (2019) 13 *International Journal of Communication* 603, 616.

be truthfully informed. Any decision on a potential infringement brought about by lack of due care in sharing truthful information should be based on a specific provision of law and made by a court in a due process of law. It should not be the result of a social media company's policy and its outsourcing of editorial duties to a piecework subcontractor, as is the case with Meta or Google.[47] Even when these processes are automated with the deployment of robots, AI, or simply algorithms, the questions on attribution and liability for infringements remain valid. Although, one might wish to investigate the potential liability or responsibility of software or AI developers rather than those of the social media company directly. The EU risk-based approach would likely, however, still point to service providers, requiring them to ensure risk assessments that would make the deployed AI human rights compliant.[48]

The pertaining challenge of intermediary liability and its limits is gaining prominence as the fight against disinformation becomes another facet of inter-state data disputes.[49] Data carries information. Information influences human behaviour. It can bring progress or harm. The free flow of data is the free flow of information. The free flow of information means the free flow of disinformation, that states and internet users want to see stopped. In the era of global election tampering and online psychological operations, the free flow of data is limited and access to information deemed untrue or detrimental, is restricted. States take different approaches to this challenge and once again, data is at its core. Most recently, these concerns were reflected in national debates and security decisions regarding the availability of the Chinese-owned TikTok, although the arguments used by governments restricting access to the platform usually cited privacy and cybersecurity concerns, rather than potential disinformation as such.[50]

As with privacy, Europe takes the lead in tackling disinformation through regulatory means and stands strong on protecting the rights of the individual. This includes their right to be diligently informed, and protection against abuse through hate speech or other harmful content. The 2018 European Commission 'Guidance on Strengthening the Code of Practice on Disinformation' (Guidance)[51] builds upon the 'European Democracy Action Plan' (EDAP),[52] the 'Communication on

[47] See, eg, AV Banchik, 'Disappearing Acts: Content Moderation and Emergent Practices to Preserve At-Risk Human Rights-Related Content' (2021) 23 *New Media & Society* 1527.

[48] See, eg, T Mahler, 'Between Risk Management and Proportionality: The Risk-Based Approach in the EU's Artificial Intelligence Act Proposal' (2021) *Nordic Yearbook of Law and Informatics* 245.

[49] See, eg, I Popović, 'The EU Ban of RT and Sputnik: Concerns Regarding Freedom of Expression' (*EJIL: Talk!*, 30 March 2022) www.ejiltalk.org/the-eu-ban-of-rt-and-sputnik-concerns-regarding-freedom-of-expression.

[50] S Maheshwari and A Holpuch, 'Why Countries are Trying to Ban TikTok' (*New York Times*, 23 May 2023) www.nytimes.com/article/tiktok-ban.html.

[51] European Commission, 'Guidance to strengthen the Code of Practice on Disinformation', 26 May 2021, Brussels.

[52] European Commission, 'Communication from the Commission To The European Parliament, The Council, The European Economic And Social Committee And The Committee Of The Regions On the European democracy action plan'; COM/2020/790 final.

Tackling Online Disinformation: A European Approach' (the Communication),[53] and various other initiatives taking place across Europe to address the challenges posed by the dissemination of disinformation. In this series of documents and accompanying actions, the European Commission attempts to tackle disinformation through co-regulation, and encourages private companies to sign up and follow a Code of Practice.[54] According to the Code of Practice, the broad category of 'disinformation' is made up of false information, disinformation in and of itself, information that influence operations, and foreign interference in the information sphere. These categories have been respectively defined in the EDAP, as pointed out in the Code of Practice.[55]

The Code of Practice encourages all actors to undertake 'multiple operational policies and tools' which may 'vary between signatories but aim to address the challenges described'.[56] Complementarily, the European Commission insists

> that all actions taken to challenge disinformation should strictly respect freedom of expression and include safeguards that prevent their misuse, for example, the censoring of critical, satirical, dissenting, or shocking speech (and) strictly respect the European Commission's commitment to an open, safe, and reliable Internet.[57]

This difficult task can only be completed with the active participation of all stakeholders. Hence the Code of Practice will serve more as a reference framework than a directly effective piece of legislation.

This co-regulatory measure is not a universal answer to all data-related disputes. It is, however, an interesting example of good practice that takes into due account the nature of the digital environment that the Commission is trying to co-regulate. It offers an interesting, and, hopefully, feasible balance between hard, top-down regulation, as exercised for example in Central Asia, and the direct reliance on the all-ruling hand of the free market as in the US. While not an ultimate solution to potential data disputes, this approach offers an interesting example of

[53] European Commission, 'Communication From The Commission To The European Parliament, The Council, The European Economic And Social Committee And The Committee Of The Regions Tackling online disinformation: a European Approach', COM/2018/236 final.

[54] European Commission, 'The Strengthened Code of Practice on Disinformation 2022' (16 June 2022) digital-strategy.ec.europa.eu/en/library/2022-strengthened-code-practice-disinformation.

[55] ibid 1. False or misleading content shared without harmful intent though the effects can still be harmful, eg, when people share false information with friends and family in good faith is 'misinformation'. False or misleading content that is spread to deceive or secure economic or political gain and which may cause public harm is 'disinformation'. Coordinated efforts by either domestic or foreign actors to influence a target audience using a range of deceptive means, including suppressing independent information sources in combination with disinformation, are referred to as 'information influence operation'. Foreign interference is to be understood as coercive and deceptive efforts to disrupt the free formation and expression of individuals, political will by a foreign state actor or its agents. Disinformation does not include misleading advertising, reporting errors, satire and parody, or clearly identified partisan news and commentary, and is without prejudice to binding legal obligations, self-regulatory advertising codes, and standards regarding misleading advertising.

[56] ibid.

[57] ibid.

good practice to follow. Another alternative would be to rely on self-regulation, such as in the challenging example of Meta's Oversight Board.

Attesting to the shifting power balance in the global information society, social media companies have the ultimate say about the scope of online free expression and data flows. Tipping the balance on inter-state dispute resolution methods towards contract-based conflict resolution, the largest social media platform grabbed the initiative and the authority on settling international data disputes over the transboundary services they offer. Meta has gone as far as to set up its own global, quasi-judicial institution – the Oversight Board – to review individual complaints about potential freedom of expression violations. As pointed out by substantiated criticism, the 'private *quasi* tribunal' fails to enforce rule of law provisions, to ensure structural independence, and to ensure equal representation.[58] Flawed as it may be, its decisions ultimately shape the limits of free expression and the data that carry them for Meta's three billion users.

This privatised dispute resolution mechanism, addressing long-standing international human rights law issues and their online application, does not directly address the potential inter-state aspect of the dispute or the dispute itself. As with any conflict mediation, all applicable judicial means are still open to parties. It might, however, offer the added value of a prompt and cost-effective way of settling a complex, transborder legal matter. As the *Gonzalez v Google*[59] and *Twitter v Taamneh*[60] cases (pending at the time of writing before the US Supreme Court) have shown, a swift and cheap alternative to lengthy and costly judicial proceedings might seem attractive to individuals seeking a prompt and effective resolution to a data dispute, notwithstanding all its due process and legitimacy challenges.

V. Peaceful Settlement of International Data-Related Disputes

As explained above, privacy and free expression are the legal normative frameworks to review when identifying potential inter-state data disputes. Should these indeed arise, international law offers dedicated measures to ensure their peaceful resolution. One should, however, start from the definition of 'dispute' and ask whether data disputes would constitute a legal dispute for international law purposes.

[58] K Klonick, 'The Facebook Oversight Board: Creating an Independent Institution to Adjudicate Online Free Expression' (2020) 129 *Yale Law Journal* 2418. For reference see Oversight Board, 'Independent Judgment. Transparency. Legitimacy' (2 November 2022) www.oversightboard.com/.

[59] Case pending before the US Supreme Court, '*Gonzalez v Google LLC* (Docket 21-1333)' www.supremecourt.gov/docket/docketfiles/html/public/21-1333.html on intermediary liability for terrorist content made available online.

[60] Case pending before the US Supreme Court, '*Twitter, Inc v Taamneh* (Docket 21-1496)' www.supremecourt.gov/docket/docketfiles/html/public/21-1496.html.

The very notion of a dispute in international law is formulated in the context of inter-state adjudication. This is because the existence of a dispute is required for an international court to recognise jurisdiction over the case and disputing parties. As a result, when defining an international dispute, one must consider international court proceedings and admissibility decisions. When attempting to identify a dispute under international law, the International Court of Justice's adjudication and decisions on admissibility should be used as a guide.[61]

The International Court of Justice (ICJ) stated in its interpretation of peace treaties with Bulgaria, Hungary, and Romania that the existence of an international dispute is a matter of objective determination.[62] States have objected in international practice to the perception of a conflict or disagreement as a dispute when such conflict or disagreement does not involve or impact any material interests of governments or nationals.[63] The ICJ did not share this understanding, determining that even in the absence of material interests, a conflict or disagreement may be perceived as a dispute under the ICJ Statute.[64] For a dispute to exist, 'it must be demonstrated that the claim of one party is positively opposed by the other'.[65] Crawford argues that the presence of a state's legal interest is separate from the presence of an inter-state controversy. As per international adjudication, the existence of legal interests may be considered the 'indispensable basis of a justiciable dispute'.[66] This implies that no dispute can be identified where no direct state interest exists. For inter-state data disputes, it could be argued that only a specific case, such as that of *Gonzales v Google*, can lie at the foundation of an inter-state claim.

In light of these considerations, inter-state data disputes can be defined as a difference of opinions between state parties as to the conduct legally required from them regarding digital information. These different opinions can cover questions on the limits of technological autonomy, digital sovereignty, cybersecurity, free expression, or, most significantly for this discussion, privacy and the free flow of personal data. They are also directly impacted by local or regional economic and political considerations. Here the EU's approach to data as part of their Single

[61] See the Introduction to this volume and chapters by Tsagourias (ch 1 in this volume) and Antonopoulos (ch 4 in this volume).

[62] *Interpretation of Peace Treaties with Bulgaria Hungary and Romania* (Advisory Opinion of 30 March 1950) [1950] ICJ Rep 65, 74.

[63] *South West Africa Cases (Ethiopia v South Africa; Liberia v South Africa)* (Preliminary Objections, Judgment of 21 December 1962) [1962] ICJ Rep 319, 327.

[64] J Crawford, *Brownlie's Principles of Public International Law*, 8th edn (Oxford, Oxford University Press, 2019) 694. See also *Obligations Concerning Negotiations Relating to Cessation of the Nuclear Arms Race and to Nuclear Disarmament (Marshall Islands v United Kingdom)* (Preliminary Objections, Judgment of 5 October 2016) [2016] ICJ Rep 833. The Court stated that, for a dispute to exist, there must be a clear difference of opinions between the parties regarding whether certain international obligations should be complied with. It also stated that a dispute arises whenever the evidence shows that the respondent was aware – or could not have been unaware – that the applicant's opinions were in direct opposition to the respondent's.

[65] *South West Africa Cases* (n 63) 382.

[66] J Crawford, *Brownlie's Principles of Public International Law*, 8th edn (Oxford, Oxford University Press, 2019) 694. See Antonopoulos (ch 4 in this volume).

Digital Market policies can be mentioned. Data lies at the cross-section of national security and international geopolitical discussions – it would be the cause of the dispute over competing individual state interests. The way states collect, process, and share data is fundamental to the contemporary application of international law. The OECD Guidelines, Convention 108+, and the GDPR all set specific norms, principles, and procedures for the handling of data. When differences on the application of these procedures arise, judicial dispute settlement has thus far proven to be the most efficient. The CJEU in both *Schrems* cases, as well as in a variety of other privacy-related decisions,[67] specified what these principles should mean in practice. In the current geopolitical environment, the settlement of transboundary data-related disputes is primarily judicial. Most significantly, the CJEU and the European Court of Human Rights laid the foundations for understanding the principles behind personal data flows. Whether their interpretation is the most likely scenario for future data disputes is debatable. When assessing the ongoing geopolitical conflicts, ranging from the US-China digital cold war to the war in Ukraine, it seems that national security concerns will likely prevail over the European human-centric approach to privacy and personal data protection.

Resolving disputes related to non-personal data proves more challenging. When data means news, political expression, targeted advertising, or election interference, national interest tends to be given priority. International law offers disputing states the full plethora of dispute settlement measures, from negotiations to the ICJ. These traditional processes have, however, proven to be slow and inefficient. This is why there is increasing interest in shifting the approach to standard-setting and norm-making. The European Commission, for example, prioritises co-regulation when attempting to find effective consensus on disinformation.[68] It is perhaps the way forward that the social responsibility of business, whether in line with the Ruggie Principles[69] or with the Facebook Oversight Board paradigm, will provide immediate and effective – if not always legitimate – online dispute resolution.

VI. Conclusion and Prospects

International data disputes are potentially a significant challenge for the application of international law in cyberspace. They cover a broad range of issues and

[67] Just to mention a few: CJEU Grand Chamber judgment in Joined Cases C-511/18, C-512/18 and C-520-18 *La Quadrature du Net v France* ECLI:EU:C:2020:791; CJEU Grand Chamber judgment in Joined Cases C-293/12 and C-594/12 *Digital Rights Ireland and Kärntner Landesregierung* ECLI:EU:C:2014:238.

[68] For this author's discussion on a standards-based approach to international data disputes settlement, see J Kulesza, 'Peaceful Settlement of Interstate Online Disputes' (available online).

[69] United Nations, Office of the High Commissioner on Human rights, Guiding Principles on Business and Human Rights, Implementing the United Nations "Protect, Respect and Remedy" Framework, New York / Geneva 2011.

span across all jurisdictions. Yet as the application of international law in cyberspace grows, states will be more inclined to use the international law toolbox to resolve disputes involving cyberattacks or cyber threats. As global tensions rise, including those on international data disputes, international lawyers and state authorities alike should investigate the international law toolbox to identify feasible and practical means of resolving inter-state disputes. The examples mentioned in this chapter allow for the identification of the components of such a toolbox and provide a unique opportunity to advance the international dialogue on the peaceful uses of cyberspace and on solving inter-state data disputes.

These tools can help to address the evolving challenges of inter-state data disputes, in particular the challenge of the a-territoriality of cyberspace. As states engage in ever more complex discussions on digital sovereignty and technological autonomy, the jurisprudence on data protection and its safe transitional transit can assist to develop new, or advance existing, trade and innovation paradigms. It applies to peaceful as well as military deployment of ICTs.

ICT, innovation, and the intrinsic transnational data flows have affected and impacted the well-established understanding of territoriality in international law. Data travels fast while all known dispute settlement mechanisms take time. Whether through diplomatic negotiations or judicial proceedings, international law has struggled to keep up with technologies and often risk lagging behind. There is one exception: the EU GDPR and the Convention 108+ framework. Following the Snowden revelations, Europe was quick and effective in implementing its well-established privacy framework, which allowed it to apply its judicial mechanism to data disputes as well. This does not, however, come without costs. Judicial dispute settlement is always suitable for states. It should therefore remain the default mechanism for data-related disputes also. The existing case law discussed in this chapter, combined with good co-regulation practices and further development of the multistakeholder Internet governance model, will likely aid the application of judicial dispute settlement mechanisms discussed in this volume as the best-suited means for settling data-related inter-state disputes.

It is likely that other jurisdictions will also investigate this method of transboundary governance to solve their data disputes. They will aim to implement their regional or national understandings of data governance globally. This poses the risk of the global network dividing into smaller regional or national sections. Though interconnected at singular junctions, it will result in a splinternet scenario. If this scenario is avoidable, the benefits of a global interconnected network should be protected. The Internet is being viewed as a precondition to sustainable development, innovation, and human growth. A splinternet will not allow for any of these aspirational goals to be achieved. This is why the settlement of international data disputes should happen at the international level, rather than being monopolised by individual jurisdictions.

9

Collective and Third-Party Cyber Countermeasures

RUSSELL BUCHAN

I. Introduction

Over the past two decades, a major achievement of the international community has been to confirm that international law applies to cyberspace and it has made considerable progress in clarifying how this legal framework applies to that domain.[1] At the same time, there has been a steady rise in malicious cyber activity,[2] which has raised concerns that cyberspace may become a 'Wild West' where international law is breached with impunity.[3] This development raises important questions as to what mechanisms are available to the international community to enforce compliance with international law, whether they are adequate, and whether new ones should be established.[4]

The international legal system is primitive when compared to other legal systems because it lacks centralised machinery for law enforcement. In this decentralised system, international law enforcement lies (predominantly) in the hands of those who believe that their legal rights have been infringed. Customary international law (CIL) has long recognised that states can take countermeasures against wrong-doing states where they have been directly injured by a breach of international law. Countermeasures are prima facie unlawful measures whose wrongfulness is

[1] UNGA, 'Report of the Group of Governmental Experts on Advancing Responsible State Behaviour in Cyberspace in the Context of International Security' (14 July 2021) UN Doc A/76/135 para 69; UNGA, 'Final Substantive Report of the Open-Ended Working Group on Developments in the Field of Information and Telecommunications in the Context of International Security' (10 March 2021) UN Doc A/AC.290/2021/CRP.2 para 34.

[2] A Mascellino, 'Global Cyber Attacks Rise by 7% in Q1 2023' (*Infosecurity Magazine*, 28 April 2023) www.infosecurity-magazine.com/news/global-cyber-attacks-rise-7-q1-2023/.

[3] Quoting US President Barack Obama in B Chappell, 'Obama: Cyberspace is the New "Wild West"' (*NPR*, 13 February 2015) www.npr.org/sections/thetwo-way/2015/02/13/385960693/obama-to-urge-companies-to-share-data-on-cyber-threats.

[4] M Hathaway, 'Getting Beyond Norms: When Violating the Agreement Becomes Customary Practice: CIGI Paper No 127' (*Centre for International Governance Innovation*, April 2017) www.cigionline.org/static/documents/documents/Paper%20no.127.pdf.

precluded on the basis that they are reactions to prior breaches of international law and are designed to induce wrongdoing states into law compliance and implement their international legal responsibility. Countermeasures are thus important self-help mechanisms that enable states to protect their legal rights when faced with another state's unlawful conduct. Given their objective is the restoration of legality and cannot involve the threat or use of force,[5] countermeasures form part of the peaceful dispute settlement system provided by international law.[6]

An important question is whether states that have not been directly injured by a breach of international law can also take countermeasures against wrongdoing states, namely, whether international law recognises the doctrines of collective and third-party countermeasures. For definitional purposes, collective countermeasures involve indirectly injured states taking countermeasures against a wrongdoing state to help protect a collective legal interest, that is, to enforce compliance with *erga omnes (partes)* obligations. By contrast, third-party countermeasures do not concern the protection of *erga omnes (partes)* obligations, but instead involve third states (who are neither directly nor indirectly injured by the breach of international law) taking countermeasures on behalf of an injured state to help protect the latter's legal rights against a wrongdoing state.

Whether the doctrines of collective and third-party countermeasures are established in CIL is an old and contested question. However, due to the uptick in malicious cyber operations in recent years, state practice and *opinio juris* on collective and third-party countermeasures have developed. The advent of cyberspace therefore provides a good opportunity to re-visit the legality of these doctrines under international law and, in doing so, this chapter is structured in three parts. Section II focuses on the legality of collective countermeasures. To explain this doctrine, section II.A charts the development of multilateralism in the international legal system. Section II.B examines the International Court of Justice's (ICJ) treatment of collective countermeasures. Section II.C engages with the International Law Commission's (ILC) project on the law of state responsibility and sets out its position on collective countermeasures. Section II.D maps developments in state practice and *opinio juris* since 1945 and examines whether the doctrine of collective countermeasures has crystallised in CIL and, if so, whether it applies to cyberspace. Section III analyses the lawfulness of third-party countermeasures under the law of state responsibility. Section IV explores the potential for the development of *lex specialis* on collective and third-party cyber countermeasures. The final section offers conclusions.

[5] International Law Commission, 'Responsibility of States for Internationally Wrongful Acts' in *Yearbook of the International Law Commission. 2001, Volume II, Part Two: Report of the Commission to the General Assembly on the Work of its Fifty-Third Session* (New York, UN, 2005) (*Articles on State Responsibility*) Art 50(1)(a).

[6] '[R]ecourse to counter-measures not involving the threat or use of force is in itself a peaceful means of settling a dispute arising from an internationally wrongful act'; B Simma, 'Counter-Measures and Dispute Settlement: A Plea for a Different Balance' (1994) 5 *European Journal of International Law* 102, 103.

II. Collective Countermeasures

A. Multilateralism in International Law

Historically, international law consisted of a series of corresponding rights and duties between states.[7] In this system, countermeasures were available only to those states whose legal rights had been directly infringed by a wrongdoing state.

During the 1970s, the international legal system developed elements of a multilateral public order. In the *Barcelona Traction* ruling,[8] the ICJ recognised that international legal rules have emerged that protect community values or interests and, as such, they are owed to the international community as a whole. These rules are known as obligations *erga omnes*, and examples include the prohibitions on slavery, genocide, torture and aggression,[9] and the 'principles and rules concerning the basic rights of the human person'.[10] Importantly, the Court determined that the international community as a whole has a collective legal interest in ensuring their observance. The Court did not consider whether members of the international community can take countermeasures against a wrongdoing state to enforce compliance with obligations *erga omnes*, a doctrine known as collective countermeasures. However, the permissibility of collective countermeasures in response to breaches of *erga omnes* obligations was inevitably raised.

The ICJ later recognised the concept of obligations *erga omnes partes*.[11] This category describes obligations owed to a group of states that protect a common value or interest, typically where states are party to a multilateral convention. As with obligations *erga omnes*, the question of the permissibility of collective countermeasures arises: if members of the group have a collective legal interest in ensuring that obligations *erga omnes partes* are upheld, can they also take collective countermeasures to enforce compliance with them?

B. Collective Countermeasures before the International Court of Justice

The ICJ addressed the legality of collective countermeasures in its *Nicaragua* judgment. The ICJ held that the United States of America (USA) committed prima

[7] J Crawford, *The International Law Commission's Articles on State Responsibility. Introduction, Text and Commentaries* (Cambridge, Cambridge University Press, 2002) 258, para 8.

[8] *Barcelona Traction, Light and Power Company, Limited (Belgium v Spain)* (Judgment of 5 February 1970) [1970] ICJ Rep 3.

[9] ibid para 34.

[10] ibid. On the identification of *erga omnes* obligations, see BD Lepard, *Customary International Law: A New Theory with Practical Applications* (Cambridge, Cambridge University Press, 2012) ch 18.

[11] *Questions Relating to the Obligation to Prosecute or Extradite (Belgium v Senegal)* (Judgment of 20 July 2012) [2012] ICJ Rep 422 para 68.

facie breaches of the principles of non-intervention and non-use of force by providing support to armed groups acting against Nicaragua.[12] The USA claimed its actions were justified on the basis of the collective self-defence of Honduras, El Salvador, and Costa Rica. The ICJ ruled out the USA's reliance on collective self-defence because it was not able to determine that Nicaragua had committed an armed attack against Honduras, El Salvador, or Costa Rica. Moreover, Honduras, El Salvador, and Costa Rica did not request assistance from the USA, a prerequisite for the invocation of the right of collective self-defence.

In the context of Nicaragua's alleged breach of the non-use of force principle, which is widely considered an *erga omnes* obligation aimed at the maintenance of international peace and security,[13] the Court went on to consider whether the USA's prima facie unlawful measures could be justified as collective countermeasures. For the Court:

> The acts of which Nicaragua is accused, even assuming them to have been established and imputable to that State, could only have justified proportionate countermeasures on the part of the State which had been the victim of these acts, namely El Salvador, Honduras or Costa Rica. They could not justify countermeasures taken by a third State, the United States, and particularly could not justify intervention involving the use of force.[14]

The Court seemed to reject the proposition that the doctrine of collective countermeasures is established in CIL. Some commentators caution against this reading of the *Nicaragua* decision, claiming the Court did not reject the doctrine of collective countermeasures per se but instead ruled out its invocation where the countermeasures undertaken involve a threat or use of force.[15] It is correct that, since 1945 and the consecration of the principle of non-use of force in Article 2(4) of the United Nations (UN) Charter 1945, countermeasures cannot take the form of a threat or use of force.[16] The Court therefore correctly concluded that the USA's support for armed opposition groups – which breached the non-use of force principle – could not be justified as a countermeasure. But the Court also addressed the legality of *non-forcible* collective countermeasures. In rejecting collective countermeasures in both their non-forcible and forcible modes, the Court held Nicaragua's actions 'could not justify countermeasures taken by a third State, the United States, *and particularly could not justify intervention involving the use of force*'.[17]

[12] *Case Concerning Military and Paramilitary Activities in and against Nicaragua (Nicaragua v United States of America)* (Merits, Judgment of 27 June 1986) [1986] ICJ Rep 14 paras 209, 228.

[13] ILC, 'Peremptory Norms of General International Law (*Jus Cogens*). Ch IV. Report of the International Law Commission on the Work of its Seventy-Third Session' (2022) UN Doc A/77/10 Conclusion 17, Commentary, para 1.

[14] *Military and Paramilitary Activities in and against Nicaragua* (n 12) para 249.

[15] 'The best reading of the judgment restricts the court's observations on collective countermeasures to instances involving the use of force'; MN Schmitt and S Watts, 'Collective Cyber Countermeasures?' (2021) 12 *Harvard National Security Journal* 373, 391.

[16] *Articles on State Responsibility* Art 50(1)(a).

[17] *Military and Paramilitary Activities in and against Nicaragua* (n 12) para 249 (emphasis added).

The ICJ's *Nicaragua* decision was rendered in 1986. As the international legal order has developed a more prominent multilateralist structure, the question is whether there have been subsequent developments in international law in favour of the doctrine of collective countermeasures.

C. Articles on State Responsibility

The ILC's 50-year project on the law of state responsibility involved a detailed consideration of the law of countermeasures and, in particular, which states are permitted to take them. The ILC adopted the Articles on State Responsibility (ASR) with commentaries in 2001, and the United Nations General Assembly (UNGA) has 'commended' this project to UN Member States on several occasions.[18] The ASR project is, therefore, an important reference point when considering the legality of collective countermeasures, even if there is a legitimate question as to whether the ILC's 2001 position on this doctrine continues to reflect *lex lata*.

The ASR concludes that 'injured' states can take countermeasures against wrongdoing states and proceeds to define this category. As Article 42 of the ASR explains:

> A State is entitled as an injured State to invoke the responsibility of another State if the obligation breached is owed to:
>
> (a) that State individually; or
>
> (b) a group of States including that State, or the international community as a whole, and the breach of the obligation:
>
> (i) specially affects that State; or
>
> (ii) is of such a character as radically to change the position of all the other States to which the obligation is owed with respect to the further performance of the obligation.

The immediate question is whether, apart from injured states, any other states can invoke the responsibility of a wrongdoing state and take countermeasures against it. This issue is in part addressed in Article 48 of the ASR:

> 1. Any State other than an injured State is entitled to invoke the responsibility of another State in accordance with paragraph 2 if:
>
> (a) the obligation breached is owed to a group of States including that State, and is established for the protection of a collective interest of the group; or
>
> (b) the obligation breached is owed to the international community as a whole.

[18] UNGA, 'Resolution Adopted by the General Assembly: 56/83. Responsibility of States for Internationally Wrongful Acts' (28 January 2002) UN Doc A/RES/56/83; UNGA, 'Resolution Adopted by the General Assembly: 59/35. Responsibility of States for Internationally Wrongful Acts' (16 December 2004) UN Doc A/RES/58/35; UNGA, 'Resolution Adopted by the General Assembly: 62/61. Responsibility of States for Internationally Wrongful Acts' (8 January 2008) UN Doc A/RES/62/61; and UNGA, 'Resolution Adopted by the General Assembly: 65/10. Responsibility of States for Internationally Wrongful Acts' (10 January 2011) UN Doc A/RES/65/19.

Article 48(1) therefore permits states who form part of a group to which the breached obligation is owed (obligations *erga omnes partes*), or where the breached obligation is owed to the international community as a whole (obligations *erga omnes*), to invoke the responsibility of the wrongdoing state. As the commentary to Article 48 explains, these states have a 'legal interest' in ensuring that *erga omnes (partes)* are upheld,[19] and are often referred to as 'indirectly injured' states. Article 48(2)(a)-(b) of the ASR explains that while indirectly injured states are entitled to invoke the responsibility of a wrongdoing state under Article 48(1), they can only demand cessation and reparations on behalf of the injured state or the beneficiaries of the obligation. Evidently, Article 48(2) does not go so far as to authorise an indirectly injured state to take countermeasures against a wrongdoing state in order to protect a collective legal interest.

Guided by James Crawford, the ILC's final Special Rapporteur on the law of state responsibility, the ILC adopted a draft set of Articles on State Responsibility in 2000.[20] Interestingly, Draft Article 54 permitted collective countermeasures in two situations: first, where there had been a breach of an *erga omnes (partes)* obligation in conjunction with a request for assistance from the injured state (Draft Article 54(1)), and second, where there had been a serious breach of an *erga omnes (partes)* obligation (Draft Article 54(2)). Some states supported the ILC's approach to collective countermeasures.[21] However, Draft Article 54 met with resistance from other states.[22] Mexico, for example, noted that 'the position expressed in [Draft] article 54 is not supported by international law'.[23] Israel concluded that the provisions contained in Draft Article 54 'went beyond existing law and were unwarranted'.[24] Similarly, the United Kingdom (UK) explained:

> A further substantial difficulty concerns the provision in draft article 54, paragraph 2, which would permit any State, in the case of "serious breach", to take countermeasures

[19] *Articles on State Responsibility* Art 48, Commentary, paras 2–8.

[20] ILC, 'Report of the International Law Commission on the Work of its Fifty-Second Session' (2000) UN Doc A/55/10, 65.

[21] Austria (UNGA, 'Sixth Committee: Summary Record of the 17th Meeting' (14 November 2000) UN Doc A/C.6/55/SR.17 para 76); Cuba (UNGA, 'Sixth Committee: Summary Record of the 18th Meeting' (4 December 2000) UN Doc A/C.6/55/SR.18 para 59); Poland (UNGA, 'Sixth Committee: 18th Meeting' UN Doc A/C.6/55/SR.18 para 48); Costa Rica (UNGA, 'Sixth Committee: 17th Meeting' UN Doc A/C.6/55/SR.17 para 63); Italy (UNGA, 'Sixth Committee: Summary Record of the 16th Meeting' (13 November 2000) UN Doc A/C.6/55/SR.16 para 28); Russia (UNGA, 'Sixth Committee: 18th Meeting' UN Doc A/C.6/55/SR.18 para 51); Spain (UNGA, 'Sixth Committee: 16th Meeting' UN Doc A/C.6/55/SR.16 para 13).

[22] Special Rapporteur Crawford described collective countermeasures as 'the most difficult and controversial aspect of the whole regime of State responsibility'; ILC, 'Report of the ILC on the Work of its Forty-Eighth Session, 6 May-26 July 1996' in *Yearbook of the International Law Commission. 1996, Volume II, Part Two: Report of the Commission to the General Assembly on the Work of its Forty-Eighth Session* (New York, UN, 1998) 66.

[23] ILC, 'State Responsibility: Document A/CN.4/515 and Add 1-3' in *Yearbook of the International Law Commission. 2001, Volume I: Summary Records of the Meetings of the Fifty-Third Session* (New York, UN, 2006) 91.

[24] UNGA, 'Sixth Committee: Summary Record of the 15th Meeting' (13 November 2000) UN Doc A/C.6/55/SR.15 para 25.

> "in the interests of the beneficiaries of the obligation breached". Even where, on the basis of the *Barcelona Traction* dictum, there may be a legal interest of States at large in respect of violations of certain obligations, it does not necessarily follow that all States can vindicate those interests in the same way as directly injured States.[25]

This disagreement among states created a dilemma for the ILC: it did not want to remove the provision on collective countermeasures given the support for this doctrine among some states, but at the same time felt unable to retain Draft Article 54 in its existing form given that other states had pushed back against this doctrine. In response, the UK proposed a compromise: to insert a 'saving' (or 'without prejudice') clause into the ASR that left the resolution of the matter of collective countermeasures to future developments in international law and practice.[26] Ultimately, this was the path taken by the ILC, and after its adoption of the ASR in 2001, the newly formulated Article 54 reads:

> This chapter does not prejudice the right of any State, entitled under article 48, paragraph 1, to invoke the responsibility of another State, to take lawful measures against that State to ensure cessation of the breach and reparation in the interest of the injured State or of the beneficiaries of the obligation breached.

The ILC's commentary on Article 54 is revealing and gives further insights into its position on collective countermeasures. After reviewing state practice, the ILC concludes:

> [T]he current state of international law on countermeasures taken in the general or collective interest is uncertain. State practice is sparse and involves a limited number of States. At present, there appears to be no clearly recognized entitlement of States referred to in article 48 to take countermeasures in the collective interest.[27]

The ILC identified six examples of state practice on collective countermeasures: US-Uganda (1978); various Western States-Poland and the Soviet Union (1981); collective measures against Argentina (1982); US-South Africa (1986); collective measures against Iraq (1990); and the collective measures against the Federal Republic of Yugoslavia (1998).

Those commentators in favour of the CIL status of the doctrine of collective countermeasures criticise the ILC for missing examples of state practice prior to 2001.[28] Moreover, they claim there have been developments in state practice since the conclusion of the ILC's project in 2001 to support the argument that the doctrine of collective countermeasures is established in CIL.

[25] ILC, 'State Responsibility: Document A/CN.4/515 and Add 1-3' 94.

[26] UNGA, 'Sixth Committee: Summary Record of the 14th Meeting' (10 November 2000) UN Doc A/C.6/55/SR.14 para 32.

[27] *Articles on State Responsibility* Art 54, Commentary, para 6.

[28] M Dawidowicz, *Third-Party Countermeasures in International Law* (Cambridge, Cambridge University Press, 2017); EK Proukaki, *The Problem of Enforcement in International Law: Countermeasures, the Non-Injured State and the Idea of International Community* (London, Routledge, 2010).

With these issues in mind, this chapter now considers whether the doctrine of collective countermeasures has crystallised as CIL. This review analyses state practice and *opinio juris* since 1945, which is a logical starting point for this inquiry given that the modern law of countermeasures emerged after the UN Charter came into force. Before the Charter's adoption, countermeasures took the form of reprisals and often involved armed reprisals. However, the doctrine of reprisals was revised and reformulated as the doctrine of countermeasures with the inception of the UN Charter and, in particular, its prohibition on the threat or use of force.

D. Collective Countermeasures under Customary Law

According to Article 38(1)(b) of the ICJ Statute 1945, two elements must be present for CIL to form: (i) a general state practice that is (ii) accepted as law (*opinio juris*).[29]

Before examining whether these elements are met in the context of collective countermeasures, a few words of caution are necessary. When evaluating whether CIL has formed, we must be careful to ensure that the state practice relied on actually supports the use of collective countermeasures. This is important because, while states often engage in restrictive measures to protect collective legal interests, they do not expressly identify the legal basis for their actions.[30] There is a tendency in some of the academic literature to place this conduct (almost as a matter of default) into the category of collective countermeasures.[31] However, just because restrictive measures are designed to enforce community rules does not automatically and necessarily mean that they qualify as collective countermeasures.[32] If a state deploys a restrictive measure in defence of a collective legal interest but does not justify it as a matter of international law, it may be the case that the state sees its conduct as inherently lawful (that is, the measure does not conflict with a primary rule of international law) and, as such, does not require justification under international law.[33] These types of restrictive measures are known as retorsion – unfriendly but intrinsically lawful acts.

[29] Art 38(1)(b) of the Statute of the International Court of Justice (San Francisco, 26 June 1945).

[30] 'While a sanctioning State will often provide a political explanation for taking unilateral coercive measures against another State, it is uncommon for it to conclusively refer to a legal basis for the action'; M Dawidowicz, 'Public Law Enforcement without Public Law Safeguards: An Analysis of State Practice on Third-Party Countermeasures and their Relationship to the UN Security Council' (2006) 77 *British Yearbook of International Law* 333, 350.

[31] Dawidowicz (n 28) ch 4.

[32] '[There are] a variety of measures to which States [can] resort in order to secure fulfilment of the obligations deriving from, or otherwise react to, the commission of an internationally wrongful act … [including] sanctions, retortion, reprisals, reciprocity, countermeasures, termination and suspension of treaties, [and] *inadimplenti non est adimplendum*'; G Arangio-Ruiz, 'Third Report on State Responsibility. UN Doc. A/CN.4/440/ and Add.1' in *Yearbook of the International Law Commission. 1991, Volume II, Part One: Documents of the Forty-Third Session* (New York, UN, 1994) 8, para 8.

[33] '[I]nternational practice does not always distinguish clearly between measures constituting violations of international obligations and those which do not cross that threshold'; Arangio-Ruiz (n 32) 11, para 19.

Consider the situation where states respond to breaches of *erga omnes (partes)* obligations by deploying restrictive economic measures without UN authorisation, such as restrictions on trade, arms embargoes, and the freezing of assets. As we know, the UNGA has adopted various resolutions condemning unilateral restrictive economic measures as unlawful,[34] and these resolutions tend to be supported by largely developing states through the so-called non-aligned movement. Yet importantly, certain states (including mainly western states) have voted against (or at least abstained from) these resolutions because they do not see these measures as breaching general international law,[35] and indeed their practice is replete with examples of them engaging in such measures.[36]

A freestanding prohibition on unilateral restrictive economic measures has not therefore crystallised under CIL,[37] and the key question is whether they breach the pre-existing CIL principle of non-intervention. The exercise of (i) coercion within (ii) the *domaine réservé* of the target state are the two conditions precedent for establishing a breach of this principle.[38] In the *Nicaragua* case, the ICJ held that the unilateral restrictive economic measures deployed by the USA against Nicaragua (such as the suspension of economic aid, the blocking of loans, and a trade embargo) did not breach the principle of non-intervention.[39] Similarly, in its

[34] See, eg, UNGA, 'Declaration on the Inadmissibility of Intervention in the Domestic Affairs of States' (21 December 1965) UN Doc A/RES/2131(XX); UNGA, 'Declaration on Principles of International Law Concerning Friendly Relations and Cooperation among States' (24 October 1979) UN Doc A/RES/2625(XXV); UNGA, 'Charter on the Economic Rights and Duties of States' (12 December 1974) UN Doc A/RES/3281(XXIX); UNGA, 'Declaration on the Inadmissibility of Intervention and Interference in the Internal Affairs of States' (9 December 1981) UN Doc A/RES/36/103; UNGA, 'Economic Measures as a Means of Political and Economic Coercion against Developing Countries' (20 December 1991) UN Doc A/RES/46/210 and subsequent annual resolutions with the same title; UNGA, 'Human Rights and Unilateral Coercive Measures' (12 December 1996) UN Doc A/RES/51/103. See also Human Rights Council, 'Report of the Special Rapporteur on the Negative Impact of Unilateral Coercive Measures on the Enjoyment of Human Rights' (4 October 2021) UN Doc A/HRC/48/59/Add.2 para 82.

[35] The USA argued that these resolutions have 'no basis in international law ... [they] undermine the ability of the international community to respond to acts that were offensive to international norms. Unilateral and multilateral sanctions were a legitimate means to achieve foreign policy, security, and other national and international objectives. The United States was not alone in that view or practice'; Statement made on 20 November 2015 by the USA before the UNGA, 'Third Committee: Summary Record of the 52nd Meeting' (15 January 2016) UN Doc A/C.3/70/SR.52 para 32. For similar statements by the USA before the UNGA Third Committee, see: 12 November 2009 (UNGA, 'Third Committee: Summary Record of the 42nd Meeting' (4 March 2010) UN Doc A/C.3/64/SR.42 para 56); 15 November 2011 (UNGA, 'Third Committee: Summary Record of the 44th Meeting' (15 February 2012) UN Doc A/C.3/66/SR.44 para 60); 26 November 2012 (UNGA, 'Third Committee: Summary Record of the 44th Meeting' (28 December 2012) UN Doc A/C.3/67/SR.44 para 12; 21 November 2013 (UNGA, 'Third Committee: Summary Record of the 49th Meeting' (20 January 2014) UN Doc A/C.3/68/SR.49 para 54; and 24 November 2014 (UNGA, 'Third Committee: Summary Record of the 52nd Meeting' (15 January 2015) UN Doc A/C.3/69/SR.52 para 33).

[36] H Lauterpacht, 'Boycott in International Relations' (1993) 14 *British Yearbook of International Law* 125, 130 and 140; SH Cleveland, 'Norm Internalization and US Economic Sanctions' (2001) 26 *Yale Journal of International Law* 1, 53; BE Carter, 'Economic Sanctions' in R Wolfrum (ed), *Max Planck Encyclopedia of Public International Law* (Oxford, Oxford University Press, 2011).

[37] A Hofer, 'The Developed/Developing Divide on Unilateral Coercive Measures: Legitimate Enforcement or Illegitimate Intervention?' (2017) 16 *Chinese Journal of International Law* 175, 192–97.

[38] *Military and Paramilitary Activities in and against Nicaragua* [1986] ICJ Rep 14 para 205.

[39] ibid para 245 (where the Court held that it was 'unable to regard such action on the economic plane as is here complained of as a breach of the customary-law principle of non-intervention').

commentary on the ASR, the ILC determined that 'embargoes of various kinds' constitute acts of retorsion and do not therefore breach international law.[40] This suggests that unilateral restrictive economic measures do not usually qualify as 'coercion' within the meaning of the principle of non-intervention, except perhaps where they are so comprehensive and intense that they compel the target state into acting (or abstain from acting) in a manner that it is permitted by international law to freely decide.[41] Even if unilateral restrictive economic measures amount to 'coercion', some commentators claim that they do not violate the principle of non-intervention where they respond to a breach of international law by the target state, the reason being that such measures do not coerce the target state in relation to policies or choices that fall within its *domaine réservé*.[42]

Some commentators argue that the freezing of assets may breach the law of state immunity.[43] The UN Convention on Jurisdictional Immunities and their Property 2004 is not in force, but its core provisions are nevertheless considered reflective of CIL.[44] While this legal framework explains that state immunity applies to state property (which covers financial assets), conventional wisdom holds that state immunity only extends to measures of constraint 'linked to a judicial proceeding'.[45] Thus, beyond the context of judicial proceedings, such as a government's decision to freeze the assets of another state, the law of state immunity does not apply.[46] While some commentators claim that the rationale for the law of state immunity is to protect foreign governments and their assets from all forms of interference by other states[47] and should therefore apply to executive and administrative decisions as well as judicial proceedings, this is not how the law has developed and, ultimately, does not reflect *lex lata*.[48]

[40] *Articles on State Responsibility* ch II, para 3.

[41] M Jamnejad and M Wood, 'The Principle of Non-Intervention' (2009) 22 *Leiden Journal of International Law* 345, 371 (explaining that coercion requires the state's sovereign will to be 'overborne').

[42] R Barber, 'An Exploration of the General Assembly's Troubled Relationship with Unilateral Sanctions' (2021) 70 *International and Comparative Law Quarterly* 343, 354 ('The vast majority of unilateral sanctions relate not to matters falling within the targeted State's *domaine reserve*, but to matters regulated by international law'). See also M Milanovic, 'Revisiting Coercion as an Element of Prohibited Intervention in International Law' (2023) 117 *American Journal of International Law* 601, 622–23.

[43] J-M Thouvenin, 'Gel des Fonds des Banques Centrales et Immunite D'execution' in A Peters et al (eds), *Immunities in the Age of Global Constitutionalism* (Leiden, Brill, 2015).

[44] *Jones v Ministry of Interior of Saudi Arabia* [2006] UKHL 26; [2007] 1 AC 270, 26.

[45] ILC, 'Draft Articles on Jurisdictional Immunities of States and their Property, with Commentaries' in *Yearbook of the International Law Commission. 1991, Volume II, Part Two: Report of the Commission to the General Assembly on the Work of its Forty-Third Session* (New York, UN, 1994) Commentary to Art 18, para 1.

[46] This analysis excludes a consideration of specialised regimes, such as diplomatic and consular law, which may provide states with additional immunities.

[47] Thouvenin (n 43).

[48] T Ruys, 'Non-UN Financial Sanctions against Central Banks and Heads of State: In Breach of International Immunity Law?' (*EJIL:Talk!*, 12 May 2017) www.ejiltalk.org/non-un-financial-sanctions-against-central-banks-and-heads-of-state-in-breach-of-international-immunity-law/.

Restrictive measures may breach conventional rules of international law to which the states are party. For instance, a trade embargo may conflict with World Trade Organization (WTO) law or a free trade agreement (FTA).

Even if restrictive measures are deployed to protect a collective legal interest and are prima facie unlawful, they may be justified on legal bases other than the doctrine of collective countermeasures. For example:

- Restrictive measures adopted by states in response to a breach of an obligation *erga omnes (partes)* may be deployed pursuant to a decision of an international organisation (most notably, the UN's collective security system).
- Measures undertaken by an injured state in response to a breach of an obligation *erga omnes partes* may be justified under the law of treaties. For example, Article 60 of the Vienna Convention on the Law of Treaties 1969 permits states to suspend treaty obligations or terminate a treaty where the opposing state has committed a material breach of the treaty. Likewise, Article 62 permits termination of, or withdrawal from, a treaty where there has been a fundamental change of circumstances that radically transforms the extent of the obligations to be performed under that agreement.
- Certain treaty regimes contain provisions permitting state parties to take restrictive measures against other parties where specific conditions are met. For instance, Article XXI of the General Agreement on Tariffs and Trade (GATT) 1994 contains a national security exemption permitting a state party to take 'any action which it considers necessary for the protection of its essential security interests … in time of war or other emergency in international relations'. Such provisions can be therefore invoked to justify the use of restrictive measures that otherwise breach the obligations owed under the treaty.
- Restrictive measures – even if non-forcible – may be justified as acts of (individual or collective) self-defence under Article 51 of the UN Charter where they are designed to halt and repel an armed attack.[49]

The critical point is that where states deploy restrictive measures to protect collective legal interests, it cannot be *assumed* that the impugned conduct is deployed as a collective countermeasure. In short, other explanations and justifications may be available and, as we shall see below, this creates significant problems when determining whether there is sufficient state practice and *opinio juris* to support the doctrine of collective countermeasures under CIL.

Commentators have identified various examples of state practice and *opinio juris* on collective countermeasures since 1945. This chapter revisits these examples and considers whether they represent bona fide instances of state practice and *opinio juris* in support of the doctrine of collective countermeasures.

[49] R Buchan, 'Non-Forcible Measures and the Law of Self-Defence' (2023) 72 *International and Comparative Law Quarterly* 1.

USA-North Korea and China (1950)

In 1950, North Korea and China committed an act of 'aggression'[50] by invading South Korea. As we saw above, the ICJ has determined that an act of aggression amounts to a breach of an *erga omnes* obligation.[51] The UN Security Council (UNSC) was unable to take enforcement action due to the threat of the veto and the USA therefore acted unilaterally and imposed arms embargoes against North Korea and China and froze their assets.[52] US policymakers saw these actions as lawful but did not identify or explain their legal basis.[53] According to the above analysis, the arms embargoes can be seen as acts of retorsion.

Some commentators argue that the freeze orders constituted a prima facie breach of general international law and must have been deployed as collective countermeasures.[54] However, as explained, it is not necessarily the case that asset freezing breaches general international law. An equally plausible explanation is that the USA saw the freeze orders as lawful acts of retorsion and, as such, they did not require justification under international law.

Various States-South Africa (1960–1964)

During the early 1960s, South Africa's policy of apartheid breached the prohibition on racial discrimination and the right to self-determination. As the ICJ has explained, these provisions qualify as *erga omnes* obligations.[55] In response, Malaysia, Ghana, Indonesia, Kuwait, Nigeria, Pakistan, Sierra Leone, Tanganyika, and Uganda imposed trade embargoes against South Africa in prima facie breach of Articles XI and XIII of the GATT.[56]

These states did not articulate a legal justification for their conduct. Article XXI of the GATT permits state parties to take measures necessary to protect their essential security interests in time of war or other emergency in international relations. Yet, this provision does not seem applicable to the situation at hand because the repressive human rights practices *within* South Africa did not threaten the essential security interests of the embargoing states. This has led certain commentators to conclude that these states deployed the embargoes as collective countermeasures,[57]

[50] UNGA, 'Intervention of the Central People's Government of the People's Republic of China in Korea' (1 February 1951) UN Doc A/RES/498(V). See also UNSC, 'Resolution 81' (25 June 1950).

[51] *Barcelona Traction* (n 8) para 34.

[52] US Department of State Bulletin (25 December 1950) 1004.

[53] ibid.

[54] Dawidowicz (n 30) 351–52.

[55] *Barcelona Traction* (n 8) para 34 (holding that the prohibition against racial discrimination is an obligation *erga omnes*) and *Legal Consequences of the Construction of a Wall in the Occupied Palestinian Territory* (Advisory Opinion of 9 July 2004) [2004] ICJ Rep 136 para 155 (determining that the right of peoples to self-determination has attained *erga omnes* status).

[56] *Keesing's Contemporary Archives* (1961–1962).

[57] CJ Tams, *Enforcing Obligations* Erga Omnes *in International Law* (Cambridge, Cambridge University Press, 2005) 90; Dawidowicz (n 28) 116–17.

although it should be stressed that these states did not identify this doctrine as the legal basis for their conduct.

European Economic Community-Greece (1967–1970)

During the late 1960s, the Greek government committed serious human rights abuses against the local population, including acts of torture. The prohibition on torture is widely recognised as an *erga omnes* obligation.[58] In response, the Member States of the European Economic Community (EEC) decided to suspend the EEC-Greece Association Agreement 1963 and withhold the development assistance owed to Greece under Protocol 19 of that agreement.[59]

The withdrawal of assistance could not be justified under the treaty because the treaty did not make the assistance contingent upon Greece's protection of human rights. Also, it is not possible to justify these states' withdrawal of assistance under the law of treaties because there had not been a material breach of the treaty or a fundamental change of circumstances. On this basis, some commentators suggest that the prima facie unlawful withdrawal of financial assistance can be seen as a collective countermeasure.[60] That said, it is important to note that the EEC did not offer a legal justification for its conduct.

USA/EEC-Uganda (1978)

In 1978, the USA imposed an import and export embargo against Uganda in response to its 'genocide' against the local population,[61] and there is no doubt that genocide constitutes a breach of an *erga omnes* obligation.[62] The USA recognised that its embargoes ran into conflict with the obligations it owed to Uganda under the GATT and could not be justified under the national security exception contained in Article XXI of that agreement.[63]

Member States of the EEC also undertook restrictive measures against Uganda. The EEC provided only five per cent of the development assistance owed to Uganda under the Lomé I Convention.[64] EEC officials accepted that withholding development assistance constituted a prima facie breach of the convention,[65] but did

[58] *Prosecutor v Furundzija* (Trial Chamber Judgment of 10 December 1998) ICTY IT-95-17/1-T para 151 ('the prohibition of torture imposes upon States obligations *erga omnes*, that is, obligations owed towards all the other members of the international community').

[59] Association Agreement between Greece and the European Economic Community [1963] OJ 294/63.

[60] Dawidowicz (n 28) 119; Tams (n 57) 91.

[61] Uganda Embargo Act (1978) s 5(a)–(b).

[62] *Barcelona Traction* (n 8) para 34.

[63] *United States–Uganda Relations: Hearings before the Subcommittee on Africa*, 95 Congress, 2nd Session (1978) Hearings, 61, 64, 98–100, 105–06.

[64] EC Bulletin 1977, No. 6, para 2.2.59.

[65] OJ Supp. 214/71 (1977–1978).

not offer any legal justification. As noted above, this agreement does not permit suspension or termination because one of the parties has committed human rights abuses. Moreover, it is difficult to justify the EEC's conduct under the law of treaties.

In light of these conclusions, certain commentators argue that the conduct undertaken by the USA and EEC must be seen as collective countermeasures.[66] However, it is again important to underscore that these actors did not expressly invoke this doctrine to justify their action.

EEC-Central African Republic (1979)

During the late 1970s, the Central African Republic (CAR) committed severe human rights abuses against the local population, including the massacre of school children in the state's capital city, Bangui.[67] As noted above, the ICJ has held that the 'principles and rules concerning the basic rights of the human person' have attained *erga omnes* status.[68] There is little doubt that the right to life concerns 'the basic rights of the human person', which means its breach amounts to a violation of an *erga omnes* rule.[69] In response, Member States of the EEC withheld development assistance owed to the CAR under the Lomé I Convention.[70] The EEC did not identify a legal basis for its withdrawal of development assistance.

As we have seen, the Lomé I Convention does not contain a human rights break clause. Some commentators therefore argue that these prima facie unlawful measures must have been deployed as collective countermeasures.[71] But yet again, it should be stressed that the EEC did not expressly invoke this doctrine to justify its withdrawal of development assistance.

EEC-Liberia (1980)

The violent military coup in Liberia in 1980 breached the right to self-determination[72] which, as we saw above, is an *erga omnes* rule. In response, the Member States of the EEC withheld development assistance owed to Liberia under the Lomé I Convention.[73] While certain commentators suggest that the withdrawal

[66] Dawidowicz (n 28) 123.

[67] *Keesing's Contemporary Archives* (1979) 29750–29751.

[68] *Barcelona Traction* (n 8) para 34.

[69] UN Human Rights Committee, 'General Comment No 6: Article 6 (Right to Life Adopted at the Sixteenth Session of the Human Rights Committee, on 30 April 1982)' www.refworld.org/docid/45388400a.html para 1 (describing the right to life as a 'supreme right from which no derogation is permitted' and as one 'which should not be interpreted narrowly').

[70] *Keesing's Contemporary Archives* (1979) 29751.

[71] Dawidowicz (n 28) 126.

[72] Human Rights Watch, 'Liberia: A Human Rights Disaster' (26 October 1990) www.hrw.org/reports/1990/liberia/.

[73] Europe, Vol. 28, No. 2495 (New Series) 11.

of development assistance should be seen as a collective countermeasure,[74] the EEC did not provide any legal justification for the prima facie breach of the treaty.

Canada/New Zealand-Soviet Union (1980)

In 1979, the Soviet Union invaded Afghanistan,[75] which constituted a prohibited use of force and thus a breach of an *erga omnes* obligation. Western states imposed restrictive measures against the Soviet Union, but these largely took the form of retorsion – for example, the US's refusal to export grain to the Soviet Union.

In early 1980, Canada and New Zealand suspended the Soviet Union's fishing rights in their exclusive economic zones, which breached bilateral treaties they had concluded with the Soviet Union. Neither Canada nor New Zealand identified a legal basis for this prima facie unlawful conduct. In the absence of a provision within these bilateral treaties that permitted the immediate suspension of fishing rights, and given that the law of treaties did not permit the suspension of these treaties in the circumstances, some commentators claim that Canada's and New Zealand's actions must be seen as collective countermeasures.[76] Importantly, however, these states did not expressly rely on this doctrine to justify their suspension of the treaties.

Various Western States-Poland and the Soviet Union (1981)

In response to civil unrest in 1981, the Polish government (and allegedly at the behest of the Soviet Union) imposed martial law and interned over 12,500 people.[77] This conduct breached the right to liberty, which is one of the 'basic rights of the human person' and therefore an *erga omnes* rule.[78] Given that *jus cogens* obligations are by definition owed *erga omnes*,[79] the fact that the right to liberty is *jus cogens* also points to its *erga omnes* status.[80]

Various western states suspended the landing rights of Soviet and Polish planes in their territories in breach of the bilateral treaties they had concluded with the Soviet Union and Poland. For example, under Article XV of the 1972 bilateral treaty between the USA and Poland, landing rights could be suspended only when

[74] Dawidowicz (n 28) 127.

[75] UNGA, 'Credentials of Representatives to the Sixth Emergency Special Session of the General Assembly' (14 January 1980) UN Doc E/RES/ES-6/2.

[76] C Focarelli, *Le Contromisure nel Diritto Internazionale* (Rome, University of Rome, 1994) 112.

[77] *Keesing's Contemporary Archives* (1982) 31453–67.

[78] As the ICJ explained in *Barcelona Traction* [1970] ICJ Rep 3 para 34.

[79] ILC, 'Peremptory Norms' UN Doc A/77/10 Conclusion 17, Commentary, para 1 ('Peremptory norms of general international law (*jus cogens*) give rise to obligations owed to the international community as a whole (obligations *erga omnes*)').

[80] OHCHR, 'Report of the Working Group on Arbitrary Detention' (24 December 2012) UN Doc A/HRC/22/44, 6 ('the prohibition of arbitrary deprivation of liberty is part of treaty law, customary international law and constitutes a *jus cogens* norm').

a party gave 12 months' notice to the other party. In rescinding Poland's landing rights, the USA accepted that it had not complied with the 12 months' notice period required by Article XV but nevertheless saw its conduct as lawful.[81] With regard to the Soviet Union, the USA immediately suspended the US-USSR Civil Air Transport Agreement 1966. This was in breach of Article XVII of that agreement, which required at least a six month notice period before a suspension could be implemented.

While certain commentators argue that the USA must have justified its prima facie breach of these treaties as collective countermeasures,[82] the USA did not in fact identify a legal basis for its action.

Various Western States-Argentina (1982)

In 1982, Argentina invaded the Falkland Islands and the UNSC quickly condemned it as a 'breach of the peace'.[83] Argentina's invasion therefore violated the prohibition on the use of force, which is widely seen as an *erga omnes* obligation.

The UK invoked its right of self-defence under Article 51 of the UN Charter and launched military action against Argentina. At the request of the UK,[84] in April 1982 ten European states imposed an import embargo on Argentinian goods.[85] Days later, the EEC,[86] Australia,[87] Canada,[88] and New Zealand[89] also imposed an import embargo against Argentina. Argentina subsequently lodged a complaint before the GATT Council of Representatives, arguing that the embargoes breached the GATT.[90]

Some commentators claim that these embargoes were deployed as collective countermeasures.[91] However, on closer analysis, it seems that these states saw *collective self-defence* as the legal basis for their measures. After all, the UK had fallen victim to an armed attack, engaged the right of individual self-defence to

[81] 93 CAB Reports 479 (1981).

[82] Dawidowicz (n 28) 134–39.

[83] UNSC, 'Resolution 502 (1982) Adopted by the Security Council at its 2350th Meeting, on 3 April 1982' (3 April 1982) UN Doc S/RES/502(1982).

[84] *Keesing's Contemporary Archives* (1982) 31532.

[85] UNSC, 'Letter Dated 13 April 1982 from the Permanent Representative of Belgium to the United Nations Addressed to the President of the Security Council' (14 April 1982) UN Doc S/14976 (Belgium, Denmark, France, Germany, Greece, Ireland, Italy, Luxembourg, Netherlands, and the UK).

[86] Council Regulation (EEC) No 877/82 of 16 April 1982 suspending imports of all products originating in Argentina [1982] OJ L102/1.

[87] 'Australian Practice in International Law 1981 to 1983' (1983) 10 *Australian Yearbook of International Law* 573.

[88] 'Canadian Practice in International Law During 1982' (1983) 21 *Canadian Yearbook of International Law* 337.

[89] *Keesing's Contemporary Archives* (1982) 31533.

[90] GATT, 'Trade Restrictions Affecting Argentina Applied for Non-Economic Reasons' (30 April 1982) GATT Doc L/5317.

[91] F Paddeu, 'Self-Defence as a Circumstance Precluding Wrongfulness: Understanding Article 21 of the Articles on State Responsibility' (2015) 85 *British Yearbook of International Law* 90, 110–11.

justify its own response, and requested assistance from third states to help repel Argentina from the Falkland Islands. Moreover, Australia, Canada, and the EEC issued a joint communiqué justifying any infraction of the GATT on the basis of 'their inherent rights of which Article XXI of the General Agreement is a reflection'.[92] The communiqué's assertion that the legal basis of the embargoes was a 'reflection' of Article XXI suggests that the source of their legal authority was located in general international law.[93]

Importantly, the language of 'inherent right' points to the conclusion that these actors justified their embargoes on the basis of the collective self-defence of the UK because, after all, Article 51 of the UN Charter uniquely describes self-defence as an 'inherent right'.[94] Countermeasures cannot be described as an inherent right but are instead referred to as a 'circumstance precluding wrongfulness'.[95] Canada was even clearer in identifying collective self-defence as the legal basis for its measures:

> What is of great concern to Canada and to other peace abiding countries is that Argentina has chosen to try to settle a dispute over territory by recourse to force of arms and that the United Kingdom has had to have recourse to self-defence in order to regain those islands. That is the position that Canada has taken. It is in pursuance of that position that we have banned the export of war material to Argentina and that we have, like the members of the Common Market, imposed similar kinds of restrictions with respect to the entry of Argentinian imports to Canada.[96]

In sum, Australia, Canada, New Zealand, and the EEC seem to have justified their measures on the basis of collective self-defence rather than the doctrine of collective countermeasures.[97]

USA-South Africa (1985–1986)

In its continued pursuit of apartheid policies in the mid-1980s, South Africa committed breaches of the prohibition on racial discrimination and the right to self-determination which, as noted above, are *erga omnes* rules. In response, the USA passed the Anti-Apartheid Act 1986. This Act suspended the landing rights of South African aircraft on US territory, a right guaranteed to South Africa by a 1947 bilateral treaty it had signed with the USA. The USA justified its suspension of this treaty right on the basis that it would lead 'toward the establishment

[92] GATT, 'Joint Communiqué (EC, Canada, Australia), Trade Restrictions Affecting Argentina Applied for Non-Economic Reasons' (18 May 1982) GATT Doc L/5319/Rev.1 para 1(b).
[93] Tams (n 57) 216.
[94] New Zealand also explained that it 'had an inherent right to take such action as a sovereign State'; GATT, 'Minutes of Meeting Held on 7 May 1982' (22 June 1982) GATT Doc C/M/157, 9.
[95] *Articles on State Responsibility* ch V.
[96] 'Canadian Practice in International Law During 1982' (n 88) 337.
[97] Buchan (n 49).

of a non-racial democracy'[98] in South Africa. The USA gave South Africa 10 days' notice of its plan to suspend the treaty. This was in breach of Article XI of the treaty, which stipulated that the agreement could be suspended only upon 12 months' notice. While some commentators maintain that the USA must have undertaken this prima facie unlawful conduct as a collective countermeasure,[99] the USA did not identify a legal basis for its conduct.

Various Western States-Iraq (1990)

On 2 August 1990, Iraq invaded Kuwait and sought to annex part of its territory.[100] Before the UNSC took collective security action on 6 August, the USA imposed a trade embargo against Iraq and froze its assets. The USA justified these measures on the basis of Iraq's 'blatant use of military aggression', which constituted a 'violation of the United Nations Charter' and a breach of an *erga omnes* obligation.[101] Similarly, Italy[102] and France[103] froze Iraqi assets, with France justifying this measure as a necessary response to a 'major violation of international law'. Japan and Switzerland also froze Iraqi assets and imposed trade embargoes.[104]

These states did not identify the legal basis for their restrictive measures. In line with previous analysis, it is unlikely that the trade embargoes ran into conflict with general international law. Some commentators argue that the freezing of Iraqi assets was prima facie unlawful under general international law and must have been deployed as collective countermeasures.[105] However, as explained, it is far from clear whether asset freezing qualifies as a breach of general international law; it may equally be the case that these states saw their measures as lawful acts of retorsion.

African States-Burundi (1996)

In July 1996, Burundi's democratically elected government was overthrown in a military coup. The military regime was accused of ethnically motivated killings

[98] US Department of Transportation, 'Termination of Air Carrier Operations between the United States and South Africa' (1987) 26 *International Legal Materials* 104, 105.

[99] Dawidowicz (n 28) 158.

[100] The UNSC characterised Iraq's actions as a 'breach of international peace and security'; UNSC, 'Resolution 660 (1990) Adopted by the Security Council at its 2932nd Meeting, on 2 August 1990' (2 August 1990) UN Doc S/RES/660(1990).

[101] UNSC, 'Provisional Verbatim Record of the 2932nd Meeting' (2 August 1990) UN Doc S/PV.2932, 13.

[102] UNSC, 'Letter Dated 6 August 1990 from the Chargé d'affaires a.i. of the Permanent Mission of Italy to the United Nations Addressed to the Secretary-General' (6 August 1990) UN Doc S/21444.

[103] UNSC, 'Provisional Verbatim Record of the 2933rd Meeting' (6 August 1990) UN Doc S/PV.2933, 21.

[104] UNSC, 'Letter Dated 5 August 1990 from the Permanent Representative of Japan to the United Nations Addressed to the Secretary-General' (6 August 1990) UN Doc S/21449 (Japan); UNSC, 'Note Verbale Dated 22 August 1990 from the Chargé d'affaires a.i. of the Permanent Observer Mission of Switzerland to the United Nations Addressed to the Secretary-General' (22 August 1990) UN Doc S/21585 (Switzerland).

[105] Dawidowicz (n 28) 162.

and the arbitrary detention of civilians,[106] which breached several *erga omnes* rules including the rights to life and liberty. Ethiopia, Kenya, Rwanda, Tanzania, Uganda, and Zaire responded to the violence by imposing trade embargoes against Burundi.[107] A month later, Zambia imposed a trade embargo.[108] With the exception of Ethiopia and Zaire, these states were members of the GATT, which meant their embargoes constituted a prima facie breach of Burundi's rights under Articles XI and XIII of that agreement. These states did not invoke the national security exception contained in Article XXI of the GATT to justify their measures.

Moreover, the embargoes imposed by Rwanda and Zaire breached the Convention Establishing the Economic Community of Great Lakes Countries 1976. Under Article 39, states parties can only suspend the application of the treaty by giving the other parties three years' notice, which Rwanda and Zaire did not do.

Some commentators suggest that the legal basis for these prima facie breaches of the GATT and Great Lakes treaty must have been the doctrine of collective countermeasures.[109] However, these states did not expressly identify the legal basis for their measures and certainly did not invoke the doctrine of collective countermeasures.

European Community and the US-Burma (1997–2005)

During the 1990s and early 2000s, the ruling military regime in Burma committed severe human rights abuses against the local population, including extrajudicial killings, sexual offences, and forced disappearances.[110] In response to these breaches of *erga omnes* obligations, the USA and European Community (EC) imposed arms embargoes against Burma and froze its assets.[111]

These actors did not identify a legal basis for their measures. As already explained, the arms embargoes were most likely lawful acts of retorsion. Subscribing to the view that asset freezing breaches general international law, some commentators claim that the only legal basis for their deployment was the doctrine of collective countermeasures.[112] But as mentioned previously, asset freezing may not breach

[106] For an account of the severity of the human rights abuses in Burundi, see US Department of State, 'Burundi Country Report on Human Rights Practices for 1996' (30 January 1997) 1997–2001.state.gov/global/human_rights/1996_hrp_report/burundi.html.

[107] 'Letter Dated 2 August 1996 from the Permanent Representative of the United Republic of Tanzania to the United Nations Addressed to the Secretary-General' (2 August 1996) UN Doc A/51/264-S/1996/620.

[108] *Keesing's Contemporary Archives* (1996) 41214.

[109] Tams (n 57) 222.

[110] For an overview, see US Department of State, 'Burma Country Report on Human Rights Practices for 1998' (26 February 1999) 1997–2001.state.gov/global/human_rights/1998_hrp_report/burma.html/.

[111] See, eg, Council Common Position 2000/346/CFSP of 26 April 2000 extending and amending Common Position 96/635/CFSP on Burma/Myanmar [2000] OJ L122/1; President Clinton's Executive Order 13047 (WJ Clinton, 'Executive Order 13047: Prohibiting New Investment in Burma' (*The American Presidency Project*, 20 May 1997) www.presidency.ucsb.edu/documents/executive-order-13047-prohibiting-new-investment-burma).

[112] Dawidowicz (n 28) 202.

general international law, and it may be the case that these actors saw their measures as lawful acts of retorsion.

EC-Yugoslavia (1998)

During the 1990s, the Yugoslav government undertook a campaign of ethnic cleansing against the Kosovar Albanian population in Kosovo.[113] This conduct breached the prohibition on racial discrimination which, as we have seen, is an *erga omnes* obligation. As the humanitarian crisis worsened, the EC froze Yugoslavia's assets and imposed a flight ban against its aircraft.[114] For France and the UK, their immediate implementation of the flight ban was in breach of bilateral navigation agreements they had signed with Yugoslavia, which required 12 months' notice before they could be suspended or terminated. The UK initially explained that it was only willing to implement the flight ban after the required 12 months' notice period had elapsed. However, under pressure from European allies, it imposed an immediate flight ban in breach of its treaty obligations. Foreign Minister Robin Cook justified this action in the following terms:

> President Milosevic's … worsening record on human rights means that, on moral and political grounds, he has forfeited the right … to insist upon the 12 months notice which would normally apply.[115]

Evidently, Foreign Minister Cook justified the ban on 'moral and political grounds', and his failure to justify it as lawful under international law prevents it from being construed as a collective countermeasure. France did not offer any legal justification for its imposition of the flight ban. Determining this conduct to be prima facie unlawful, some commentators conclude that it must have been deployed as a collective countermeasure.[116] That said, France did not invoke this doctrine to justify the flight ban.

Various States/International Organisations-Zimbabwe (2002–2006)

In 2002, the policies pursued by President Robert Mugabe led to the deterioration of the humanitarian situation in Zimbabwe, which triggered breaches of fundamental human rights of *erga omnes* status such as the rights of freedom of expression, association, and assembly.[117] In order to protect human rights, the European Union (EU), Commonwealth, and the USA imposed arms embargoes, travel bans,

[113] US Department of State, 'Ethnic Cleansing in Kosovo: An Accounting' (December 1999) 1997–2001. state.gov/global/human_rights/kosovoii/homepage.html.

[114] Council Common Position of 7 May 1998 defined by the Council on the basis of Article J.2 of the treaty on European Union concerning the freezing of funds held abroad by the Federal Republic of Yugoslavia (FRY) and Serbian Governments (98/326/CFSP) [1998] OJ L143/1.

[115] *Keesing's Contemporary Archives* (1998) 42520–21.

[116] Dawidowicz (n 28) 192.

[117] Amnesty International, 'Zimbabwe: Human Rights Defenders under Siege' (9 May 2005) www.amnesty.org/en/documents/afr46/001/2005/en/.

and asset freezes against Zimbabwe.[118] Neither the EU, Commonwealth, nor the USA identified an explicit legal justification for their restrictive measures, even if the EU explained that it deployed them based on the 'serious human rights violations' in Zimbabwe and the government's policies which 'seriously infringe on the right to freedom of speech, assembly and association'.[119] Some commentators argue that these measures constituted a prima facie breach of general international law and must have been deployed as collective countermeasures.[120] However, for reasons previously stated, it is not clear whether these measures were internationally wrongful and thus required justification; rather, these states and organisations may have seen their measures as lawful acts of retorsion.

USA-Syria (2003–2004)

To halt Syria's support for international terrorism and end its occupation of parts of Lebanon (and which constituted breaches of *erga omnes* rules), in 2003 the USA froze Syrian assets and imposed an export embargo.[121] The USA did not justify these measures in international law terms.

It is unlikely that the trade embargoes breached general international law and, as Syria is not a WTO member, WTO law is not relevant. Certain commentators argue that the freezing of assets was prima facie unlawful and must have been deployed as collective countermeasures.[122] Again, we must resist rushing to classify these acts as collective countermeasures. Asset freezing may not breach general international law and it may be the case that the USA saw these measures as lawful acts of retorsion.

EU-Iran (2006–)

Due to its lack of transparency over its nuclear programme, the International Atomic Energy Agency has been unable to provide assurances to the international community that Iran's development of nuclear power is intended for exclusively peaceful purposes. In 2006, this led to allegations that Iran had breached its obligations under Articles II and III(1) of the Treaty on the Non-Proliferation of Nuclear Weapons 1968, which are almost certainly *erga omnes partes* norms.[123]

[118] *Keesing's Contemporary Archives* (2002) 44541.

[119] See, eg, Council Common Position of 18 February 2002 concerning restrictive measures against Zimbabwe (2002/145/CFSP) [2002] OJ L50/1.

[120] Tams (n 57) 224–25.

[121] President Bush's Executive Order 13338 (GW Bush, 'Executive Order 13338: Blocking Property of Certain Persons and Prohibiting the Export of Certain Goods to Syria' (*The American Presidency Project*, 11 May 2004) www.presidency.ucsb.edu/documents/executive-order-13338-blocking-property-certain-persons-and-prohibiting-the-export-certain).

[122] Dawidowicz (n 30) 397.

[123] For an overview, see Congressional Research Service, 'Iran's Nuclear Program: Tehran's Compliance with International Obligations' (2 August 2022) crsreports.congress.gov/product/pdf/R/R40094/133.

In response, the UNSC imposed a range of sanctions against Iran, including an import and export embargo on certain items and technologies relating to nuclear weapons and other military applications, as well as freezing the financial assets of a number of Iranian officials.[124] Subsequently, the US[125] and EU[126] imposed various sanctions against Iran.

Some of these sanctions ran into prima facie conflict with the treaty obligations that EU Member States owed to Iran.[127] The EU indicated that the legal basis for these sanctions resided in the UN Charter because, under Article 103 of the Charter, UN obligations prevail over any other conflicting treaty commitments.[128] Yet, certain commentators claim that the EU misinterpreted the Security Council's resolutions and, consequently, the sanctions went beyond what was permitted by UN law.[129] For these commentators, the sanctions must be seen as collective countermeasures in defence of *erga omnes partes* obligations.[130]

This analysis misses the point, however. Regardless of whether the EU's sanctions did in fact exceed UNSC authorisation, the EU nevertheless justified them on the basis that it was implementing the will of the UNSC. In this way, the EU saw

[124] UNSC, 'Resolution 1696 (2006) Adopted by the Security Council at its 5500th Meeting, on 31 July 2006' (31 July 2006) UN Doc S/RES/1696(2006); UNSC, 'Resolution 1737 (2006) Adopted by the Security Council at its 5612th Meeting, on 23 December 2006' (27 December 2006) UN Doc S/RES/1737(2006); UNSC, 'Resolution 1747 (2007) Adopted by the Security Council at its 5647th Meeting on 24 March 2007' (24 March 2007) UN Doc S/RES/1747(2007); UNSC, 'Resolution 1803 (2008) Adopted by the Security Council at its 5848th Meeting, on 3 March 2008' (3 March 2008) UN Doc S/RES/1803(2008); UNSC, 'Resolution 1835 (2008) Adopted by the Security Council at its 5984th Meeting, on 27 September 2008' (27 September 2008) UN Doc S/RES/1835(2008); and UNSC, 'Resolution 1929 (2010) Adopted by the Security Council at its 6335th Meeting, on 9 June 2010' (9 June 2010) UN Doc S/RES/1929(2010).

[125] For an overview, see US Department of the Treasury, 'Iran Sanctions' (*Office of Foreign Assets Control*) ofac.treasury.gov/sanctions-programs-and-country-information/iran-sanctions.

[126] Council Regulation (EC) No 423/2007 of 19 April 2007 concerning restrictive measures against Iran [2007] OJ L103/1; Council Regulation (EU) No 961/2010 of 27 October 2010 on restrictive measures against Iran and repealing Regulation (EC) No 423/2007 [2010] OJ L281/1; Council Decision 2012/35/CFSP of 23 January 2012 amending Decision 2010/413/CFSP concerning restrictive measures against Iran [2012] OJ L19/22.

[127] For example, these measures were in prima facie breach of the Agreement on Reciprocal Promotion and Protection of Investments between the Government of the Republic of Austria and the Government of the Islamic Republic of Iran (Tehran, 15 February 2001); the Treaty between the Federal Republic of Germany and the Empire of Iran Concerning the Promotion and Reciprocal Protection of Investments (Tehran, 11 November 1965); the Accord entre le Gouvernement de la Republique francaise et le Gouvernement de la Republique islamique d'Iran sur l'encouragement et la protection reciproques des investissements, signe a Teheran le 12 mai 2003 (Agreement between the Government of the French Republic and the Government of the Islamic Republic of Iran on the Reciprocal Promotion and Protection of Investments (Tehran, 12 May 2003)).

[128] Council Decision 2010/413/CFSP of 26 July 2010 concerning restrictive measures against Iran and repealing Common Position 2007/140/CFSP [2010] OJ L195/39.

[129] P-E Dupont, 'Countermeasures and Collective Security: The Case of EU Sanctions against Iran' (2012) 17 *Journal of Conflict and Security Law* 301, 319 ('[UNSC Res. 1969] can hardly provide a legal basis for a comprehensive embargo on Iran's oil and gas … such interpretation of Resolution 1969 (2010) may be seen as [an] instance of *misinterpretation*').

[130] GI Hernandez, *International Law* (Oxford, Oxford University Press, 2019) 364.

its restrictive measures as UN-authorised sanctions under Chapter VII of the UN Charter. While its interpretation of these resolutions may have been erroneous, the key point is that the EU did not see its sanctions as collective countermeasures.

EU and the USA-Belarus (2006–)

In 2006, there were widespread protests on the streets of Minsk following allegations of corruption in the Belarusian presidential election. The incumbent government brutally repressed the protests, leading to severe human rights abuses such as unlawful detentions and forced disappearances, and thus breached a range of *erga omnes* obligations concerning the basic rights of the human person.[131]

In response, the USA froze the assets of the Belarusian President Alexander Lukashenko.[132] In October 2010, the Member States of the EU froze the assets of President Lukashenko.[133] Neither the USA nor EU identified the legal basis for their measures. Concluding that the freezing of assets breached general international law, some authors argue that these prima facie unlawful measures must have been deployed as collective countermeasures.[134] But in line with previous analysis on asset freezing, an equally plausible explanation is that these actors saw their measures as lawful acts of retorsion.

Various States-Libya (2011)

Colonel Muammar Ghaddafi's brutal repression of the 2011 pro-democracy demonstrations in Libya, including the killing and torture of civilians, triggered a severe humanitarian crisis and breached a range of *erga omnes* obligations.[135] Prior to collective security action by the UNSC, various states froze assets belonging to Libyan officials, with the USA justifying its action because of the 'extreme measures taken against the people of Libya, including by using weapons of war, mercenaries, and wanton violence on unarmed civilians'.[136] These states did not

[131] Council of Europe Parliamentary Assembly, 'Belarus in the Aftermath of the Presidential Election of 19 March 2006, Resolution 1496' (13 April 2006) assembly.coe.int/nw/xml/XRef/Xref-XML2HTML-en.asp?fileid=17430.

[132] See President Bush's Executive Order 13405 (GW Bush, 'Executive Order 13405: Blocking Property of Certain Persons Undermining Democratic Processes or Institutions in Belarus' (*The American Presidency Project*, 19 June 2006) www.presidency.ucsb.edu/documents/executive-order-13405-blocking-property-certain-persons-undermining-democratic-processes); Belarus Democracy and Human Rights Act 2011.

[133] Council Decision 2010/639/CFSP of 25 October 2010 concerning restrictive measures against certain officials of Belarus [2010] OJ L280/18.

[134] Dawidowicz (n 28) 216.

[135] J Adetunji, P Beaumont and M Chulov, 'Libya Protests: More than 100 Killed as Army Fires on Unarmed Demonstrators' (*The Guardian*, 20 February 2011) www.theguardian.com/world/2011/feb/20/libya-protests-benghazi-muammar-gaddafi.

[136] President Obama's Executive Order 13566 (B Obama, 'Executive Order 13566: Blocking Property and Prohibiting Certain Transactions Related to Libya' (*The White House*, 25 February 2011)

clearly articulate the international law basis for their restrictive measures. Some commentators argue that the freezing of assets was prima facie unlawful under general international law and, as such, their legal basis must have been the doctrine of collective countermeasures.[137] However, it may be the case that these states saw their measures as lawful acts of retorsion.

Notably, the Council of the League of Arab States suspended Libya from its organisation. Article 18 of the League's Charter permits the Council – when acting unanimously (but without the participation of the state whose membership is under consideration) – to suspend a member where it fails to fulfil its obligations under that agreement. While the Council suspended Libya based on its breaches of international human rights law and international humanitarian law, the League's Charter does not require Member States to respect these legal frameworks. Some commentators therefore maintain that the Council's decision to suspend Libya must have been deployed as a collective countermeasure.[138] However, it is important to stress that neither the Council nor the League's members invoked the doctrine of collective countermeasures to justify the suspension.

Various States/International Organisations-Syria (2011–)

After Syria fell into civil war in 2011, UN bodies documented the massive human rights abuses being committed by the Syrian government.[139] In response to breaches of various *erga omnes* obligations, the EU,[140] US,[141] Australia,[142] Switzerland,[143]

obamawhitehouse.archives.gov/the-press-office/2011/02/25/executive-order-13566-libya). Other states that froze Libyan assets include Switzerland (Swiss Federal Council, 'Libyan Ordinance' (21 February 2011)) and the UK (N Watt, 'Britain Freezes Gaddafi Family Assets as £900m of Libyan Currency Impounded' (*The Guardian*, 27 February 2011) www.theguardian.com/world/2011/feb/27/gaddafi-family-assets-frozen-queen).

[137] Dawidowicz (n 28) 220.

[138] ibid 218.

[139] UN Human Rights Council, 'Resolution Adopted by the Human Rights Council: 22/24. Situation of Human Rights in the Syrian Arab Republic' (12 April 2013) UN Doc A/HRC/RES/22/24. See also UNSC, 'Resolution 2165 (2014) Adopted by the Security Council at its 7216th Meeting, on 14 July 2014' (14 July 2014) UN Doc S/RES/2165(2014); and UNGA, 'Resolution Adopted by the General Assembly on 23 December 2015: 70/234. Situation of Human Rights in the Syrian Arab Republic' (23 December 2015) UN Doc A/RES/70/234.

[140] Council Decision 2011/273/CFSP of 9 May 2011 concerning restrictive measures against Syria [2011] OJ L121/11. These asset freezes were broadened by Council Implementing Decision 2011/302/CFSP of 23 May 2011 concerning restrictive measures against Syria [2011] OJ L136/91. See also Council Decision 2012/634/CFSP of 15 October 2012 amending Decision 2011/782/CFSP concerning restrictive measures against Syria [2012] OJ L282/50.

[141] President Obama's Executive Order 13573 (B Obama, 'Executive Order 13573: Blocking Property of Senior Officials of the Government of Syria' (*The White House*, 18 May 2011) obamawhitehouse.archives.gov/the-press-office/2011/05/18/executive-order-13573-blocking-property-senior-officials-government-syri.

[142] Australian Department of Foreign Affairs and Trade, *Sanctions Regimes: Syria* (13 May 2011).

[143] Swiss Secretariat for Economic Affairs, *Syrian Sanctions* (18 May 2011).

Canada,[144] Japan,[145] and Turkey[146] imposed embargoes against Syria, imposed travel bans on Syrian officials, adopted an aviation ban against Syrian aircraft, and froze Syrian assets in their territories. The Arab League also froze assets belonging to key Syrian officials and imposed travel bans against them.[147]

These states and organisations did not provide any international law justification for their restrictive measures. Applying previous analysis, it is unlikely that the trade embargoes breached international law. Some commentators claim that the freezing of Syrian assets was prima facie unlawful under general international law and must therefore have been undertaken as collective countermeasures.[148] Again, however, this is not the only possible legal basis for their deployment – instead, it may be the case that these states and organisations saw their measures as lawful acts of retorsion.

In November 2011, the Council of the League of Arab States suspended Syria's membership of the organisation. Substantively, and as already seen, the Charter of the Arab League does not give the Council the power to suspend a Member State for breaching international humanitarian law and international human rights law. Procedurally, the Council's suspension of Syria was not supported by a unanimous vote of its members, with Lebanon and Yemen voting against the motion and Iraq abstaining. The Council's decision to suspend Syria from the organisation, therefore, seems to be in breach of the Charter's substantive and procedural obligations, and some commentators claim that the legal basis for the suspension must have been the doctrine of collective countermeasures.[149] That said, neither the Council nor the League's members relied on this doctrine to justify Syria's suspension.

Various States/EU-Russia (2014–)

In 2014, Russia invaded and occupied Crimea. The EU characterised the invasion as an act of 'military aggression' that 'breaches fundamental principles of international law'.[150] The EU imposed a range of restrictive measures against Russia including the freezing of assets, denying Russian financial institutions access to

[144] Canadian Department of Foreign Affairs, *Trade and Development, Canadian Sanctions Related to Syria* (24 May 2011).

[145] Ministry of Foreign Affairs of Japan, 'Implementation of Measures to Freeze the Assets of President Bashar Al-Assad and his Related Individuals and Entities in Syria' (9 September 2011) www.mofa.go.jp/announce/announce/2011/9/0909_02.html.

[146] I Black, 'Turkey Imposes Sanctions on Syria' (*The Guardian*, 30 November 2011) www.theguardian.com/world/2011/nov/30/turkey-imposes-sanctions-on-syria.

[147] League of Arab States, 'Resolution 7442 of the League of Arab States' (27 November 2011) issuu.com/openbriefing/docs/resolution7442.

[148] Dawidowicz (n 28) 222–223.

[149] ibid 225.

[150] Council Decision 2014/512/CFSP of 31 July 2014 concerning restrictive measures in view of Russia's actions destabilising the situation in Ukraine [2014] OJ L229/13; Resolution on the Russian military aggression against Ukraine and the urgent need for a peaceful resolution to the conflict (2015/C 315/06) [2015] OJ C315/24.

European capital markets, an arms embargo, and banning technology exports to Russia's oil industry. Australia,[151] Canada,[152] Japan,[153] Switzerland,[154] and the USA[155] adopted similar measures. Neither the EU nor these states identified an international legal basis for their restrictive measures.

Some commentators argue that these measures constituted a prima facie breach of international law and must have been deployed as collective countermeasures.[156] However, this conclusion does not necessarily follow. First, and as explained previously, the asset freezes may have been lawful acts of retorsion. Second, while the embargoes constituted a prima facie breach of WTO law, the fact that an armed conflict was underway between Ukraine and Russia may mean that the embargoing actors deployed the restrictive measures pursuant to the national security exception contained in Article XXI of the GATT (and corresponding WTO agreements) rather than the doctrine of collective countermeasures.

Various States-Qatar (2017)

In 2017, Bahrain, Saudi Arabia, and the United Arab Emirates alleged that Qatar had breached its obligations under the Riyadh Agreements and general international law by supporting international terrorism. In response, these states imposed a land, air, and sea blockade against Qatar. Egypt, which is not a party to the Riyadh Agreements, imposed a similar blockade, alleging that Qatar had breached the principle of non-intervention by supporting terrorist activity against it.[157]

Qatar argued that the blockade breached various international legal rules, including those enshrined in the Chicago Convention 1944 and the UN Convention on the Law of the Sea 1982. The blockading states claimed their 'measures were intended to induce Qatar to comply with its international obligations, and thus constitute lawful countermeasures under customary international law'.[158] Note that the blockading states did not justify their actions as *collective* countermeasures, but as 'countermeasures'. Some of the blockading states saw themselves as 'injured' within the meaning of Article 42 of the ASR. For example, Bahrain alleged that Qatar breached the Riyadh Agreements and the principle of non-intervention

[151] Australian Department of Foreign Affairs and Trade, *Sanctions Regimes: Russia* (19 March 2014).

[152] Government of Canada, 'Special Economic Measures (Russia) Regulations' (17 March 2014) laws-lois.justice.gc.ca/eng/regulations/SOR-2014-58/index.html.

[153] Ministry of Foreign Affairs of Japan, 'Statement by the Minister for Foreign Affairs of Japan on the Additional Measures Imposed on Russia in Connection with the Ukraine Situation' (25 September 2014) www.mofa.go.jp/press/release/press4e_000445.html.

[154] Swiss Federal Council, *Russian Sanctions (Ukraine)* (27 August 2014).

[155] B Obama, 'Statement by the President on New Sanctions Related to Russia' (*The White House*, 11 September 2014) obamawhitehouse.archives.gov/the-press-office/2014/09/11/statement-president-new-sanctions-related-russia.

[156] Dawidowicz (n 28) 235.

[157] *Memorial of the United Kingdom of Bahrain, the Arab Republic of Egypt, the Kingdom of Saudi Arabia, and the United Arab Emirates, Vol I* (27 December 2018) [2018] ICJ Rep 1, 48–60.

[158] ibid 53.

by supporting terrorism within its territory and, as said, Egypt took the view that Qatar breached the principle of non-intervention by supporting terrorist activity against it. As injured states, they were permitted to take bilateral countermeasures against Qatar under the law of state responsibility.

Yet, Saudi Arabia and the United Arab Emirates focused their complaint on Qatar's general support for terrorism, such as its financial support for known terrorist organisations, allowing Qatari media to be used to air terrorist propaganda, refusing to support resolutions of the Council of the Arab League condemning the Islamic State of Iraq and the Levant (ISIL), and its failure to prosecute and extradite terrorists living and operating in Qatar.[159] Saudi Arabia and the United Arab Emirates alleged that this support breached various provisions of the Riyadh Agreements.[160] Although these states did not expressly determine that these provisions were *erga omnes partes* obligations, this seems to be the logical inference given that all parties to the Riyadh Agreements have a legal interest in suppressing terrorism and the threat it poses to international peace and security. If this reading is correct, Saudi Arabia and the United Arab Emirates saw themselves as 'indirectly injured' states within the meaning of Article 48(1) of the ASR and, consequently, their blockades can be seen as *collective* countermeasures in defence of *erga omnes partes* obligations. As noted, however, these states did not expressly invoke the doctrine of *collective* countermeasures to justify their conduct.

Estonia (2019)

In 2019, Estonia issued a statement outlining its position on the application of international law to cyberspace. It explains:

> Estonia is furthering the position that states which are not directly injured may apply countermeasures to support the state directly affected by the malicious cyber operation …
>
> The threats to the security of states increasingly involve unlawful cyber operations. It is therefore important that states may respond collectively to unlawful cyber operations where diplomatic action is insufficient, but no lawful recourse to use of force exists.[161]

Most scholars interpret Estonia's statement as supporting the doctrine of collective countermeasures.[162] Yet, the statement explains that 'states which are not directly injured may apply countermeasures to support the state directly affected by the malicious cyber operation'. The statement does not expressly state that collective countermeasures can be taken to protect *community* obligations. Instead, it

[159] ibid 40–53.

[160] ibid.

[161] K Kaljulaid, *President of Estonia, Opening at CyCon 2019* (29 May 2019) www.vm.ee/en/international-law-cyber-diplomacy/cyber-diplomacy/international-law-and-cyberspace.

[162] See, eg, Schmitt and Watts (n 15); P Roguski, 'Collective Countermeasures in Cyberspace – *Lex Lata*, Progressive Development or a Bad Idea?' in T Jancarkova et al (eds), *The Next Decade* (Tallinn, CCDCOE Publications, 2020).

explains that countermeasures can be carried out 'to support the state directly affected by the malicious cyber operation'. A reasonable reading of this sentence is that Estonia endorses (what this chapter calls) the doctrine of third-party countermeasures rather than the doctrine of collective countermeasures.

France (2019)

In 2019, France published its statement on the application of international law to cyberspace. It explains:

> Collective countermeasures are not authorised, which rules out the possibility of France taking such measures in response to an infringement of another State's rights.[163]

Some commentators interpret this statement as rejecting the doctrine of collective countermeasures under international law.[164] But while France uses the language of 'collective countermeasures', it may be referring to third-party countermeasures. This is because France explains that countermeasures cannot be taken 'in response to an infringement of another State's rights'. If the statement refers to collective countermeasures (as understood in this chapter), presumably it would have ruled out the use of countermeasures to protect *community* rights rather than the rights of other states. France's statement may therefore leave open the possibility of collective countermeasures.

New Zealand (2020)

In 2020, New Zealand published its statement on the application of international law to cyberspace. It states:

> Given the collective interest in the observance of international law in cyberspace, and the potential asymmetry between malicious and victim states, New Zealand is open to the proposition that victim states, in limited circumstances, may request assistance from other states in applying proportionate countermeasures to induce compliance by the state acting in breach of international law.[165]

Schmitt interprets this paragraph as supporting the doctrine of collective countermeasures.[166] This conclusion is far from obvious. For example, this

[163] République Française, Ministère des Armées, *Droit International Appliqué aux Opérations dans le Cyberespace* (2019) www.defense.gouv.fr/sites/default/files/ministere-armees/Droit%20international%20appliqu%C3%A9%20aux%20op%C3%A9rations%20dans%20le%20cyberespace.pdf 8.

[164] MN Schmitt, 'France's Major Statement on International Law and Cyber: An Assessment' (*Just Security*, 16 September 2019) www.justsecurity.org/66194/frances-major-statement-on-international-law-and-cyber-an-assessment/.

[165] New Zealand, 'The Application of International Law to State Activity in Cyberspace' (1 December 2020) www.dpmc.govt.nz/publications/application-international-law-state-activity-cyberspace para 22.

[166] MN Schmitt, 'Canada Takes on International Law in Cyberspace' (*EJIL:Talk!*, 14 July 2022) www.ejiltalk.org/canada-takes-on-international-law-in-cyberspace/.

paragraph does not expressly state that collective countermeasures in support of *erga omnes (partes)* obligations are permissible. In fact, the statement explains that 'victim States … may *request assistance* from other states in applying proportionate countermeasures to induce compliance by the state acting in breach of international law'.[167]

An interesting question is whether third states can *assist* an injured state in conducting countermeasures (and where that assistance does not itself qualify as an internationally wrongful act). Commentators are divided on this issue. While some argue that a third state's provision of assistance to an injured state is permissible because the impugned conduct is lawful per se, others take a more restrictive approach and claim that the provision of material assistance is akin to taking the countermeasure and that the exculpatory effect of the doctrine of countermeasures cannot be extended to third parties.[168] A reasonable interpretation of New Zealand's statement is that it is 'open' to the approach adopted by the first group of commentators; that is, third states can, upon request, assist an injured state in conducting countermeasures. If this is the case, New Zealand's statement cannot be read as support for the doctrine of collective countermeasures.

EU-Belarus (2021)

In May 2021, the Belarusian government forced a Ryanair flight bound for Vilnius to land in Minsk because of a 'potential security risk'.[169] This conduct constituted a breach of Belarus's obligations under Article 3*bis* of the Chicago Convention 1944 and Article 10(1) of the Montreal Convention 1971, which are *erga omnes partes* norms.[170]

The EU described the landing of the flight as 'forced' and 'unlawful'.[171] In response, the EU imposed several restrictive measures against Belarus, including a ban on overflights of EU airspace by Belarusian carriers.[172] This measure was implemented by EU Member States and arguably in prima facie breach of their

[167] ibid (emphasis added).

[168] For a discussion see M Jackson and F Paddeu, 'The Countermeasures of Others: When Can States Collaborate in the Taking of Countermeasures?' (2024) 118 *American Journal of International Law* 231 and MN Schmitt (ed), *Tallinn Manual 2.0 on the International Law Applicable to Cyber Operations*, 2nd edn (Cambridge, Cambridge University Press, 2017) 132.

[169] A Sytas and A Ostroukh, 'Belarus Forces Airliner to Land and Arrests Opponent, Sparking US and European Outrage' (*Reuters*, 23 May 2021) www.reuters.com/world/europe/belarus-forces-vilnius-bound-ryanair-plane-land-detain-blogger-2021-05-23/.

[170] M Jackson and A Tzanakopoulos, 'Aerial Incident of 23 May 2021: Belarus and the Ryanair Flight 4978' (*EJIL:Talk!*, 24 May 2021) www.ejiltalk.org/aerial-incident-of-23-may-2021-belarus-and-the-ryanair-flight-4978/.

[171] Council of the EU, 'EU Bans Belarusian Carriers from its Airspace and Airports' (4 June 2021) www.consilium.europa.eu/en/press/press-releases/2021/06/04/eu-bans-belarusian-carriers-from-its-airspace-and-airports/.

[172] Council Regulation (EU) 2021/907 (4 June 2021) eur-lex.europa.eu/legal-content/EN/TXT/PDF/?uri=CELEX:32021R0907&from=EN#:~:text=%27Article%208b-,1.,landing%20or%20an%20emergency%20overflight.

obligations under the Chicago Convention, which only permits such bans where they do not make a distinction as to the nationality of the aircraft.

Certain EU Member States were directly injured by the forced landing of the Ryanair flight (eg, Poland, Ireland, and Lithuania). Some commentators argue that the other EU Member States were indirectly injured because Belarus had breached *erga omnes partes* rules and thus their bans must be seen as collective countermeasures.[173] However, it is important to note that these states did not justify their bans as collective countermeasures.

Canada (2022)

In 2022, Canada published its statement on the application of international law to cyberspace and rejected the CIL status of collective cyber countermeasures. It explains:

> Canada has considered the concept of "collective cyber countermeasures" but does not, to date, see sufficient State practice or *opinio juris* to conclude that these are permitted under international law.[174]

Various States/EU-Russia (2022–)

In February 2022, Russia continued its military assault against Ukraine by launching a full-scale invasion. The UNGA characterised Russia's invasion as an 'act of aggression',[175] which as we have seen is a breach of an *erga omnes* obligation. Various states and international organisations, including the US, Canada, Japan, South Korea, and the EU, imposed restrictive measures against Russia.[176] These included the freezing of assets belonging to Russian politicians and government-affiliated business leaders; preventing Russian banks and financial institutions from operating in their territories and from engaging in transactions with the Russian Central Bank; banning Russian airlines and vessels entering their territories; banning exports to Russia that may assist its war effort; and removing Russia's Most Favoured Nation (MFN) treatment under WTO law.

In line with previous analysis, many of these restrictive measures can be classified as lawful acts of retorsion. That said, some of them are likely to conflict with

[173] S Talmon, 'Banning Belarusian Airlines in Response to Belarus' Diversion of Ryanair Flight FR4978 as a Third-Party Countermeasure' (*German Practice in International Law*, 4 October 2023) gpil.jura.uni-bonn.de/2023/10/banning-belarusian-airlines-in-response-to-belarus-diversion-of-ryanair-flight-fr4978-as-a-third-party-countermeasure/.

[174] Government of Canada, 'International Law Applicable in Cyberspace' (2022) www.international.gc.ca/world-monde/issues_development-enjeux_developpement/peace_security-paix_securite/cyber_policy-politique_cyberspace.aspx?lang=eng para 37.

[175] UNGA, 'Resolution Adopted by the General Assembly on 2 March 2022: ES-11/1: Aggression against Ukraine' (18 March 2022) UN Doc A/RES/ES-11/1.

[176] For an overview, see BBC News, 'What are the Sanctions on Russia and are they Hurting its Economy?' (27 June 2022) www.bbc.co.uk/news/world-europe-60125659.

treaty regimes and are prima facie unlawful. For example, most states (including the EU) sanctioning Russia are WTO members (as is Russia), which means their trade embargoes prima facie breach WTO law. For instance, under the WTO's MFN clause, Russian exports must receive the same regulatory and tariff treatment accorded to products of other WTO members, and its service suppliers must enjoy non-discriminatory market access in certain sectors.

Russia regarded the trade embargoes as breaches of WTO law and announced its intention to challenge them before the WTO.[177] While the embargoing actors have not yet sought to justify these prima facie breaches of WTO law under international law, some commentators argue that they can be seen as collective countermeasures.[178] However, perhaps the most obvious legal basis for these measures is Article XXI of the GATT (and corresponding provisions in other WTO agreements), which permits members to protect their essential security interests during times of war or other emergencies in international relations. If these actors go down this route, their measures cannot be regarded as customary practice of collective countermeasures. Either way, at present, these actors have not expressly invoked the doctrine of collective countermeasures to justify their conduct.

Norway-Belarus/Russia (2022)

In 2022, Norway suspended a bilateral agreement with Belarus on international road transport due to Belarus's complicity in Russia's invasion of Ukraine. By way of Royal Decree, Norway justified its prima facie breach of this treaty as a collective countermeasure 'to support international law and world society where conflicts are resolved peacefully'.[179] The Royal Decree explains that 'State practice underpins the existence of exceptional access to countermeasures for third countries in the most serious cases of breach of community obligations' and that international law confers 'an extraordinary and exceptional right to take countermeasures against Russian and Belarus, even if Norway is not directly affected by the Russian violations of international law'.[180]

Interestingly, Norway claims that it only supports the use of collective countermeasures in response to 'the most serious breaches' of community obligations, which seems to be drawn from Draft Article 54(2) of the Draft Articles on State Responsibility 2001 (discussed above). Some commentators take a similar

[177] V Hughes et al, 'Russia Will Challenge Economic Sanctions at the WTO' (*Bennett Jones*, 22 March 2022) www.bennettjones.com/Blogs-Section/Russia-Will-Challenge-Economic-Sanctions-at-the-WTO.

[178] See, eg, P Zelikow, 'A Legal Approach to the Transfer of Russian Assets to Rebuild Ukraine' (*Lawfare*, 12 May 2022) www.lawfaremedia.org/article/legal-approach-transfer-russian-assets-rebuild-ukraine.

[179] Government of Norway, 'Determination of Regulations on Amendments to Regulations 15 August 2014 No 1076 on Restrictive Measures Regarding Actions that Undermine or Threaten Ukraine's Territorial Integrity, Sovereignty, Independence and Stability' (29 April 2022) www.regjeringen.no/no/dokumenter/kglres_sanksjoner2/id2910739/ (my translation).

[180] ibid (my translation).

approach, claiming 'there is overwhelming support among commentators and governments for the view that only a serious breach of an *erga omnes* obligation might potentially justify resort to [collective] countermeasures'.[181] In this context, an important question is whether every breach of an *erga omnes (partes)* obligation is ipso facto serious. While it may be said that every breach of an *erga omnes* obligation is by definition serious, this argument is less persuasive when it comes to breaches of *erga omnes partes* obligations. However, Article 48(1) of the ASR permits indirectly injured states to invoke state responsibility for any breach of an *erga omnes (partes)* obligation. Moreover, the commentary to Article 48 does not indicate that indirectly injured states can only invoke the responsibility of a wrongdoing state where there has been a serious breach of an *erga omnes (partes)* obligation. Similarly, the commentary to Article 54 of the ASR does not suggest that state practice on collective countermeasures is limited to serious breaches of *erga omnes (partes)* obligations.

Poland (2022)

In late 2022, Poland published its statement on the application of international law to cyberspace. It explains:

> At the same time, the Republic of Poland expresses the view that the evolution of customary international law over the last two decades provides grounds for recognising that a state may take countermeasures in pursuit of general interest as well.[182]

This statement appears to reference the ILC's 2001 project on the law of state responsibility when it explains that, 'over the last two decades', CIL has evolved to recognise the doctrine of collective countermeasures. Evidently, Poland's statement supports the legality of collective countermeasures.

Moreover, Poland may have undertaken a collective countermeasure in March 2023 when it refused to implement certain provisions of the Treaty on Conventional Armed Forces in Europe 1990 'in relation to the Republic of Belarus, due to its participation in the aggression against Ukraine'.[183] That said,

[181] Dawidowicz (n 30) 347. In 2005, the Institut de Droit International explained that collective countermeasures can be undertaken only in response to 'a grave breach of an *erga omnes* obligation'; MG Gaja, 'Obligations and Rights *Erga Omnes* in International Law' (*Institut de Droit International*, 2005) www.idi-iil.org/app/uploads/2017/06/2005_kra_01_en.pdf Art 5.

[182] Ministry of Foreign Affairs, Republic of Poland, 'The Republic of Poland's Position on the Application of International Law to Cyberspace' (29 December 2022) www.gov.pl/web/diplomacy/the-republic-of-polands-position-on-the-application-of-international-law-in-cyberspace 8.

[183] Ministry of Foreign Affairs, Republic of Poland, 'Request for the Consent of the Council of Ministers for the Non-Implementation by the Republic of Poland of the Treaty of Conventional Armed Forces in Europe' (21 March 2023) www.gov.pl/web/premier/wniosek-o-udzielnie-zgody-rady-ministrow-na-niewykonywanie-przez-rzeczpospolita-polska-artykulow-v-ust-2-ix-ust-2-x-ust-1-x-ust-8-x-ust-11-xi-ust-3-xi-ust-7-xii-ust-2-xiii-xiv-traktatu-o-konwencjonalnych-silach-zbrojnych-w-europie-podpisanego-w-paryzu-dnia-19-listopada-1990-r-dz-u-z-1995-r-poz-73-w-stosunku-do-republiki-bialorusi-z-powodu-jej-udzialu-w-agresji-na-ukraine-wraz-z-projektem-zapisu-protokolarnego (my translation).

Poland did not expressly identify the doctrine of collective countermeasures as the legal basis for its conduct.

Ireland (2023)

Ireland's 2023 statement on the application of international law to cyberspace also addresses the doctrine of collective countermeasures. It reads:

> On the question of third party or collective countermeasures, Ireland considers that since the adoption of the ARSIWA in 2001, state practice indicates that such measures are permissible in limited circumstances, in particular in the context of violations of peremptory norms.[184]

The statement refers to 'third party or collective countermeasures' without indicating whether it regards them as the same or different doctrines. As we have seen, these are different doctrines, with each requiring distinct evidence to establish their legality under CIL. The reference to developments in state practice since the ILC's 2001 ASR indicates that the statement focuses on collective rather than third-party countermeasures. However, the statement also explains that such measures are permissible '*in particular* in the context of violations of peremptory norms',[185] which implies that they are available beyond breaches of peremptory norms, ie, any breach of international law. This suggests that Ireland may consider third-party countermeasures to be lawful under CIL. The best characterisation of Ireland's statement is that it regards the doctrine of collective countermeasures as established in CIL, but has not ruled out the potential for third-party countermeasures.

Denmark (2023)

Denmark's 2023 national position on the application of international law to cyberspace deals with collective countermeasures. It explains:

> The question of collective countermeasures does not seem to have been fully settled in state practice and needs careful consideration. As a general observation Denmark finds that there may be instances where one State suffers a violation of an obligation owed to the international community as a whole, and where the victim State may request the assistance of other States in applying proportionate and necessary countermeasures in collective response hereto.[186]

[184] Ireland, Department of Foreign Affairs, 'Position Paper on the Application of International Law in Cyberspace' (July 2023) www.dfa.ie/media/dfa/ourrolepolicies/internationallaw/Ireland---National-Position-Paper.pdf para 26.

[185] ibid (emphasis added). Intriguingly, the Irish statement explains that collective countermeasures can be taken in response to breaches of 'peremptory norms' (*jus cogens*) rather than *erga omnes* obligations. *Jus cogens* and *erga omnes* are different categories of rules, even if (as said above in n 79) *jus cogens* rules are by definition owed *erga omnes*.

[186] Government of Denmark (with introduction by JM Kjelgaard and U Melgaard), 'Denmark's Position Paper on the Application of International Law in Cyberspace' (2023) 92 *Nordic Journal of International Law* 446, 454.

Evidently, Denmark's support for the doctrine of collective countermeasures is lukewarm; as it notes, '[t]he question of collective countermeasures does not seem to have been fully settled in state practice', even if it accepts that there 'may be' instances where collective countermeasures are permissible. That collective countermeasures 'may be' permissible hardly constitutes a strong showing of *opinio juris* in favour of this doctrine.

Costa Rica (2023)

In 2023, Costa Rica published its national position on the application of international law to cyberspace and addressed the topic of collective countermeasures. The position explains:

> [C]ountermeasures may be taken by the injured State, i.e., the State specifically affected by the breach, as well as third States in response to violations of obligations of an *erga omnes* nature or upon request by the injured State.[187]

Costa Rica therefore expresses support for the doctrines of collective countermeasures. This is an important statement because it provides a rare example of a Latin American state endorsing the legality of collective countermeasures under CIL. The statement also supports the use of third-party countermeasures insofar as it determines that 'third States' can take countermeasures 'upon request by the injured State'.

Evaluation

This chapter now evaluates whether there is sufficient evidence of state practice and *opinio juris* to establish the doctrine of collective countermeasures in CIL. If so, this doctrine applies to cyberspace 'by default' as part of the law of state responsibility, and does not require additional evidence of cyber-specific state practice and *opinio juris*.[188] Indeed, states have used this approach to determine that the law of bilateral countermeasures applies to cyberspace.[189]

[187] Costa Rica, 'Costa Rica's Position on the Application of International Law in Cyberspace' (2023) docs-library.unoda.org/Open-Ended_Working_Group_on_Information_and_Communication_Technologies_-_(2021)/Costa_Rica_-_Position_Paper_-_International_Law_in_Cyberspace.pdf para 15.

[188] '[A]ll relevant existing rules of international law are by default applicable to the conduct of States with respect to ICTs'; D Akande, A Coco and T de Souza Dias, 'Drawing the Cyber Baseline: The Applicability of Existing International Law to the Governance of Information and Communication Technologies' (2022) 99 *International Law Studies* 4, 9. But for a different view, see Israel: R Schondorf, 'Israel's Perspective on Key Legal and Practical Issues Concerning the Application of International Law to Cyber Operations' (*EJIL:Talk*!, 9 December 2020) www.ejiltalk.org/israels-perspective-on-key-legal-and-practical-issues-concerning-the-application-of-international-law-to-cyber-operations/.

[189] See, eg, UK Attorney General, 'Speech: Cyber and International Law in the 21st Century' (23 May 2018) www.gov.uk/government/speeches/cyber-and-international-law-in-the-21st-century; Finland, 'International Law and Cyberspace: Finland's National Position' (2020) um.fi/documents/35732/0/Cyber+and+international+law%3B+Finland%27s+views.pdf/41404cbb-d300-a3b9-92e4-a7d675d5d585?t=1602758856859.

Turning to the first element of CIL, state practice must be 'sufficiently widespread and representative, as well as consistent',[190] within the international community. In the *North Sea* case, the ICJ looked for a 'settled practice'[191] among states.

Determining whether there is state practice in support of collective countermeasures is difficult because states rarely claim that their restrictive measures are deployed on this basis. Commentators arguing in favour of the CIL status of collective countermeasures tend to fall into the trap of interpreting the context in which restrictive measures are undertaken and *assuming* that they must have been deployed as collective countermeasures. This is often an erroneous assumption because, as shown above, in many instances the restrictive measures undertaken may have been lawful acts of retorsion; that is, states sought to protect collective legal interests through unfriendly but inherently lawful measures. Given that countermeasures involve the use of otherwise unlawful measures, it cannot be assumed that these restrictive measures constitute state practice in favour of collective countermeasures.

Admittedly, since the ILC concluded its work on state responsibility in 2001, there is a growing state practice of collective countermeasures. In 2022, for example, Norway deployed collective countermeasures against Belarus. Poland (2022), Ireland (2023), and Costa Rica (2023) have also expressed support for the legality of collective countermeasures under CIL and, as we know, official pronouncements can constitute evidence of state practice.[192] That said, state practice on collective countermeasures remains relatively limited[193] and, in light of this, it cannot be considered sufficiently widespread to establish CIL.[194]

Moreover, this practice is drawn from largely western states and, as such, is not representative of the international community. It is correct that non-western states have engaged in collective countermeasures – for example, Saudi Arabia and the United Arab Emirates appear to have resorted to collective countermeasures against Qatar. However, certain constituencies within the international community have not engaged in this practice. For instance, there is little evidence of state

[190] ILC, 'Draft Conclusions on Identification of Customary International Law, with Commentaries' in *Yearbook of the International Law Commission. 2018, Volume II, Part Two: Report of the Commission to the General Assembly on the Work of its Seventieth Session* (New York, UN, 2022) Conclusion 8.

[191] *North Sea Continental Shelf Cases (Federal Republic of Germany/Denmark; Federal Republic of Germany/Netherlands)* (Judgment of 20 February 1969) [1969] ICJ Rep 3 para 77.

[192] ILC, 'Draft Conclusions on Identification of Customary International Law', Conclusion 6, Commentary, para 2 (explaining that 'it is now generally accepted that verbal conduct (whether written or oral) may also count as practice'). See also *Prosecutor v Tadić* (Appeals Chamber, Decision on the Defence Motion for Interlocutory Appeal on Jurisdiction, 2 October 1995) ICTY Case No IT-94-1-AR72 para 99.

[193] In the *North Sea* case, the ICJ held that 15 instances of state practice represented only 'a very small proportion … [of] the world as a whole' and could not therefore form the basis of a customary rule; *North Sea Continental Shelf Cases* (n 191) para 75.

[194] As Denmark explains, the doctrine of collective countermeasures 'does not seem to have been fully settled in state practice'; Government of Denmark, 'Denmark's Position Paper', para 26.

practice on collective countermeasures from African or Asian states or, with the exception of Costa Rica (2023), Latin American states.[195]

State practice on collective countermeasures has also been described as 'inconsistent in the extreme'.[196] This observation is fair. While there are examples of western states deploying collective countermeasures in response to severe human rights abuses, in similar instances they have not taken such measures against wrongdoing states, for example, against Cambodia in the 1970s or Rwanda in the 1990s.[197] Although states are entitled to decline to exercise a legal right based on political (and other) considerations, when it comes to the formation of CIL their failure to consistently invoke this right militates against the conclusion that a concordant practice has emerged.

Given that official pronouncements can constitute evidence of state practice, there is also state practice rejecting the doctrine of collective countermeasures. During the ILC's ASR project, states such as Mexico, Israel, and the UK protested against the use of collective countermeasures. Canada made a similar protestation in 2022 when issuing its national position on the application of international law to cyberspace.

In the *Asylum* case, the ICJ rejected the claim that CIL had crystallised on diplomatic asylum because:

> The facts brought to the knowledge of the Court disclose so much uncertainty and contradiction, so much fluctuation and discrepancy in the exercise of diplomatic asylum … that it is not possible to discern in all this any constant and uniform usage … with regard to the alleged rule.[198]

This description of state practice on diplomatic asylum reflects state practice on collective countermeasures: limited, uncertain, contradictory, and fluctuating. In other words, state practice on collective countermeasures is in a state of flux and, in this condition, cannot support a rule of CIL.

If we assume *arguendo* that there is widespread, representative, and consistent state practice on collective countermeasures, for CIL to develop it must be 'undertaken with a sense of legal right or obligation'.[199] Whereas state practice is

[195] *Texaco Overseas Petroleum et al v Libya* (1977) 53 ILR 389 (where the arbitrator rejected the claim that several General Assembly resolutions had crystalised as customary law because certain sections of the international community had voted against them).

[196] ILC, 'State Responsibility (Continued) (A/CN.4/513, sect. A, A/CN.4/515 and Add.1-3, A/CN.4/517 and Add.1, A/CN.4/ L.602 and Corr.1 and Rev.1)' in *Yearbook of the International Law Commission. 2001, Volume I: Summary Records of the Meetings of the Fifty-Third Session* (New York, UN, 2006) 35, para 2 (Mr Brownlie). Commissioner Bruno Simma explained that 'selectivity was widespread'; ILC, 'State Responsibility (Continued) (A/CN.4/504, sect. A, A/CN.4/507 and Add.1–4, A/CN.4/L.600)' in *Yearbook of the International Law Commission. 2000, Volume I: Summary Records of the Meetings of the Fifty-Second Session* (New York, UN, 2005) 305, para 31 (Mr Simma).

[197] ILC, 'State Responsibility' in *Yearbook of the International Law Commission. 2000, Volume I* 304, para 18 (Mr Kateka), 312, para 4 (Mr Goco).

[198] *Colombian-Peruvian Asylum Case* (Judgment of 20 November 1950) [1950] ICJ Rep 266, 277.

[199] ILC, 'Draft Conclusions on Identification of Customary International Law', Conclusion 9.

the objective element of CIL, *opinio juris* is the subjective component and serves to 'distinguish between those practices of States that result merely from political expedience, diplomacy, domestic policy, or habit – and those that flow from legal obligations'.[200]

Commentators supporting the CIL status of collective countermeasures maintain that it can be 'presumed that consistent practice is accompanied by normative intent (*opinio juris*)'.[201] However, presuming or inferring *opinio juris* from consistent state practice is problematic.[202] This approach ignores the fact that these states have not expressly claimed these legal rights for themselves and imposes on them legal views that they *could* or *should* have articulated but, for whatever reason, did not. In the words of the ICJ, we need to be careful not to 'ascribe to States views which they have not themselves advanced'[203] – and this is particularly the case when the practice in question can be explained or justified on other legal bases.[204] As we have seen, states deploying restrictive measures have justified this conduct based on the right of self-defence or other security exceptions contained in international agreements. Albeit exceptionally, it may even be the case that states deploy restrictive measures in full recognition of their illegality under international law.

Another argument in the literature is that the international community's reluctance to invoke international law to condemn state practice on collective countermeasures is 'astonishing' and indicates a tacit acceptance of this doctrine.[205] In this context, the formula is that the failure of states to protest against collective countermeasure is tantamount to acceptance which in turn equals *opinio juris*. It is well accepted that state silence can generate *opinio juris*.[206] But this approach must be used cautiously lest we fall into the trap of ascribing to states legal views that they have not advanced themselves. Thus, it is only where 'the circumstances called for some reaction'[207] that state silence can be construed as *opinio juris*, the rationale being that the only reasonable explanation for why a state did not

[200] JH Currie, *Public International Law: Essentials of Canadian Law* (Toronto, Irwin Law, 2001) 170.
[201] Dawidowicz (n 28) 253.
[202] R Buchan, *Cyber Espionage and International Law* (Oxford, Hart Publishing, 2018) ch 7.
[203] *Military and Paramilitary Activities in and against Nicaragua* (n 12) para 207. Although for a different view, see *Question of the Delimitation of the Continental Shelf Between Nicaragua and Colombia Beyond 200 Nautical Miles from the Nicaraguan Coast (Nicaragua v Colombia)* (Judgment of 13 July 2023) [2023] ICJ Rep 1, Dissenting Opinion of Judge Charlesworth (available at icj-cij.org/sites/default/files/case-related/154/154-20230713-jud-01-07-en.pdf) para 29 ('In the view of States' silence, it is the Court's task to articulate the legal rule to which the general practice conforms. Practice will invariably be subject to multiple interpretations … The Court should then identify a legal rule that accommodates the broadest variety of practice, that conforms to the established principles concerning the relevant legal field').
[204] *Question of the Delimitation of the Continental Shelf Between Nicaragua and Colombia* (n 203), Dissenting Opinion of Judge Tomka (available at icj-cij.org/sites/default/files/case-related/154/154-20230713-jud-01-01-en.pdf) paras 52–53 and Dissenting Opinion of Judge Robinson (available at icj-cij.org/sites/default/files/case-related/154/154-20230713-jud-01-04-en.pdf) para 14.
[205] Tams (n 57) 236.
[206] ILC, 'Draft Conclusions on Identification of Customary International Law', Conclusion 10(3).
[207] ibid.

condemn the impugned behaviour as a breach of international law was because it saw that conduct as lawful.

When it comes to collective countermeasures, it is difficult to assume that the lack of protest by members of the international community constitutes acceptance and thus *opinio juris*. The reason for this is because, as we have seen, states taking collective countermeasures often fail to articulate a clear legal basis for their action and, in fact, there are often various possible legal justifications available. If this is the case, state silence cannot be interpreted as acceptance of the lawfulness of collective countermeasures.

Importantly, some states have rejected the claim that collective countermeasures are lawful under CIL, thereby preventing the formation of a stable *opinio juris* in favour of this doctrine.[208] For example, during the ILC's work on the law of state responsibility, states such as Mexico, Israel, and the UK pushed back against the claim that the doctrine of collective countermeasures is established in CIL. In 2022, when discussing collective countermeasures Canada did not 'see sufficient … *opinio juris* to conclude that these are permitted under international law'.

The above approach to the identification of CIL is known as the inductive method: CIL is induced into existence by state practice accompanied by *opinio juris*. There is, however, another approach that is sometimes used to identify CIL: the deductive approach identifies specific rules of CIL by extracting them from established general rules of CIL.

Some scholars utilise the deductive method and argue that states can deploy collective countermeasures to enforce compliance with communitarian norms due to the structure of the law of state responsibility.[209] They argue that if states have a legal interest in ensuring that communitarian norms are upheld and can therefore invoke the responsibility of a wrongdoing state for breaching such norms (as Article 48(1) of the ASR explains), the only logical conclusion is that they can also take countermeasures to protect collective norms.[210] In essence, this approach uses a deductive methodology to identify CIL; namely, that new rules of CIL can be deduced from existing rules of CIL, which in the present context means that a customary rule permitting collective countermeasures can be deduced from the existing CIL on state responsibility.[211] For those in favour of collective

[208] *Legality of the Threat or Use of Nuclear Weapons* (Advisory Opinion of 8 July 1996) [1996] ICJ Rep 226 para 67 (where the ICJ could not identify *opinio juris* supporting a prohibition against the use of nuclear weapons because nuclear-armed states had consistently objected to such a prohibition).

[209] O Schachter, 'International Law in Theory and Practice' (1982) 178 *Recueil des Cours* 1, 183; N Tsagourias, 'The Law Applicable to Countermeasures against Low-Intensity Cyber Operations' (2015) 14 *Baltic Yearbook of International Law* 105.

[210] Eg, UNGA, 'Seventh Report on State Responsibility by Mr Gaetano Arangio-Ruiz, Special Rapporteur' (9 May 1995) UN Doc A/CN.4/469, 14, para 35; T Meron, 'International Law in the Age of Human Rights' (2003) 301 *Recueil des Cours* 1, 296.

[211] On deduction, see S Talmon, 'Determining Customary International Law: The ICJ's Methodology between Induction, Deduction and Assertion' (2015) 26 *European Journal of International Law* 417.

countermeasures, the attraction of the deductive approach is that it side-steps the difficult task of having to demonstrate that the doctrine of collective countermeasures is supported by a widespread, representative, and consistent state practice accompanied by *opinio juris*.

Importantly, this approach is not purely deductive – it utilises induction insofar as these commentators point to state practice and *opinio juris* on collective countermeasures to *strengthen* and *confirm* this interpretation of the law on state responsibility (while recognising that contrary state practice weakens it). As we saw above, there is support for the doctrine of collective countermeasures among states, even if state practice is not widespread, representative, and consistent.

Several commentators find the deductive approach unpersuasive in the context of collective countermeasures, maintaining that there is a critical difference between a state being entitled to invoke the responsibility of a wrongdoing state for a breach of a communitarian norm and being entitled to take otherwise unlawful measures to enforce compliance with it.[212] In short, they argue that the right to take collective countermeasures is not an 'automatic consequence' of the right of indirectly injured states to invoke the responsibility of wrongdoing states for breaches of *erga omnes (partes)* obligations.[213] The UK adopted this view when, during the ILC's work on the law of state responsibility, it explained:

> Even where, on the basis of the *Barcelona Traction* dictum, there may be a legal interest of States at large in respect of violations of certain obligations, it does not necessarily follow that all States can vindicate those interests in the same way as directly injured States.[214]

When it comes to the ICJ, the Court invariably declares that CIL must be found in the actual practice and *opinio juris* of states and, in doing so, expresses fidelity to the inductive approach: CIL forms where it is induced into existence through a widespread, representative, and consistent state practice coupled with *opinio juris*. On a limited number of occasions, however, the ICJ has been prepared to combine the inductive and deductive methods when identifying CIL.[215] In this way, deduction seems to be used to lower the bar for the amount of state practice and *opinio juris* needed to establish CIL.

In its work on the identification of CIL, the ILC endorses the inductive method but explains that it 'does not in fact preclude a measure of deduction as an aid, to be deployed with caution, in the application of the two-element [inductive] approach'.[216] The ILC therefore takes a more traditional approach: induction is the

[212] Tams (n 57) 202–04.

[213] Dawidowicz (n 28) 53.

[214] ILC, 'State Responsibility' in *Yearbook of the International Law Commission. 2001, Volume I* 94 (emphasis added).

[215] *Military and Paramilitary Activities in and against Nicaragua* (n 12) paras 202–07; *Jurisdictional Immunities of the State (Germany v Italy: Greece Intervening)* (Judgment of 3 February 2012) [2012] ICJ Rep 99 paras 55–56. See generally Talmon (n 211).

[216] ILC, 'Draft Conclusions on Identification of Customary International Law', Conclusion 2, Commentary, para 5.

correct method for identifying CIL, and deduction can only be used to confirm the existence of such rules. Certainly, the ILC does not permit the use of deduction to compensate for insufficient state practice and *opinio juris* under the inductive approach. Thus, given that states have expressed a range of different views on the CIL status of collective countermeasures, deduction cannot be used to somehow lower the threshold for inductive evidence and thereby establish this doctrine in CIL.

III. Third-Party Countermeasures

There is some discussion in the academic literature as to whether states can take third-party countermeasures.[217] To avoid conceptual confusion, third-party countermeasures must be distinguished from collective countermeasures. As said, third-party countermeasures refer to situations in which a wrongdoing state breaches an obligation owed to an injured state and the injured state requests third states to take countermeasures on its behalf against the wrongdoing state to protect its legal interests. In this context, no breach of a collective obligation occurs.

Some commentators claim that third-party countermeasures are lawful because of the close analogy with collective self-defence,[218] which permits a state that has fallen victim to an armed attack to request third states to take defensive measures against the attacking state.[219] However, countermeasures and self-defence are very different doctrines. Countermeasures are law enforcement mechanisms insofar as they are designed to implement state responsibility for prior breaches of international law – in other words, countermeasures are responses to illegality. By contrast, self-defence is a reaction to an event, namely, an armed attack against a state.[220] Self-defence therefore concerns the preservation of state sovereignty and evokes a war-like paradigm. It thus stands to reason that victim states can invite third states to help protect them from violent attacks, but injured states cannot invite third states to take countermeasures to help them protect their legal rights.

Regarding third-party countermeasures, there is no relationship of illegality between the wrongdoing state and the third state. This means that, unlike the doctrine of collective countermeasures where indirectly injured states have a legal interest in securing compliance with the breached *erga omnes (partes)* obligation, no argument can be made that the structure of the law on state responsibility gives third states the right to take countermeasures against the wrongdoing state. This

[217] S Haataja, 'Cyber Operations and Collective Countermeasures under International Law' (2020) 25 *Journal of Conflict and Security Law* 33, 47.

[218] ibid.

[219] Art 51 UN Charter (referring to 'collective self-defence').

[220] DW Bowett, 'Economic Coercion and Reprisals by States' (1972) 13 *Virginia Journal of International Law* 1, 8.

means the only legal basis for the doctrine of third-party countermeasures is that it is established in CIL through extensive state practice coupled with *opinio juris*.

It is difficult to sustain the argument that CIL permits third-party countermeasures. There are very few – if any – clear-cut instances of third states engaging in countermeasures on behalf of an injured state simply because the injured state has requested assistance. And to the best of the author's knowledge, only Estonia (2019) and Costa Rica (2023) (and perhaps Ireland (2023)) have expressed support for the legality of third-party countermeasures under CIL. In addition, France (2019) seems to have ruled out recourse to third-party countermeasures under CIL.

IV. *Lex Specialis*: Cyber-Specific Collective and Third-Party Countermeasures

Assuming the doctrines of collective and third-party countermeasures are not established in CIL, can the argument be made that specialised regimes (*lex specialis*) of CIL have formed (or are forming) on the doctrines of collective and third-party *cyber* countermeasures? The scenario, here, is whether CIL permits states to take cyber-specific collective and third-party countermeasures in response to cyber-specific internationally wrongful acts. This question is pertinent because Article 55 of the ASR accepts that specialised regimes on the law of state responsibility can emerge:

> These articles do not apply where and to the extent that the conditions for the existence of an internationally wrongful act or the content or implementation of the international responsibility of a State are governed by special rules of international law.

Lex specialis on collective and third-party cyber countermeasures may seem desirable given the volume and frequency of internationally wrongful behaviour in cyberspace. While some states and commentators may see the doctrines of collective and third-party countermeasures as destabilising, they may regard these cyber-specific doctrines as an acceptable compromise.

However, as we have seen, there is currently a lack of state practice and *opinio juris* to support the development of cyber-specific doctrines on collective and third-party countermeasures. Moreover, it is difficult to see how such doctrines would work in practice. This is because various states have determined that countermeasures taken in response to unlawful cyber operations need not be 'in-kind', meaning that states can take non-cyber countermeasures to confront unlawful cyber operations.[221] Instead, the key factor in determining the legality of a

[221] 'It is also clear that countermeasures need not be of the same character as the threat and could involve non-cyber means'; UK Attorney General, 'Speech: International Law in Future Frontiers' (19 May 2022) www.gov.uk/government/speeches/international-law-in-future-frontiers. See also B Egan, 'Remarks on International Law and Stability in Cyberspace' (10 November 2016) 2009–2017. state.gov/s/l/releases/remarks/264303.htm.

particular countermeasure is the principle of proportionality, which requires that countermeasures 'must be commensurate with the injury suffered, taking into account the gravity of the internationally wrongful act and the rights in question'.[222]

V. Conclusion

This chapter has drawn a critical distinction between collective and third-party countermeasures. Collective countermeasures involve indirectly injured states taking countermeasures against wrongdoing states to protect *erga omnes (partes)* obligations. As noted, a sharp rise in internationally wrongful cyber activity appears to have galvanised some states into expressing support for the doctrine of collective countermeasures. To a certain extent, there seems to be greater acceptance of collective countermeasures nowadays than in 2001. Ultimately, however, this direction of travel is checked by the fact that most states have not opined on the legality of collective countermeasures (and have not, therefore, *claimed* the legality of this doctrine); acceptance of this doctrine is limited to mainly western states; and some states have actually rejected it (including western states). Given the high threshold that must be met for custom to develop, this chapter concludes that – at present – the doctrine of collective countermeasures is not established in CIL.

Third-party countermeasures involve third states taking countermeasures on behalf of an injured state to help protect the latter's legal rights against a wrongdoing state. This chapter has found very little evidence of state practice and *opinio juris* to support the existence of this doctrine in CIL.

[222] *Articles on State Responsibility* Art 51.

10

The Obligation to Settle Cyber Disputes Peacefully: Arbitration, Conciliation, Fact-Finding and Other Mechanisms

PÅL WRANGE*

I. Introduction

States are reluctant to settle their cyber disputes in the public eye and even more reluctant to involve third parties. There are several reasons for that, as will be discussed in this chapter, including the lack of agreement on how international law applies to cyberspace, the various difficulties involved in the collection and assessment of evidence, and – surely, in some cases – the perception that cyber operations are 'what states do'. Nevertheless, with the growing number of public attributions of cyber incidents and the accompanying refutations, as well as the growing sense that there is a need for some form of order in cyberspace, it may well be the case that states are becoming more interested in seeking ways to resolve their disputes and, in that process also develop and clarify legal rules. The purpose of this chapter is to contribute to a nascent debate about these issues, with a focus on the question whether established dispute resolution procedures such as arbitration, conciliation and fact-finding, may need to be complemented or amended for that purpose.

This chapter is structured as follows: Section II delimits the subject. Section III discusses the obligation to settle disputes peacefully and its implications for the resolution of cyber disputes. Section IV continues with a review of some features of cyber disputes which are problematic from a dispute settlement perspective. In section V, I discuss how to address these problems in relation to arbitration,

*I want to thank François Delerue and the editors for very useful comments on earlier drafts. Disclosure: I am a member of the Permanent Court of Arbitration and an alternate arbitrator of the OSCE Court of Conciliation and Arbitration, which means that I have a (very modest) self-interest in promoting the increased use of arbitration in this field. In spite of that interest, this chapter will explain why states may be reluctant to submit cyber disputes to arbitration.

conciliation and fact-finding, but also in relation to alternative dispute settlement mechanisms. Section VI provides some concluding remarks. The underlying theme of this chapter is the critical role of dispute settlement procedures for maintaining international peace and security in cyberspace.

II. What are Cyber Disputes?

'Dispute' has been defined elsewhere in this volume as an international law-framed claim followed by rejection or denial by the other state.[1] As will be noted below, many allegations by states of malicious cyber activities by other states have not been made in legal terms. However, they have been made in normative language which could be framed in international law terms, for instance in the terms of the United Nations (UN) 'norms of responsible state behaviour in cyberspace', adopted by the UN Groups of Governmental Experts since 2013.[2]

Following this, the predicate 'cyber' will be used in this chapter to mean phenomena related to ICTs.[3] The term 'cyberspace', by contrast, carries little analytical value from a legal point of view. 'Cyberspace' is not a new domain in any legal sense. In particular, it is not an unregulated 'space'. I will nevertheless occasionally use the term 'cyberspace', since it is an established term, but only as a shorthand to signify several different types of phenomena having to do with ICTs.

Today 'cyber is everywhere'.[4] Just as hardly any dispute scenario is without elements in 'cyberspace', disputes which may seem to focus on 'cyberspace' are not isolated from effects in 'real life'. Harm to computer networks for example have also kinetic knock-on effects. Events that one may think of as 'ordinary' and not cyber-related are, in all likelihood, to a very large extent guided, enabled or even performed by computers. Hence, it is difficult, if not impossible, to establish

[1] Tsagourias (ch 1 in this volume). The Tallinn Manual adopts the definition from the *Mavrommatis* case: 'a disagreement on a point of law or fact, a conflict of legal views or interests between parties'. MN Schmitt (ed), *Tallinn Manual 2.0 on the International Law Applicable to Cyber Operations*, 2nd edn (Cambridge, Cambridge University Press, 2017) 304.

[2] UNGA, 'Reports of the Group of Governmental Experts on Developments in the Field of Information and Telecommunications in the Context of International Security' (24 June 2013) UN Doc A/68/98; UNGA, 'Reports of the Group of Governmental Experts on Developments in the Field of Information and Telecommunications in the Context of International Security' (22 July 2015) UN Doc A/70/174; and UNGA, 'Report of the Group of Governmental Experts on Advancing Responsible State Behaviour in Cyberspace in the Context of International Security' (14 July 2021) UN Doc A/76/135.

[3] One could also include other computer networks which are air-gapped from the Internet. Such networks share some relevant traits with the Internet, not least that they involve computers. Damage to such networks, just as well as damage to computers which are not connected at all, may also involve issues on how to assess damage.

[4] See, for instance, J Seffinga, 'Cyber, Cyber Everywhere: Is Your Cyber Strategy Everywhere Too?' (*Deloitte*) www2.deloitte.com/ch/en/pages/technology/articles/cyber-cyber-everywhere.html.

a particular category of disputes that are purely cyber disputes, and disputes over events in 'cyberspace' must be settled according to the same rules and principles as events that mainly take place offline. The difference between what is 'cyber' and what is not is one of degree, not of kind. Having said that, and as will be discussed, 'cyber' brings several legal complications that did not exist before computers or the Internet were invented, including new phenomena such as cloud computing and has radically changed existing phenomena such as espionage.

As stated by one observer, '[t]here is by far no uniform understanding of cyber disputes'.[5] The scope of 'cyber disputes' covered in this chapter will be delimited along three axes. The first is that the dispute must have significant cyber elements, typically relating to the technology itself and/or its impact on geography.

Second, disputes on cyber issues may concern different legal and policy areas.[6] Although many other types of disputes could credibly be called 'cyber disputes', the cyber disputes dealt with here will be those that have an international security dimension, in particular cyber operations with security implications. The reason why I focus on security issues is because the current chapter is published in a collection in which most authors (including the present one) have been involved in discussions on cyber and international security, broadly defined. Also, the main global inter-state discussions conducted in the six Groups of Governmental Experts (GGEs) and the two Open-Ended Working Groups (OEWGs) focus on ICTs and international security and in academic circles, the *Tallinn Manual*[7] is an important reference point. Nevertheless, much of what is said here will also be relevant to cyber disputes in a broader sense.

The third axis is that the chapter focuses on 'cyber disputes' between states which is also the focus of this collection in general even if cyber threats often emanate from non-state actors and disputes may involve private actors. Disputes with or action against non-state actors are relevant only to the extent that a state invokes the responsibility of another state for the acts of such actors. Hence, the definition of 'cyber dispute' adopted by this chapter is narrower than certain other definitions.[8]

[5] J Kulesza, 'Peaceful Settlement of Interstate Online Disputes' in Special Issue: International Law as a Driver of Internet Governance (2022) 11 *Laws* 1, 3.

[6] Issues related to ICTs and the Internet are treated under different headings with different predicates, like cyber, Internet, data, ICT, information, tech, digital, etc, and with different nouns, like governance, law, regime, etc. This chapter notes that the different labels used are related to different policy fields and different areas of law and often have different histories, but the chapter is not concerned with these differences.

[7] Schmitt (n 1).

[8] *cf* Kulesza (n 5) 4; SJ Shackelford, 'The Law of Cyber Peace' (2017) 18 *Chicago Journal of International Law* 1; *cf* Delerue, who draws the line for cyber operations and the physical hostile acts against computers and computer networks, where 'cyber operations' are all acts taking place in cyberspace. F Delerue, *Cyber Operations and International Law* (Cambridge, Cambridge University Press, 2020).

III. The Obligation to Settle Cyber Disputes Peacefully

It is pertinent to start with a discussion of the basic obligation to settle disputes peacefully. The two main provisions are Article 2(3) and Article 33 of the UN Charter which have different consequences for state behaviour.[9] The report of the sixth UN Group of Governmental Experts stated that:

> in accordance with their obligations under Article 2(3) and Chapter VI of the Charter of the United Nations, States party to any international dispute, including those involving the use of ICTs, the continuance of which is likely to endanger the maintenance of international peace and security, shall, first of all, seek a solution by such means as described in Article 33 of the Charter, namely negotiation, enquiry, mediation, conciliation, arbitration, judicial settlement, resort to regional agencies or arrangements, or other peaceful means of their own choice.[10]

Despite the reference to Article 2(3), this statement focuses on the obligation in Article 33. The *Tallinn Manual*, however, clearly differentiates between the two obligations:

> Rule 65 – Peaceful settlement of disputes (a) States must attempt to settle their international disputes involving cyber activities that endanger international peace and security by peaceful means. (b) If States attempt to settle international disputes involving cyber activities that do not endanger international peace and security, they must do so by peaceful means.[11]

The first obligation relates to Article 33 and the second to Article 2(3). Regarding the type of disputes falling under the Article 33 obligation, the group of experts that produced the *Tallinn Manual*:

> agreed that situations involving cyber activities that risk leading to the outbreak of an international armed conflict …, or even isolated uses of force …, clearly qualify. So too do cyber activities that destabilise relations between States in a manner that creates an environment foreseeably susceptible to escalation to uses of force and armed conflict. This means there is an obligation to make a *bona fide* effort to actually settle (or at least freeze) any dispute which endangers peace and security, such as 'cyber activities that destabilise relations between States in a manner that creates an environment foreseeably susceptible to escalation to uses of force and armed conflict'.[12]

[9] See the Introduction to this volume.

[10] UNGA, 'Report of the GGE' UN Doc A/76/135 para 71(a). Regarding the corresponding 'norm', this is further elaborated on in para 25.

[11] Schmitt (n 1) 303. Indeed, in contrast to Art 2(3), Art 33 and the entire Chapter VI of the Charter of the United Nations (San Francisco, 26 June 1945) are limited to those disputes 'the continuance of which is likely to endanger the maintenance of international peace and security'. T De Souza Dias, 'Applying Chapters VI and VII of the Charter of the United Nations in the Cyber Context: The Challenges and Opportunities of Information and Communications Technologies' (*UNIDIR*, 2021) www.unidir.org/sites/default/files/2021-09/UNIDIR_UN_Charter_in_Cyber_Context.pdf 12.

[12] Schmitt (n 1) 306. See the very thoughtful analysis of this obligation in DB Hollis and E Tikk, 'Peaceful Settlement in International Law' (2022) 57 *Texas International Law Journal* 1, 26–38.

Article 33 enjoins states to make efforts to be creative and overcome the many difficulties in order to settle a dispute. As argued by Peters, even if states have a free choice of mechanisms to settle their disputes (unless there are specific contractual obligations), 'in the event of an objective failure of one strategy, the principle of good faith obliges the parties to continue to strive for settlement with a new means'.[13]

Regarding Article 2(3) the obligation is limited to the means used and has implications for the use of countermeasures[14] as will be discussed below, but it is not an obligation to actually settle their disputes. Article 2(3) also requires that those dispute settlement means are employed 'in such a manner that international peace and security, and justice, are not endangered'. If this is to have a meaning independent of Article 2(4) on the use of force, it must entail that states should avoid 'action which could make things worse'.[15] In the words of Hollis and Tikk, 'States must, in such situations, avoid escalatory behaviour independent of the use of force threshold.'[16]

How does the imposition of sanctions relate to the obligation to avoid escalatory behaviour? Two examples are indicative. In 2019, within the framework of its 'cyber diplomacy toolbox', the European Union (EU) established a cyber-related sanctions regime which includes 'targeted restrictive measures' on natural and legal persons.[17] Such sanctions, amounting to travel bans and asset freezes, were first imposed against individuals associated with the Russian, North Korean and Chinese governments in July 2020.[18] In 2021, the USA attributed the Solar Winds hack to the Russian Federation and imposed economic sanctions on Russian nationals and assets.[19] Russia not only denied any involvement in the operation but also challenged the legality of those sanctions.[20]

There are, broadly speaking, two different (but not necessarily contradictory) interests involved here: peace and justice. Both interests are served (though in different ways) by the law on dispute settlement as well as by the law on

[13] A Peters, 'International Dispute Settlement: A Network of Cooperational Duties' (2003) 14 *European Journal of International Law* 1, 16.

[14] See Buchan (ch 9 in this volume).

[15] JG Merrills, 'The Means of Dispute Settlement' in MD Evans (ed), *International Law*, 5th edn (Oxford, Oxford University Press, 2018) 564; Hollis and Tikk (n 12) 28.

[16] Hollis and Tikk (n 12) 33. 'This obligation is enshrined in paragraph 4 principle 2 of the 1970 *UN Declaration* as well as in paragraph 8 of the *Manila Declaration*.' Kulesza (n 5) 5.

[17] Y Shany and MN Schmitt, 'An International Attribution Mechanism for Hostile Cyber Operations' (2020) 96 *International Law Studies* 196, 212. The latest iteration of this regime can be found in Council of Europe, Decision (CFSP) 2021/796 amending Decision (CFSP) 2019/797 concerning restrictive measures against cyber-attacks threatening the Union or its Member States [2021] OJ L174I/1. See also A Bendiek and M Schulze, 'Attribution: A Major Challenge for EU Cyber Sanctions. An Analysis of WannaCry, NotPetya, Cloud Hopper, Bundestag Hack and the Attack on the OPCW. SWP Research Paper 2021/RP 11' (*German Institute for International and Security Affairs*, December 2021) www.swp-berlin.org/10.18449/2021RP11/ 15.

[18] Bendiek and Schulze (n 17) 3.

[19] The White House, 'Fact Sheet: Imposing Costs for Harmful Foreign Activities by the Russian Government' (15 April 2021) www.whitehouse.gov/briefing-room/statements-releases/2021/04/15/fact-sheet-imposing-costs-for-harmful-foreign-activities-by-the-russian-government/.

[20] De Souza Dias (n 11) 14.

countermeasures, and they must be balanced. Some sanctions amount to retorsion[21] while others, which prima facie are illegal, may constitute countermeasures. Even though countermeasures can be justified under the law of state responsibility,[22] they must be implemented in the light of the obligation to settle disputes in a peaceful manner.[23] Under customary international law, as codified in Article 52 of the articles on state responsibility for internationally wrongful acts (ARSIWA), an injured state must, before resorting to countermeasures, 'call upon the responsible State' to cease the internationally wrongful act and make full reparation and 'notify the responsible State of [the] decision to take countermeasures and offer to negotiate' unless 'urgent countermeasures … are necessary to preserve its rights'.[24] This balances the rights and interests of the states involved and serves the interest of maintaining peace as part of the obligations of peaceful settlement. While the legal and factual basis of a countermeasure will be assessed by the acting state in the first instance,[25] that state does so at its own risk. If there has not been a prior wrongful act justifying the countermeasure, then the responding state itself has committed an internationally wrongful act.[26]

A related matter is whether the state that takes countermeasures needs to 'publicly provide evidence of the basis upon which it attributed cyber operations

[21] For instance, it is legal as such to prosecute persons suspected of having committed computer crime, provided that the state in question has a jurisdictional basis for the prosecution.

[22] Art 22 of the ILC, 'Responsibility of States for Internationally Wrongful Acts' in *Yearbook of the International Law Commission. 2001, Volume II, Part Two: Report of the Commission to the General Assembly on the Work of its Fifty-Third Session* (New York, UN, 2005) (ARSIWA).

[23] According to what is probably the overwhelmingly dominant view, countermeasures are *ipso jure* legal, regardless of whether they are escalatory or not. DD Caron and C Tomuschat, 'Article 2, para 3 UN Charter' in A Zimmermann et al (eds), *The Statute of the International Court of Justice: A Commentary*, 3rd edn (Oxford, Oxford University Press, 2019) para 30. The thoughtful discussion in Hollis and Tikk is more nuanced, and notes that '[p]eaceful settlement also incorporates obligations of a more positive character, requiring behavior of its subjects'. Hollis and Tikk (n 12) 34. See Buchan (ch 9 in this volume).

[24] Art 52(1) and (2) of ARSIWA. See Delerue (n 8) 443. See also Fan Yang, 'The Problem with Ill-Substantiated Public Cyber Attribution: A Legal Perspective' in AE Levite et al (eds), *Managing US-China Tensions over Public Cyber Attribution* (Washington DC, Carnegie Endowment for International Peace, 2022) 6. This is reflected to some extent in the report of the sixth GGE: 'States that are subject to malicious ICT activity, and States from whose territory such malicious ICT activity is suspected to have originated, are encouraged to consult among relevant competent authorities.' UNGA, 'Report of the GGE' UN Doc A/76/135 para 23. See Buchan (ch 9 in this volume).

[25] *cf* Delerue (n 8) 438.

[26] ILC, 'Draft Articles on Responsibility of States for Internationally Wrongful Acts, with Commentaries' in *Yearbook of the International Law Commission. 2001, Volume II, Part Two: Report of the Commission to the General Assembly on the Work of its Fifty-Third Session, as Corrected* (New York, UN, 2007) p 130. This was noted by the Tallinn experts. Schmitt (n 1) 116, 120–21. See also Yang (n 24) 12; *cf* Delerue (n 8) 438. The UK has a different position: 'Prior notice may not be a legal obligation when responding to covert cyber intrusion with countermeasures or when resort is had to countermeasures which themselves depend on covert cyber capabilities.' UNGA, 'Official Compendium of Voluntary National Contributions on the Subject of How International Law Applies to the Use of Information and Communications Technologies by States Submitted by Participating Governmental Experts in the Group of Governmental Experts on Advancing Responsible State Behaviour in Cyberspace in the Context of International Security Established Pursuant to General Assembly Resolution 73/266' (13 July 2021) UN Doc A/76/136, 118. See Buchan (ch 9 in this volume).

to another State when responding thereto pursuant to the law of State responsibility', which is the view of some states.[27] There have also been debates about whether evidence should be disclosed even in case of a public attribution without sanctions. In paragraph 71(g) of its report, the sixth GGE 'notes that accusations of organizing and implementing wrongful acts brought against States should be substantiated'.[28] States like the USA, UK and France claim that there is no such obligation (note the use of 'should' as well as the vagueness of the term 'substantiated'),[29] while China, Russia, and some other countries hold that accusations must be substantiated.[30] The Tallinn Manual did not find that there 'is an established basis under international law for … an obligation' to provide evidence before sanctions,[31] and that is probably a correct assessment. However, to show the evidence supporting an attribution claim may help defuse a situation, particularly if the assessment is mistaken.[32] At any rate, even if a state that takes countermeasures does not provide evidence, it must still justify these measures by explaining in legal terms why it believes that the target state has violated international law.[33] After all, under Articles 22 and 49 of ARSIWA, countermeasures may only be taken 'in order to induce that State to comply with its obligations under Part Two' of the articles, that is, to cease the illegal action, to offer appropriate assurances and guarantees of non-repetition (Article 30), and to provide reparation.[34] Such justifications – to date very rare – will also serve to contribute to the formation or crystallisation of customary international law.

IV. Particular Issues Related to Cyber Disputes

This chapter will now proceed to discuss some particular problems related to cyber disputes which are relevant from a dispute settlement perspective, and which may call for new or modified dispute settlement procedures. Most of them can be linked to the UN GGEs' Norms of Responsible State Behaviour or the GGEs' statements about international law.[35]

[27] Schmitt (n 1) 83.

[28] UNGA, 'Report of the GGE' UN Doc A/76/135, 18.

[29] N Tsagourias and M Farrell, 'Cyber Attribution: Technical and Legal Approaches and Challenges' (2020) 31 *European Journal of International Law* 941, 955. See also Kulesza (n 5) 2; Shany and Schmitt (n 17) 212.

[30] Fan Yang (n 24) 8. Yang finds, though, that 'Legal consequences for making factually incorrect or wrongful public attributions are not clearly defined'. ibid 9.

[31] Schmitt (n 1) 83.

[32] *cf* the remark in the *Tallinn Manual* on the requirement of notification that this 'is especially apropos because the originator of a cyber operation might be spoofed'. Schmitt (n 1) 120.

[33] Art 22 of ARSIWA provides that 'An injured State may only take countermeasures against a State which is responsible for an internationally wrongful act in order to induce that State to comply with its obligations under Part Two' (that is, to cease the illegal activity and to provide reparation).

[34] Art 49 of ARSIWA.

[35] UNGA, 'Report of the GGE' UN Doc A/76/135.

Disputes often revolve around allegations that one state has hacked into the cyber infrastructure in another state. Hacking may be done to prepare for future cyber operations or to gather information related to national security or to economic assets that can be used later.[36] The hack in itself may violate the territorial sovereignty of the victim state.[37] It may also be followed by other operations, such as attacks against electrical grids or financial systems, which may cause further direct damage in ways that violate international law. The information gathered, such as technical know-how, may be used for economic purposes which may violate, for instance, international intellectual property law.[38] In addition to their own hacks, states may support hacking operations by non-state actors[39] or fail to cooperate with the victim state to stop, investigate and prosecute such actors.[40] Further, states may survey individuals in third states through their own cyber operations or through intermediaries (for instance, platform companies) in ways which may violate the right to privacy of these individuals. As reactions to such actions, the alleged victim state may prosecute individuals that are suspected to be responsible, it may impose sanctions,[41] or it may simply make a public allegation against the other country.

In all of these instances, the victim state will be interested in having such actions ceased, and it will in some cases also want compensation or to simply know the truth. In addition, and perhaps even more importantly, the victim state may be interested in real assurances of non-repetition, as well as an authoritative confirmation that it has suffered a wrong and that its view of the law is correct. A state which feels that it has been wrongly accused of a violation will want confirmation that it was innocent and reparation in the form of an apology. These different goals may call for different approaches to dispute settlement and different mechanisms of dispute settlement, depending on what the parties deem important.[42]

[36] *cf* Schmitt (n 1) 304.

[37] For views along this line, see R Buchan, *Cyber Espionage and International Law* (Oxford, Hart Publishing, 2018); S Watts and T Richard, 'Baseline Territorial Sovereignty and Cyberspace' (2018) 22 *Lewis & Clark Law Review* 771; P Wrange, 'Intervention in National and Private Cyberspace and International Law' in D Langlet et al (eds), *International Law and Changing Perceptions of Security* (Leiden, Brill, 2014).

[38] *cf* Bendiek and Schulze (n 17) 11.

[39] Under norm 13(f): 'A State should not conduct or knowingly support ICT activity contrary to its obligations under international law that intentionally damages critical infrastructure or otherwise impairs the use and operation of critical infrastructure to provide services to the public.' According to para 71(g) of the report, the GGE 'reaffirms that States must not use proxies to commit internationally wrongful acts using ICTs' and should seek 'to ensure that their territory is not used by non-State actors to commit such acts'. UNGA, 'Report of the GGE' UN Doc A/76/135, 12 and 18.

[40] Under norm 13(d): 'States should consider how best to cooperate to exchange information, assist each other, prosecute terrorist and criminal use of ICTs and implement other cooperative measures to address such threats.' According to norm 13(h): 'States should respond to appropriate requests for assistance by another State whose critical infrastructure is subject to malicious ICT acts. States should also respond to appropriate requests to mitigate malicious ICT activity aimed at the critical infrastructure of another State emanating from their territory, taking into account due regard for sovereignty.' UNGA, 'Report of the GGE' UN Doc A/76/135, 13.

[41] *cf* the Solar Winds incident. See De Souza Dias (n 11) 14. See Franchini (ch 3 in this volume).

[42] I am grateful to François Delerue for having pointed this out. I have not been able to pursue this question consistently in this chapter, however.

There is also the general interest of the international community – to the extent that such an interest can be ascertained[43] – that disputes are resolved so that peace is maintained, that wrongful acts cease so that the stability of cyberspace is upheld and, arguably, that the law be clarified.

However, as will be discussed in this section, there are several difficulties involved in the settlement of cyber disputes, namely, the controversies regarding the content of the law, the difficulty of establishing the facts (including for attribution), and the need of expertise to deal with the above. I will now explain further these issues.

A. Contested Law

Perhaps the most difficult aspect in settling cyber disputes is the lack of legal clarity.[44] Although states, and almost all commentators, agree that international law as we know it applies to cyberspace, there are conceptual, technical and structural aspects in cyberspace that pose new problems, and which may call for authoritative clarifications or adjustments of existing rules. Even though there is a growing body of *opinio juris*, in particular from many small and medium-sized western states,[45] there is very little in terms of state or court practice to be found for anyone looking for specifics. In public attributions, states generally do not use legal language and they do not demand reparation.[46]

The uncertain status of law is also one important reason why states feel uncomfortable to make claims in legal terms. But there are also less innocent reasons. One observer avers that 'Washington may not yet be ready to constrain itself from conducting similar cyber operations of its own.'[47] Whatever the reasons, the reluctance to speak in legal terms is an obstacle to the crystallisation or development of international law and for international law to provide the framework of dispute settlement.[48]

[43] See P Wrange, 'Is There a General Interest *hors la loi*?' in H Ruiz Fabri, E Jouannet and V Tomkiewic (eds), *Select Proceedings of the European Society of International Law: Volume I 2006* (Oxford, Hart Publishing, 2008).

[44] Law is not determinate, which is not to say that law is never predictable. See also Tsagourias (ch 1 in this volume).

[45] National position papers can be found at UNIDIR, 'Cyber Policy Portal' cyberpolicyportal.org/. Neither India nor Russia submitted such papers. It should be noted, though, that Russia made proposals for international treaties, including the Cybercrime Convention which is currently being negotiated in the UN.

[46] *cf* Tsagourias and Farrell (n 29) 946; J Bateman, 'The Purposes of US Government Public Cyber Attribution' in AE Levite et al (eds), *Managing US-China Tensions over Public Cyber Attribution* (Washington DC, Carnegie Endowment for International Peace, 2022) 20. See Tsagourias (ch 1 in this volume).

[47] Bateman (n 46) 20.

[48] 'In the view of skeptical States, legal clarity constrains the cyber operations of "rule of law" States.' Shany and Schmitt (n 17) 217.

An even more important difficulty is that states are hesitant to submit to dispute settlement mechanism if they do not have a fair idea of how these mechanisms approach the law. Furthermore, at least some states are weary of the law-making function of dispute settlement bodies.[49]

If states nevertheless submit to a dispute settlement procedure, the results of such a procedure may have quite important precedential value. Therefore, while the primary purpose of a dispute settlement body is to settle a concrete dispute, at least in the cyber context, it should also have its law-making or 'constitutive' function in the back of its mind, if not up front.[50] Therefore, important interests are at stake for other states and for the international community. This may justify the involvement of third parties, for instance in the form of interventions in the process or as amicus curiae, as will be discussed in the subsection on arbitration.

B. Proof: Means and Standards

If a cyber dispute arises, it needs to be established what happened, including the damage that was caused, and to whom the malicious act is attributed. As explained by Delerue, '[i]n the case of cyber operations, the facts are generally articulated around two main axes: the identification of the cyber operation and its consequences and the attribution of the cyber operation'.[51]

When one state alleges that another state has conducted an illegal cyber operation against it, the standard of proof and the methods for establishing the facts are matters dealt with by international law but the law is not always clear. Also legal questions about admissibility of evidence as well as about the proper methodology for assessing evidence are raised. That said, establishing the facts in cyber is also a technical question.

Usually, the most contentious factual issues concern cyber attribution, which is an issue that received significant attention in both scholarly and policy circles. The first state-to-state attribution took place in 2014, when the USA attributed the hack against Sony Pictures to North Korea, without submitting any public evidence.[52] An even more important event was the US disclosure of some evidence that corroborated its allegation that the hack in 2016 against the Democratic National Committee could be attributed to the Russian Federation. The allegation was made on 7 October 2016, in a 'Joint Statement from the Department of Homeland Security and Office of the Director of National Intelligence on Election Security', and evidence in the form of a 'Joint Analysis Report' was released on

[49] *cf* CPR Romano, 'International Dispute Settlement' in D Bodansky, J Brunnée and E Hey (eds), *The Oxford Handbook of International Environmental Law* (Oxford, Oxford University Press, 2008) 1041.

[50] Hollis and Tikk (n 12) 46.

[51] *cf* Delerue (n 8) 94.

[52] ibid 102; Tsagourias and Farrell (n 29) 944.

29 December.[53] Since then, there have been many more state-to-state attributions, some coordinated. For example, in 2021 there was a joint attribution by the USA, EU, UK, Australia, Canada, New Zealand, Japan, and NATO of 'malicious cyber activities' to China,[54] and in November 2022, China alleged that the USA hacked into a Chinese university and 'took away a group of core technical data'.[55] Nevertheless, most attributions have been made by private entities, including cyber security companies and news media.[56]

Legal attribution[57] is a difficult exercise and will rarely lead to certainty.[58] As opined by two experts, '[m]atching an offender to an offence is an exercise in minimising uncertainty on several levels'.[59] The ensuing passage deserves a quotation:

> On a technical level, attribution is an art as much as a science. … Finding the right clues requires a disciplined focus on a set of detailed questions – but also the intuition of technically experienced operators. … On an operational level, attribution is a nuanced process, not a simple problem. That process of attribution is … not black-and-white, yes-or-no, but appears in shades. … On a strategic level, attribution is a function of what is at stake politically. The political stakes are determined by a range of factors, most importantly by the incurred damage.[60]

In a typical attribution process, a cyber activity operation is attributed first to a machine, thereafter to a human and lastly to a state.[61] 'During the event of a cyber operation, a number of traces are usually left and may be collected as evidence. Most of these traces can be presented in the form of written documents to constitute documentary evidence.'[62] This may involve 'malware samples, compiler language, programming language, IP addresses, domain names, registration information for infrastructure, payment information for infrastructure, patterns/ordering of execution events, keyboard layout for malware creation, scripts and programmes used on a victim network or host'.[63]

If and when technical attribution is performed, one then needs to determine who was at the keyboard, and which state – if any – is responsible for the acts

[53] *cf* Delerue (n 8) 89–90.

[54] The White House, 'The United States, Joined by Allies and Partners, Attributes Malicious Cyber Activity and Irresponsible State Behavior to the People's Republic of China' (19 July 2021) www.whitehouse.gov/briefing-room/statements-releases/2021/07/19/the-united-states-joined-by-allies-and-partners-attributes-malicious-cyber-activity-and-irresponsible-state-behavior-to-the-peoples-republic-of-china/.

[55] People's Republic of China, 'China Urges US to Stop Irresponsible Accusations on Cyber Security' (*State Council Information Office*, 17 November 2022) english.scio.gov.cn/pressroom/2022-11/17/content_78523581.htm.

[56] M Mueller et al, 'Cyber Attribution: Can a New Institution Achieve Transnational Credibility?' (2019) 4 *The Cyber Defense Review* 107, 112. See also Tsagourias and Farrell (n 29) 944.

[57] See for instance Art 2 of ARSIWA.

[58] Tsagourias and Farrell (n 29) 950.

[59] T Rid and B Buchanan, 'Attributing Cyber Attacks' (2015) 38 *Journal of Strategic Studies* 4, 7.

[60] ibid 7.

[61] *cf* Delerue (n 8) 55.

[62] ibid 95. See also Bendiek and Schulze (n 17) 7; Tsagourias and Farrell (n 29) 956.

[63] Tsagourias and Farrell (n 29) 956.

of that individual. Technical data may be useful for such determinations, but it is usually necessary to also bring in different kinds of evidence, such as 'geopolitical factors, indicators of origin, motivation, the degree of sophistication of the attack, the scale and timing of the attack, linguistic indicators, common tooling, infrastructure and so on'.[64] Such evidence must be assessed properly in order to establish a legally relevant link to a state.

Full attribution is usually only available to states, and only the most resourceful ones.[65] For instance, the EU relies on NATO capabilities to a large extent, and according to some observers, not even China has that capacity.[66]

In its 2015 report, the fourth GGE suggested the following relevant norm in its list of Norms of Responsible State Behaviour:

> Norm 13(b): In case of ICT incidents, States should consider all relevant information, including the larger context of the event, the challenges of attribution in the ICT environment, and the nature and extent of the consequences.

This was developed by the sixth GGE:

> 22. This norm acknowledges that attribution is a complex undertaking and that a broad range of factors should be considered before establishing the source of an ICT incident.
>
> …
>
> 24. A State that is victim of a malicious ICT incident should consider all aspects in its assessment of the incident. Such aspects, supported by substantiated facts, can include the incident's technical attributes; its scope, scale and impact; the wider context, including the incident's bearing on international peace and security; and the results of consultations between the States concerned.[67]

In paragraph 71(g)

> the Group recalls that the indication that an ICT activity was launched or otherwise originates from the territory or the ICT infrastructure of a State may be insufficient in itself to attribute the activity to that State …. The invocation of the responsibility of a State for an internationally wrongful act involves complex technical, legal and political considerations.[68]

The GGE report is not binding as such, and it does not even claim that 'norms' express existing international law. However, the report was the result of careful deliberations, and the language on norm 13(b) (paragraphs 22–24) is echoed in paragraph 71, which explicitly purports to set out international law norms. To the extent that this has a legal *porté*, for instance with reference to the admissibility of evidence, it means that a dispute settlement body should allow and assess evidence of different kinds.

[64] ibid 958.

[65] Rid and Buchanan (n 59) 31. See also Fan Yang (n 24) 6; Bateman (n 46) 16.

[66] Bendiek and Schulze (n 17) 37–8; G Perkovich and L Chuanying, 'Conclusions and Recommendations' in AE Levite et al (eds), *Managing US-China Tensions over Public Cyber Attribution* (Washington DC, Carnegie Endowment for International Peace, 2022) 50.

[67] UNGA, 'Report of the GGE' UN Doc A/76/135, 9.

[68] ibid 18.

There is not much international court practice on the required standard of proof.[69] According to one commentator, there are at least four different levels of proof:

> 1. The *prima facie* possibility, which requires only indicative evidence of the claim. 2. A preponderance of evidence, which concerns mainly the balance of probabilities of the two sides. 3. The 'clear and convincing' standard, which requires the party to prove the factual claims are substantially more likely true. 4. Proof beyond reasonable doubt, which requires a full chain of evidence weighing together heavily toward one direction that is virtually indisputable.[70]

As for cyber disputes (at least regarding cyberattacks), Fan Yang finds that the appropriate standard is 'clear and convincing',[71] while Tsagourias and Farrell hold that 'preponderance of the evidence' is the most appropriate standard for 'less serious malicious cyber operations', and this view is based partly on the argument that it is difficult to produce 'clear and convincing evidence' for cyber disputes.[72] In my opinion, the interests of the parties to a dispute are equally strong, and there seem to be no valid reason for putting the burden of proof on the claimant above 'preponderance of the evidence', regardless of the seriousness of the matter.[73] Having said that, states must still strive for maximum certainty before taking action.

A related issue is the distribution of the burden of proof or, to be more precise, how the maxim *semper necessitas probandi incumbit ei qui agit* ('the necessity of proof always lies with the person who lays charges') shall be applied. For instance, if the alleging State A has established prima facie that the attack seems to come from a computer operated by a government agency in State B, is the burden then transferred to State B to prove that the IP address was actually spoofed? Such questions need to be decided based on thorough assessments of the technical issues.[74]

Another issue is what damages are included in relevant claims. This is a question of law (for example foreseeability) but also a matter of evidence. The *Tallinn Manual* states that 'loss includes costs naturally associated with the injury concerned'.[75] Exactly what counts as damages is not determined in practice. It could include reduced uptime of servers that causes reduced availability of files, reduced integrity of data, incapacitated hardware, reputational costs, loss as a result of violations of intellectual property rights facilitated by economic espionage, etc,

[69] R Pietrowski, 'Evidence in International Arbitration' (2006) 22 *Arbitration International* 373, 379.

[70] Fan Yang (n 24) 11.

[71] ibid.

[72] Tsagourias and Farrell (n 29) 966.

[73] See, however, Pietrowski (n 69) 379.

[74] For a fine-grained analysis of this issue, see J Pauwelyn, 'Defenses and the Burden of Proof in International Law' in L Bartels and F Paddeu (eds), *Exceptions in International Law* (Oxford, Oxford University Press, 2017).

[75] Schmitt (n 1) 151.

as well as other costs caused by loss of confidentiality of data.[76] The above would also require different type of supporting evidence.

Another important issue is secrecy. Public attributions are seldom accompanied by the release of the supporting evidence.[77] States have established ways of sharing secret evidence with one another and with international bodies such as the UN or the ICC, but only very reluctantly and in a piecemeal fashion.[78] Secrecy is an impediment even for regional mechanisms between cooperating states, for instance the EU's cyber-related sanctions regime.[79] There are probably extremely few cases where both parties would be comfortable to submit secret evidence to an international body,[80] due to the risk of revealing intelligence sources and methods as well as cyber capabilities.[81] Another reason is that the evidence might have been acquired in a way which violates foreign sovereignty.[82]

C. The Need for Expertise

All these problems relating to the content of the law and the assessment of evidence suggest that special expertise is needed. The technical features of cyber disputes constitute an obvious new aspect. It is true that judges and lawyers always have to apply their expert knowledge of the law to phenomena on which they have little expertise. Many types of legal disputes involve difficult technical aspects, and it

[76] Rid and Buchanan (n 59) 24–25. Whether states are liable for damages caused by loss of confidentiality depends, of course, inter alia on whether cyber espionage through hacking is illegal or not. In my view it is, but that may be a minority view.

[77] Shany and Schmitt (n 17) 213.

[78] See for instance S Chesterman, 'Does the UN Have Intelligence?' (2006) 48 *Survival* 149.

[79] Shany and Schmitt (n 17) 214. See also Bendiek and Schulze (n 17) 5; Tsagourias and Farrell (n 29) 957; Rid and Buchanan (n 59) 26.

[80] The difficulties can be gleaned from a few cases in US courts. The US issued several indictments against hackers from China and other states. In the very first case, from 2014, the indictments are public. See Office of Public Affairs, 'US Charges Five Chinese Military Hackers for Cyber Espionage Against US Corporations and a Labor Organization for Commercial Advantage' (*US Department of Justice*, 19 May 2014) www.justice.gov/opa/pr/us-charges-five-chinese-military-hackers-cyber-espionage-against-us-corporations-and-labor; United States District Court Western Pennsylvania, 'Indictment of Wand Dong and Others' (*US Department of Justice*, 1 May 2014) www.justice.gov/iso/opa/resources/5122014519132358461949.pdf. The hacking method used was spearfishing, and the Federal Bureau of Investigation (FBI) (and other authorities) evidently determined that the description of their modus operandi could be made public. In cases against Chinese hackers from 2020, one indictment is made public in full while two others are available only in redacted form. Office of Public Affairs, 'Seven International Cyber Defendants, Including "Apt41" Actors, Charged in Connection with Computer Intrusion Campaigns against More than 100 Victims Globally' (*US Department of Justice*, 16 September 2020) www.justice.gov/opa/pr/seven-international-cyber-defendants-including-apt41-actors-charged-connection-computer. In two charges against sponsors of the Russian Internet Research Agency, the charges were withdrawn, evidently because US law enforcement would otherwise have to disclose classified information. G Hinck and T Maurer, 'Foreign Hackers have Made It Harder for the US to Prosecute Them' (*Carnegie Endowment for International Peace*, 8 April 2020) carnegieendowment.org/2020/04/08/foreign-hackers-have-made-it-harder-for-u.s.-to-prosecute-them-pub-81512.

[81] Shany and Schmitt (n 17) 196.

[82] *cf* Delerue (n 8) 101–02. See also Bendiek and Schulze (n 17) 16; Tsagourias and Farrell (n 29) 957.

is not uncommon for courts to hear technical evidence, like forensic evidence in criminal cases. However, while most such issues can be fitted within a framework of quotidian experience, that is not necessarily true for cyberspace, which seems not to fit easily with our sensory perceptions or even basic categories of space and time. This suggests that the dispute settlers may be selected at least partly because of their understanding of cyber issues as well as their experience. The required degree of expert knowledge will depend on the issues involved. A dispute settlement body might also want to add an advisory panel of experts as will be further discussed in relation to fact-finding.

V. Cyber Characteristics and Existing Dispute Settlement Mechanisms

For the settlement of cyber disputes there are the generally available dispute settlement mechanisms enumerated in Article 33 of the UN Charter, to wit, 'negotiation, enquiry, mediation, conciliation, arbitration, judicial settlement, resort to regional agencies or arrangements, or other peaceful means of their own choice'.[83] To the above, the existence of special dispute settlement mechanisms with regard to specific cyber matters should be added. For instance, Article 56 of the Constitution of the International Telecommunications Union (ITU) lays down dispute settlement methods for disputes over the interpretation or application of the Constitution.[84] With regard to disputes arising from the Convention on Consular Relations, there is the Optional Protocol on the Compulsory Settlement of Disputes Relating to the Convention.[85] There are also dispute settlement provisions in several agreements on criminal cooperation, including Mutual Legal Assistance Treaties.[86] The Budapest Convention on Cybercrime[87] provides in Article 45 that, in case of a dispute over the interpretation or application of the Convention, parties should seek a settlement through:

> negotiation or any other peaceful means of their choice, including submission of the dispute to the [the European Committee on Crime Problems], to an arbitral tribunal whose decisions shall be binding upon the Parties, or to the International Court of Justice, as agreed upon by the Parties concerned.

[83] See also Schmitt (n 1) 307.

[84] ITU, 'Constitution of the International Telecommunication Union' www.itu.int/en/council/Documents/basic-texts/Constitution-E.pdf. This concerns, for instance, alleged violations of Art 37 of the Constitution, in which Member States agree to take all possible measures, compatible with the system of telecommunication used, with a view to ensuring the secrecy of international correspondence.

[85] Optional Protocol concerning the Compulsory Settlement of Disputes Done at Vienna on 24 April 1963 legal.un.org/ilc/texts/instruments/english/conventions/9_2_1963_disputes.pdf.

[86] However, the Council of Europe's Convention on Mutual Assistance in Criminal Matters (Strasbourg, 20 April 1959) CETS No 030 does not contain a dispute settlement clause, neither does the UN Model Treaty on Mutual Assistance in Criminal Matters (UNODC, 'Mutual Legal Assistance (MLA)' www.unodc.org/e4j/zh/organized-crime/module-11/key-issues/mutual-legal-assistance.html).

[87] Convention on Cybercrime (Budapest, 23 November 2001) rm.coe.int/1680081561.

If a cyber dispute involves human rights (for instance breaches of the right to privacy), human rights dispute settlement or monitoring mechanisms such as the European Court of Human Rights or the UN Human Rights Committee accept individual petitions, but they are also open to inter-state applications.[88]

In addition to the above, domestic courts may be able to adjudicate on cyber related disputes for example sanctions against individuals such as the freezing of assets.[89] Under EU law, there is also the right under the Treaty on the Functioning of the European Union[90] for individuals targeted by sanctions to challenge them before the Court of Justice of the European Union.[91]

Be that as it may, the remaining of this section will discuss three dispute settlement methods – arbitration, conciliation, and fact-finding (or enquiry) – and how they can deal with the challenges identified earlier namely contested law, proof and expertise.

A. Arbitration[92]

Arbitration is a legal but not judicial method of dispute settlement which involves third party adjudication. Although the parties to the dispute have some freedom regarding the choice of applicable law and the selection of arbitrators, the decisions of the arbitral tribunal are final and binding on the parties. In this sub-section I will discuss how the challenges identified earlier of contested law, proof and expertise can be addressed in arbitration proceedings.

i. Contested Law

A challenge facing arbitration in settling cyber disputes is the controversies surrounding the content and scope of application of international law to cyberspace. For this reason, states may not want to submit cyber disputes to arbitration if they cannot predict the outcome[93] or because they 'believe that a policy of deterrence unfettered by normative strictures offers a more promising way to prevent harmful cyber operations than reliance on international law norms and institutions'.[94] Even if a dispute is submitted to arbitration, states may be reluctant

[88] A significant number of cases before the European Court of Human Rights concerned such issues, though all of them individual complaints. ECHR, 'Factsheet: New Technologies' (January 2023) www.echr.coe.int/documents/fs_new_technologies_eng.pdf.

[89] See Franchini (ch 3 in this volume).

[90] Art 263, para 4 of the Consolidated Version of the Treaty on the Functioning of the European Union [2012] OJ C326/47. See Bendiek et al (ch 5 in this volume).

[91] Bendiek and Schulze (n 17) 3.

[92] In distinction to subsections on conciliation and fact-finding, the institution of arbitration will not be presented, since it is assumed that it is familiar to the reader.

[93] *cf* JI Charney, 'Third Party Dispute Settlement and International Law' (1998) 36 *Columbia Journal of Transnational Law* 65, 70.

[94] Shany and Schmitt (n 17) 199.

to say much about the law in their pleadings, because they do not want to commit themselves to a certain interpretation of the norm.

If arbitration would occur, this lack of legal clarity suggests that the precedential aspect of the arbitral award must take a prominent place in the deliberations of the arbitrators. A settlement of a bilateral cyber dispute through arbitration may constitute a rare example of juridical practice, which should be given the requisite weight by commentators and interested parties and therefore have a de facto law-making function (regardless of the weight one attributes to judicial practice as a source of the law). For this reason, the choice of arbitrators is critical. The panel should include jurists with good knowledge of the technical issues raised by cyberspace but also jurists with broad generalist knowledge and good judgment, to ensure that the award fits into the general system of international law (unless states have agreed to apply special rules).

Furthermore, it is recommended that the procedure be open. This will allow the arbitrators to receive necessary input from external stakeholders but openness will also increase the public legitimacy of the award. For instance, one could invite observations by other states or allow amicus curiae, as is now common in investor state dispute settlement.[95] It is also possible to allow intervention from third states.[96] The rules of the Permanent Court of Arbitration (PCA) provide for a limited possibility of intervention by third states, when it 'concerns the interpretation of a Convention to which Powers other than those concerned in the dispute are parties'.[97]

The parties may also allow an arbitral tribunal to settle a dispute *ex aequo et bono*, as provided for in arbitration before both the PCA and the Organization for Security and Co-operation in Europe (OSCE) Court of Conciliation and Arbitration.[98] This means that an arbitral tribunal can go beyond international law in its deliberations.[99] These extra sources could, perhaps, include the GGE Norms of Responsible State Behaviour. To go beyond black-letter substantive law would, of course, diminish the law-making function of the award, but that may be a price worth paying to settle a dispute. The arbitral tribunal would also be at liberty to fill gaps in the law, where a *non liquet* might otherwise arise. Other ways to get around the problem of the contested content of the law is to limit the jurisdiction of the court to particular issues, for example the assessment of damages or the future

[95] WJ Miles (ed), *Dispute Resolution and Climate Change: The Paris Agreement and Beyond* (Paris, International Chamber of Commerce Services, 2017) 29 and 32.

[96] BW Daly, 'Permanent Court of Arbitration' in C Giorgetti (ed) *The Rules, Practice, and Jurisprudence of International Courts and Tribunals* (Leiden, Martinus Nijhoff, 2012) 45.

[97] Art 84(2) of the Convention for the Pacific Settlement of International Disputes (The Hague, 18 October 1907). See also Daly (n 96) 44.

[98] Arts 33(2) and 27(2) of the PCA, 'Optional Rules for Arbitrating Disputes between Two States' (1992) docs.pca-cpa.org/2016/01/Optional-Rules-for-Arbitrating-Disputes-between-Two-States_1992.pdf.

[99] As stated above, it is my view that existing international law covers all aspects of cyberspace, but there is controversy over exactly how international law applies, and some of the generally applicable rules and principles need to be adapted to 'cyberspace'.

behaviour of the parties. This would bring arbitration closer to conciliation which will be discussed below.

ii. Proof

With regard to the issue of collecting and assessing evidence, the bulk of the evidence submitted to an arbitral tribunal will be indirect (secondary or circumstantial).[100] Such evidence is generally admissible before arbitral tribunals, and, as was pointed out in the 2021 GGE report quoted above, such evidence is necessary to establish the facts in disputes of this nature. As also noted by one arbitration practitioner, '[t]he evaluation of the evidence is entirely within the discretion of the tribunal'.[101]

That said, states as mentioned above are often reluctant to provide evidence for their public assertions of attribution for security or other reasons. The PCA rules try to accommodate such sensitivities. According to Article 25(4), '[h]earings shall be held in camera unless the parties agree otherwise' and Article 32(5) provides that '[t]he award may be made public only with the consent of both parties'. However, this will not always reassure a party, in particular if secrecy is important.

Under Article 24 of the PCA Optional Rules, '[e]ach party shall have the burden of proving the facts relied on to support its claim or defence'.[102] Hence, it is up to each state to balance its interest in proving its case against its interest in keeping secrets. Of course, it may be the case that a party withholds information because that information may assist the other party. Under the PCA Rules, 'the arbitral tribunal may call upon the parties to produce documents, exhibits or other evidence within such a period of time as the tribunal shall determine', although that is less likely to occur in inter-state arbitration.[103] If a party refuses, '[t]he tribunal shall take note of any refusal to do so as well as any reasons given for such refusal'.[104] This may suggest that adverse inferences can be drawn from the refusal.[105]

iii. Expertise

As indicated above, cyber disputes require certain expertise, and that has a bearing on the appointment of arbitrators. In an arbitral process, the parties can agree on the requisite qualifications of the arbitrators. The PCA has a list of a specialised

[100] Pietrowski (n 69) 380.
[101] ibid 373–74.
[102] See ibid 374.
[103] ibid.
[104] Art 24(3). If an arbitral tribunal appoints an expert, '[t]he parties shall give the expert any relevant information or produce for his/her inspection any relevant documents or goods that he/she may request of them'. Art 27(2) of the PCA, 'Optional Rules for Arbitrating Disputes between Two States'.
[105] JK Sharpe, 'Drawing Adverse Inferences from the Non-Production of Evidence' (2006) 22 *Arbitration International* 549, 549.

panel of arbitrators for disputes relating to outer space activities as well as to the environment.[106] Similar lists could also be established for disputes involving significant cyber matters.

It may also be necessary to involve technical experts to help the arbitrators assess the submitted evidence.[107] According to the procedure regarding the production and assessment of evidence before the International Court of Justice,[108] experts can be appointed by the parties to the dispute, act as informal consultants to the judges or act as assessors with the right to vote.[109] This can be replicated before arbitral tribunals. The PCA's Optional Rules for Arbitrating Disputes between Two States, Article 27(1) provides that '[t]he arbitral tribunal may appoint one or more experts to report to it, in writing, on specific issues to be determined by the tribunal'.[110] Experts appointed to arbitral proceedings can also make their own enquiries. They can collect information from private sources like cyber security companies, network operators, etc, and from public sources, as will be discussed below in relation to fact-finding.[111] The Optional Rules for Arbitration of Disputes Relating to Outer Space Activities and the Optional Rules for Arbitration of Disputes Relating to Natural Resources and/or the Environment have similar provisions and they further provide for special lists of experts.[112] Such a list could be established also for disputes involving significant cyber issues. As one commentator noted, 'one can expect that most of the future battles will likely focus on the selection of expert panels'.[113]

B. Conciliation

If states are reluctant to commit themselves to an arbitral process which they cannot predict or fully control, conciliation presents itself as an alternative

[106] PCA, 'Optional Rules for Arbitration of Disputes Relating to Outer Space Activities' (2011) docs.pca-cpa.org/2016/01/Permanent-Court-of-Arbitration-Optional-Rules-for-Arbitration-of-Disputes-Relating-to-Outer-Space-Activities.pdf; PCA, 'Optional Rules for Arbitration of Disputes Relating to Natural Resources and/or the Environment' (2001) docs.pca-cpa.org/2016/01/Optional-Rules-for-Arbitration-of-Disputes-Relating-to-the-Environment-and_or-Natural-Resources.pdf. See C Qiong Wu, 'A Unified Forum? The New Arbitration Rules for Environmental Disputes under the Permanent Court of Arbitration' (2002) 3 *Chicago Journal of International Law* 263, 263.

[107] See *cf* Delerue (n 8) 103.

[108] ibid 88.

[109] ibid 103–07. For instance, under Art 50 of the Statute of the International Court of Justice (San Francisco, 26 June 1945) '[t]he Court may, at any time, entrust any individual, body, bureau, commission, or other organisation that it may select, with the task of carrying out an enquiry or giving an expert opinion'.

[110] Art 27(1) of the PCA, 'Optional Rules for Arbitrating Disputes between Two States'.

[111] *cf* also Miles (n 95) 29.

[112] Art 29 of the PCA, 'Optional Rules for Arbitration of Disputes Relating to Outer Space Activities'; Art 27 of the PCA, 'Optional Rules for Arbitration of Disputes Relating to Natural Resources and/or the Environment'.

[113] Wu (n 106) 266.

mechanism of dispute settlement which is more state friendly. Conciliation has been defined as

> a method for the settlement of international disputes of any nature according to which a Commission set up by the Parties, either on a permanent basis or on an ad hoc basis to deal with a dispute, proceeds to the impartial examination of the dispute and attempts to define the terms of a settlement susceptible of being accepted by them, or of affording the Parties, with a view to its settlement, such aid as they may have requested.[114]

Cot describes conciliation as 'a half-breed method for the settlement of disputes … between diplomatic methods … on the one hand, and arbitral or judicial settlement on the other'.[115] Whereas the borderline between mediation and conciliation is not crystal clear, mediation is usually under the control of a political authority, which typically has its own interest, while conciliation is performed by a body of independent persons.

Many bilateral treaties on conciliation were concluded in the inter-war years,[116] and conciliation was one of the three dispute settlement means set out in the General Act on the Pacific Settlement of International Disputes 1928, revised in 1949.[117] Conciliation has also featured in a number of multilateral treaties such as the Vienna Convention on the Law of Treaties 1969, the Law of the Sea Convention 1982 and a number of multilateral environmental treaties, including the Convention on Biological Diversity 1992.[118] Conciliation has not been used very often lately, but a recent and successful example is the conciliation in 2016–2018 between Timor-Leste and Australia over maritime boundaries in the Timor Sea.[119]

Conciliation can take place under the auspices of the PCA, which has laid down optional rules for that purpose[120] although there have only been a few cases of conciliation.[121] Conciliation can also take place within a multilateral framework.

[114] Art 1 of the ILL, 'Regulations on the Procedure of International Conciliation' (1961) www.idi-iil.org/app/uploads/2017/06/1961_salz_02_en.pdf. See also J-P Cot, 'Conciliation' in *Max Planck Encyclopedia of Public International Law* (Oxford, Oxford University Press, 2006) 2.

[115] Cot (n 114) para 3. Kulesza (n 5). See also SV Scott and RC Andrade, 'Political Disputes: Inter-State Dispute Settlement' in *Max Planck Encyclopedia of Public International Law* (Oxford, Oxford University Press, 2022) para 33 et seq.

[116] JG Merrills, *International Dispute Settlement*, 5th edn (Cambridge, Cambridge University Press, 2011) 60; also see Cot (n 114) para 5 et seq.

[117] Pacific Settlement of International Disputes – General Act, 1928, League of Nations, *Treaty Series*, vol 93, p 343.

[118] Vienna Convention on the Law of Treaties (adopted 23 May 1969, entered into force 1 January 1980) 1155 UNTS 331; United Nations Convention on the Law of the Sea (adopted 10 December 1982, entered into force 16 November 1994) 1833 UNTS 3; Convention on Biological Diversity (adopted 5 June 1992, entered into force 29 December 1993) 1760 UNTS 79. See also Scott and Andrade (n 115) 10; Cot (n 114) para 8. See also Peters (n 13) 32.

[119] Scott and Andrade (n 115) 9; D Tamada, 'The Timor Sea Conciliation: The Unique Mechanism of Dispute Settlement' (2020) 31 *European Journal of International Law* 321.

[120] PCA, 'Optional Conciliation Rules' (1996) docs.pca-cpa.org/2016/01/Permanent-Court-of-Arbitration-Optional-Conciliation-Rules.pdf.

[121] JJ van Haersolte-van Hof, 'The Revitalization of the Permanent Court of Arbitration' (2007) 54 *Netherlands International Law Review* 395, 407.

This may provide an element of pressure on the parties but also, arguably, some reassurance for parties who participate in good faith.[122] For instance, in 2016 the OSCE introduced a number of confidence-building measures in cyberspace[123] which can be linked to existing conciliation procedures. The OSCE Council, or the Committee of Senior Officials, may direct the parties to a dispute to seek conciliation under the Valletta Procedure or under the Stockholm Convention on Conciliation and Arbitration in the OSCE.[124]

Different model rules on conciliation outside the PCA are also available, including the 1995 UN Model Rules for the Conciliation of Disputes Between States[125] or those adopted by UNCITRAL, WIPO and ICSID.[126] According to Article 8 of the UN Model Rules, the Conciliation Commission can adopt its own procedure.[127] Indeed, in the *Timor Sea Conciliation*, the Commission adopted a very flexible approach. The process opened with the adoption of confidence-building measures because as explained by the Commission, a significant element of its efforts was 'concerned with building trust between the Parties and removing obstacles to productive and successful conciliation on the substance of the Parties' dispute'.[128]

After that, the Commission met with the parties separately or jointly in different constellations, at different levels, and in different forms.[129] Furthermore, 'each Party would have complete control over information and documents submitted by it, including with respect to whether they were communicated to the other Party or made public'.[130] The Commission also avoided being restrained by the parties' conceptions: 'Rather than restrict itself to the most immediate or prominent elements of the Parties' dispute identified at the outset of the proceedings, the Commission has sought to comprehensively engage with the Parties to address the issues necessary to achieve an amicable and durable settlement.'[131] Regarding the applicable law, the Commission found that it may 'as a matter of course engage

[122] Cot (n 114) para 31.

[123] OSCE, 'Decision No 1202. OSCE Confidence-Building Measures to Reduce the Risks of Conflict Stemming from the Use of Information and Communication Technologies' (10 March 2016) PC.DEC/1202.

[124] Convention on Conciliation and Arbitration within the CSCE 15 December 1992 www.osce.org/court-of-conciliation-and-arbitration/111409. C Tomuschat, 'Conciliation within the Framework of the OSCE Court of Conciliation and Arbitration: An Assessment from the Viewpoint of Legal Policy' in C Tomuschat, R Pisillo Mazzeschi and D Thürer (eds), *Conciliation in International Law: The OSCE Court of Conciliation and Arbitration* (Leiden, Brill/Nijhoff, 2017) 90; Kulesza (n 5) 9.

[125] UNGA, 'Resolution Adopted by the General Assembly: 50/50. UN Model Rules for the Conciliation of Disputes between States' (29 January 1996) UN Doc A/RES/50/50. See Kulesza (n 5).

[126] See Cot (n 114) 3. The UNCITRAL Conciliation Rules were endorsed in UNGA, 'Resolution Adopted by the General Assembly: 35/52. Conciliation Rules of the United Nations Commission on International Trade Law' (4 December 1980) UN Doc A/RES/35/52.

[127] Scott and Andrade (n 115). See also Tomuschat (n 124) 98.

[128] *Timor Sea Conciliation* (*Timor Leste v Australia*) (Report and Recommendations of the Compulsory Conciliation Commission between Timor-Leste and Australia on the Timor Sea of 9 May 2018) [2018] PCA Case No 2016-10, 95.

[129] *Timor Sea Conciliation* [2018] (n 128) 29–30.

[130] ibid 31.

[131] ibid 32.

with the parties on their legal positions, but may engage with these matters to the extent that so doing will likely facilitate the achievement of an amicable settlement'.[132] One could imagine that in a cyber dispute, a conciliation commission might want to broaden the scope of the dispute. Rather than to only focus on the interests of the parties linked to the dispute, it could ask states about their wider interests, both in the resolution of the dispute at hand and in the regulation of cyber operations in general.[133]

Be that as it may, I will now discuss how the issues of contested law, proof and expertise can be dealt with in conciliation procedures.

i. Contested Law

A conciliation commission is not necessarily inhibited by the lack of legal clarity. In fact, it is not bound by international law in its proposals.[134] According to Article 20(2) of the UN Model Rules, the Commission 'shall refrain from presenting in its report any final conclusions with regard to facts or from ruling formally on issues of law, unless the parties have jointly asked it to do so'. Further, not only are the recommendations of the Commission not binding on the parties, but their legal positions are also entirely preserved regarding anything that has transpired during the proceedings.[135] Article 28 of the UN Model Rules reads:

> 1. Except as the parties may otherwise agree, neither party shall be entitled in any other proceedings, whether in a court of law or before arbitrators or before any other body, entity or person, to invoke any views expressed or statements, admissions or proposals made by the other party in the conciliation proceedings, but not accepted, or the report of the commission, the recommendations submitted by the commission or any proposal made by the commission, unless agreed to by both parties.
> 2. Acceptance by a party of recommendations submitted by the commission in no way implies any admission by it of the considerations of law or of fact which may have inspired the recommendations.

These advantages, however, come at a cost. A conciliation procedure will most likely not contribute to the development (or crystallisation) of international law in cyberspace, nor will it be very useful in a dispute with a party that is not willing to participate in good faith. That said conciliation 'favours … mutual understanding and trust instead of confrontation'[136] and provides a 'framework of dialogue', 'from which all elements of surprise are removed'.[137] Hence, while a conciliation

[132] ibid 35.

[133] For instance, national security agencies may have different views on international law from government agencies (or civil society organisations) concerned with privacy.

[134] UNGA, 'UN Model Rules' UN Doc A/RES/50/50 (29 January 1996) See Cot (n 114) para 27.

[135] Scott and Andrade (n 115) 10.

[136] D Thürer, 'Peaceful Settlement of International Disputes: About the Essence and Role of Conciliation' in C Tomuschat, R Pisillo Mazzeschi and D Thürer (eds), *Conciliation in International Law: The OSCE Court of Conciliation and Arbitration* (Leiden, Brill/Nijhoff, 2017) 49.

[137] Tomuschat (n 124) 87 and 100.

may not necessarily settle a dispute fully, at least it is disposed to help de-escalate tensions. A conciliation commission can be asked to provide its legal views on some or all of the issues raised by the parties and to assess some or all of the facts. It can provide recommendations for future behaviour and/or suggest means for the parties to settle, or at least manage, the current as well as future disputes. Although the commission's proposals are not binding, and can be rejected by the parties[138] even in that case they can provide a framework of communication and a roadmap of accepted behaviour.

ii. Proof

Since a conciliation procedure will not result in a legally binding decision, the rules on evidence and proof can be adapted to what the parties find useful.

A commission can obtain information on the dispute in different ways.[139] Under Article 14 of the UN Model Rules, a commission 'may use all means at its disposal, such as … consultation with experts, to ascertain the facts'. As will be discussed below, there are also several existing inter- and transnational bodies that may be helpful in this respect. As set out in Article 15 of the UN Model Rules:

> The commission may propose to the parties that they jointly appoint expert advisers to assist it in the consideration of technical aspects of the dispute. If the proposal is accepted, its implementation shall be conditional upon the expert advisers being appointed by the parties by mutual agreement and accepted by the commission and upon the parties fixing their emoluments.

This procedure may – ideally – create a professional atmosphere based on shared knowledge, in which the appointed experts come to joint understandings about the appropriate standards of proof and about what the various pieces of evidence indicate. If that fails, a commission could at least identify the points where the parties agree and where they disagree.

As discussed above, the willingness of parties to provide information is important, and confidentiality of the proceedings may be of some help in that respect.[140] This is recognised in Article 25 of the UN Model Rules:

> The commission's meetings shall be closed. The parties and the members and expert advisers of the commission, the agents and counsel of the parties, and the secretary and the secretariat staff, shall maintain strictly the confidentiality of any documents or statements, or any communication concerning the progress of the proceedings unless their disclosure has been approved by both parties in advance.

As noted with regard to the Timor Sea Commission, the commission may also decide that evidence produced by one party will not be disclosed to the other side.

[138] Cot (n 114) para 3.
[139] Merrills (n 116) 67.
[140] ibid 68. See also Tomuschat (n 124) 98–99.

iii. Expertise

With regard to expertise, the same considerations as regards arbitration apply to conciliation. To reiterate, the parties are free to choose the conciliators and a conciliation commission could include technical experts as well.[141]

C. Fact-finding

Since many inter-state cyber disputes revolve around attribution[142] and given the difficulty in applying legal rules to cyber disputes, a reasonable course of action may be to reduce the scope of the dispute to facts and involve a fact-finding commission to establish the technical facts behind a malicious cyber operation. Fact-finding may also create a less adversarial environment where claims and counter claims can be discussed.

Although fact-finding and cyber attribution has been examined in more detail elsewhere,[143] I will still discuss this method in this section due to its close relation with arbitration and conciliation since the findings of a fact-finding mission can also feed into other forms of dispute resolution.

Fact-finding (or commissions of enquiry) as an international dispute settlement institution was introduced by the Hague Convention for the Pacific Settlement of International Disputes 1899.[144] There have been a few instances where fact-finding commissions have been provided for in some multilateral treaties, such as in Article 33 of the Convention on the Law of the Non-Navigational Uses of International Watercourses 1997.[145] Most fact-finding commissions were instituted by the United Nations. Article 34 of the UN Charter provides the UN Security Council with the power to 'investigate any dispute, or any situation, which may lead to international friction or give rise to a dispute', and in recent years fact-finding has been used many times regarding human rights issues, for instance in Syria, Myanmar, Libya, Yemen, Sudan/Darfur and the Central African Republic.[146]

[141] Kulesza (n 5) 9.

[142] De Souza Dias (n 11) 13.

[143] N Tsagourias and F Middleton, 'Fact-Finding and Cyber Attribution' in R Buchan, D Franchini and N Tsagourias (eds), *The Changing Character of International Dispute Settlement: Challenges and Prospects* (Cambridge, Cambridge University Press, 2023) 439–466.

[144] Convention for the Pacific Settlement of International Disputes (adopted 29 July 1899, entered into force 5 September 1900) docs.pca-cpa.org/2016/01/1899-Convention-for-the-Pacific-Settlement-of-International-Disputes.pdf.

[145] Convention on the Law of the Non-navigational Uses of International Watercourses (adopted by the General Assembly of the United Nations on 21 May 1997, entered into force on 17 August 2014), at legal.un.org/ilc/texts/instruments/english/conventions/8_3_1997.pdf. See also A Jachec-Neale, 'Fact-Finding' in *Max Planck Encyclopedia of Public International Law* (Oxford, Oxford University Press, 2021) 7.

[146] Jachec-Neale (n 145) 8. Another example is the investigation by the International Civil Aviation Organization of the KE 007 incident, which involved the shooting down of a South Korean jumbo jet over the Soviet Union. Merrills (n 116) 55.

Model provisions on fact-finding have been adopted by the PCA[147] and by the UN.[148] The brief model rules of the PCA are relevant for commissions created through inter-state agreement.

As with the other methods, I will now discuss how the issues of contested law, proof and expertise can be dealt with by fact-finding commissions.

i. Contested Law

Even though there are examples of fact-finding commissions which have delivered legal findings,[149] the main virtue of referring a cyber dispute to a fact-finding body is that such a body will not have to make pronouncements on substantive law. This is particularly important when the legal terrain is unclear.[150] Having said that, the scope of the factual investigation may be determined by the legal claims of the parties, which may need to be interpreted by the commission.

ii. Proof

To obtain and assess evidence is the key task of a fact-finding commission. Article 12 of the PCA Rules provides the following:

> 1. Subject to these Rules and the agreement of the parties, the Commission may conduct the fact-finding proceedings in such manner as it considers appropriate, provided that the parties are treated with equality and that at any stage of the proceedings each party is given a full opportunity to present its case.
> 2. The Commission shall give the parties every opportunity to be present at hearings and investigations, and to submit documents, present evidence and have witnesses and experts called. The Commission may also take initiative in asking for documents and calling witnesses and experts.

While the model rules do not suggest any obligation on the parties to cooperate and submit evidence, a fact-finding commission has the power to determine what evidence and burden of proof it will apply.[151] Its power is due to the fact that its findings are not binding. Although its 'report shall state in detail the facts established by the Commission, and the reason why certain facts may not be considered as having been established',[152] it is for the parties to accept or reject the report,[153]

[147] PCA, 'Optional Rules for Fact-Finding Commissions of Inquiry' (1997) docs.pca-cpa.org/2016/01/Permanent-Court-of-Arbitration-Optional-Rules-for-Fact-finding-Commissions-of-Inquiry.pdf.

[148] UNGA, 'Resolution Adopted by the General Assembly: 46/59. The Declaration on Fact-finding by the United Nations in the Field of the Maintenance of International Peace and Security' (9 December 1991) UN Doc A/RES/46/59. See also Jachec-Neale (n 145) 5 and 12.

[149] Merrills (n 116) 53.

[150] *cf* ibid 51.

[151] ibid 46.

[152] Art 15 of the PCA, 'Optional Rules for Fact-Finding Commissions of Inquiry'.

[153] Merrills (n 116) 46.

and at any rate the implications of the findings will remain in the hands of the parties.[154]

The issue of secrecy is addressed in Article 10 of the PCA Rules:

> Unless the parties agree otherwise, or unless disclosure is required by the law applicable to a party, the members of the Commission and the parties shall keep confidential all matters relating to the fact-finding proceedings, including the investigations, hearings, deliberations and findings of the Commission. Unless the parties agree otherwise, the Commission shall meet in camera.

Even though this provision may alleviate some concerns of the parties, the problem of secrecy remains, and will likely prevent a fact-finding commission from assessing all available information. Nevertheless, it may be helpful to have even a limited amount of evidence assessed by an impartial body, which can distinguish between facts which have been 'established' and those which may be just implied by the available material.

It is pertinent to mention in this regard that several organisations could be enrolled to assist a fact-finding commission in its mission. Kulesza indicated that information on particular incidents or information of a more general nature could be found in organisations such as the Internet Corporation for Assigned Names and Numbers, the Internet Society, the Internet Engineering Task Force, Europol, Interpol, the ITU or the Council of Europe.[155]

iii. Expertise

As remarked, '[c]ommissions of enquiry would be the perfect fit for cyber disputes given both: their focus on professional technical assistance and the high level of technical expertise needed to understand the Internet environment, its operations, and the technical background for cyber disputes'.[156] A fact-finding commission is typically composed of technical experts, but commissioners may also be lawyers, as the Red Crusader inquiry of 1962 demonstrates.[157] Legal expertise is particularly relevant to ensure that the evidence is assessed according to legal standards.

D. Other Mechanisms: Attribution Mechanisms, Regional Bodies, Bilateral Commissions

Arbitration, conciliation and fact-finding are flexible mechanisms that can be tailor-made to meet the needs of the parties to a cyber dispute. However, to be set in motion, the consent of all parties to the dispute is necessary.

[154] ibid 51.
[155] Kulesza (n 5) 7–8.
[156] ibid 8.
[157] Merrills (n 116) 49.

Instead, the last few years, several proposals for a permanent international attribution body have been made[158] ranging from private-sector membership, private-public partnership to an intergovernmental agency.[159] One prominent initiative is the CyberPeace Institute, which is co-sponsored by the Hewlett Foundation, Mastercard, and Microsoft. It is not a proper attribution mechanism but rather an entity producing information that can help other entities to effectively perform attribution.[160]

Shany and Schmitt mention the Organisation for the Prohibition of Chemical Weapons (OPCW) as a source of inspiration for a future attribution institution and note how the OPCW helped investigate the Salisbury incident of 2017, when two Russian citizens were poisoned by Russian agents. The OPCW can investigate alleged violations of the Convention for the Prohibition of Chemical Weapons under Articles IX (challenge inspections) and X (invited inspection). Such investigations seek to establish whether chemical weapons have been used as well as provide relevant information that may serve to identify the origin of such weapons.[161]

The proponents of an attribution institution hope that such a mechanism 'could serve as a neutral global platform',[162] which could 'lend credibility to attribution in the cyber realm'.[163] For sure, an inter-governmental attribution body may be caught in politicking and a private body – likely financed by tech companies – may not be credible in the eyes of many states. Nevertheless, attribution reports from a third body may appear more trustworthy to the public than attributions by governments or by single cyber security companies. Such reports would also be difficult to completely ignore. If done well, the work of such a body, however formed, could contribute to 'the standardization of attribution by establishing its own attribution methodology, rules of evidence and decision-making process',[164] which in and of itself will be useful for both political and dispute settlement conversations.

That said, proposals of this nature are controversial and perhaps premature.[165] Also 'States wielding significant cyber capability have little interest in creating an international attribution mechanism for cyber incidents'.[166] However, there is some resonance for ideas of this nature among states. In the Chair's cautiously formulated Summary from the first OEWG, it was noted that:

> Some States suggested that developing a universally-accepted, common approach and understanding of the source of ICT incidents at the technical level under the

[158] Some of these proposals are discussed also in Tsagourias and Middleton (n 143).
[159] Tsagourias and Farrell (n 29) 959; Mueller et al (n 56) 115–16.
[160] Shany and Schmitt (n 17) 216.
[161] Convention on the Prohibition of the Development, Production, Stockpiling and Use of Chemical Weapons and on their Destruction (adopted 3 September 1992, entered into force 29 April 1997), 1975 UNTS 45. OPCW, 'Responding to the Use of Chemical Weapons' www.opcw.org/our-work/responding-use-chemical-weapons.
[162] Mueller et al (n 56) 115.
[163] Shany and Schmitt (n 17) 215.
[164] Tsagourias and Farrell (n 29) 960.
[165] ibid 961.
[166] Shany and Schmitt (n 17) 201.

> auspices of the United Nations, through the sharing of good practices, bearing in mind respect for the principle of State sovereignty, could lead to greater accountability and transparency, and could help support legal recourse for those harmed by malicious acts.[167]

International organisations – global and regional – can also be engaged in dispute settlement at the request of parties to a dispute or as monitors. At the regional level, in Europe the OSCE is an obvious candidate and has already engaged in the field of ICTs and security.[168] The African Union has been involved in cyber security issues, including the hosting of a convention.[169] Other regional organisations could also be entrusted with such tasks.[170]

A different approach is to establish bilateral commissions between states to manage and resolve disputes. It is a common practice to establish such commissions to deal with shared interests, such as trade or common watercourses.[171] Such commissions can deal with disputes from both a legal and a political perspective, and even when they are not able to resolve a dispute, they can help the parties understand exactly where the disagreement lies – in factual and/or in legal terms. A shared professional ethos between the expert members of a commission will be helpful in this regard. In the ICT domain, even though some states have frequent conflicts with one another, they still have a common interest in protecting cyber stability and may want to prevent escalation. A commission of this nature might benefit from engagement with the national Computer Security Incident Response Teams (CSIRTs).

VI. Concluding Thoughts

This chapter identified three main factors that make it difficult to settle cyber disputes:

1. The law is to a very large extent unsettled, because even if international law does apply in 'cyberspace', states have different views on how it applies;

[167] UNGA, 'Chair's Summary: Open-Ended Working Group on Developments in the Field of Information and Telecommunications in the Context of International Security, Third Substantive Session' (10 March 2021) UN Doc A/AC.290/2021/CRP.3 para 20.

[168] See, for instance, OSCE, 'Decision No 1202. OSCE Confidence-Building Measures' PC.DEC/1202.

[169] See UJ Orji, 'The African Union Convention on Cybersecurity: A Regional Response Towards Cyber Stability?' (2018) 12 *Masaryk University Journal of Law and Technology* 91, 91.

[170] Most regional organisations are created for economic cooperation. However, that is not necessarily a bar to engaging in security matters. A famous example is ECOWAS, the Economic Community of West African States, which established a peacekeeping force, ECOMOG, in 1990. ECOMOG was deployed in the Manu River wars in Liberia, Sierra Leone and Guinea.

[171] Perhaps the most famous commissions are those that have been established to deal with various issues relating to the border between the USA and Canada, including 'The International Joint Commission'. See DML Farr, 'Joint Commission' (*The Canadian Encyclopedia*, 16 December 2013) www.thecanadianencyclopedia.ca/en/article/joint-commission.

2. It is difficult to establish the facts of a cyber incident, in particular the attribution (or non-attribution) to a state, not least because the available information is to a very large extent secret; and
3. The technical aspects may be difficult to grasp for a lawyer without subject-matter expertise in law and technology.

At present, it may appear unrealistic to expect that cyber disputes could be settled through established third-party procedures like arbitration, conciliation or even fact-finding. States hurl allegations and sanctions against each other, perhaps with a sound factual basis but without presenting evidence or justifying their measures in legal terms. Some important states have not even set out their views on international law and ICTs.

States need to be reminded of their obligation to settle cyber disputes pacifically as well as their obligation to seriously attempt to settle cyber disputes that endanger international peace and security. In order to comply with these obligations, they must endeavour to find ways to overcome these difficulties. The well-established and tried mechanisms of arbitration, conciliation and fact-finding are flexible and can be adjusted to fit the needs of the disputing states but also the general interest. There are also methods less often described in international law terms, such as bilateral commissions, that can be considered.

INDEX

www.ingramcontent.com/pod-product-compliance
Ingram Content Group UK Ltd.
Pitfield, Milton Keynes, MK11 3LW, UK
UKHW021910150926
475560UK00003B/287

9 781509 960910